LONDON BRIDGE AND ITS HOUSES,
c. 1209–1761

Detail from Anthonis van den Wyngaerde's panorama of London in about 1544, showing London Bridge from the south-east.

LONDON BRIDGE AND ITS HOUSES, c. 1209–1761

DORIAN GERHOLD

New revised edition

Oxford & Philadelphia

Originally published in 2019 by the London Topographical Society

Published in the United Kingdom in 2021 by
OXBOW BOOKS
The Old Music Hall, 106–108 Cowley Road, Oxford, OX4 1JE

and in the United States by
OXBOW BOOKS
1950 Lawrence Road, Havertown, PA 19083

© Oxbow Books and the author 2021

Hardback Edition: ISBN 978-1-78925-751-9
Digital Edition: ISBN 978-1-78925-752-6

A CIP record for this book is available from the British Library

Library of Congress Control Number: 2021939544

All rights reserved. No part of this book may be reproduced or transmitted in any form or by any means, electronic or mechanical including photocopying, recording or by any information storage and retrieval system, without permission from the publisher in writing.

Printed in India by Replika Press
Text design and layout by Frabjous Books, UK

For a complete list of Oxbow titles, please contact:

UNITED KINGDOM
Oxbow Books
Telephone (01865) 241249
Email: oxbow@oxbowbooks.com
www.oxbowbooks.com

UNITED STATES OF AMERICA
Oxbow Books
Telephone (610) 853-9131, Fax (610) 853-9146
Email: queries@casemateacademic.com
www.casemateacademic.com/oxbow

Oxbow Books is part of the Casemate Group

Contents

Author's acknowledgements ix
Abbreviations and notes on house numbering, measurements and currency xi

1. Introduction 1
   The bridge 2
   Plans and views 8

2. Reconstructing the bridge and its houses 12
   The roadway 12
   Widths and depths of the houses 14
   The cross buildings 15
   Reconstructing the plan of the bridge and its houses 17
   Piers and hammer beams 19

3. The houses from c. 1209 to 1358 23
   Origins 23
   The houses in 1358 24
   The 'hautpas' of 1358 29

4. The major buildings 31
   The chapel 31
   The stone gate 35
   The drawbridge tower 38
   Other structures 40

5. The houses from 1358 to 1633 42
   Houses on new sites 42
   Merging of plots..43
   Rebuilding of houses...44
   The house with many windows 49
   Nonsuch House 50
   Enlarging the houses 53
   Landlord and tenants: leases...54
   Landlord and tenants: repairs and rebuilding 56

6. Inside the houses in the seventeenth century..58
   Cellars and shops 61
   Upper rooms 64
   Services..67

7. Fires and rebuildings 1633–82 69
   The fire of 1633 69
   The new building of 1645–49...71
   The Great Fire of 1666 and the sheds 75

8. Trading on the bridge 80
   The fourteenth and fifteenth centuries 81
   The sixteenth and seventeenth centuries 88
   Bridge customers...91
   Booksellers 93
   From the 1680s to the 1750s 96

9. Families and community 103
   Bridge families...103
   The bridge population in the late seventeenth century 107
   Community...109

10. The great rebuilding of 1683–96	112
The northern end	112
Growing traffic and the keep-right rule	117
The middle part and the drawbridge houses	118
South of the stone gate	123
The new houses	124
11. From the fire of 1725 to the removal of the houses	127
The fire of 1725	127
The falling in of leases in the 1740s	128
The new houses of 1745	129
Managing the existing houses	135
Removing the houses	136
Survey of the houses on London Bridge, 1604–83	143
Appendices	
1. Reconstructing the plan of London Bridge	167
2. The reliability of the views of the bridge	170
3. Tracing the bridge houses back to 1358	172
4. The hearth tax of 1664–66	176
5. Rents on the bridge	178
6. The northern end of the bridge	180
Notes	185
Image credits	200
Index	201

AUTHOR'S ACKNOWLEDGEMENTS
(FROM THE FIRST EDITION)

I am grateful to the Council of the London Topographical Society for agreeing to publish this book. Sheila O'Connell, as LTS editor, has been extremely helpful, as have Linda Fisher and Steve Hartley of Scorpion Creative. The Comptroller and City Solicitor's Department, especially Tina Armstrong and Ann Harrison, made it possible for me to examine the leases of the bridge houses. Caroline Barron kindly read and commented on the text, as did Peter Cross-Rudkin for sections with engineering content. Staff at London Metropolitan Archives have as usual been unfailingly helpful. Staff of many other organisations were helpful in providing images. John Goodall of *Country Life* magazine commissioned the reconstruction drawings that form Figures 15 and 21, and I am fortunate to be able to use the excellent drawings by both Stephen Conlin and Pete Urmston. Others who have helped in various ways have included Jeremy Ashbee, Stewart Brown, David Harrison, Derek Keene, James Nye, Robert Peberdy, Andrew Roberts and Timothy Walker. My wife Lis has been sympathetic towards my sudden obsession with London Bridge and provided much encouragement throughout.

Note on the revised edition

It has been a pleasure working with Oxbow Books on this new edition. Only minor changes have been made to the text. All the original illustrations are included, and three have been added.

ABBREVIATIONS

BHJ	LMA, Journals of the bridge estates committee (e.g. COL/CC/BHC/01/001 becomes BHJ, 001; BHJ, A, is LMA, CLA/007/EM/05/01/001)
BHP	LMA, Papers of the bridge estates committee (e.g. COL/CC/BHC/03/001 becomes BHP, 001)
BHR	LMA, Bridge House rentals and accounts (e.g. LMA, CLA/007/FN/02/001 becomes BHR, 001)
BHV 1	Bridge House views 1647–67, LMA, COL/CCS/CO/06/003
BHV 2	Bridge House views 1675–82, LMA, CLA/007/EM/06/04
CCLD	City Corporation, Comptroller's City Lands deeds, Bridge House (e.g. COL/CCS/RM11/02699 becomes CCLD, 02699)
Harding	Vanessa Harding and Laura Wright (eds), *London Bridge: selected accounts and rentals, 1381–1538*, London Record Society, vol. 31 (1995)
Home	Gordon Home, *Old London Bridge* (1931)
Journals	LMA, Journals of the Common Council
LLT	Ancestry website, London land tax, Bridge Ward [accessed on 4 December 2018]
LMA	London Metropolitan Archives
Repertories	LMA, Repertories of the Court of Aldermen
Sharpe LB	R.R. Sharpe, *Calendar of letter-books ... City of London ... Letter-Book C* (1901) (and subsequent volumes for Letter-Books E to K (1903–11))
Stow	C.L. Kingsford (ed.), *A survey of London by John Stow* (1908), 2 vols
Survey	Survey of the houses on London Bridge, 1604–83, pp. 143–66 below
TNA	The National Archives
Watson	Bruce Watson, Trevor Brigham and Tony Dyson, *London Bridge: 2000 years of a river crossing*, MOLAS monograph 8 (2001)

Note on house numbering

In this book, PE and PW refer to houses on the east and west sides of the principal or northern part, ME and MW to those on the middle part and SE and SW to those on the south part. The houses were known by their signs rather than by numbers, but these tended to change, so they are given numbers here. The numbers are those in Figure 14 and in the Survey (e.g. ME1 or SW13), with A and B added for formerly separate houses which were later merged. Note that, on the principal part, the layout changed several times upon rebuilding, so the same house number relates to a different point on the bridge according to whether it is up to 1633, between 1645 and 1666 or after 1682.

Note on measurements and currency

There are 12 inches to a foot. One foot is equivalent to 0.3048 metres. There were 12 pence in a shilling and 20 shillings in a pound. Pounds, shillings and pence are expressed in the following form: £12.6s.8d.

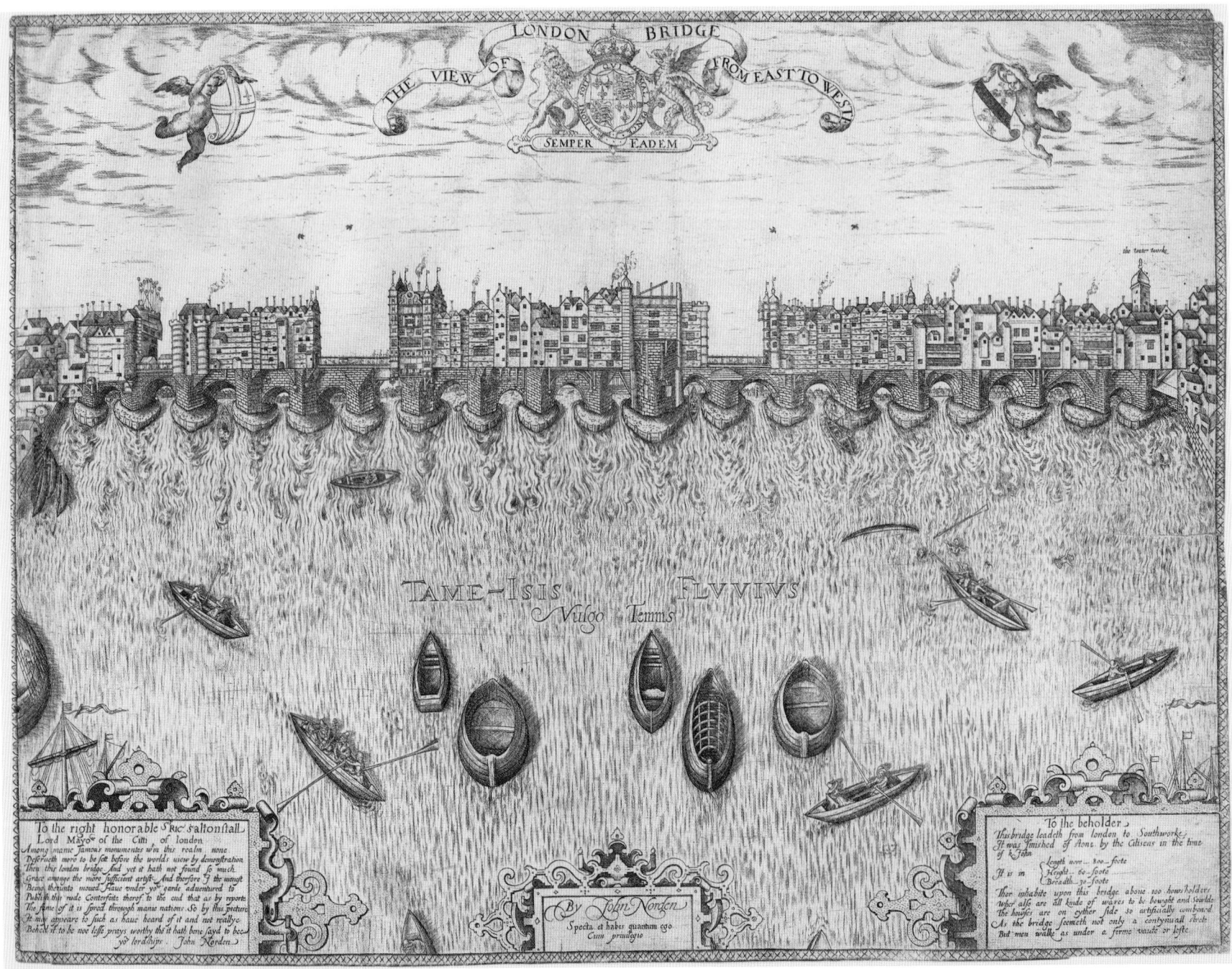

CHAPTER 1

Introduction

Fig. 1 John Norden's view of the east side of the bridge in 1597–98. It is dedicated to Sir Richard Saltonstall, who was Lord Mayor in 1597–98, and bears the arms of Saltonstall and the City. In the foreground a boat has overturned and its passengers are in the water, probably after making the dangerous passage through the arches.

Views of London Bridge lined with houses from end to end are among the most familiar images of London in the past. Up to the late seventeenth century they show a higgledy-piggledy collection of houses apparently developed piecemeal (Frontispiece and Figs 1–2). Thereafter a more regular set of houses lined the bridge, until these were eventually removed in 1757–61 (Fig. 84). The very familiarity of the views has perhaps dulled our sense of the extraordinary fact that 500 or more people lived directly above the Thames, with the water rushing through the arches below them. The equivalent of a small town was perched on the bridge, and probably some people lived their entire lives there. Inhabited bridges were common in western Europe from medieval times until the eighteenth century, but none was as long as London Bridge.[1]

Little has been written about the houses, and some important questions remain unanswered. When were the buildings in the views constructed? How were they prevented from falling into the river? How were they organised internally? How did they change over time? Who occupied them? What were the advantages of trading on the bridge? Also, the views show only the backs of the houses facing away from the bridge, and nothing has been known for certain about their fronts facing the roadway.

The houses are in fact unusually well documented, and some of the most valuable sources have not previously been exploited. Apart from the views, there are the extensive records of the Bridge House, which maintained the bridge and owned the buildings on it. These include annual or near-annual rentals in house-by-house order back to 1460, listing the leaseholders, together with rentals of 1358 and 1404–21.[2] Accounts of expenditure also go back to 1460, and less informatively, with a gap, to 1404, and provide much useful information, especially about the rebuilding of houses.[3] However, the rentals and accounts are of limited value without knowing exactly where the individual houses were. For this, the leases, which are plentiful from the early seventeenth century onwards, are essential. From about 1604 to 1660 almost all of them list the rooms in each dwelling with their dimensions, providing a detailed survey of nearly all the houses on the bridge, and of some at more than one date (see the Survey below). Only one of them has ever previously been used, and that in an unsatisfactory way without the dimensions.[4] There is especially good coverage for the 1650s, when all the

bridge houses were re-let. The other new source, and the single most illuminating document, is a table of measurements drawn up in 1683 covering most of the houses then standing, hitherto unnoticed among the papers of the committee which managed the Bridge House estates.[5] As explained below, the leases and the table of measurements are the key to understanding the information in the rentals and accounts.

With this evidence the questions posed above can be answered, and we can greatly increase our understanding of the houses and the community they contained. Much of what the documents tell us is surprising, and contrary to what has previously been believed about the bridge. The measurements of 1683 will provide our starting point, but first the bridge itself and the views and plans of it must be introduced.

The bridge

London Bridge, linking the City to Southwark and south-east England, was the only fixed crossing of the Thames

Fig. 2 View of the west side of the bridge in the Pepys Library, Cambridge, referred to in this book as the Pepys view. The date is unknown, but it cannot be earlier than 1590 (the date of the mills at the south end) or later than 1633 (when the principal part was burnt), unless compiled from earlier materials.

downstream of Kingston-upon-Thames until 1729. There were earlier timber bridges, but the first with stone arches was built between about 1176 and 1209, at the time when such bridges were becoming common in England.[6] Timber used in the southern abutment was felled in 1187 or 1188, and a datestone of 1192 was found 'in the arch work' in a cellar close to the north end in the eighteenth century.[7] This was the bridge that remained in use until 1831, and on which the houses stood. It was about 150 feet east of the present London Bridge (see Fig. 106). Its length was 926 feet, and it had nineteen piers linked by nineteen arches and a wooden drawbridge.[8] It is usually said to have been built by Peter of Colechurch, who was chaplain of St Mary Colechurch in the City and had earlier rebuilt London's wooden bridge. However, it is possible that his main role was as fundraiser rather than builder, at least from 1202 until his death in 1205. In 1202 King John intended Isembert of Saintes to complete the bridge and add houses to it, and Isembert may well have done so, though there is no direct evidence of him coming to London. Isembert had experience of building bridges in France, and had constructed houses on the bridge at La Rochelle to help pay for it.[9]

Constructing a bridge over such a large river was a major undertaking, comparable to building an important cathedral or castle. There is no evidence that before the nineteenth century anyone was capable of building coffer dams (watertight structures to exclude water from an area of riverbed) in the Thames at London. Instead, piles were driven into the riverbed from a boat at low tide, creating an enclosure that could be filled with rubble (forming the base of the pier) and across which planks could be laid to provide a firm working surface. Larger piles could then be driven in to form the 'starling' around the pier, after which the pier could be completed, with its stone facing (Figs 3–5). The starlings were essential, because the method of construction meant that the piers had relatively shallow foundations, which would soon have been undermined without the starlings. The price paid for this was that a great part of the river's flow was obstructed: at high tide, when the starlings were covered, the width of flow was reduced to 508 feet, and at low tide, when the starlings were exposed, it was reduced to 237 feet, only 26% of its full width.[10] The bridge was almost a dam, and, depending on the tide, the difference in the level of the water upstream and downstream could be as much as 5 feet; Ned Ward wrote in

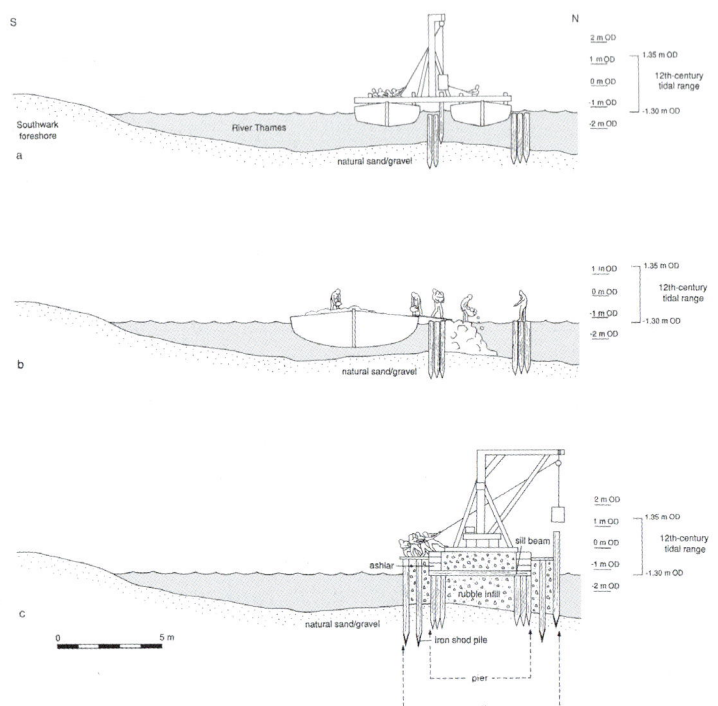

Left: **Fig. 3** Reconstruction drawing by Museum of London Archaeology of three stages of the bridge's construction.

Right: **Fig. 4** Reconstruction drawn by Peter Jackson in about 1970 showing the bridge under construction, demonstrating the challenging conditions under which the bridge was built. The bridge in the background reflects an earlier belief, since disproved, that the preceding timber bridge was further east.

about 1700 of 'the frightful roaring of the bridge water-falls'.[11] The river flowed with great force through the arches, scouring the foundations, and constant and expensive maintenance of the starlings was necessary throughout the bridge's life. To build a bridge that endured for more than six centuries in such conditions and with such limited technology was an immense achievement (Fig. 6). Only twice in that long history, in 1281 and 1437, did parts of the structure collapse (five arches and two arches respectively), a better record than many major bridges.

The arches seemed unnecessarily small to later generations, and the piers unnecessarily numerous and wide (from north to south).[12] In fact the arches were slightly larger than was usual at the time, averaging about 24 feet, compared with usually less than 18 feet. Only from about the mid-thirteenth century were much larger bridge arches built, mainly in northern England.[13] Wide piers made it easier to build one pier at a time, as they could more easily withstand unequal loads on their two sides, and it was less likely that the collapse of one pier would endanger neighbouring ones. In the eighteenth century Hawksmoor suggested that the exceptionally large pier on which the bridge's chapel stood was intended as a buttress, which would withstand shocks such as the collapse of an arch and prevent such a collapse spreading.[14] The number of piers and arches increased the cost of maintaining the bridge but, as we shall see, made it easier to build houses on it, and the houses provided revenue for maintenance.

At first the administration of the bridge may have been a shared responsibility of lay officials, described as the warden and proctors, and the 'brethren and chaplains ministering in the chapel of St Thomas' on the bridge. From 1282 onwards that responsibility belonged to the bridge wardens – from 1311 two in number and chosen from among the citizens of London.[15] They headed an organisation known as the Bridge House, which operated under the supervision of the City and never became an independent body.[16] It had premises just east of the bridge in Southwark. The bridge was the first in England known to have had a permanent endowment.[17] Three-quarters or more of its revenues in the fifteenth century came from the rents of its properties on the bridge and elsewhere and from quit rents, the rest being the income from the Stocks Market and from tolls on carts passing over the bridge and boats passing under the drawbridge. The houses on the bridge were a third of the rents, and therefore about a quarter of total revenue,

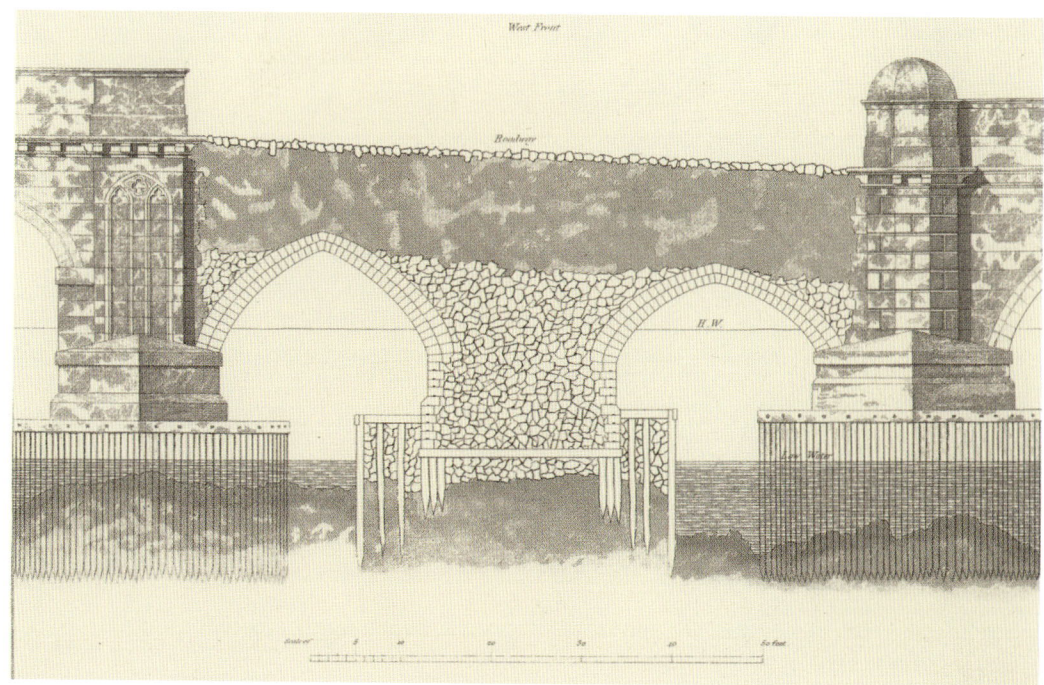

Fig. 5 William Knight's cross-section of several piers and arches of the bridge in 1826–27, during the removal of a pier and its adjoining arches, showing the relatively shallow piles of the piers and the deeper ones of the starlings.

6 LONDON BRIDGE AND ITS HOUSES, *c.* 1209–1761

Fig. 6 Reconstruction drawn by Peter Jackson in about 1990 showing the bridge in about 1600. Some changes would be needed to reflect subsequent research, especially the greater length of the piers and the buildings on them, but the drawing brilliantly captures the audacity of laying a ribbon of stone across such a powerful river.

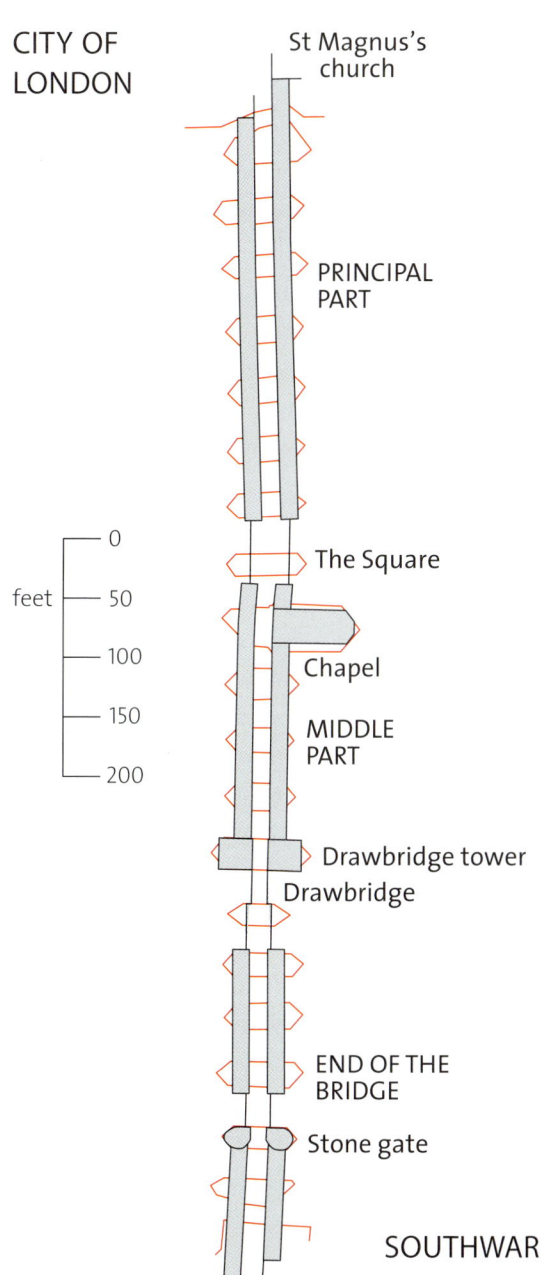

Fig. 7 Outline plan of the bridge. North is at the top. The starlings are not shown.

though this was of course the gross income, ignoring the cost of building and maintaining them.[18]

By the time views began to be drawn of the bridge in the sixteenth century, it bore three major buildings and four groups of houses (Fig. 7). The most important building was the chapel, standing on by far the largest pier and dedicated to St Thomas Becket. On the second pier from the Southwark end was the stone gate, which was one of the City's defensive gates. Five piers north of that was the tower from which the drawbridge was operated, later replaced by Nonsuch House. The drawbridge allowed ships to pass to and from quays upstream, notably Queenhithe, and was an important defensive feature, though it had almost entirely fallen out of use by the late fifteenth century.

All the houses had shops on the ground floor. The largest group was at the north end, stretching from St Magnus's church, which adjoined the northern abutment, to an open space known as the Square. These houses were usually described as the principal east part and the principal west part of the bridge, though that terminology died out after the fire of 1633. In the fifteenth and sixteenth centuries the principal part yielded as much rent as all the other houses. The next group of houses lay between the Square and the drawbridge, and was known as the middle east part and the middle west part. Between the drawbridge and Southwark was 'the end of the bridge', where there were two separate groups (usually treated as one) either side of the stone gate. The two groups will be referred to here as the drawbridge houses and the houses south of the stone gate, or together as the south part. The individual houses were known by their signs rather than by numbers, but these tended to change, so they are identified in this book by the part of the bridge (PE and PW for the principal part, ME and MW for the middle part and SE and SW for the south part) followed by the number used in Figure 14 and the Survey.[19]

The whole of the bridge was in the City's Bridge Ward Within, forming three 'precincts', corresponding to the south, middle and principal parts of the bridge, except that the precincts containing the south and principal parts included a few additional houses. The south part was in the parish of St Olave, Southwark, and the other two parts were in St Magnus parish, the dividing line being at the drawbridge.

Traffic over the bridge was so important to London that works that required it to be closed were usually carried out at night.[20] When the drawbridge had to be replaced in 1722, resulting in the bridge being closed during the day, the watermen undertook to provide thirty extra boats.[21] But the bridge was not just a way of crossing the river: it was also an important part of London's identity. It dominated the view of anyone approaching London along the Thames and was a constant presence to people on the river or the waterfront. It was a place for pageants and for ceremonial entrances to the City. Its maintenance was the largest single collective endeavour of London's citizens, many of whom made bequests towards it in their wills, and it symbolised their wealth and corporate identity.[22]

Foreign visitors were loud in their praise, at least in the sixteenth century. According to a Frenchman, L. Grenade, in 1578, it was

> a great and powerful bridge, the most magnificent that exists in the whole of Europe. It is … completely covered with houses which are all like big castles. And the shops are great storehouses full of all sorts of very opulent merchandise. And there is nowhere in London which is more commercial than this bridge. … I reiterate that there is no bridge in the whole of Europe which is on a great river like the Thames and as formidable, as spectacular and as bustling with trade as this bridge in London.[23]

For Grenade it was one of the four most impressive structures in London, along with St Paul's Cathedral, the Royal Exchange and the Tower of London. A visiting Moravian in 1597 described London Bridge as 'one of the finest bridges in the whole of Europe for size and beauty'. For a German visitor in 1592, it was a 'beautiful long bridge, with quite splendid, handsome and well-built houses, which are occupied by merchants of consequence'.[24]

Plans and views

What was probably the first plan of the bridge was drawn for the Bridge House in 1587 by Arthur Gregory, who worked for Francis Walsingham.[25] It has not survived, and nor have the plans drawn in connection with the removal of the houses in 1757–61.[26] There are three surviving plans of part or all of the bridge, all of them highly informative in different ways. That of 1633, made on the orders of the Privy Council following a fire, shows the northern abutment and the first seven piers and starlings, including the roadway (widened after the fire) and what seem to be the cellars in the piers (Fig. 8).[27] South of that it omits the piers and starlings but shows the roadway and buildings for a short distance. It is to scale, and is helpful for reconstructing the houses on the north part of the bridge both before and after 1633. For example, without it we would not know that the roadway curved slightly between the principal

Fig. 8 The plan of the north end of the bridge drawn for the Privy Council in 1633 after the fire of that year. North is to the right. In the burnt area, covering the seven northernmost piers, it shows the starlings, the piers and the roadway, together with the waterworks to the west. The black shapes are almost certainly cellars. Further south, the piers and starlings are not shown, but the roadway and houses are, including the chapel house, though not with much accuracy. The roadway in the burnt area is shown 20 feet wide, as the Privy Council was demanding, and two lines mark the six-foot wide footway it wanted on each side. The plan is particularly informative about the layout on the northern abutment (see Appendix 6).

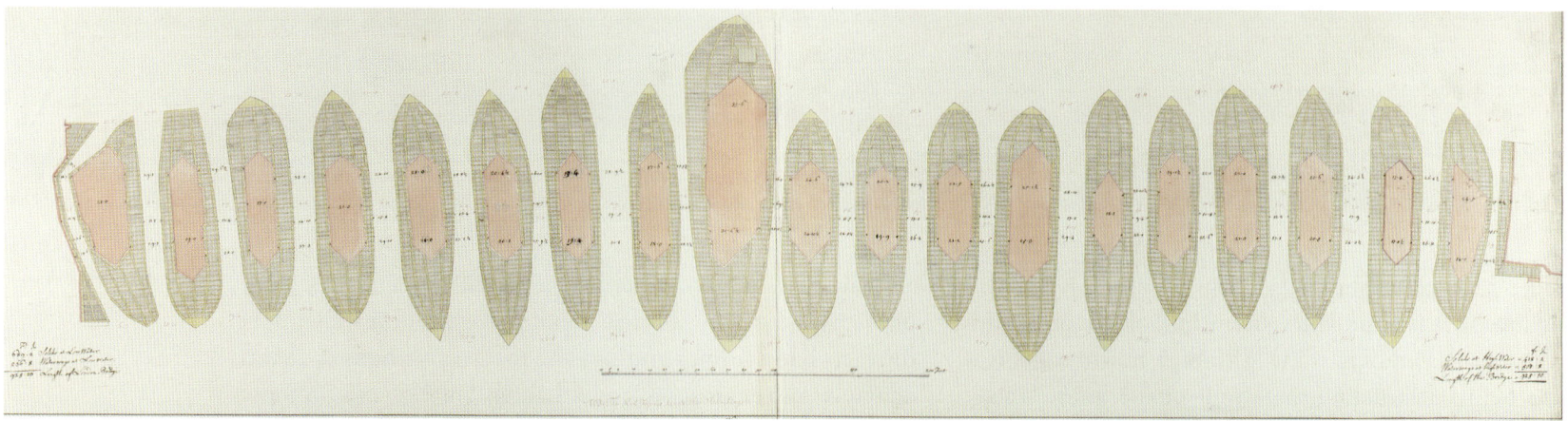

Fig. 9 Charles Labelye's plan of the starlings and piers of the bridge as they were in 1746. North is to the left. The houses are not shown, but this is the only plan of the whole bridge before the houses were removed and other alterations were made around 1760.

10 LONDON BRIDGE AND ITS HOUSES, c. 1209–1761

Fig. 10 Detail from Wenceslaus Hollar's Long View of London in 1647.

and middle parts of the bridge. A plan of about 1725, also drawn following a fire, provides an outline of the properties south of the stone gate (Fig. 114).[28] Though not to scale, it is invaluable for reconstructing the layout of the houses there. It reveals, for example, that the southernmost house on the east side in the rentals was well south of the bridge abutment and not contiguous to other Bridge House property. The third plan covers the whole bridge, and is to scale, but it shows only the piers and starlings and not the roadway or houses. It was drawn by the engineer, Charles Labelye, in 1746 to promote his proposal to cut the cost of maintenance either by improving the piers and reducing the size of the starlings or by removing every other pier and starling (Fig. 9).[29] It has been used in this book as the basis for the reconstruction plan. Only one of the three plans shows both piers and roadway, and none shows both piers and houses in relation to each other. Reconstructing the houses and how they were supported therefore requires the bringing together of information and measurements from different sources, as discussed in Appendix 1.

There are many views of the bridge and houses before the 1680s, but some are highly inaccurate, such as the famous one by Claude de Jongh,[30] and almost all had to simplify the complicated jumble of houses too much to be of great value. Four of the views are reasonably detailed and comprehensive, although even these, where they show the same features, do not always agree, and they do not always seem to correspond to the lease descriptions. Wyngaerde's drawing of London in about 1544 looks at the east side of the bridge from a point high up to the south-east, showing some features that were soon to disappear, such as the drawbridge tower and the chapel (Frontispiece). Norden's view of the east side was drawn in 1597–98 (Fig. 1). The west side of the bridge also features in his general view of London in 1600, though the bridge houses are much simplified (Fig. 45). An anonymous view in the Pepys Library (referred to here as the Pepys view) shows the west side in detail (Fig. 2). Its date is unknown, except that it is after waterwheels were set up at the south end of the bridge in 1590 and before a fire destroyed the houses at the north end in 1633, unless of course it was compiled wholly or partly from earlier work. It shows the houses in perspective, which is highly informative. Fourthly, there is Hollar's Long View of London in 1647, showing in detail the west sides of the middle and south parts (Fig. 10). The reliability of these views is examined in Appendix 2.

For the bridge after the 1680s, the most comprehensive image is Sutton Nicholls's print of 1711, showing both sides (Fig. 84). There are also drawings and paintings, including those by Samuel Scott and Canaletto (Figs 98, 99).

CHAPTER 2

Reconstructing the bridge and its houses

In 1683, just before the houses on the middle part and the drawbridge houses were rebuilt, a detailed set of measurements was made of them, probably by William Leybourn, who dominated surveying in London from about 1669 to 1694.[1] As indicated above, a document containing those measurements has survived among the papers of the bridge estates committee (Fig. 11).[2] It is the single most informative record of the bridge houses, and is crucial for understanding the structure of both the bridge and the houses and for reconstructing a plan of them. Among other things, it states the width of the roadway at various points, the width of each house, the depth of each house and the breadth of their 'cross buildings' above the roadway. Some other measurements have also survived from this period.

The roadway

Strype stated in 1720 that the width of the roadway across London Bridge was from 12 to 14 feet, and one later writer made it only 12 feet wide on average.[3] In 1831 it was observed that cellars at the south end left space for a roadway 12 to 14 feet wide.[4] However, Strype was writing long after the bridge had been widened, and the assumption made in 1831 that the width between the cellars was the width of the roadway was not a safe one.[5] The contemporary measurements indicate that the roadway was in fact somewhat wider, except where it passed though defensive features. The narrowest point measured in 1683 was 12 feet 5 inches under Nonsuch House, which had replaced just such a defensive feature. Elsewhere on the middle part of the bridge the width ranged from 14 feet to 16 feet. Between the drawbridge houses the roadway was 16 feet 3 inches wide at the north end and 15 feet 4 inches wide at the south end, though another set of measurements indicates 15 feet 6 inches at the north end and in the middle and 14 feet 6 inches at the south end.[6] Measurements also exist for the other parts of the bridge. The principal part was stated in 1633 to have been 15 feet wide before the fire of that year.[7] South of the stone gate the roadway was much wider: as measured in 1693 (before any widening) it was 17 feet 2 inches between the first houses south of the gate and a curiously precise 18 feet 5⅛ inches between the last houses before Tooley Street.[8]

RECONSTRUCTING THE BRIDGE AND ITS HOUSES 13

Fig. 11 The table of measurements of the middle part and the drawbridge area made in 1683.

As the stone gate itself was a defensive feature, the roadway through it was of course narrower. After being widened in the 1520s, it was 13 feet wide under the arch and only 11 feet wide at the gate itself.[9]

We can conclude that the roadway was generally around 15 feet across, and occasionally 16 feet, but narrower at Nonsuch House and the stone gate (and probably the drawbridge) and wider south of the stone gate. Even without taking into account the ground occupied by the houses, this made London Bridge one of the wider medieval bridges. The great majority of surviving medieval bridges were originally 9 to 15 feet wide, but about fifteen of them, usually important ones on major roads in towns, were 15 feet wide or more, and London Bridge falls into that category, as one would expect. Twelve feet was probably the minimum needed for two carts to pass each other, and London Bridge more than fulfilled that requirement.[10]

The document of 1683 does not indicate the full width of the bridge including the part occupied by the houses, but there are other sources for this. In the 1680s the City insisted that the houses, when rebuilt, must leave a roadway 20 feet wide, which gives us the minimum possible width.[11] The plan of 1633 shows the principal part of the bridge to have varied from 21 to 24 feet wide (Fig. 8), and that corresponds to the later estimate by George Dance the Younger and others that before the changes made around 1760 the whole bridge was from 20 feet to 24 feet 4 inches wide.[12] Just south of the drawbridge, where there were no houses, the space between the parapet walls was 19 feet 3 inches in 1684, which would be just over 20 feet with the width of the walls added.[13] There was a greater width only at the Square – about 33 feet on the 1633 plan. Knowing the full width of the bridge tells us something important: the houses were not firmly founded on the bridge itself, just slightly overhanging the edge, but instead had only a toe-hold on the bridge, occupying anything from 2 to 5 feet of its width on each side. We will therefore need to examine carefully how they were supported.

Widths and depths of the houses

The widths of the houses (i.e. the length of the street frontage) varied greatly in 1683. Five on the middle part of the bridge were between 10 and 11 feet wide, while four were between 27 and 28 feet wide. One of the drawbridge houses was 32 feet 5½ inches wide. The variety of widths seems at first sight to rule out any idea that there was originally a standard width, but this will be examined later.[14] Many small houses were merged over the centuries to form larger ones, but the remaining east–west boundaries are likely to have been one of the bridge's more persistent features. One interesting aspect is that the widths of the houses on the east and west sides largely matched each other, allowing for the occasional amalgamation and a margin of error of a few inches. This was not the case, however, at the northern end of the middle part, probably because of the chapel there.

The depths of the houses (i.e. from front to back) also varied considerably. Four were from 14 to 15 feet deep, and two between 30 and 31 feet deep, while the two parts of Nonsuch House were both 32 feet 2 inches deep. Even the two houses on the middle west part rebuilt together in the 1650s had different depths: 19 feet 1 inch and 25 feet (MW7–8). The depths seem almost random. Until, that is, they are plotted against the piers, as shown in Figure 14 below. Houses wholly or largely on the piers were usually deeper than those which were over the channels or gullets, as the Pepys view confirms (Fig. 2). That explains, for example, the varying depths of the two houses rebuilt in the 1650s. The pattern was not entirely consistent however, probably because houses over gullets were being enlarged towards the river by the 1630s.[15] In the case of the drawbridge houses the piers apparently affected the widths too, as they seem to have been planned so that some houses were almost entirely over piers and others entirely over gullets. As we shall see, the piers were crucial to the houses, and not just to the ones directly over them.

The cross buildings

One of the most useful pieces of information provided in 1683 is the location and width of the 'cross buildings'. The views of the bridge indicate roof structures extending over the roadway, in places appearing to cover it completely. However, this cannot possibly have been the case, as it would have turned the roadway into a dark tunnel. The measurements of 1683 tell us that there were buildings across the roadway only between roughly every other house. About 52% of the middle part of the bridge was covered, and 54% of the stretch occupied by the drawbridge houses. The cross buildings only occasionally corresponded exactly to the width of the houses they formed part of, for reasons that will be examined later.[16]

What the document of 1683 does not tell us is what form the cross buildings took. They have often been described or shown in reconstruction drawings as little more than tie-overs at an upper level,[17] and it has even been doubted that in most parts of the bridge there was any link between the houses on opposite sides.[18] However, when the middle part and the drawbridge houses were rebuilt in 1684–86, the stated purpose was not just so that the roadway could be widened, but also so that the height of the roadway could be raised from one storey to two.[19] The lease descriptions confirm that the cross buildings began in the first storey and continued upwards to the tops of the houses, as shown in Figure 12. Two of them were measured in 1683, and they were only 10 feet 2 inches and 10 feet 3 inches above the roadway (at the north and south ends of the drawbridge houses respectively).[20] Some of these first-storey cross buildings can be seen in the views of the bridge, such as that in the middle of the drawbridge houses in Wyngaerde's drawing and those at the south end of the drawbridge houses and at Nonsuch House in Hollar's view.

With this information it is possible to reconstruct the appearance of the roadway and to begin to understand what it was like to cross the bridge (Fig. 13). The roadway was not a tunnel, but it must nevertheless have been fairly dark, and travellers using it would have experienced a constant alternation

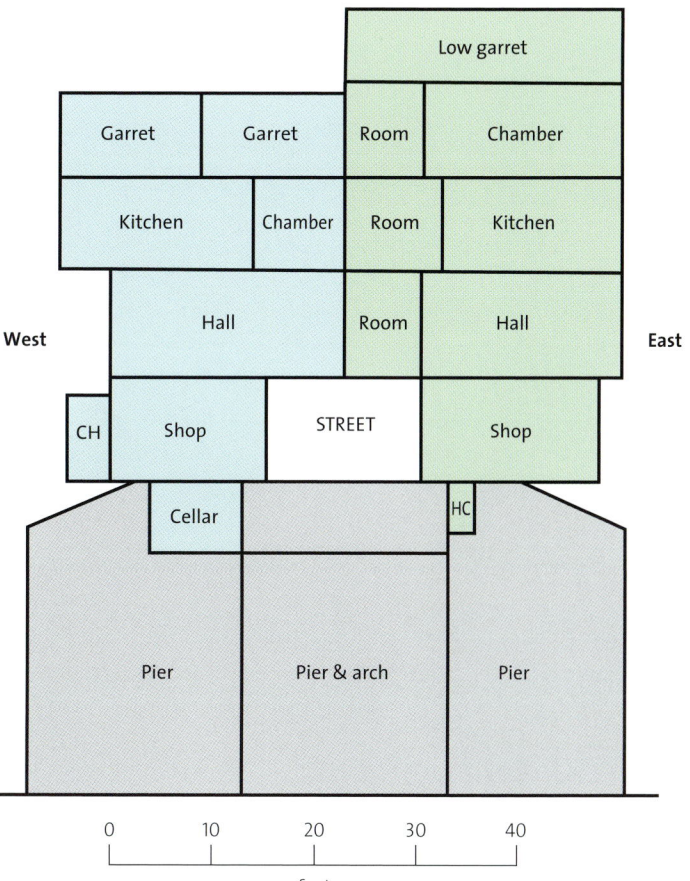

Fig. 12 Reconstructed cross-section of two houses on the middle part, based on descriptions in leases. 'CH' indicates a counting house; 'HC' a hanging cellar. The houses are those of Martha Charlton, widow, in 1653 (MW9) and Lawrence Warkman, citizen and vintner, in 1649 (ME7). The two houses were partly over a pier and partly over a gullet. Warkman's house was occupied in 1649 by Daniel Stockwell, a haberdasher, but by 1656 was the Three Bibles bookshop.

Fig. 13 Reconstruction drawing by Pete Urmston of the roadway on the principal part of the bridge in about 1600, looking north.

of light and shade. The cross buildings make sense of some of the contemporary remarks about the bridge. According to Norden, 'the howses are on eyther side so artificially combyned as the bridge seemeth not only a contynuall strete but men walke as under a ferme vaute [vault] or lofte'.[21] According to Grenade, writing in 1578 and exaggerating somewhat, 'Another singular feature of this bridge is that it is covered along its whole length'.[22] In 1637 the bridge's inhabitants stated that they 'formerly were accustomed in the winter nights to hang forth at their doores a small light which by reason of the closenesse of the place their houses hanging over the streete, could hardly be seene', and sought permission to hang out 'seven greate lights' instead, at their own charge.[23]

What was the reason for the cross buildings? Obviously they increased the size of some of the houses and the rents that could be charged for them. However, they had the considerable disadvantages of making the roadway darker and increasing the risk of fires spreading. Their purpose was not to prevent the houses toppling backwards into the river,[24] as it is inconceivable that houses would have been built that were so unbalanced that they depended on the cross buildings to hold them upright. Their main purpose must have been to provide greater stability to the houses, which were frequently buffeted by high winds. When an additional 'cross building or tye over' was proposed between two of the new houses on the middle part in 1688, the reason given was 'for the strengthneing of the buildings on both sides & preservacon of the stone worke',[25] the latter presumably because the pressure of the timbers under high winds damaged the bridge's stonework.

Reconstructing the plan of the bridge and its houses

We have still far from exhausted the value of the measurements made in 1683. Documents relating to the houses rarely state more about their location than which part of the bridge they stood on. They virtually never indicate even which properties were abutted on north and south. Admittedly the rentals are in house-by-house order, but they do not make it possible to identify the exact location of a house (except those at the ends of each part) or its size and shape. For this, the measurements of 1683, supplemented by the lease descriptions, are crucial. Using Labelye's plan of 1746 as the base, the position of the houses on the middle part and the drawbridge houses can be plotted, making it possible to identify their relationship to the piers and which houses they were in the views of the bridge. This provides some clues as regards the rest of the bridge, such as that the deeper houses and houses with large cellars were over piers. To reconstruct the rest of the bridge we have to rely largely on the measurements in the leases, using the rentals to place the houses in the correct order. This works well south of the stone gate, where the leases provide a complete record and there is a rough plan. It is harder for the principal part, as this was destroyed by fire in 1633 and leases have not survived for every house. Nevertheless, there is enough information of various sorts to build up a reasonably reliable picture, as explained in Appendix 1. Thus the plan of the whole of the bridge as it was before the fire of 1633 and the rebuilding of the 1680s can be reconstructed, as shown in Figure 14.

That reconstruction is the key to unlocking the entire history of the houses. The next step is to trace them back through the rentals as far as 1358, only a century and a half after the completion of the bridge, noting on the way the merging of adjoining properties to form larger ones. There are certain difficulties in this process, which have been overcome as explained in Appendix 3. There is therefore a firm basis for reconstructing the bridge and its houses in 1358, and thereby for examining how the houses developed both before and after that date. In fact it becomes possible to identify how the houses were laid out when the bridge was new.

The reconstruction reveals some unexpected features. It has always been clear that, like many medieval bridges, London Bridge had piers that were irregularly spaced, perhaps reflecting the builders' need to use the most stable parts of the river's bed in such challenging conditions, and that the piers were of varying widths and lengths. But, in addition, the piers of the principal part were not at right angles to the roadway, and the roadway there was decidedly off-centre in relation to the piers, as the depths of the houses on each side make clear – averaging 18 feet on the east side and 26 feet on the west. Probably as a consequence of the irregularity, the roadway was not absolutely straight from one end to the other. Its alignment changed between the principal and middle parts and also, slightly, south of the stone gate. If Isembert did arrive to complete the bridge in 1202, the greater regularity of the middle and south parts may have been one of the consequences. Curiously, some of the houses over piers on the principal part did not extend the full length of the pier, perhaps because they were among the older houses.

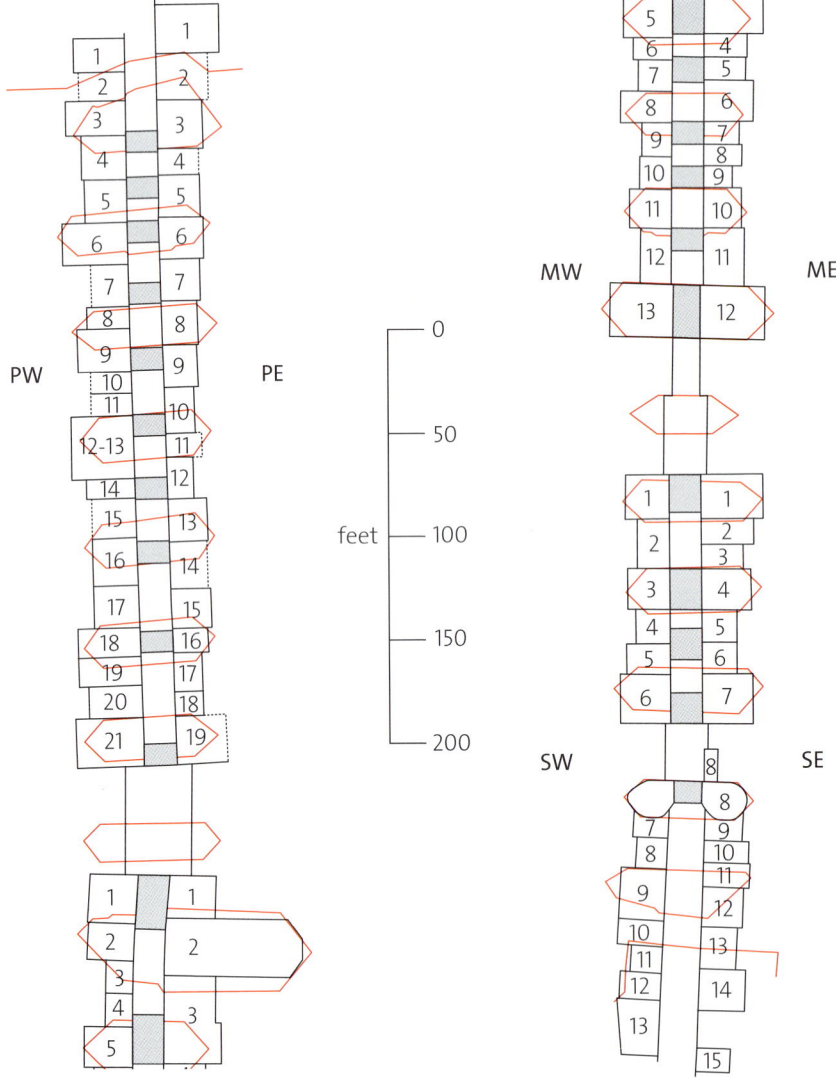

Fig. 14 Reconstructed plan of the bridge, as far as possible showing it before the fire of 1633. It is based largely on seventeenth-century leases and the table of measurements of 1683, as discussed in Appendix 1. On this and other reconstruction plans in this book, the piers are shown in red and grey shading on the roadway indicates cross buildings above it. On the principal part, the back lines of houses for which no information is available are indicated by dotted lines, which are entirely conjectural.

Piers and hammer beams

The discussion so far has made clear the importance of the piers. Some houses were firmly founded on them, perhaps overhanging somewhat at the river end of the pier. Others were over the gullets between the piers, with only a few feet of their depth resting on stonework. They could not have been cantilevered out from the arches, as there was simply not enough weight there to balance that of an entire house extending at least 12 feet from the bridge and with three or four storeys; nor would struts from the arches have been much use. How, then, were these houses supported? The answer is that they rested on 'hammer beams' laid from pier to pier parallel to the roadway (Fig. 15). One lease explicitly refers to the repair of 'the hammer beams from peer to peer'.[26] This use of hammer beams for substantial houses was possible because the piers of London Bridge were unusually and perhaps uniquely long from east to west – an oddity which ought to have attracted more attention from historians. The piers of medieval bridges generally projected beyond the roadway, if at all, only a few feet as a triangular cutwater. Many reconstruction drawings and models show London Bridge's piers in that form, despite the availability of plans showing that its piers were completely different.[27] In fact, the rectangular parts of London Bridge's piers extended well beyond the carriageway on both sides, in some cases by 15 or more feet, at least by the seventeenth century (Figs 8, 9). Without the long piers, only much shallower houses would have been possible.

Some inhabited bridges elsewhere, such as some of those in Paris and Pulteney Bridge in Bath, had piers and arches that were the same width as each other from one side of the bridge to the other and also the same width as houses plus roadway. The houses therefore rested firmly on the stonework and overhung the sides only a little, if at all.[28] For a bridge as long as London's, that was probably ruled out by the extra cost. Some other inhabited bridges had short piers and either houses that projected only a little beyond the stonework, as at Bristol, or just a few shallow buildings only or mainly on the piers, as at Newcastle.[29] If the aim was to build substantial houses the full length of a major bridge without excessive cost, the answer was apparently to build long piers, so that some houses could rest on the piers and others could be supported by beams or stone ribs between the piers. It is hard to see any purpose for London Bridge's long piers other than their usefulness for supporting houses. Hammer beams as such were not unique to London Bridge: beams between the piers supported the few houses of Exeter's Exe Bridge,[30] and hammer beams can still be seen today at the Krämerbrücke at Erfurt in Germany, though they add only a little to the depth of the houses because the piers are short. What was unique about London Bridge was the long piers and their use as a platform for hammer beams along the whole of a major bridge.

As might be expected, the hammer beams used at London Bridge were extremely large timbers. Those specified for new houses on the principal part in 1682–83 measured 18 inches by 14 inches in cross-section, and this was increased to 20 inches by 18 inches for the middle part in 1684.[31] The new houses of 1745 had hammer beams 14 inches by 14 inches.[32] Not surprisingly, bridge officials often rode long distances looking for suitable timber.[33] The term 'hammer beam' is first encountered in Bridge House records in 1602.[34] Where a hammer beam was supported by an arch brace, as shown under ME3 to 6 in Norden's view (Fig. 111), it had the same position in relation to any such brace as a hammer beam in a

20 LONDON BRIDGE AND ITS HOUSES, c. 1209–1761

Fig. 15 Reconstruction drawing by Stephen Conlin of the middle part of the bridge in about 1590, seen from the south-east. It shows the starlings and piers, the hammer beams between the piers, the roadway with cross buildings above it, and cutaway views of Nonsuch House, ME5 and several of the cross buildings.

timber roof, which was perhaps why the term was used on the bridge. The hammer beams of the hall of Hampton Court were described as such in the 1520s, whereas those of Westminster Hall seem to have been referred to in the 1390s as corbels.[35]

The hammer beams, or some of them, were supported by stone corbels, as can be seen on some of the piers in Norden's view. The 1633 plan shows small projections from some of the piers on the east side, which may have been corbels. Building agreements for houses on the middle part in 1684 required the Bridge House to provide 'such new corbells or other beareings of stoneworke' as the builder proposed.[36] Some hammer beams were given extra support by braces sprung from the piers or the bridge itself, as Norden shows.[37]

Some houses had more than one hammer beam, as there was an 'inward hammerbeame' under the houses of Mrs Lever and John Woller (PE9 and 10) in 1619, though John Amy at SE13 was told by the bridge estates committee in 1726 that only one hammer beam would be provided for his rebuilding.[38] Where there was a single hammer beam it was presumably towards the back of the house. Problems with hammer beams evidently resulted in sagging rather than collapse: the hammer beam referred to in 1619 was 'broken', and there were other defects, 'besydes the whole house of Mrs Lever buckled and settled'. Indeed there is no record of any of the bridge houses collapsing, other than on the two occasions when parts of the bridge itself gave way. A decayed hammer beam could sometimes be repaired or supplemented without the house having to be taken down,[39] and repairs were not always hugely expensive.[40] A hammer beam set up to support two houses in 1684 cost £32.[41]

Some houses, especially on the principal part, were instead supported by stone ribs between the piers (Fig. 16). The plan of 1633 shows two ribs between each pair of neighbouring piers on the west side of the north end (Fig. 8).[42] The committee considering the rebuilding of the houses at the north end in 1682 recommended that 'there bee foure new ribbs built where the same are wanting crosse the gulletts on ye east side of the bridge for the better support of the houses to bee built thereupon', and four new ribs were duly built over the fourth to seventh gulletts.[43] In 1694, a rib was to be erected where several houses were to be rebuilt south of the stone gate, and Mrs Turner, one of the lessees, petitioned the bridge wardens to

Fig. 16 Plan by William Leybourn on a lease of a plot on the west side of the bridge to Humphrey Caseby in 1683, showing the stone ribs between the piers. Caseby built four houses here.

set up 'ye ribb or arch which is to be ye foundacon on which her house is to be built'.[44]

As noted earlier, the smallness of the bridge's arches and the number of piers were criticised in later centuries, as the numerous piers and starlings impeded the river's flow and contributed to high maintenance costs. But if the arches had been much larger and the piers fewer, it would have been significantly harder to build houses along the full length of the bridge, as longer hammer beams would have been required. This does not mean that the arches were made deliberately small for that purpose, but it does indicate that not only the length of the piers but also the smallness of the arches were necessary for London Bridge to have houses along its full length.

CHAPTER 3

The houses from c. 1209 to 1358

Origins

Houses on the bridge seem to have been envisaged from the start, probably drawing on precedents from France, where there were several inhabited bridges before 1176.[1] Part of the evidence is the design of the bridge, with its long piers, as discussed above. The houses were an integral part both of the finances of the bridge and of its physical design. We do not know, of course, exactly how long the piers were when first built. George Dance the Elder observed in 1746 that 'the points of the piers have been much extended in order to erect houses thereon', noting that in some piers there were fresh casings of stone beyond the original ashlar facing.[2] There are a few references to piers being enlarged or widened in the 1470s.[3] But it seems unlikely that the unusual length of the piers was wholly the result of later alterations, or that every one of the piers had been significantly extended, especially given the size of the two piers that never bore any houses. The one next to the drawbridge was 26½ feet long, or 54 feet including the triangular ends, and the eighth pier from the north end was 53 feet long, or 69 feet including the triangular ends.

The evidence from the design is supported by the written record. According to King John in 1202,

> We will and grant, that the rents and profits of the several houses that the said Master of the Schools [Isembert] shall cause to be erected upon the bridge aforesaid, be for ever appropriated to repair, maintain and uphold the same.[4]

The Southwark fire of July 1212 or 1213 spread across the southern part of the bridge at least as far as the chapel, which was destroyed, strongly indicating that there were buildings on the bridge by means of which the fire could spread.[5] A grant of 1221 of land in the parish of St Olave, Southwark, refers to 'the highway leading to the houses of the bridge', which probably indicates houses on the bridge rather than simply houses forming part of the bridge estate. Leases or other documents relating to individual properties on the bridge have survived from the 1220s and 1230s and subsequently. In about 1250, for example, Eufemia, daughter of Andrew le Ferun, granted to the master of the bridge 'all right in her tenement adjoining the stone gate of the bridge of London on the south, which Andrew her father held of the master and brethren of the bridge aforesaid'.[6] In 1280 it was said that the expected collapse of the bridge would result in 'the destruction of innumerable people dwelling upon it'.[7]

Houses may have been regarded as a way of protecting the bridge as well as generating revenue. When the case for rebuilding the one next to St Magnus's church (PE1) was considered in 1667, an argument in favour was that it 'will much preserve the arch there', whereas not rebuilding would be 'prejudicall to the arch'.[8] In 1678, some of the northern piers were said to be 'much prejudiced for want of being built over', and the sheds built after the Great Fire were claimed to be 'a preservacon to the peeres whereupon they are built'.[9]

Exactly what the earliest houses consisted of is unrecorded. New timber-framing methods were being developed around 1200, just at the time the bridge was built, using substantial squared timbers, interdependent components and pegged, closely fitting mortise and tenon joints. One result was that, whereas previously almost all houses were single-storeyed, they now increasingly had two storeys.[10] The 1358 rental describes all the bridge houses as shops, and clearly their main purpose was to be shops on a busy thoroughfare, but a street of lock-up shops on the bridge, with valuable goods left unguarded overnight, is implausible. In the thirteenth and fourteenth centuries shops in and around Cheapside, London's main shopping area, were referred to simply as shops, but invariably had rooms or 'solars' (meaning a private room on an upper floor) above them, and sometimes rooms on more than one upper storey.[11] There are many references from the thirteenth century to houses, messuages or tenements on the bridge, as well as one of 1235/36 to shops and solars,[12] so two storeys was probably the norm. More than two storeys is likely to have become common only in the fourteenth century, as discussed

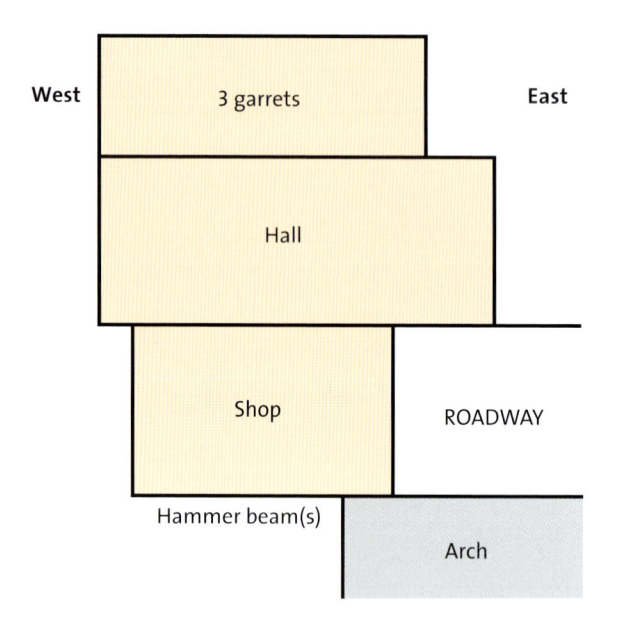

Fig. 17. Reconstructed cross-section of MW10 in 1640, based on a lease of that year. Apart from the garrets, its form is that of a shop and solar.

later.[13] Like other institutional landowners in the thirteenth century, the Bridge House both built and maintained the structures on its property, and it long continued to do so.[14]

Remarkably, one house retained something close to its original form until 1640. MW10, which was probably built before 1460, consisted of a shop, a hall above it, extending over the street, and garrets above that; there was no kitchen (Fig. 17).[15] The garrets had probably been added within the hall's roof space.

The houses in 1358

The first comprehensive evidence of the bridge houses is the rental of 1358.[16] Within each part of the bridge it numbers the shops and states the rents (e.g. 'prima schopa xxvi.s.viii.d'), adding in some cases that the shop had a 'hautpas'. It does not name the lessees or occupants. It is immensely informative, especially as the houses or shops can be linked to those in the rental of 1404–21 and then to the continuous series of rentals from 1460 onwards (Appendix 3). Its information is summarised in Table 1.

Table 1 Houses on the bridge in the 1358 rental

Location	Frontage to roadway (feet)	No. of shops or houses	Average width (feet)	Total rent (shillings)	Average rent (shillings)	Rent per foot of frontage (shillings)
Principal east, northern houses (PE1–9)	183	17	10.8	594	34.9	3.08
Principal west, northern houses (PW2–9)	145	14	10.4	415	29.6	
Principal east, southern houses (PE10–19)	180	17	10.6	359	21.1	2.06
Principal west, southern houses (PW10–21)	190	18	10.6	402	22.3	
Middle east	193	18	10.7	320	17.8	1.55
Middle west	221	20	11.1	323	16.2	
Drawbridge houses, east side	121	7	17.3	160	22.9	1.35
Drawbridge houses, west side	122	7	17.4	167	23.9	
South of stone gate, east side	110	10	11.0	190	19.0	1.43
South of stone gate, west side	122	10	12.2	142	14.2	
Totals or overall average	1587	138	–	3072	22.3	1.93

The figures for the drawbridge houses were added to the rental after 1358. Frontages and rents are given to the nearest whole number. Frontages are from Appendix 1 (principal part), Fig. 11 (middle part and drawbridge houses, in the latter case assuming the same frontages as in 1683) and the Survey (south of the stone gate); they exclude the chapel and a notional 17 feet each for the drawbridge tower and the stone gate. The two houses in the stone gate are excluded.

The most important fact to emerge from the 1358 rental is that there were then no houses between the stone gate and the drawbridge tower. Houses on that part of the bridge are listed, but they are an addition made in the margin (Fig. 18). It is easy to see why that area was not at first built on. It was a military area, between the bridge's two main defensive structures. Evidently, the desire for additional rent eventually overcame the military logic, but the disadvantages were demonstrated when the houses built there were twice destroyed during revolts, in 1450 and 1471.

Without the drawbridge houses, there were 124 houses, plus two dwellings in the stone gate, though in fact eleven of them were wholly or largely on the bridge abutments rather than on the bridge itself. With the drawbridge houses added, the total number would have been up to 138, plus the two in the stone gate.[17] This was the largest number ever, as subsequently many of the small plots were amalgamated.

The next major conclusion is that, apart from the addition of the drawbridge houses, the parts of the bridge occupied by buildings were almost identical in 1358 and 1633. This can be demonstrated by tracing the seventeenth-century houses back through the rentals to 1358 (see Appendix 3). The only other changes were a new house at the north end of the middle west part by 1404 (MW1A) and a possible extension northwards of the opposite house (ME1). The grouping of the houses into three blocks therefore dated back before 1358, and once the drawbridge houses were added as a fourth block (not later than 1381), the pattern that remained in place for centuries was established.[18] While the gap between the drawbridge tower and the stone gate had a military purpose, the gap at the Square, where the superstructure of the bridge itself was wider, may have had the purpose of providing an approach to the chapel and space for processions and other activities, and of making the chapel more visible to travellers.

As we now know the area occupied by the bridge houses, we can conclude on the basis of the 1358 rental that the plots on the bridge averaged about 10½ to 11 feet wide, though slightly more on the west side south of the stone gate. In fact, we can go further and demonstrate that, contrary to what the 1683 measurements seem to suggest, there was a fairly consistent plot size throughout the bridge. There was a long process after 1358, and probably before it, of merging plots, and by following the houses through the rentals between 1358 and the seventeenth century it is possible to identify which plots were merged and when (Appendix 3). Knowing the widths of the seventeenth-century houses and how many of the plots of 1358 each of them incorporated means that we should then be able to identify the widths of the latter. This works extremely well in some parts of the bridge, such as the middle east part, and less well in others, probably for three reasons. The first is that the process was sometimes more complicated than simply merging two plots. For example, the rentals, including the sums specified, make clear that one was divided between its two neighbours in 1523 (MW7 and 8). The second is that boundaries may have shifted when several houses were rebuilt together – for example, where three plots of 1358 had become two plots of roughly equal width by the seventeenth century (e.g. MW9 and 10), although the Bridge House often seems to have recreated what existed before. The third is that the process of merging plots had probably already begun by 1358, and the numbering of that year may sometimes have treated two formerly separate plots as one, or in one case a formerly single plot as two (SW12); hence two cases in 1358 of plots double the usual width.

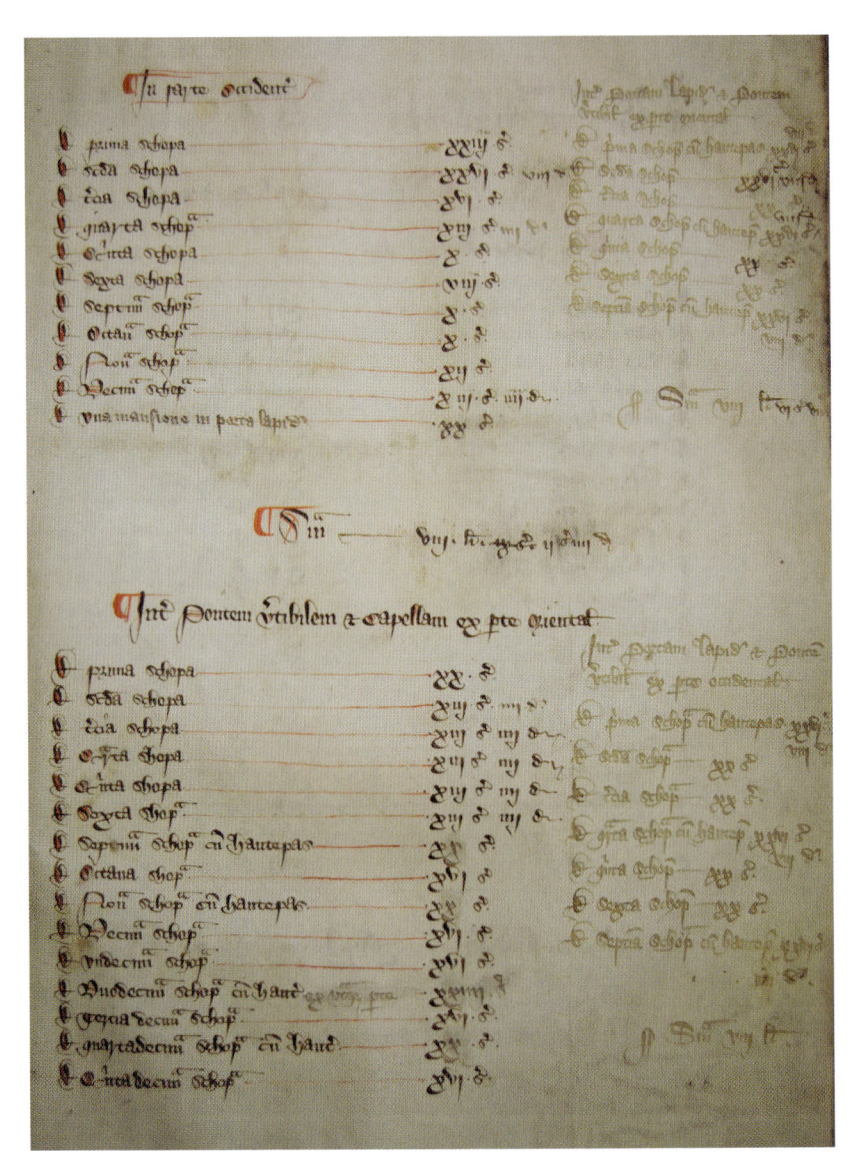

Fig. 18 A page from the Bridge House rental of 1358. It covers the houses south of the stone gate on the west side and most of those between the drawbridge and the chapel on the east side. In the margin the drawbridge houses have been added, possibly in the same hand but clearly at a later date.

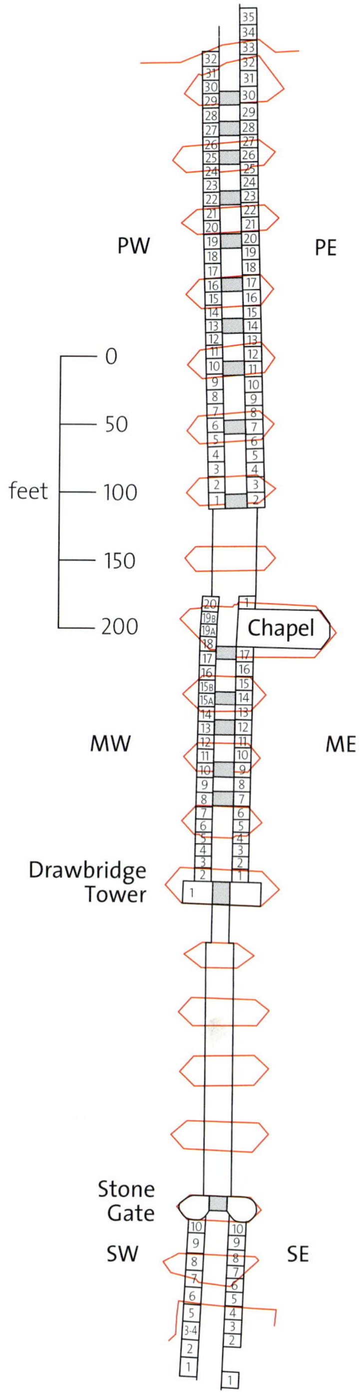

Fig. 19 Reconstructed plan of the layout of the bridge in the thirteenth century, showing the 10-foot plots and the gap in the houses between the stone gate and the drawbridge tower. The house numbers are those assigned in the survey of 1358 (see Appendix 3). A standard plot depth of 13 feet has been assumed, without any variation between houses over piers and those over gullets, and the piers are shown as they were in 1746. The least certain part of the reconstruction is the houses adjoining the drawbridge tower.

THE HOUSES FROM C. 1209 TO 1358   27

Despite the uncertainties, there is no doubt that the bridge was originally laid out with plots around 10 or 11 feet wide, and with this information we can reconstruct the original layout and what the bridge may have looked like (Figs 19–21). The total number of 10-feet wide plots when first laid out was apparently 124, apart from dwellings in the gate and drawbridge tower. Houses on opposite sides of the roadway largely matched each other, except south of the stone gate, which could indicate that one side there was developed later than the other. As for the drawbridge houses, on the reasonable assumption that they occupied about the same area as their successors in 1683, their greater width, of just over 17 feet each, testifies to their later origin.

The original layout, with narrow and roughly standard-sized plots, resembled that of the typical medieval new town, and especially those that consisted of both sides of a linear market place on a main road.[19] As in a medieval new town, the original layout was hard to change subsequently, and some plots only about 10 feet wide survived on the middle and south parts of the bridge until the houses were removed around 1760. The bridge's shops were wider than those of Cheapside, which up to the 1320s were typically only 6 to 7 feet wide. However, Cheapside was London's prime shopping area, and in less prominent locations shops were wider, such us about 13½ feet in Poultry, and 15 to 20 feet in Broad Street and Cornhill.[20] The bridge's shops fell between the two extremes.

The pattern of rents in 1358 is also interesting. Rents per foot of frontage were highest on the northern half of the principal part, which was obviously the part of the bridge most accessible from the City. They were only 67% of that level on the southern half of the principal part, 50% on the middle part and 45% on the south part. Despite the Black Death and the consequent

Fig. 20 Reconstruction drawing by Pete Urmston of the bridge in about 1250, based on the evidence discussed in this book. The drawbridge is being opened to let ships through.

THE HOUSES FROM c. 1209 TO 1358

Although the 1358 rental does not list tenants or their trades, many of them are recorded in the earliest surviving accounts, from 1381 to 1397. The great majority of those named were haberdashers, glovers, cutlers, bowyers or fletchers (thirty-six out of fifty).[22]

The 'hautpas' of 1358

The 1358 rental has one further important thing to tell us. As already indicated, many of the houses were said to have a 'hautpas' or high place. There were nine or ten of these on each side on the principal part and four or five on each side on the middle part, to which the drawbridge houses later added another three on each side; there were none south of the stone gate. They have usually been interpreted as links across the street between the tops of the houses, or even as galleries or other structures built out over the river.[23] However, there was nearly always a cross building in exactly the same place in the seventeenth century, and there can be no doubt that the hautpas were the structures described later as cross buildings, spanning the roadway at first-floor level and above. On the middle part, in four of the five cases the leases indicate cross buildings in about 1650 in the same position as those of 1358. The northernmost cross building of 1358 (between ME3 and MW3) had apparently gone by the 1650s, and instead there was a new one between ME1 and MW1, almost certainly added in 1539–41, when ME1 and MW1 to 5 were all rebuilt. On the principal part, although the lease descriptions rarely explicitly identify the cross buildings, there is good seventeenth-century evidence for all but two of the ten in the places where they were recorded in 1358.[24] The placing of the cross buildings was therefore a fairly stable feature

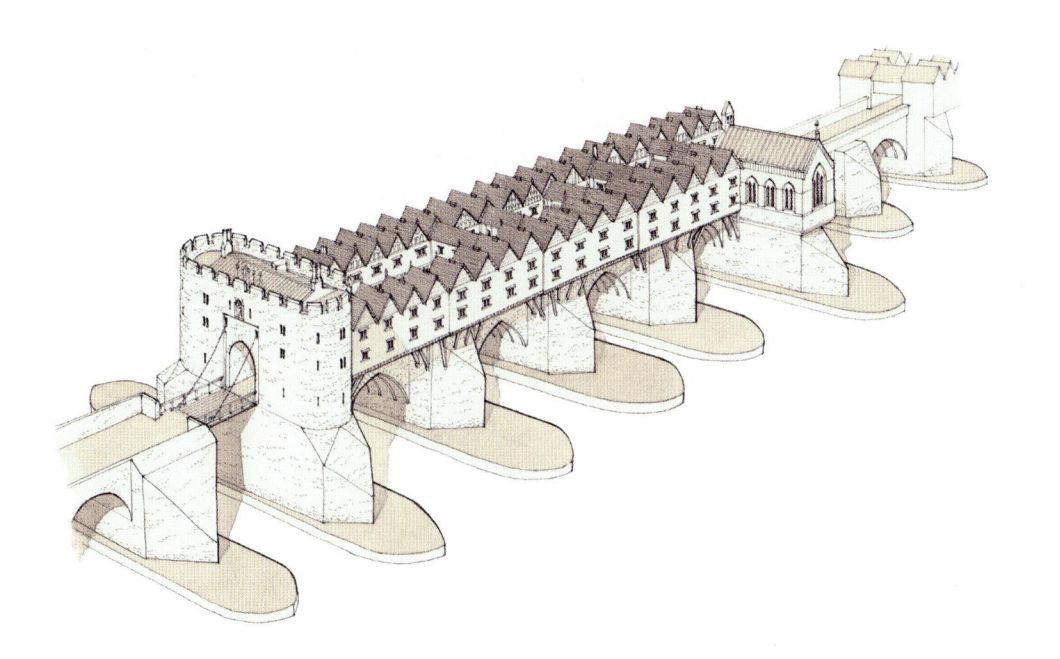

Fig. 21 Reconstruction drawing by Stephen Conlin showing the middle part of the bridge (the same area as in Fig. 15) as it might have appeared in about 1250, with two-storey dwellings each about 10 feet wide.

reduction in population, London rents were fairly stable from about 1330 to 1400, and sometimes for much longer; those for Canterbury Cathedral Priory's London properties remained at their probable pre-1100 level throughout the medieval period.[21] Only a few changes are noted on the 1358 rental itself, and hardly any had changed at all by 1404. On the middle part, for example, plots without a hautpas paid 13s. 4d. or 16s. (except one) and those with a hautpas 20s. or 24s.; the equivalent figures on the southern half of the principal part were 20s. or 21s. without a hautpas (except one) and 22s. or 23s. with a hautpas (except one). The regularity suggests a set of customary and probably long-established rents, little affected by piecemeal changes subsequently, and may take us close to the origin of the bridge houses. The drawbridge houses, similarly, paid 20s. without a hautpas (except one) and 26s. 8d. with a hautpas.

of the bridge. In fact, given the difficulty of creating new ones, because of the effect on neighbouring houses and on the light reaching the roadway, they were probably an even more stable feature than the boundaries between plots. Their early origin explains why they started at first-floor level: when they were created it is likely that most or all of the houses had no more than two storeys. When extra storeys were added, the cross buildings would have been extended upwards at the same time.

Several cross buildings on the principal and middle parts were 10 or 11 feet wide (from north to south) in the seventeenth century.[25] The likelihood is that, except at the drawbridge tower and the stone gate, they were all that width in 1358, since, if they had been much wider (e.g. 20 feet), they would have been shared by neighbouring houses, whereas the rental records no such sharing. In other words, the width of the cross buildings was the same as or similar to the width of the houses they adjoined. In 1683, ME9 was a surviving example of house and cross building having the same width – in this case 10 feet 9 inches – whereas most other cross buildings had been widened by then. Enlarging of cross buildings was a different process from the merging of houses, which might also proceed differently on opposite sides of the roadway, and that must be why in the seventeenth century the widths of the cross buildings usually differed from those of the houses to which they belonged.

The 1358 rental is the only comprehensive record of where the cross buildings were, as the 1683 measurements covered only part of the bridge, and it is therefore the basis for placing the cross buildings of the principal part on the reconstruction plans, even for the seventeenth century. For the reconstruction of the bridge in the thirteenth century it is assumed that all the cross buildings were 10 to 11 feet wide. Once they are reduced to that width and plotted on a map, it becomes clear that they were irregularly spaced, and also that their placing was independent of the piers (Fig. 19). Their location and spacing must have been determined by the Bridge House, which built all the houses. Two different conclusions could be drawn. One is that the lack of regularity indicates that they were not part of the original scheme and were added piecemeal later, for structural or financial reasons, or both. The other, which seems more likely, is that the Bridge House learnt from experience and adapted its planning, perhaps having learnt that the cross buildings had disadvantages and not so many were needed. On the principal part, the first three cross buildings from the north were each separated by only one 10-feet-wide house; there were two houses without cross buildings before each of the next five, and then three houses and four houses without cross buildings before the last two. On the middle part the cross buildings were generally separated by one or two 10-feet-wide houses, though there was a gap of about six houses at its southern end, where a new cross building had been added by the mid-seventeenth century.

The absence of cross buildings south of the stone gate may have been because an unobstructed view from the gate was needed, because the wider street made them harder to build, or because the stability provided by cross buildings was not required on the bridge abutment, though Wyngaerde's drawing does show beams linking two of the houses. The difference between the numbers of cross buildings recorded in 1358 on the east and west sides on both the principal and middle parts was because not all were shared between the two opposite houses; instead, in two cases the whole cross building belonged to a house on one side. The lease description for ME5 in 1653 makes clear that this situation persisted for centuries.

CHAPTER 4

The major buildings

The chapel

All three of the bridge's major buildings are mentioned within sixty years of the bridge's completion, and all seem to have been part of the original plan. All three were at some stage used wholly or partly as dwellings. The chapel of St Thomas the Martyr (Thomas Becket) stood on an exceptionally large pier near the centre of the bridge on the east side. Chapels were common on medieval bridges and a number survive today, such as those at Wakefield and St Ives (Cambridgeshire). The building of bridges was a work of piety; chapels were regarded as a means of encouraging divine protection of those bridges; and travellers, especially pilgrims, might call at a chapel at the start and end of their journeys. Numerous pilgrim badges have been recovered from the Thames around the chapel site.[1] Becket had been murdered in 1170 and canonised in 1173, and quickly became one of the most popular saints. In addition to the chapel dedicated to him, there was later a painted image of him 'over the bridge', repainted in 1420–21, and an image of him on one of the arches on the west side near the chapel in the 1520s.[2]

Peter of Colechurch was buried in the chapel. As already noted, 'the brethren and chaplains ministering in the chapel of St Thomas upon the said bridge' at first played a part in administering the bridge and its estates.[3] Later, when that was wholly the responsibility of the bridge wardens, it was they who maintained the chapel and paid for the chaplains and other expenses.

The original chapel was presumably destroyed or damaged in the fire of 1212/13, and nothing is known about either that chapel or its successor. Between 1387 and 1396 the chapel was rebuilt in the perpendicular style, and that building is much better recorded. It is shown in the view of London in about 1500 and in Wyngaerde's drawing (Figs 22, 23), and some features are recorded in later views, including interior features (Figs 24, 25). The builder was Henry Yevele, master mason to the king from 1360 until his death in 1400, and one of the bridge wardens from 1365 to 1396. He lived on the west side of Bridge Street (the northern approach to the bridge) opposite St Magnus's church. He not only designed the new chapel but also largely paid for it.[4] The main chapel at street level measured about 70 feet by 28 feet, and had a five-sided apse at the east end.[5] A stair turret on the south side allowed access from the starling for people arriving by boat. Much later, the chapel was said to have had a plain gable facing the street, surmounted by a cross.[6] There was an undercroft or lower chapel, 14 feet high and paved with black and white marble.[7] Eighteenth-century sources indicate that the former lower chapel, then a cellar, was remarkably dry, despite being close to the water, and this seems to indicate the use of waterproof mortar.[8]

In 1539–40, following Henry VIII's condemnation of Thomas Becket as a traitor, the dedication of the chapel was changed to St Thomas the Apostle. At about the same time the number of clerks was reduced from five to one.[9] In 1548, benches from the chapel were disposed of, as was the timber of the steeple, though weekly payments for singing there apparently continued for the whole year. In 1549 the decision was taken that the chapel should be 'defaced', reflecting the Protestant policies of Edward VI's government, and a new timber frame was to be constructed in order to convert it into a house. In 1550 images in the windows were replaced by new plain windows, and the organ was sold, but further action was slow. In early 1553 masons were paid for 'the breakinge

Above: **Figs 22–23** The chapel as seen in the view of *c.* 1500 and in Wyngaerde's view of *c.* 1544.

Left: **Fig. 24** George Vertue's engraving of the former lower chapel, later the cellar of the chapel house, seen from the west in 1744.

Right: **Fig. 25** George Vertue's engraving reconstructing the interior of the upper chapel, looking east, published in 1748. Vertue had no evidence with which to reconstruct the vaulted roof, and some of the windows he shows on the right would have been obstructed by the houses there.

THE MAJOR BUILDINGS   33

up of the chappell' and carpenters for setting up a new frame there.[10] Building probably continued for some time, as it was not until June 1556 that William Bridger, a grocer, paid an entry fine – the large sum of £133 6s. 8d. – for what became known as the chapel house.[11]

The lease description of 1627 and later views and a plan (Figs 26–30) indicate what had been done. The lower chapel became a cellar ('a great large cellar'), with two levels in part of it. The walls of the upper chapel were retained at ground-floor level, but the upper walls and the roof were removed and new upper storeys were added by means of the timber frame. The result was a very large four-storey house, by far the largest house on the bridge. On the ground floor was a shop about 24 feet wide and 36 feet deep, with a large warehouse behind it. On the first floor was a 'great hall', 30 feet by 23 feet, together with two parlours and a kitchen. On the second floor, over the hall was a 'fair chamber', 23 feet by 22 feet, with windows to north and south and a chimney to the west, together with a gallery (39 feet by 11 feet), three chambers and some small rooms. There were five more chambers on the top

Left to right:
Figs 26–28 The chapel house as seen in Norden's view of 1597–98, a print of 1710 and Sutton Nicholls's view of 1711.

floor.[12] There was a staircase projecting beyond the line of the walls to the south. The print of about 1710 is more convincing than Norden's, which makes the chapel house too wide, shows no windows on the ground floor and crams in three storeys above with implausibly little headroom.

At one end of the starling on which the chapel house stood was a small rectangular fishpond or well where fish were trapped when the tide fell, and this probably dated back to when the chapel still existed (Fig. 27). In 1622 there was a dispute between the Bridge House workmen and the tenant, Anne Dye, over both the stonework of the pier and the well, and in 1627 Robert Osbolston's lease of the chapel house forbade him and his servants from taking the fish or interfering with the well and the stonework.[13] After most repair obligations for other houses had been transferred to tenants, the Bridge House retained responsibility for the chapel house's external stone walls, and repairing the east and south sides cost the large sum of £250 in 1647–48.[14]

By 1682, the chapel house (sometimes referred to as 'the stonehouse')[15] was divided into two. John Savage, a grocer, had the front shop, known as the Cross Keys, and half of the rest of the house, while Nicholas Smith had a passage from the street, the back part of the ground floor, known as the Swan and presumably a shop, and the other half of the house.[16] When the roadway in the middle part of the bridge was widened in the mid-1680s, the street front of the chapel house was set back, and the stonework at that end of the building must then have been removed (Fig. 30). The ground lost was 5½ feet at the south end of the front and 2½ feet at the north end, reflecting the fact that the roadway had not been straight at this point.[17] Even after this, the depth of the chapel house was about 66 feet. Its cellar was not truncated, and now projected three feet under the roadway.[18] The plan of the house (Fig. 30) dates from the 1740s, and shows that on the ground floor most of the stonework of 1387–96, apparently including original window openings, survived.

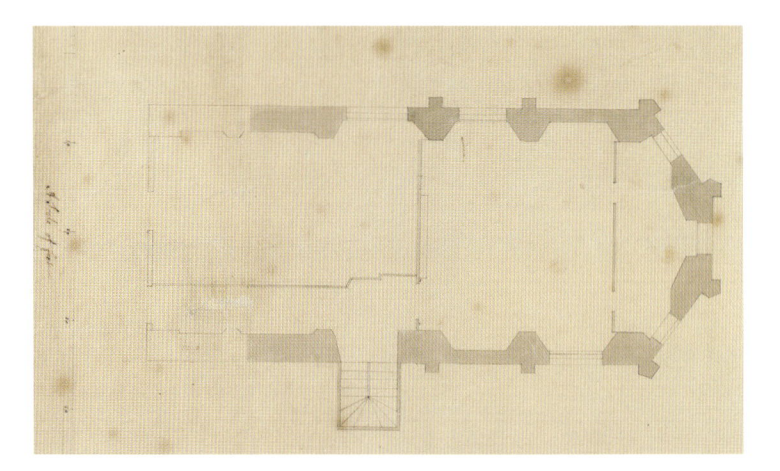

Fig. 29 The chapel house seen from the west in 1758 after all the other houses on the middle part had been demolished apart from ME1 to its left (detail from the print at Fig. 101). It seems to make the chapel house too wide.

Fig. 30 Plan of the chapel house in about 1744, when it was proposed to create a 'piazza' or covered walkway across the bridge, about 12 feet wide, and to take it through the west part of the house. As the plan shows the proposed piazza and openings to the street, it must be at ground-floor level, and therefore shows the remains of the upper chapel. North is at the top.

The stone gate

The gatehouse near the south end of the bridge, first mentioned in about 1250, defended one of the main approaches to London (Figs 31–33). It was known as the stone gate or the great gate, and together with the drawbridge and drawbridge tower was a formidable barrier against anyone seeking to enter London if the bridge was defended. In 1471, during a rebellion against the restoration of Edward IV, the stone gate fell to Thomas Fauconberg but the drawbridge tower did not, whereas in 1554 Sir Thomas Wyatt, rebelling against Queen Mary, was deterred from attacking the stone gate.[19] The last occasion on which the stone gate had military importance was in 1647, when men of Southwark held the bridge against the City in support of the New Model Army. The Bridge House accounts record 18s. 'for lettinge downe and pullinge up the portcullice at the bridge gate, upon the approach of Sr Thomas Fairefax armie'.[20]

In 1394, two statues of Richard II and his queen were placed on the gate, together with their arms and those of Edward the Confessor, and large canopies over them. This was by order of Richard II himself, shortly after he had placed statues of kings in Westminster Hall. The ones on the stone gate were carved by Thomas Wrenke, mason, and cost £10, while painting them cost £20.[21] In January 1437 the stone gate

Left to right:
Figs 31–33 The stone gate, as seen from the south side in Wyngaerde's view of *c.* 1544 and from the north side in Norden's view of 1597–98 and Nicholls's view of 1711. The last two of these both show the heads of executed traitors.

and the two adjoining arches collapsed, following a period in which maintenance of the bridge had been neglected. Funds were being collected for rebuilding in 1439, and work probably started fairly soon afterwards,[22] but in 1450 the gate is likely to have been damaged by fire during Cade's rebellion. Work on rebuilding it again seems to have been completed in 1465–70, when there are references in the accounts to 'the new tower' at the south end of the bridge.[23] This was just in time for it to be damaged once more during Fauconberg's rebellion of 1471. In his will of 1472 (not proved until 1476) Sir John Crosby left £100 'towards the making of a new toure of stone, to be set and stand at Stulpes [the staples or posts marking the end of the bridge], at south end of London Bridge, or there about, toward Southwark', provided the work was done within ten years.[24] There are references in 1472–76 to the new tower and gate at the south end of the bridge.[25] Probably the stone gate always consisted of two towers and a gateway between them, as it did when a plan was drawn in about 1728 (Fig. 34). The towers were then about 17 feet in diameter, with walls about 2½ feet thick.

Changes were made in 1521–24. In 1521 stone images of Saints Peter, Paul, Michael and George, carved by a Spaniard, Matthew Peter, were set up on the 'great gate', and in 1523 Andrew Wright, a painter, painted two gold lions on the gate. In 1522 £50 was received from the Grocers' Company out of the estate of Sir John Crosby towards the cost of 'enlarging of the weye at the grete gate of London brigge', and in 1524 Alderman Sir William Butlar gave £20 towards the same work. Their arms were to be set up on the gate as a result, and this was done with 'ii plates of copur and gylte graven with scripture' in 1527.[26] Perhaps Crosby's £100 had been withheld because the work he left it for had already been completed by the time of

Fig. 34 Plan of the stone gate and elevation of its north side in about 1728, before the alterations made in that year.

his death in 1476, and £50 for a somewhat different purpose was agreed instead. The stone gate as altered in the 1520s is clearly shown in Wyngaerde's drawing of c. 1544, where it is adorned on the south side by what seems to be a coat of arms with statues either side (Fig. 31). After the drawbridge tower was demolished in 1577, the heads of executed traitors, previously displayed there, were put up on the stone gate

THE MAJOR BUILDINGS   37

Left to right:

Fig. 35 Plan of the stone gate showing the proposal to widen the roadway and provide a second postern for pedestrians, together with an elevation of the north side of the gateway. Whether the alterations were carried out exactly in this form in 1728 is unknown.

Fig. 36 View of the south side of the stone gate dated 1737, showing the changes made to the central part of the structure in 1728.

Fig. 37 The royal arms from the stone gate, as altered from those of George II to George III, now set in the facade of the King's Arms public house, Newcomen Street, Southwark.

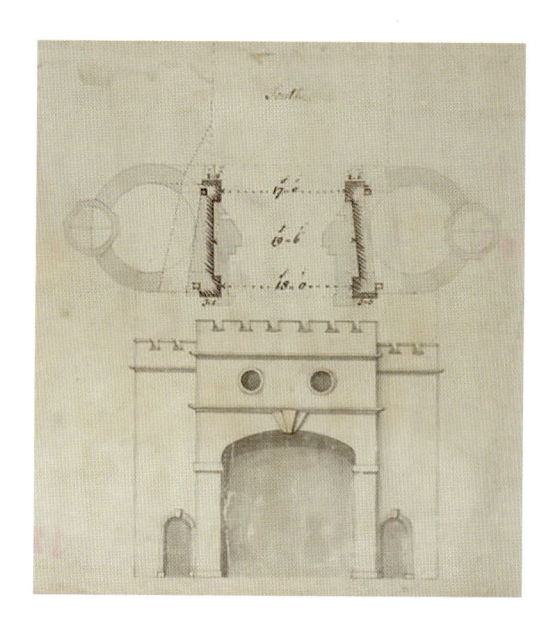

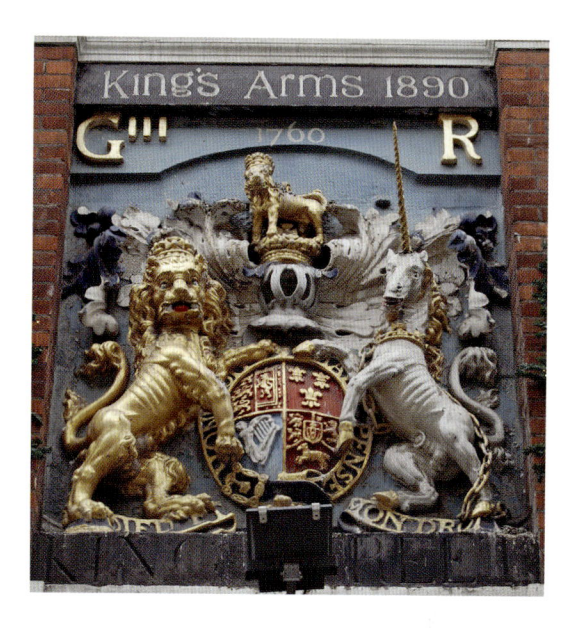

instead. The last was apparently installed in 1661, and from 1684 they were placed on Temple Bar.[27]

After the 1520s there is no evidence of any further widening of the roadway at the gate until 1728,[28] so the width up to 1728 is what was achieved in the 1520s. It was 11 feet at the gate itself and 13 feet at the gateway arch. It must have been even less before the 1520s. The one change, recorded in 1726 as having been made 'some years since', was the creation of a postern for pedestrians on the west side.[29] After the gate was damaged by fire in 1725 there was renewed pressure to widen the passage under it. Although it has usually been said that the gate was then rebuilt, the papers of the bridge estates committee show that only the middle part of the gate was rebuilt, leaving the outer parts of the two towers intact. This was done in 1728, at a cost of £670, resulting in a roadway 18 feet wide and postern gates on both sides for pedestrians (Figs 34–36).[30] A plaque recorded the widening of the passage from 11 feet to 18 feet. Also, the arch over the roadway was higher, corresponding to the greater height of the rest of bridge's roadway from the 1680s. In this altered form the stone gate survived until it was removed with the bridge's houses in 1760. The royal arms from the gate, originally those of George II but later altered to those of George III, can still be seen in the facade of the King's Arms public house in Newcomen Street, Southwark (Fig. 37).

The gate's two towers provided houses, usually for officials. In 1358 and 1460–73 the western tower was occupied by the keeper of the gate, but in 1399 it was granted to William Est, Mayor's Serjeant and Bailiff of Southwark, and in 1421 to John Hastyng, 'Mayor's Esquire', for good service past and future.[31] Subsequently, it seems to have been let out, but from 1557 it was occupied by the Beadle of Bridge Ward, apparently rent-free. An attempt in 1658 to impose a rent of £6 a year evidently failed, as in 1699 the bridge estates committee found the Beadle still living there rent-free. They asked what right he could claim, to which he replied that he was 'only relyeing on a custome that he had lived in it about 22 yeares without any molestation', and that an alderman had promised him a house rent-free when he became Beadle. The committee ordered that he be ejected, but eventually agreed that the ward should pay 10s. per year.[32] In 1734, it was ordered that the west side of the gate be fitted up for the gatekeeper to live there.[33]

Until the early 1550s the eastern tower was occupied by the Beadle of Bridge Ward, but by 1557 John Peere, described as a Mayor's officer and clerk of the market, was living there. In 1630 it was found that a City official called the Yeoman of the Channel had for some years claimed the east part of the gate and had let it out, and it was agreed to pay him 50s. a year in lieu of his claim.[34] Subsequently, the Bridge House let it out. By 1551 there was a shed or single-storey shop outside the stone gate on the east side, and in 1630 it was noted that the shop would yield little rent if let separately from the east part of the gate. It was a bookshop from 1595 to 1654 and from about 1667 to 1700, as discussed later.[35] In 1630 the gate tower had a cellar and four storeys above, including a ground-floor hall 12 feet in diameter. By 1654 there was an extra storey, and the rooms were cellar, kitchen, 'inner shop', hall, chamber and another chamber, one over the other.[36] In about 1730 the lease was bought in by the Bridge House, and from 1737 the rooms in the gate (presumably excluding the west side) were the residence of the junior bridge warden. He complained in 1741 that the windows in the 'great room' above the arch were 'very much exposed to the wind and weather', and requested shutters.[37]

The stone gate evidently had an impact on the houses to its south, as they lacked cross buildings and are shown as uniformly low in the Pepys view (Fig. 2). There was little point in a fortified gate if the view from it was obstructed and enemies could look down on it from above. Even as it was, the houses may have compromised the gate, as shown by events during Wyatt's rebellion of 1554. At 11 p.m. one February night, after the rebels had occupied Southwark, Wyatt and a few others broke through the wall of an adjoining house and gained access to the leads of the gate. Then they descended through the porter's house, finding him asleep by the fire downstairs. Leaving him unharmed, but 'greatlie amazed', they advanced as far as the drawbridge, from which they could see the Lord Mayor and others discussing the defence of the bridge. This persuaded the rebels to withdraw from Southwark and seek another way into the City, but if the City had been less well prepared there might have been a different outcome.[38] By the seventeenth century the military role of the gate was clearly not considered so important, as many of the houses south of the gate then acquired extra storeys.[39]

The drawbridge tower

The drawbridge tower is first mentioned in 1258. It contained the machinery for raising and lowering the drawbridge and was probably also a second fortified gate preventing access to London from the south. The drawbridge enabled large ships to pass upstream to Queenhithe and elsewhere, and tolls paid by ships doing so provided part of the bridge's income. According to Stow, the drawbridge tower began to be rebuilt in 1426.[40] Wyngaerde's drawing of *c.* 1544 provides the only detailed view

THE MAJOR BUILDINGS 39

Above: **Fig. 38** Detail from Wyngaerde's view of c. 1544 showing the drawbridge tower.

Right: **Fig. 39** Detail from the so-called Agas map of London of about 1561 (based on an earlier map of about 1557) showing London Bridge, including the houses with towers at the south end of the principal part, the drawbridge tower and what seems to be the house with many windows. The awkward junction with the Borough and Tooley Street is also shown.

of it (Fig. 38), though it can also be seen on the so-called Agas map (Fig. 39). It had four circular or polygonal corner towers, a gallery on the south side from which the drawbridge could be observed, and three or four storeys. At the top it carried the heads of executed traitors on poles (see Fig. 38), the first recorded of these being that of Sir William Wallace in 1305.[41] At least after 1426, the structure was much larger than was needed for operating the drawbridge, and it incorporated two substantial houses, one on each side. Each was known, for obvious reasons, as the stone house or stone tenement ('the stonehouse nexte the drawebridge' in 1559).[42] William Stede, Alderman and grocer, held both of the stone houses from 1484 to 1506.[43] From 1515 the occupant of the eastern house also rented one or two chambers in the main part of the drawbridge tower. When Robert Branches, described as a widow, held the eastern house in 1568, her lease excluded the room containing the two wheels which wound up the drawbridge.[44]

The drawbridge tower was probably damaged during the revolts of 1450 and 1471, and from 1476 the accounts record that the drawbridge could no longer be raised because the tower's stonework needed repair.[45] It never was repaired, probably because the tolls gathered were not sufficient to make it worthwhile. In 1481, because of the state of the tower, it was ordered that the drawbridge be raised only when absolutely necessary, such as for the defence of the City. What were apparently the last two occasions on which it was raised, in 1485 and 1500, were both to allow Henry VII's barge to pass through.[46] Repairs in 1488 dealt with the tower's roof and battlements. In 1494 the Bridge House's masons and carpenters viewed 'the great jupardy' of the defects in the tower. Aldermen did the same in 1497–98, when rebuilding was considered, but nothing was done.[47] In 1554, as Wyatt's rebels approached, it proved impossible to raise the drawbridge, so it was thrown into the river instead.[48] Nevertheless, the tower continued to stand until 1577, when it was replaced by Nonsuch House, discussed later.[49]

Other structures

Medieval London had a system of public conveniences, some of them very large, with up to 128 seats.[50] Two of these latrines, or 'common sieges', were at the north and south ends of the bridge, and scattered references make it possible to piece together some of their story. The one at the north end is first recorded in 1306, when a debtor gave his creditor's servant the slip by entering it and then leaving by another entrance.[51] Two entrances suggest an above-ground structure rather than a cellar, and so does the fact that it was reconstructed by a carpenter using timber in 1383, costing £11, and was repaired by carpenters in 1464.[52] In 1358 the Bridge House owned quit rents from a shop and solar at the staples at the London end of the bridge abutting west on the highway, north on a tenement of Roger Clovile and south on the common latrine.[53] Another survey, possibly of similar date, records a shop and solar at the staples on the east side between the highway to the west, tenements north and east and the way leading to the common latrine south. Both indicate that the latrine was at the northernmost part of the bridge, and the latter suggests that it was behind the bridge houses on the riverbank or the first pier.[54] A common latrine at the south end of the bridge probably existed by 1481, when it was ordered that the bridge's two latrines be repaired.[55]

In 1481 disaster struck: according to Stow, 'an house called the common siege on London bridge fell downe into the Thames, through the fall whereof five men were drowned'. A payment in 1481 for making clean the stairs at the entrance to the privy at the north end of the bridge could indicate that the northern latrine was then moved into a cellar, as happened later to the southern one.[56] However, nothing more is recorded. After the Great Fire, residents of the Billingsgate area pressed for a common latrine there, which suggests that there was no longer one at the north end of the bridge.[57]

At the south end, the common latrine was rebuilt in 1505. John Styvar was paid 'for taking downe of the comon seege at the southende of the bridge', and Thomas Pullen and Lawrence Cotton were paid for the 'new making' of it.[58] In 1540 Southwark residents petitioned the City to rebuild 'the common house of easement' at the foot of the bridge, and in 1542 the City ordered the bridge wardens to do so, 'where in time past a like house hath been'. Certain householders nearby were assessed at a halfpenny each per quarter to pay the man who kept it 'for opening and shutting of the same'.[59] The latrine of 1542 was probably in a cellar, as in 1591 Edward Muschampe was granted the lease of a space 'under his house (having byn a common privy)'; it appears in the rental as 'the common vault'.[60] Muschampe's house was SE14, which was on the bridge abutment rather than the bridge itself, so again the common latrine was at the end of the bridge. From the 1570s the City insisted that dwellings and alleys have their own privies, so the common latrines declined, except those at markets.[61] Nevertheless, in 1591 the Court of Aldermen ordered the 'newe erectinge of a pryvye howse nere the watergate at thende of London Bridge'.[62] Whether the order was obeyed and, if so, how long the common latrine lasted is unknown, as there are no more references to it.

Fig. 40 The stocks and the cage on the bridge, with the stone gate in the background. This view is from an eighteenth-century edition of Foxe's *Book of Martyrs*.

Also on the bridge were the stocks and the cage, for imprisoning people (Fig. 40). The one indication of where the stocks were is from the Bridge House's 'view' (or inspection) of 1682, which places them on the west side, just north of the stone gate. It states that within the gate

> on ye west side there is an aple woman pays 8d per weeke to ye Beadle [of Bridge Ward] for her standing at ye stockes and yet ye ward desire ye Bridgehouse to repair ye penthouse over ye stockes.[63]

When a postern for pedestrians was made through the west side of the gate 'some years' before 1726 the stocks were taken down, but in that year the bridge estates committee gave £10 to the ward to set up new ones.[64] Other structures were the staples or posts with chains marking the two ends of the bridge (the 'roadechaine' is mentioned in 1649);[65] the stone parapets, sometimes surmounted by iron railings, where there were no houses;[66] and the wheelage house where tolls were collected (SW1).

Two other structures need to be mentioned here because, though not on the bridge itself, they appear in the views and had some impact on the houses. The first was the waterworks on the west side at the north end, created by Peter Morris, a Dutchman, in 1578–82. Morris dispelled doubts about his proposal by projecting a jet of water high over the tower of St Magnus's church, and the City then leased him the first arch of the bridge. A waterwheel under the arch drove a pump that raised water to the top of a tower, from which wooden pipes conveyed it to two conduits and to individual houses. A wheel under the second arch was added in 1582/83 and one under the fourth arch in 1701.[67] The water tower and the machinery are clearly shown on the 1633 plan and in the Pepys view (Figs 2, 8).

At the south end, waterwheels for grinding corn were set up in 1590 just west of the bridge, the aim being that poorer citizens could bring their own corn to be ground at a moderate charge.[68] The Pepys view shows a building spanning the bridge abutment and the first two starlings a little way west of the bridge itself, with two waterwheels. By the eighteenth century there were wheels there pumping water to supply Southwark. The waterworks at both ends of the bridge continued to operate until 1822.[69]

CHAPTER 5

The houses from 1358 to 1633

There were four main changes from 1358 up to the fire of 1633: houses on new sites (almost entirely confined to one area), merging of plots, rebuilding of houses and enlargement of houses.

Houses on new sites

The major addition shortly after 1358 was the drawbridge houses, consisting of seven houses on each side and three cross buildings. At least some of these houses existed by 1385, when one Hytherpool paid an entry fine for a shop between the stone gate and the drawbridge.[1] They are unlikely to have been built after 1381, as the detailed accounts which begin in that year reveal no such major building project. The drawbridge houses can therefore be dated to between 1358 and 1381. Probably they spanned three piers and the gullets between them, as their successors did in the seventeenth century.

The other house inserted subsequently in the 1358 rental was at the north end of the middle west part, and became part of MW1.[2] By 1404 four houses, all with relatively low rents, had been added on the north side of the stone gate – three on the west side and one on the east – but they disappeared between 1421 and 1460, together with SE9 to 11 and SW7 and 8. The collapse of the stone gate and its two adjoining arches in 1437 probably took them with it, and, if rebuilt, they may have been destroyed again during Cade's rebellion of 1450. The drawbridge houses were probably also destroyed during Cade's rebellion, as they were described in 1471 as newly built.[3] The houses from the first pier southwards (SE12 to 15 and SW9 to 13) evidently survived, as their rents remained almost unchanged from 1421 to 1460 and even some of the tenants remained the same.

During Fauconberg's rebellion of 1471 fighting took place between the stone gate and the drawbridge tower, and the drawbridge houses, described as fourteen newly-built houses, were destroyed again.[4] (One of the bridge tenants, Richard Garnell, a bowyer at MW3, was among those killed.)[5] A few 'cabins' (presumably sheds) were created afterwards, but otherwise none of the drawbridge houses and none of those which had disappeared south of the stone gate were replaced until 1494, and the south part of the bridge was not fully

THE HOUSES FROM 1358 TO 1633   43

Figs 41–42 The earliest known views of London Bridge, drawn between 1461 and about 1475 to illustrate Jon Lydgate's *Lives of Saints Edmund and Fremund*. The text records that at 4 p.m. on 20 November 1441, the three-year-old son of a butcher was pushed by an ox and fell off the bridge. With the help of St Edmund, passing boatmen rescued him. The drawings are unlikely to be topographically accurate. Two-storey gabled houses are shown in one view, which perhaps resembled the bridge's earliest houses, but the second view shows one-storey houses.

rebuilt until 1548. Apart from the changes just described, the area on the bridge occupied by houses was unchanged between 1358 and 1633.

Merging of plots

The bridge's 10-feet plots had probably already begun to be merged by 1358, and the process was certainly under way by 1404. Similar changes took place in the Cheapside area, where the minute plots of around 1300 tended to disappear as London's population fell drastically following the Black Death, and did not reappear when the population rose again after 1500.[6] Merging of plots without permission was forbidden by Bridge House leases, and the Bridge House may have sought to prevent it; as late as 1568 a tenant occupying two adjoining houses was instructed that if she ceased to live in both of them

herself she must convert them back into two tenements, each with its own staircase and kitchen.[7] The process continued regardless, and the bridge estates committee actually required two properties to be merged in 1606.[8]

When two adjoining houses were brought into single ownership, they were often split up again later. Here, properties are regarded as merged only if they were never subsequently separated. On that definition, six plots were absorbed into others between 1358 and 1404, and another fifteen by 1460, seventeen by 1502, eleven by 1525, and four by 1560 (Appendix 3).[9] The principal part of the bridge was particularly affected. The total number of plots fell from about 138 in 1381 to ninety-two in 1560. After 1550 mergers were few, and some proved temporary. Many merged properties, especially on the principal part, continued to have rooms about 10 feet wide and sometimes very long (e.g. a hall 10 feet by 24 feet at PE9), but this was so even where properties had been rebuilt after a merger, and seems to reflect nothing more than the fact that a house 20 feet wide is likely to have rooms either 20 feet wide or 10 feet wide.

A 10-feet width evidently became inconveniently small, but there seems to have been little appetite for more than 20 feet. There are few examples of more than two 10-feet plots being merged into one, and in at least two such cases the merged property contained two separate shops (ME3 and MW12). The new houses built on the principal part in the 1640s mostly had widths from 19 feet 6 inches to 26 feet 3 inches, but when the whole of the principal part was rebuilt in the 1680s the new houses were almost all 15 to 17 feet wide.[10]

Rebuilding of houses

There was probably a fairly constant process of rebuilding the bridge houses, but it becomes visible only once the continuous series of accounts of expenditure begins in 1460.[11] Until the seventeenth century new building and even repairs were carried out by the Bridge House itself, so rebuilding of houses should be recorded in the accounts. In the most informative cases they have payments to the carpenters for making a new 'frame' (the timber construction that formed the skeleton of a house or group of houses), they indicate work on the new houses by other tradesmen, especially the glazier, they state the number of houses rebuilt and the location or the tenants affected, they list 'vacations' of a group of contiguous houses (i.e. lessees not expected to pay their rent for that year or quarter), they record an increase in rents for a group of contiguous houses, and they list entry fines or name the tenants of houses described as new. In the south part, where there were empty sites after 1471, the rentals reveal the existence of new houses. In the least informative case, the rebuilding following a fire in 1504, the accounts make clear that rebuilding is taking place, but do not indicate either the number of houses rebuilt or the precise location. We have to rely on chronicles to tell us that the fire began at a house called the Panier, near St Magnus's church, and that six houses were destroyed.[12] By the 1570s the accounts have become more standardised, and rebuildings could be hidden within payments for wages and materials. From 1570, however, there is a record of leases granted, and it includes orders to rebuild. Occasionally in the sixteenth century the Court of Aldermen ordered rebuilding or recorded it.[13]

Sometimes rebuilding was prompted by the burning of houses, as in 1504. During that fire the Lord Mayor was

Fig. 43 Detail from a view of London in c. 1500, showing 2½- and 3½-storey houses on the principal part and the chapel. Like the earlier views, it is unlikely to be topographically accurate. For example, it ought to show a house on the north side of the chapel and two arches, rather than one, between that house and the principal part.

involved in giving orders, and several 'bogemen' were rewarded afterwards for bringing 'boges with water' (low trucks with four wheels), in one case doing so throughout the night.[14] Sometimes the reason given was decay or smallness. For example, the house of John Bright, clothworker (MW6), was ordered to be rebuilt in 1590 'forasmuch as the same howse is verye smale and in greate ruyne'. Similarly, two years later, John Edmeade's house (PW15) was 'a small tenement and ruynous'.[15] In some cases, rebuilding was evidently connected with the reconstruction of arches or piers, and it must have been difficult to carry out such work without removing and rebuilding the houses, though perhaps the causation sometimes worked the other way and the need to rebuild houses provided the opportunity to work on a pier. In 1476–77 the fifth and sixth piers from the north on the east side were enlarged and three houses on or near the fifth pier were rebuilt (PE12–14), though not those above the sixth pier. In 1488 two piers were reconstructed on the west side near the drawbridge tower and some of the houses there were rebuilt. And in 1531 the carpenters made a new frame for four tenements 'upon an arche and pyer of stone of late newe made' (PW10–13).[16] The other factor affecting the timing of rebuilding was the state of the Bridge House's finances.

Sometimes it was difficult to rebuild one house on its own. For example, PW14 and 15 stood over the same gullet, presumably sharing a hammer beam or beams. Having ordered in 1592 that the former be rebuilt, the bridge estates committee noted that this could not conveniently be done without also rebuilding the latter, and so ordered that they be rebuilt as a single frame.[17] (Apparently PW13, partly over the same gullet, did not need to be rebuilt as well.) The other difficulty must have been in rebuilding houses which shared a cross building, though it was possible to prop up one end, and indeed Wyngarde shows just such a propped-up cross building at SW3 (Fig. 44). Building and repairing houses on the bridge was of course dangerous work. In 1632 Thomas Lewis, a Bridge House employee for fourteen years, was putting up scaffolding when he fell, coming to 'a sudden and lamentable death haveing the scull of his heade dashed into many peeces'; the Bridge House agreed to pay 2s. a week to his widow, Alice.[18] Scaffolding was sometimes placed underneath the houses and was dismantled at low tide,[19] which indicates that it was constructed on the starlings.

There were ninety-one houses standing on the bridge in 1605, and the dates when fifty-eight of them were built can be identified (Table 2).[20] In addition, the six houses burnt in 1504 near St Magnus's church were rebuilt shortly afterwards and were probably part of PE2 to PE11, for none of which there is any subsequent record of rebuilding, and two unidentified houses on the south part seem to have been rebuilt by Humphrey Coke under contract in about 1513 (probably within SW8 to 13). That leaves twenty-five undated houses. It seems unlikely that whole houses could have been rebuilt after 1460 without leaving a trace in the accounts, at least up to the 1570s, and therefore the undated houses were almost certainly built before 1460. It is probably significant that they included the smallest houses, as discussed later.[21]

For some time after 1460 there was apparently only one house rebuilt.[22] This may have reflected the Bridge House's lack of spare cash.[23] From 1477 was there a trickle of rebuildings, the most important before 1504 being the six houses immediately north of the drawbridge tower in 1487–90. There was another burst of activity in 1504–08, partly prompted by the fire of 1504 and giving rise to about thirteen

Table 2 Rebuilding of houses 1463–1655

1463	1 house, PW6
1477	3 houses, PE12–14
1486	1 house, SE15
1487–90	5 or 6 houses, ME10–11, MW11–12*
1495–96	2 houses, SE1, SW3
1504	1 house, SW7
1504–05	New houses at north end following a fire which destroyed six houses (probably within PE2–14)
1507–08	New houses at south end, apparently SE2–4, SW1–2B
c. 1513	2 houses at south end**
1526–29	10 houses, PE15–19, PW17–21
1529–30	3 houses, SE9–11
1531–32	4 houses, PW10–13
1535–36	2 houses, PW4–5
1539–41	6 houses, ME1, MW1–5
1547–48	6 houses, SE5–7, SW4–6
1553	ME2 (chapel house)
1559	2 houses at bridge foot, probably SE12–13***
c. 1572	At least 1 house, PE1
1577–79	ME12, MW13 (Nonsuch House)
1590	1 house, MW6
1592	2 houses, PW14–15
1596	1 house, PW3
1610	1 house, SW8
1630–31	1 house on recently-acquired plot, PW1
1644	1 house, SW10 (by tenant)
c. 1644	1 house, PE1 (by tenant)
1645–49	13 houses at north end
c. 1647	1 house, SW12 (by tenant)
1649–50	1 house, ME6 (by tenant)
1655–56	2 houses, MW7–8 (by tenant)

Sources: BHR; BHJ; CCLD, 02620.

Houses not accounted for above up to 1600: PE2–11, PW2, PW7–9, PW16, ME3–9, MW7–10, SE14, SW8–13. (PW1 was not yet acquired; SE8 was part of the stone gate.)

It is occasionally uncertain whether the accounts are referring to repair or rebuilding, i.e. (i) Richard Frecok's PW6 in 1463, included above: 'To Thomas Wareham carpenter, for timber and carpentry works had and used in a new building in the tenement of Richard Frecok, fletcher, newly built in this year, by agreement made with him in gross', £10 (BHR, 060, p. 134); (ii) Richard Gardyner's MW2 in 1497–99: said to be 'renewed, newe made and amended' by Gardyner, and £20 paid by him 'towarde the costes in bilding newe the tenement wheryn the same Richard nowe dwellith upon London Bridge' (BHR, 004, ff. 176b, 201a); (iii) Simon Lowe's PE6 in 1538: 'mendynge and makynge newe of Symonde Lowys house' (BHR, 006, f. 249a).

Four datestones were found on the south part of the bridge during demolition in 1757, proclaiming 1487, 1497, 1509 and 1514 (British Library, Add. MS 71008, ff. 64–65). That of 1497 was presumably the one at SE1 or SW3, originally intended to bear the date 1494 (BHR, 004, f. 160b).

* Previously six houses apart from the two in the drawbridge tower. Those on the east side were described both as two new tenements and three new tenements (BHR, 004, ff. 76a–b, 87b). On both sides, property held with the houses in the drawbridge tower was rebuilt, but the tower itself was not.

** In 1512–13, 26s.8d. was paid to Humphrey Coke for weatherboarding the south side of two tenements at the south end 'soe letten to hym in grete fyndying almaner of workemanship belonging to the same' (BHR, 005, f. 44b). Letting 'by the great' meant sub-contracting the whole of a project, but no payment by Coke is recorded, and there is no sign in the rentals of any new houses. Nevertheless, the datestone of 1514 suggests that one or more new houses was built (probably forming part of SW8–13).

*** The two houses (probably but not necessarily adjacent) were to continue to pay the old rent of 113s.4d. (BHR, 008, f. 64b). No houses south of the stone gate paid exactly half that sum (56s.8d.), so one of them needed to be paying more than that, which narrows it down to SE12 (86s.8d.), SW9 (ditto), SW12A (83s.4d.) and SE14 (66s.8d.). The second house therefore needed to be paying 26s.8d., 30s. or 46s.8d. SW9 was probably too far north to be regarded as 'bridge foot'; SW12A is ruled out because there was no house paying 30s.; SE14 would need to partner SE9 or SE15, both of which were fairly recent; SE12 could partner either SW7 (recently-built, and probably not really 'bridge foot') or SE13, so the latter provides the most likely combination.

THE HOUSES FROM 1358 TO 1633 47

Fig. 44 Detail from Wyngaerde's view showing the south end of the bridge in about 1544, just before the construction of the house with many windows, with the passage under the drawbridge tower in the top right corner. SE1 to 4 and SW1 to 3 had been rebuilt by 1508 (with rents from 46s.8d. to 120s.), the houses on the west side extending somewhat further south than those on the east, just as Wyngaerde shows them. South of these, up to the space in front of the stone gate, were only lower-rent properties (from 26s.8d. to 33s.4d.), with a gap at SW4. South of the gate on the east side, the gap Wyngaerde shows is hard to explain, as SE9 to 11 had rents from 40s. to 46s.8d. On the west side, the narrow building is SW7 and 8 (rents 26s.8d. and 48s.4d.). The houses linked by struts over the street are SE12 and SW9 (rents 86s.8d. in each case).

new houses. These included six south of the drawbridge, making good at last some of the damage done in 1471 (Fig. 44). Richard Rownang was paid for painting the Trinity and two angels on the frame of the six houses, and for painting in gold two weathervanes set upon it.[24]

The period of greatest activity was from 1526 to 1548, when no fewer than thirty-one houses were built. This was made possible by an improvement in the Bridge House's finances,[25] and was probably encouraged by a rising population in London. Much of it was overseen by Humphrey Coke, who was the bridge's warden carpenter from 1503 and master or chief carpenter from 1512 until his death in 1531; he was also the King's Master Carpenter from 1519 to 1531.[26] The houses built included several of the groups that gave the bridge much of its character in later views, and it is perhaps not surprising that most of the expressions of admiration of the bridge are from the second half of the sixteenth century. The largest single project was ten houses at the south end of the principal part in 1526–29. This produced a group of buildings that look extremely regular in Wyngaerde's view, but much less so in the Pepys view. Indeed, the leases suggest that they did not even have the same number of storeys, and as usual those on the

Fig. 45 Detail from Norden's panorama of London in 1600, showing the west side of London Bridge, referred to in this book as Norden's view from the west. In particular, it shows clearly the towers at the south end of the principal part and on its west side, Nonsuch House and the house with many windows.

piers were deeper than those over the gullets. Norden's view from the west clearly shows two towers flanking the roadway, as well as battlements (Fig. 45). Coke seems to have been willing to extend the houses further beyond the ends of the piers than either his predecessors or successors. The end house on the west side was the deepest on the bridge at 34 feet, apart from the chapel house. If the smaller eastern house extended a similar distance beyond the end of the pier, the length of the facade facing south was a remarkable 75 or so feet. In 1528–29 Isebrande Johnson, a joiner, was paid 'for cuttyng and carvyng of the Transfiguracon of J[es]hu set in the newe frame upon London Brigge', and for two angels for the same purpose, and John Maynard painted two lions on the new houses.[27] Here we see clearly for the first time the way that architectural display was concentrated on the ends of the groups of houses, to be seen mainly by people crossing the bridge, rather than by those observing it from the river or its banks. It seems also to have been the practice to make the houses at the ends of the groups as deep as possible, which must have contributed to the impact the bridge made on travellers. There were apparently also two towers facing the river at PW11 to 13, rebuilt in 1531-32, which are shown in Norden's view from the west (Fig. 45) but not in the Pepys view (Fig. 2). That group of houses may have been Humphrey Coke's last work.

The next major work comprised six new houses at the north end of the middle part in 1539-41, of which one was on the east side by the chapel and five were on the west side. There was a new cross building, obscuring the view of the chapel, and it is probably no coincidence that it was built shortly after the downgrading of the chapel by reducing its staff.[28] A joiner was paid for making nineteen finials to be put on the battlements and the arms of the king and the City, while a painter painted and gilded eighteen vanes with arms and 'garnyshed with flowers de lyees', 'a great lyon holdynge a great fayne in his clowes', and 'a great signe' of St Christopher.[29] (In 1682 Thomas Passinger at MW1 was ordered to repair a carved lion and a man's head at the top of his house.)[30]

The views show semi-circular projections or towers on the north side of these houses. The leases indicate that the towers flanked the roadway on either side, like those at the end of the principal part. That for ME1 refers to a 'cant window' on the first floor, and there were evidently similar windows in the upper storeys, all projecting beyond the building line. The lease for MW1 refers to a projecting window on the first floor and a 'compass window' on each of the second and third floors. A canted window was and is a bay window, while a compass window (perhaps a more precise description in this case) was usually a semi-circular bay window, the best-known sixteenth-century examples being the two compass windows of the early 1580s at Kirby Hall, Northamptonshire. The compass windows show that the Bridge House was very much up to date in terms of architectural style. The first projections consisting wholly or largely of windows seem to have been built around 1520 at Cardinal Wolsey's Hampton Court and the Duke of Buckingham's Thornbury Castle, and compass windows were apparently first installed in royal buildings in the 1530s.[31] The Bridge House probably acquired knowledge of the royal examples through its master carpenter, Richard Ambrose, who had succeeded Humphrey Coke. Ambrose was Master Carpenter in the Tower from 1535 to 1557, as well as being twice Master of the Carpenters' Company.[32] He was almost certainly the Richard Ameros who had been apprenticed in 1504 to Thomas Maunsey, the master carpenter of the bridge before Coke.[33]

The house with many windows

The next major work, the six southernmost drawbridge houses, was even more impressive. It appears prominently in Hollar's view: at its south end a three-and-a-half-storey building with four semi-circular projections and windows marching across the entire facade, together with battlements (Fig. 46). It never acquired a name, so we will use here a modern term coined

Left: **Fig. 46** Detail from Hollar's Long View of London in 1647, showing the house with many windows. The existence of the extra storeys on the right-hand part is confirmed by the lease of SE7. The windows stretching across the facade also appear in Norden's view from the west and in Morgan's panorama of 1682 (Figs 45, 118).

and a plasterer was paid for 'whiteinge' the houses.[36] A good indication of the effect provided is the courtyard windows of Little Moreton Hall, Cheshire, of 1559.

Nonsuch House

After the construction of the house with many windows in 1547–48 and the chapel house in 1553, rebuilding slowed to a trickle until the 1640s. But the most famous building of the bridge's later years belonged to this period. This was Nonsuch House, which replaced the drawbridge tower in 1577–79 (Fig. 47). According to the bridge wardens, the lessees of the tower had asked for it to be rebuilt because it was 'in very dangerous ruine' and they were afraid to remain there. Stow stated that demolition of the tower began in April 1577, the first stone of the new building's foundations was laid by the Lord Mayor on 28 August 1577, and the new building was finished in September 1579. The accounts record four men clearing 'stuff' out of the new houses (five days each) in that month. Despite the name, Nonsuch House always consisted of two houses, which were first let in December 1579.[37]

Nonsuch House was one of the largest structures on the bridge, measuring 75 feet by 25 feet and having four and a half storeys. It was a far more remarkable and innovative building than has previously been realised, and was designed by a notable Elizabethan architect. Its name meant 'no other such house', and Stow called it 'a beautifull & chargeable peece of worke'.[38] The contemporary drawings of it differ considerably. Hollar's provides what looks at first sight like the most careful depiction, but it certainly distorts the shape of the building and seems also to be incorrect as regards the three ground-floor windows

for it – the house with many windows, though it was actually two houses. It has generally being regarded as an Elizabethan building, but the accounts tell a different story. They show that it was in fact built in 1547–48.[34] The combination of projections and windows is reminiscent of Henry VIII's Nonsuch Palace of 1539–45, and this was probably the result of Richard Ambrose drawing on his knowledge of recent royal architecture. Again it shows the Bridge House being stylistically up-to-date. The lease descriptions suggest that the semi-circular projections at the front towards the river were the staircases.[35] In 1647 the timbers were painted 'in oyle colour'

THE HOUSES FROM 1358 TO 1633

each side of the roadway, the continuous bands of windows on the two storeys above and the onion domes on the towers (Fig. 10). Other views indicate two ground-floor windows on each side (as does the plan) and four-light windows above them in the first and second storeys, all the windows being flanked by columns (Figs 47, 48, 91); none shows onion domes. The Pepys view indicates that the columns had capitals which were painted gold, and, though showing only the side of the building, provides the best evidence of the richness of the decoration (Fig. 2). These views rather than Hollar's have been the basis for the reconstruction of the building in Fig. 15.[39]

Nonsuch House seems in fact to have had one of the earliest classical facades in England, comparable to advanced work of the same period elsewhere, such as Tixall Gatehouse

Fig. 47 Nonsuch House in Morgan's panorama of London in 1682, shortly before the roadway was widened and heightened.

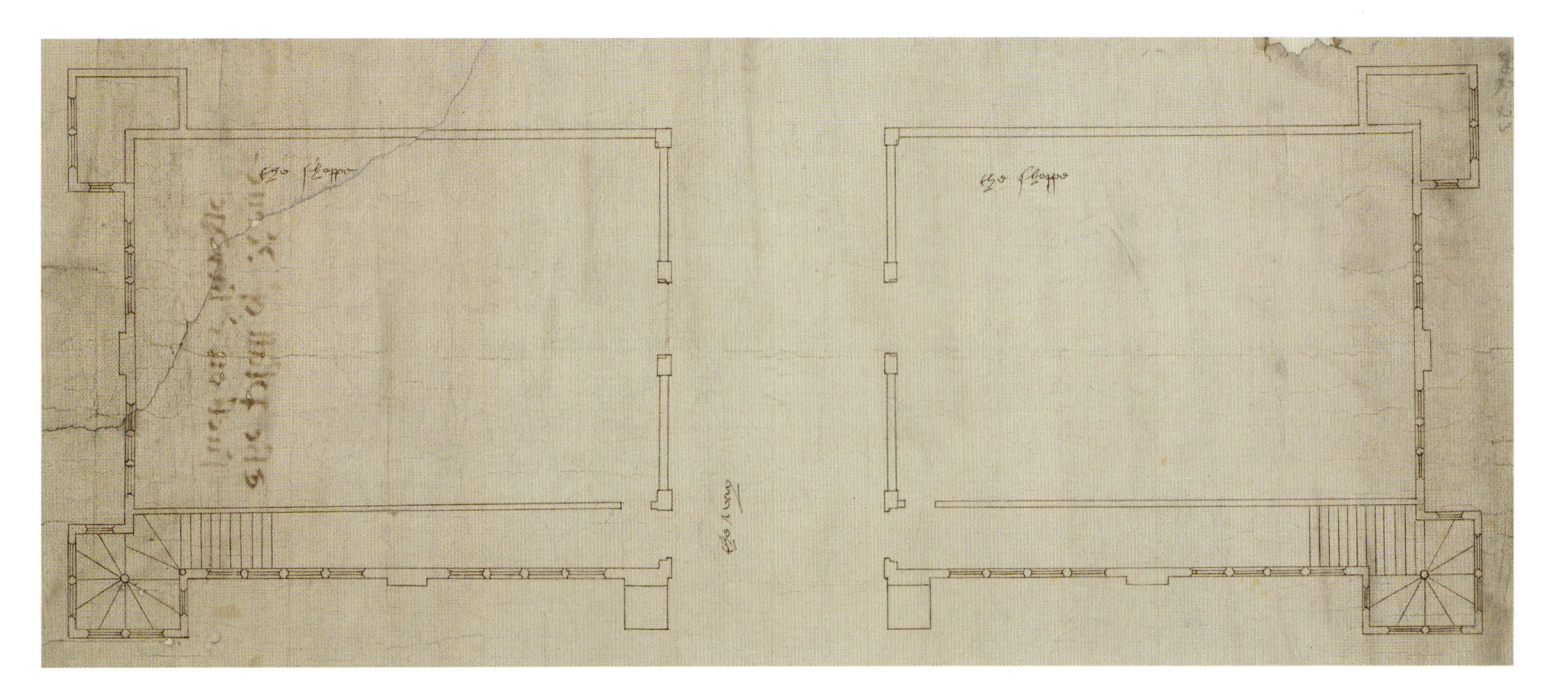

Fig. 48 Plan of Nonsuch House, probably drawn in 1577, when it was built.

52 LONDON BRIDGE AND ITS HOUSES, c. 1209–1761

Constructing Nonsuch House: selected entries from the accounts
1577
26 Oct: For carvinge tooles for the newe frame, 10s.
1578
26 July: To Peter Fillett for turninge v posts for newe frame, 20s. [and many similar payments]
30 Aug: To iiii labourers aboute the frame with the carpinters vi daies at xxs and one ii daies at xxd, 21s.8d.
6 Sept: To iiii labourers aboute the frame in the yarde ii daies, 6s.8d.
13 Sept To iiii men in the yarde to help the carpinters at the frame at iiiis a pece, 16s.
20 Sept: To iiii labourers to help the carpinters aboute the frame, 16s.
27 Sept: To iiii labourers in the yardes to help the carpinters at iiiis a pece, 16s.
1579
14 Feb: To the turnor for turninge iiii posts for the turretts at vis viiid, for ballisters iiiis viiid and for vi doosen roses ixs. [and similar payments]
To [Thomas Strutt] in rewarde aboute the newe frame for xl weekes at iiis the weeke and so ended, £6. [in addition to wages of 6s. per week]

Source: BHR, 009, accounts.
Note: Sums paid have been standardised.

and Moreton Corbet.[40] That, together with the length of the facade, probably accounts for the admiration it inspired. The architect was undoubtedly Lewis Stockett, who was the Bridge House's master carpenter from 1565 until his death in 1578.

He was also Surveyor of the Queen's Works, and had earlier worked on the Duke of Somerset's Somerset House with its classical facade in the Strand.[41] In several other respects Nonsuch House resembled the drawbridge tower it replaced, including the four corner towers, the narrow roadway under it, the first-floor cross building and the gallery overlooking the drawbridge. It is usually said to have been brightly painted, on the basis of instructions for painting the vault of the mayor's parlour at Coventry in 1585 – 'to ley the vawte in oyle colers substancially, the greate posts in jasper collur, as the newe house on London Bridge ys: all the rayles in stone coulor, the smale pillars in white leade coulours, the great pillars in perfect greene coullor'.[42] However, the wording suggests that

Far left: **Fig. 49** Cutaway view of the eastern part of Nonsuch House in about 1590 (a detail from Fig. 15 by Stephen Conlin).

Fig. 50 Cross-section of Nonsuch House (ME12 and MW13), showing the rooms listed in seventeenth-century leases. ME12 also had a counting house on the ground floor of its north-east tower. No attempt has been made to reconstruct the building's roofline.

only the columns or posts painted jasper (a brownish colour) emulated Nonsuch House, and the colour scheme at the latter was probably fairly restrained.

The idea that Nonsuch House was prefabricated in Holland is an eighteenth-century invention.[43] The problem with it is not just that it was unnecessary to seek Dutch expertise, but also that the accounts disprove it. They contain no payments for a frame brought from Holland, and they record a lengthy process by which the frame was constructed by the Bridge House carpenters in the Bridge House yard, as shown in the box opposite. The other eighteenth-century story, that the structure was built without nails, may be true but is unremarkable, as timber structures were usually built using wooden pegs.

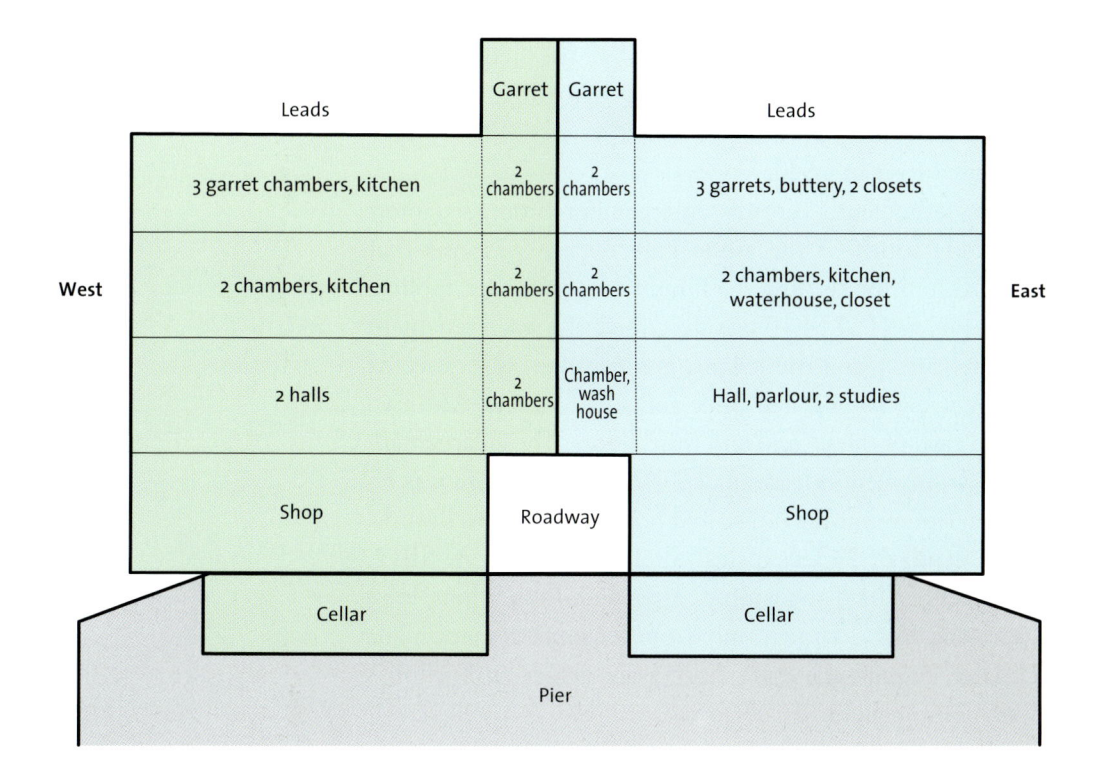

The first occupants were William Clayton, a grocer, in the western house and Thomas James, a vintner, in the eastern one. Both of them had occupied the previous houses on the site, and enlisted the help of Lord Burleigh to secure their new leases. Each paid a £200 fine and rent of £10 a year.[44] In the seventeenth century the occupants were typically haberdashers, mercers or drapers. Eighteenth-century occupants were less distinguished: in 1711 the eastern part was John Weaver's slopshop (selling ready-made clothes) and William West, described as a drysalter, was using the western part as a hemp shop.[45] The last occupants before demolition in 1757 were Andrew Bray, a stationer, in the eastern house and William West in the western one.

The internal arrangements in the mid-seventeenth century are shown in Fig. 50.[46] At the top were rails and bannisters around a terrace.[47] Edward Pitt was occupying the western house (the Bell) in 1677 and an inventory of his goods survives. He was a citizen and leatherseller, though the fabrics in his shop included linen, buckram, calico and canvas. One of the large first-floor rooms was used as the hall, with no more furniture than a Spanish table, but the other was the dining room, containing five pieces of tapestry, 12 turkey-work chairs, seven red chairs, an oval table and a chimneypiece, together worth £20. The first-floor rooms over the street were a closet and a 'little chamber' containing a bed. On the floor above was what was described as the widow's chamber, with the richest furnishings in the house (£35), including a bed with embroidered curtains. The same floor contained a kitchen and a parlour, furnished with a couch, nine chairs and a table. Otherwise only a 'loft roome', three garrets and a washhouse are mentioned. Pitt left an estate of £3,907, including £1,575 of cash in the house, together with £2,161 of debts owed to him. His own debts to others were only £287.[48]

After the completion of Nonsuch House there were only a few houses rebuilt up to the 1640s, as shown in Table 2.

Enlarging the houses

Many houses, even if not rebuilt, were significantly enlarged. Either they acquired extra storeys or they were extended backwards and became deeper. Until the late sixteenth century such changes were probably carried out by the Bridge House workmen, but thereafter they were often made a condition of the leases, and so the process becomes more visible. Even so, it is sometimes only successive lease descriptions that show that a house had been enlarged, such as one of 1653 revealing an extra storey on ME10.

In the Cheapside area, shops with more than two storeys may have been common as early as the late thirteenth century, but that reflected Cheapside's unique commercial importance.[49] In other towns and cities, and therefore almost certainly in London away from Cheapside, houses with three or four storeys were being built from the early fourteenth century, though they may not have been common until the fifteenth century. This corresponded to the multiplication of separate chambers or bedrooms in the latter century, and probably also the spread of kitchens to ordinary urban houses, about which little is known.[50] A note added to the Bridge House rental of 1404 two years later stated that it was granted to a tenant (at PW7) 'that he might have his kitchen in the said house by licence of the masters', which probably reflected this process.[51]

A reasonable conclusion is that the bridge houses began to be enlarged from two to three and a half or four and a half storeys (the half-storeys being the garrets) in the fourteenth century, and that the process was largely completed by the rebuilding from 1477 to 1548. None of the houses built from 1477 onwards had fewer than three and a half storeys in the seventeenth century, and both of those that did have fewer storeys are undated and were probably built before 1460. These were ME8 with three storeys and MW10 with two and a half. PW16B, another undated house, had 'an over storie with a garet therupon' added in 1501, making it up to three and a half storeys, presumably from two storeys.[52] In 1597 Thomas Green's lease of ME3, also an undated house, required him to add a storey, and presumably before that it had partly two and a half and partly three and a half storeys.[53] MW10 had a storey added to it in 1640.

In the seventeenth century enlargement proceeded most energetically south of the stone gate, where it seems that military reasons for keeping the houses low no longer applied. For example, in 1617 SE10 was described as a small tenement with three rooms, and the tenant, Henry Allen, was expected to enlarge it. By 1653 it had three and a half storeys, with two rooms on each of the second and third floors. The enlargement of SW9 can be seen in leases of 1607 and 1653: there was no additional storey, but the house had been extended backwards, having a depth of 23 feet instead of 12 to 18 feet. At SE12, Robert Clarke added two storeys after obtaining a long lease in 1653, and this is known only from a chance remark made much later, though the extra storeys are visible in Nicholls's view of 1711 (Fig. 115).[54]

Landlord and tenants: leases

All the houses on the bridge were owned by the Bridge House and were let out. When they were first built, London houses were either granted away in return for fixed rents, which involved loss of control, or were let to tenants at will, without any security of tenure. As the Bridge House did not lose control of the bridge houses, its tenants there were presumably all tenants at will. By about 1250 London properties were being leased to tenants for life, and by 1280 leases for a number of years were common.[55] From that time the tenants on the bridge were probably a mixture of tenants at will and leaseholders. When the first set of accounts begins in 1381, there are people paying a 'gersuma' or entry fine for houses on the bridge, though not all of those occupying such houses did so, and hardly any of those occupying the Bridge House's properties elsewhere did so. The fines were small – usually less than a year's rent[56] – and perhaps in this period the benefits were small too, consisting mainly of greater security of tenure, though in 1442 the payers of fines were accused of selling on their leases (presumably at a profit) without permission.[57] Between 1460 and 1501 the fines were pocketed by the bridge's rent collectors, until this was remedied in the latter year.[58] Six examples of leases granted or renewed in 1518–34 were all for ten-year terms, which was typical in London,[59] though some earlier leases of bridge houses were longer, and the Bridge House sometimes bought them back.[60] There were also leases for life.[61]

From the 1540s the Bridge House, probably like other landlords, increasingly relied on large entry fines rather than higher annual rents. The first £10 entry fine was levied in 1543, the first £20 one in 1547, and the first £40 one in 1550. Much larger fines were collected for the chapel house in 1555 (£133.6s.8d; annual rent £13.6s.8d) and each part of Nonsuch House in 1579 (£200; annual rent £10). In the 1570s entry fines averaged about five times the annual rent.[62] By the 1650s the policy was apparently to take about half the value in fines and the other half as annual rent. From about the 1570s leases for somewhat longer terms (but no longer for life) were becoming the norm, as on other landlords' estates in London. The first twenty-one-year lease of a house on the bridge was recorded in 1558, and by the 1570s terms were usually of twenty-one years or slightly longer.[63] The last lease for a life or lives seems to have been granted in 1559, though at least one remained in force until 1607, when Agnes Palmer agreed to surrender it.[64] Probably the last tenant at will was James Lusher or Lasher, a haberdasher (ME4). He was offered a lease in 1603 for an entry fine of £25 and 'utterly refuseth the same', but a threat to eject him persuaded him to pay £20 for a lease.[65] These changes corresponded to trends elsewhere in London, but they may also have reflected competition for the bridge houses. The City's bridge estates committee, which took over the granting of leases of Bridge House properties in 1592,[66] seems never to have had difficulty finding tenants for them. By the late sixteenth century it was even granting reversions after existing leases expired, and some would-be tenants obtained heavyweight backing for their applications: for example from Lord Burleigh for his servant Humphrey Plessington in 1581, and from the Queen of Bohemia for Richard Whetstone, a haberdasher, in 1627.[67]

Large entry fines combined with small rents meant that the lessee could extract a higher rent from a sub-tenant than they themselves were paying to the Bridge House. From the earliest rental with names in 1404 there were always some tenants who held more than one house (other than adjoining ones), and a few who seem to have acquired a house to let out. This was perhaps the explanation for Richard Whittington appearing in the rental for ME4 and 5 in 1415.[68] Leases usually forbade subletting without permission, though some in the late sixteenth century allowed this provided the sub-tenant was a freeman of the City,[69] and occasionally they imposed a requirement to live in the premises.[70] Nevertheless, from the late sixteenth century leases of houses on the bridge were increasingly investments, held by people who did not live there, such as John Milton, scrivener, who was almost certainly the father of John Milton the poet, in 1631 (PW12–13).[71] Of the occupants burnt out on the principal part of the bridge in 1633, only half were direct tenants of the Bridge House, and the proportion declined after that. Only an eighth of the occupants on the middle and south parts were direct tenants in 1682, and after the 1680s hardly any.[72] In the 1650s, when the Bridge House was desperate for cash, leases were usually for sixty-one years, and entry fines were high – about sixteen times the annual rent. The building leases granted in the 1680s and later were also for sixty-one-year terms. However, when these long leases fell in in the 1740s, twenty-one-year terms were usually granted, and many were then secured by the occupants of the houses.[73]

Landlord and tenants: repairs and rebuilding

For most of the bridge's life, the Bridge House not only built the houses but repaired them as well. The accounts from the 1460s onwards show that tenants often made a contribution towards repairs, and this may have been essential for persuading the Bridge House to carry them out promptly, especially when it was short of cash.[74] In 1502 it paid compensation of 13s.4d. (a third of what he had requested) to Robert Bekyngham, grocer (SE12), 'for lacke of due reparacion uppon his tenement whiche he holdith soo that he coude not bestowe his marchaundice within the same by the space of ii yeres'.[75] Tenants on the bridge also sometimes contributed towards rebuilding.[76] Nevertheless, it was the Bridge House (or in the seventeenth-century leases the City) which had the responsibility and determined what was done.

At first that was not unusual, especially from about 1380 to 1530, when major urban landowners were investing directly in buildings and repairs. From about 1530 landowners began to shift the responsibility for repairs to tenants, and this was the usual arrangement by 1600. The Bridge House followed the trend for its other properties, but not at first for those on the bridge. When the first grant book begins in 1570, tenants of its houses elsewhere were responsible for repairs, whereas tenants of its houses on the bridge were not, except for replacement of broken windows.[77]

The probable reason for the Bridge House continuing to build and repair houses on the bridge was that it needed to be sure that they were structurally sound and that any building work did not damage the bridge itself. It needed structures well enough supported by hammer beams or ribs that they would last much longer than a lease of twenty-one or so years. Also its workmen had specific expertise, notably in the installation and repair of hammer beams and putting up scaffolding on the bridge. The bridge houses were inevitably more expensive both to build and repair than other houses, because of the hammer beams and the greater cost of scaffolding, and making lessees pay for repairs would have made the leases much less attractive. No doubt the Bridge House officials were also mindful of the potential loss of jobs.

As soon as the bridge estates committee took over the granting of leases in 1592 it sought to reduce the Bridge House's responsibility for repairs. A lease of that year was the first to do so. It specified that the Bridge House would provide the materials, except for broken windows and 'wilful decays', and the tenants would pay the workmen. It was the start of a long process of adjustment. From 1602 the obligations were reversed, with the tenants providing materials and the Bridge House paying the workmen; tenants were exempted from repairs to the street pavement, the bridge itself and the hammer beams. Leases made the tenant responsible for repairs 'from the hamerbeame (which lyeth upon the crowne of the arche) upwards', except the cost of scaffolding timber and workmen's wages.[78] The wording was changed in about 1610 to cover from the crown of the arch upwards, in 1629 to cover from the stone arch and foundations upwards and in about 1639 to make clearer that the tenant was not responsible for hammer beams. From 1629 scaffolding was covered only on the water side. The tenants argued in 1629 that they should pay only half the cost of repairs.[79]

The next major change, in 1647, resulted from a petition from the tenants, and had the perhaps unexpected effect that under future leases the Bridge House would no longer pay workmen's wages.[80] Possibly the tenants expected to pay smaller entry fines as a result. The standard wording in leases now committed the Bridge House to keep hammer beams and the street pavement in repair and to provide materials for scaffolding, and the new leases of the 1650s made this the norm. Finally, in the building leases of the 1680s onwards, the leaseholders were wholly responsible for repairs, including repairs to hammer beams and the cost of scaffolding, though for the few remaining older buildings such as Nonsuch House the former exceptions continued. From the 1640s the Bridge House also left the rebuilding of individual houses to tenants (Table 2).

CHAPTER 6

Inside the houses in the seventeenth century

The houses as they were before the destruction of the principal part in 1633 and the rebuilding of the middle and south parts in the 1680s and 1690s are well recorded in the lease descriptions of 1604–60 and in several probate inventories from slightly later (1661–94).[1] Leases listing individual rooms are available for all but thirteen of the houses on the principal part, all of those on the middle part and all but one of those on the south part, and are set out in the Survey. They also survive for all but four of the new houses built on the principal part in the 1640s, but these are discussed in the next chapter. Where the lease descriptions can be compared with the measurements of 1683 they are usually consistent with them. They are not always easy to interpret, though features baffling at first sight can sometimes be explained. For example, measurements seem usually to have been to the furthest point in a room, such as to the triangular end of a cellar within a bridge pier,[2] so they can make irregularly-shaped rooms seem larger than they really were. Sometimes, as the Pepys view makes clear, a small room might stick out into thin air, and in other cases a room apparently with nothing under it was in fact over the roadway. Probably small spaces such as privies and entries were often omitted. Despite the problems, the lease descriptions provide a wealth of information, and make it possible to reconstruct many of the houses (Fig. 51).

Virtually all the bridge houses were built of timber rather than brick, even in the eighteenth century, reflecting the need to minimise their weight. The only exceptions were those in the stone gate, the drawbridge tower and the former chapel, and, later, two of those not actually on the bridge itself – PE1, rebuilt in brick in about 1667, and SE15, rebuilt in brick after a fire in 1725.[3] This timber building of course became distinctive only after the rest of the City had become brick-built, largely in the seventeenth century and especially after 1666. Houses on London Bridge were specifically exempted in 1630 from the government's requirement that all new buildings in London have outer walls of brick or stone.[4] However, some brick was used in the bridge houses: chimneys were of brick from about 1503, before which stone had been used;[5] and some party walls may have been of brick, at least on the ground floor, such as the one between ME6 and 7 before the 1680s rebuilding.[6] Kitchen floors were paved with stone. Outside, the houses were plastered and weatherboarded, at least sometimes with weatherboarding

Fig. 51 Cutaway view by Pete Urmston of MW9 and ME7 in about 1650 (the houses also shown in Fig. 12).

INSIDE THE HOUSES IN THE SEVENTEENTH CENTURY 59

on the street side as well as the river side.[7] There were pentices to provide further protection; one was to be set up at SE10 in 1650 'all the length of the howse southward to secure the windowes from wett', and ME7 in 1655 had 'penthowse bords over the windowes towards the Thames'.[8] Ordinary London houses began to have glazed windows in the thirteenth and fourteenth centuries, and these are recorded in one of the bridge houses in 1410, almost as soon as records begin.[9]

As already indicated, the houses varied in size. In terms of plot size, the smallest identified were PE18 (10 feet 10 inches by 14 feet) and ME9 (10 feet 9 inches by 15 feet). The largest were the chapel house and ME3 (though both of these were usually divided into two shops) and the two parts of Nonsuch House. Almost all in the seventeenth century had three and a half or four and a half storeys. Three are recorded in leases as having five and a half storeys (PW4, SE7 and SE15). Two had three storeys or fewer, as already discussed.

Many houses had cross buildings, which are discussed below.[10] As for jettying, whereby the whole of a storey projected outwards further than the one below it, there is not much evidence of this in the views, except Hollar's, but the measurements in the lease descriptions show that some houses had jettying while others did not. They do not indicate whether any overhang was towards the river or towards the street, but the likelihood is that it was usually towards the river, as the existence of cross buildings restricted the scope for jettying on the street side. On the principal part, there are just three instances of the size of upper floors being so much deeper than the floor below that jettying in both directions is likely.[11] There was certainly a jetty towards the street at SE3, recorded as projecting one foot 6 inches at a level 9 feet 10 inches above the roadway.[12] Jettying was most common south of the stone gate, where there were no cross buildings: on the east side, at least four houses had jetties towards the street and at least two had them towards the river. PW21, at the end of the principal part, had jettying southwards.

The intermixing of tenancies, with different people holding rooms on different floors, was common in London,[13] but not on the bridge. The lease descriptions provide only a few clear examples: a first-floor parlour transferred from one house to its neighbour (SE11 and 12), two houses with one shop between them (PW12 and 13), one shop let separately from the house above (MW7 and 8), three cross buildings divided between different occupants on different storeys, a garret extending over the house opposite (PE16 and PW18) and some hanging cellars which extended under an adjoining house. There is also a case of a widow being allowed to occupy two chambers and a closet on a third floor for the rest of her life (MW3). Other intermixing may sometimes have happened on the infrequent occasions when a house was divided between two households, but transfer of a room from one house to another was certainly rare. Lessees were forbidden to enlarge or diminish their houses without permission, and at least in certain periods there were regular visits or 'views' to check who was occupying the houses and what repairs were needed. The surviving records of views provide only one example of intermixing (within SE14, which had been divided, in 1678).[14] The building agreements made in 1684 for the middle part included a provision for resolving 'mixed interests', but there seems to be no evidence of the provision being used.[15]

Whether large or small, the bridge houses followed a fairly standard plan until the mid-seventeenth century. On the ground floor was a shop, and often a passage or entry and a small counting house. Above the shop was a hall and usually

Cellars and shops

Starting at the bottom, there were two different sorts of cellar. Houses over a pier usually had a cellar within the pier ('within the biggness of a piere' at MW5), almost always at least 12 feet wide, unless shared. At least some of them had windows.[17] According to George Dance, the piers were solid for 10 feet above the starlings, and above that were walls 3 feet thick enclosing the cellars.[18] By far the largest cellar was the one under the chapel house, formerly the lower chapel, measuring about 64 feet by 24 feet. The Bridge House occasionally worried about occupants tampering with the stonework of the piers, but it did not question their right to use the cellars. In 1621 it complained that the arches and stonework

> are oftentymes greatly injured by the sinister carriage of the tennants there in making incrochement into the walls & blemishing ye said stoneworke and altering the walls & bounds of their said tenements by plucking them downe'.[19]

The cellars may have been an original feature of the bridge, and some certainly existed by the early sixteenth century.[20]

Houses over the gullets either lacked a cellar or had a 'hanging cellar' under the shop.[21] One was described as being below the hammer beam on which the house rested,[22] and it was presumably from the hammer beams that they hung, while also often being attached to the outside of the arches.[23] Usually they were long and thin, with dimensions such as 26 by 6 feet, or even 10 by 2½ feet or 20½ by 3 feet.[24] The smaller dimension was never more than nine feet, except for the 'great hanginge celler' at ME3 (28 feet north–south and 10 feet east–west). The longer dimension seems always to have been the north–south one, parallel to the roadway. At PW19, a

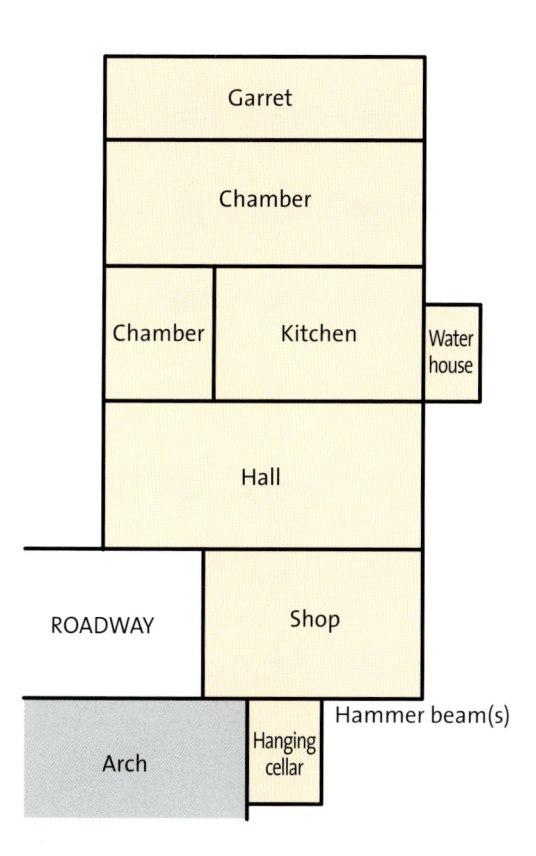

Fig. 52 Reconstructed cross section of ME9, based on the lease of 1653 to Alice Powell. The house was 10 feet 9 inches wide.

a chamber as well. On the second floor was a kitchen and usually another chamber, as well as the 'waterhouse' (discussed below).[16] On the uppermost floors were chambers and garrets. There might also be a cellar. An example of the most simple sort of house is ME9 in 1653, with cellar, shop, hall on the first floor (partly over the street), kitchen and chamber on the second floor, chamber on the third floor and garret above (Fig. 52). The larger houses differed mainly in having larger rooms and more of them, especially chambers.

house 13½ feet wide and 31½ feet deep, there was a hanging cellar 13 by 6 feet and another one towards the Thames 13½ by five feet, suggesting two hammer beams each holding up a cellar. In a few cases the hanging cellar was longer from north to south than the house itself.[25] What determined the sizes and shapes of the hanging cellars is unclear, except that they could not extend below the stonework of the arch without being at risk from boats. Cellars as narrow as 2½ feet or 3 feet would scarcely have allowed space for a person to walk in, and perhaps their contents were accessed from trap doors rather than having stairs or ladders. However, the hanging cellar at MW7–8 (26 by 6 feet), which contained a privy, must have been a walk-in one, and so must those which extended under an adjoining house. The great mystery is why the hanging cellars are not obvious in any of the views of the houses.

Inventories from the late seventeenth century suggest that the cellars were used for coal, beer and lumber, but not for trade goods. One house with a cellar also had what was described as a 'nooke' under the next house, which is visible in the Pepys view as a shed sitting on the end of the pier (MW1; Fig. 112).

Shops normally occupied the whole of the ground floor, except that many houses had a counting house or other small room or an entry leading to the stairs, and PW20 and 21 and the chapel house had warehouses. At ME7 the counting house was under the staircase, jutting out towards the Thames.[26] As the narrowness of the street and the existence of cross buildings limited the light entering from the street side, the shops presumably made the most of the light from the Thames side. Many of the shops were large, especially those at the chapel house (36 feet by 24 feet in 1627) and PW12–13 and the two parts of Nonsuch House (each about 31 feet by 25 feet).

Fig. 53 Cutaway view of ME5 in about 1590 (a detail from Fig. 15 by Stephen Conlin), showing shop, hall, kitchen and buttery, two chambers and two garrets. Two other rooms not visible here were in the adjoining cross building, the whole of which belonged to this house.

Those with a frontage of 20 feet were as wide as some of the larger Cheapside shops, but were less deep.[27]

Like shops elsewhere, those on the bridge had stalls on which goods could be displayed, no doubt with shutters which could be closed at night. They also had pentices (projecting roofs) above the shop front, which gave some protection from rain.[28] In 1581 it was ordered that no stall on London Bridge should project more than 4 inches into the roadway.[29] However, there are three reasons for thinking that most sales took place within the shop rather than across the stall. The first is the danger to shoppers of lingering in the street, especially as traffic increased. The second is that, as discussed later, most types of goods sold on the bridge required comparison between different items, rather than quick sales of fairly standard items.[30] The third is that most of the goods sold were valuable ones, and laying them out on a stall on a busy thoroughfare would have encouraged theft. From the fifteenth century some or all of the bridge shops had wooden lattices, which made it possible to display goods while also protecting them, and that was probably the main way in which the fronts of the shops were used.[31] One lattice seems to be shown in Wyngaerde's view, with a pentice above, just south of the stone gate (Fig. 44). Glass shop windows are not recorded elsewhere in London until 1667, but there are two intriguing references to glass being used in some way in shops on the bridge much earlier. 'Glazed windows in the shop' are recorded at PE7B in 1410, and glass was installed in the shop and hall of John Toker at PE13 in 1476.[32]

The inventories and other documents occasionally record shop furnishings, always including a counter and usually items for storage such as cupboards and presses. In 1682, for example, Jeremy Tawke, silkman, had two counters, two nests of drawers, a press, a stool and a form in the shop, together with a bed (ME10). In 1694 Thomas Soper, apothecary, had two counters and drawers, and he too had a bed in the shop (SE10).[33]

The lower parts of the houses were particularly vulnerable to damage by boats, recorded from 1385 onwards. In 1464, for example, a boat broke the windows of John Codde's house (PE10B). In 1568 a Dutchman 'broke' Simon Lowe's house with his ship (PE6). In 1622 a lighter hit Mr Woller's cellar (PE9) '& broke great part of hyt downe which was caried away'. Jeremy Champney had extra years added to his lease in 1623 'in regard of his poverty and losses occasioned by shippes rushing upon that parte of his house next the Thames' (PE7).[34]

The leases only occasionally mention stairs, usually by indicating that one of the dimensions given included or excluded the staircase, but that is enough to show where the stairs were. The great majority of those referred to were against the side wall. On the ground floor they often adjoined an entry at one side of the shop. In some of these cases all the flights recorded were in the same position, but in others one or more of the other flights was parallel to the roadway instead. Two houses had staircases which evidently changed direction in one of the back corners. A minority of houses had stairs which were parallel to the roadway, presumably at the back of the shop. There were also five where the leases provide dimensions, and these must have been spiral stairs or pairs of stairs. Four of these were 5 or 6 feet square and one was larger. Two of them were replaced by stairs at the back in a rebuilding of about 1650.[35] In addition, SE2 had what was described as a pair of stairs, and there is what looks like a staircase tower there in Norden's view; Nonsuch House had spiral stairs in the corner turrets (Fig. 48); and the stairs in the house with many windows were apparently in one of the semi-circular projections.

Upper rooms

On the first floor, the main or only room was the hall. The most common arrangement was a hall and a chamber, sometimes with additional small rooms such as butteries, but sometimes there was only a hall. In some cases the hall extended over the street. Where plots had not been merged, the hall tended to be long and narrow, such as 19 by 9 feet at PW14; elsewhere it could be wider. The smallest was 14 by 10 feet (PW8); the largest were 30 by 23 feet at the chapel house and about 24 by 18 feet at MW10. In all but one of the twenty-three cases where there was both a hall and chamber and the lease description indicates their location, the hall overlooked the river. The reason is obvious: a room next to the river had the best views and received the most light. (The exception, SE13, was partly on the abutment rather than the bridge.) A few large houses had two halls, whereas in several small ones the first-floor room was described as a chamber or a room rather than a hall (e.g. ME8).

Fifteen leases record a parlour in addition to a hall (two parlours at the chapel house), and all were on the first floor. At the nine houses where the position of hall and parlour is clear, the hall was towards the river and the parlour towards the street in four, the reverse was the case in two, and both hall and parlour faced the river in three.[36] Only three leases mention dining rooms, two of them in unusually large houses. One was on the first floor along with both hall and parlour (ME3); the other two were on the second floor along with the kitchen (SE5–6, SW3). Small rooms on the first floor included butteries (for storing drink and sometimes other provisions; numerous), counting houses (also numerous), closets (providing privacy and security for valuables; three examples), washhouses (probably for washing clothes; one example), studies (two examples in one house), warehouses (ditto) and privies.

Many halls were wainscoted, and settles (wooden benches with a high back) are mentioned several times. The contents recorded in inventories were often not just a table and chairs but also a bed, and the beds in many shops and halls indicate the pressure on space. The hall must usually have been the main living room, rather than a room intended primarily to display the occupant's status, though this is less clear where there was also a parlour. Nevertheless, halls may have displayed status too. In an interesting example from 1673, Thomas Ruck at ME5 had turned a second-floor room next to the kitchen into a dining room, containing two tables, two joined stools, four leather chairs and a looking glass. He still had a hall on the first floor, and it contained ten chairs, two stools, a drawing

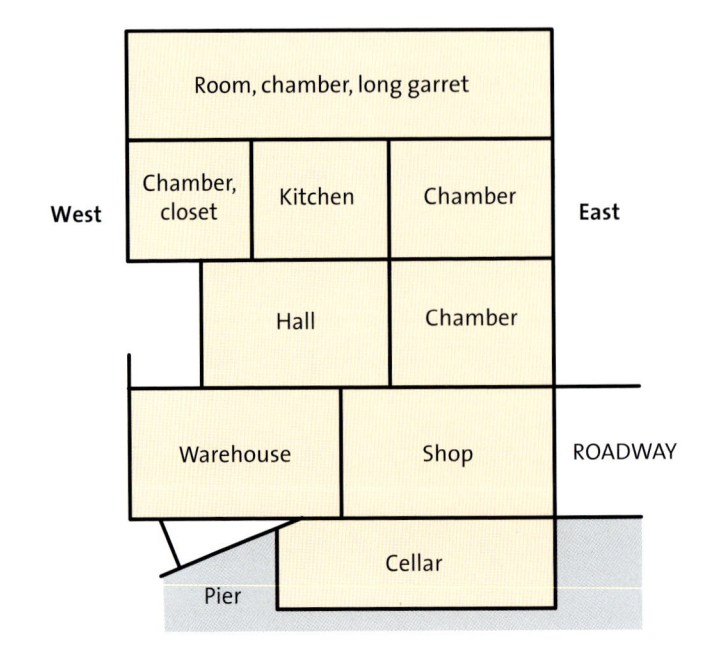

Fig. 54 Reconstructed cross section of PW21, built in 1526–29 and the deepest house on the bridge. The reconstruction relies on the measurements stated in the lease of 1615 to John Busbridge, citizen and skinner, though the second floor has been made slightly larger and the top floor slightly smaller to avoid an improbably irregular outline. The Pepys view correctly shows jettying towards the south, but makes the house too narrow. The unusual position of the kitchen reflected the fact that this house had access to the river on its south side (see Fig. 14). The adjacent cross building seems to have belonged entirely to PE19.

INSIDE THE HOUSES IN THE SEVENTEENTH CENTURY 65

table, a cupboard, three muskets, two halberds, three swords, one belt and one pair of bandoliers (ammunition belts).[37] In cities such as Bristol, merchants and others demonstrated their status by displaying weapons in impressive halls open to the roof and thus their involvement in the urban militia. There were no open halls on the bridge by the seventeenth century, but Ruck's weaponry may have had a similar purpose. From the 1670s the creation of a standing army reduced the role of urban militias and thereby the importance of the hall.[38] By the late seventeenth century the halls on the bridge were referred to as dining rooms, except that Timothy Blackwell's at SE9 in 1679 was simply the chamber over the shop.

Kitchens were invariably on the second floor until the mid-seventeenth century, other than second kitchens where there was more than one and at the chapel house and the stone gate. Only two houses lacked a kitchen.[39] The most common arrangement on the second floor was kitchen and chamber, often with one or more small rooms such as waterhouses, washhouses, butteries and closets. The chapel house had a gallery. The inventories, which are later than the leases, provide two examples of second-floor chambers that had been turned into dining rooms. Where there was space for only one room on each floor, it clearly made sense to put the kitchen above the hall, which was probably the most heavily-used room.[40] However, the kitchens on the bridge were consistently on the second floor even when they could have been placed next to the hall instead of a chamber. Examining where the kitchen was placed on the second floor provides the explanation. In the twenty-three houses where there was more than one room on the second floor and the placing of the kitchen is clear, all but three of the kitchens were on the Thames side rather than the street side.[41] The reason for this preference was clearly that the waterhouses were necessarily on that side too, and it was desirable for them to adjoin the kitchen; also the disposal of waste was far easier on the Thames side. If the preference was for both hall and kitchen to be on the river side, they could not be on the same floor; hence kitchens on the second floor.

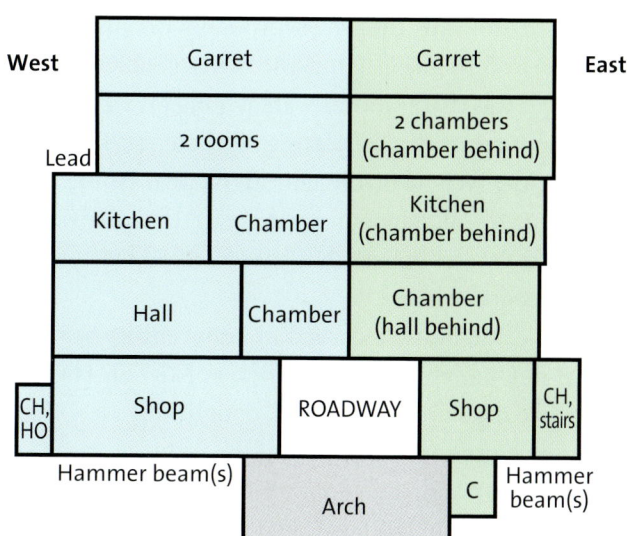

In 1748 the bridge estates committee stated that it would not let houses to pastry cooks because of the oven and the consequent fire risk.[42] This may have reflected long-established policy, but the leases do record two ovens (at PW16 and 17). Another oven is recorded in a schedule of fixtures in one of the new houses of the 1640s.[43] There may have been more, as there was no particular reason for lease descriptions to mention them.

Above the second floor almost all rooms were chambers, garrets or garret chambers, the latter being presumably garrets with reasonable headroom. Since garrets with half-height walls,

Fig. 55 Reconstructed cross section of the houses leased to William Hooke in 1625 (PE12) and John Calverley in 1631 (PW14), illustrating the greater depth of the houses on the west side of the principal part. The two houses were 20 feet and 9 feet wide respectively. Calverley's hall has been made one foot longer than stated to match the depth of his ground and second storeys. For Hooke's house, it is assumed that the kitchen was over the chamber, rather than (as stated) over the hall, as the dimensions otherwise make little sense. 'C' indicates a cellar, 'CH' a counting house and 'HO' a house of office (or privy).

as opposed to garrets wholly confined to the roof space, seem to have been introduced in London only in about 1550,[44] and most bridge houses were built before that, most garrets on the bridge were probably fairly cramped. PW13 had a waterhouse and a shed on the third floor. Other third floors included three supplementary kitchens, a counting house, a buttery and three closets. PW8 had a coal-hole in a garret, and the coal was presumably winched up from boats (the Pepys view shows some sort of container suspended from PW12).

Many lease descriptions mention the leads. A few of them may have been purely functional roof coverings, but most seem to have been an amenity for the occupants. PE13 had 'a little walkinge leade upon the first storie', apparently by the hall, and PE9 had 'a leade to walke in' at the top of the house. The most common place for a lead was next to the hall, such as the lead before the hall window towards the Thames at PE5, and these were clearly intended to be enjoyed as an adjunct to the hall. These ones varied from 3 to 6 feet in depth and could be as wide as the house itself. Two can be seen in the Pepys view at PW6 and 9 (Fig. 2), but most are not visible in the drawings. In one case the kitchen was over both hall and lead. Four houses had leaded galleries or a gallery with a lead. Of these, two adjoined the hall, one was on the first floor and one was at the top of the house. Houses at the ends of the blocks had leads the full width of the house at the top, sometimes behind battlements.

As for the cross buildings, sometimes a room occupied both the cross building and part of the main house (in the first storey this was usually the hall), but more often there were separate rooms over the roadway. In the former case, the fact that the cross buildings were usually a different width from the houses could result in irregularly-shaped rooms, such as the hall at MW9 and the first-floor chamber at PW9. Usually two houses on opposite sides of the roadway shared every floor of the cross building, with the dividing line being in the middle of the street, but several were arranged differently. At the north end of the middle part there was a complicated division between three houses, one of which had a room extending the full width of the roadway and one of which had a second-floor chamber over part of someone else's house. Towards the south end of the drawbridge houses, two eastern houses had the whole of the first floor, while the western ones had the whole of the second floor and above (SE5–6 and SW4–5). ME5 had rooms occupying the whole of the adjoining cross building, in which the house opposite (MW7) did not share at all, an arrangement which seems to have persisted since 1358. Another irregular arrangement was at PE16 and PW18 (see Fig. 110). Cross buildings must have made it hard to light the adjoining rooms, and MW7 had what were described as a void room and a dark chamber towards the street, probably because the cross building deprived them of light. The other problem with the cross buildings was that if rooms were wholly over the roadway it was difficult to provide any heating, as there was no easy way of conveying the weight of the chimney down to the bridge. The disadvantages of separate rooms over the roadway may explain why in several houses that space was added to the hall in the seventeenth century.[45]

An example of a house recorded in an inventory as well as a lease is that of Charles Tyus, bookseller, at ME7 in 1664 (Figs 12, 50). Above the shop was the hall, containing a large square table, six old chairs and eight stools. The room over the street on the same floor and the room above that were chambers. Other rooms were as in the lease, apart from a chamber within the hall, and most of them contained books forming part of

Tyus's stock.[46] Another example is Jeremy Tawke, silkman, at ME10 in 1682. Above the cellar and the shop containing silks, the first floor, formerly consisting of the hall and buttery, comprised the dining room and a chamber. The dining room contained a drawing table and six turkeywork chairs, while what was evidently the best chamber adjoining it had the house's most valuable furnishings, including a bed with green serge curtains, 'a worsted camblett bed', a table, chairs and a chest of drawers. On the second floor were the kitchen and a chamber containing a bed with grey printed stuff curtains, a table, six stools and a chest of drawers. On the third floor were two chambers, each containing a bed and not much else, apart from a cupboard and a looking glass in the back room. There was apparently nothing worth recording in the garret. Tawke's goods were worth £501 and debts owed to him totalled £646, somewhat less than his debts of £782 to others.[47] The inventory of Cornelius Bull, haberdasher, at SE14 in 1684 is notable for the dining room on the second floor (replacing a chamber), which contained four pieces of tapestry, the only tapestries recorded in any of the inventories except Edward Pitt's at Nonsuch House.[48]

Services

Probably every house had a waterhouse, as they are mentioned in the leases of twenty-seven properties and other documents record them at houses where the lease omits them.[49] They were where water was drawn up from the river. Virtually all were on the second floor, apart from one on the third floor (PW13) and one on the ground floor or the pier (PW6), and many of them can be seen in the views of the bridge. They were small rooms, the few examples for which dimensions are available ranging from 3 feet square to 7 by 5½ feet. Thomas Ruck's waterhouse at ME5 in 1673 contained a cistern, lead pipes and 'the pulley rope & winch', as well as brass and iron kettles and skillets (cooking vessels).[50] From the 1460s the Bridge House accounts contain payments for pulleys and barrels.[51] Later, buckets are mentioned,[52] and the Pepys view shows several buckets being let down into the river. Cisterns were installed in kitchens.[53] According to an Icelandic visitor in 1615, 'In the floor of every kitchen on the bridge there is a square trap-door, over the hole through which the water for household purposes is daily drawn up'.[54] For houses that were wholly on piers, the waterhouse was presumably either where the house overhung the pier or to one side.

Comparison between the lease descriptions and hearth tax assessments (Appendix 4) indicates that, as elsewhere in London by the 1660s, nearly all rooms were heated, except for shops, warehouses, some garrets and small rooms such as closets, counting houses, studies and butteries.[55] As discussed above, rooms wholly over the street were also unlikely to be heated. On that basis there is sometimes a clear match with the hearth tax assessment. For example, at ME11 the four heated rooms of Richard Love would have been the hall and parlour on the first floor and the chamber and kitchen on the second. At SW7, with three hearths, there was evidently a single chimney stack heating all three main rooms – one on each floor. In the western part of Nonsuch House the eight hearths were probably in the two halls on the first floor and the kitchen and two chambers on each of the second and third floors. In numerous other cases the assessment matches the lease description if one of the garrets was heated. There were, however, houses where one or two of the main rooms were not heated. For example, at ME4 and 5, the three hearths apiece of John Welding or Wilding and Thomas Ruck suggest a single chimney stack in each case heating one room on each floor – hall, kitchen and one of the chambers.[56] Both of these seem to have been houses built before 1460.

Elsewhere in London, chimneys were being built from the fourteenth century and added to existing houses from the fifteenth,[57] and that may have applied to the bridge houses. Presumably before that there was an open hearth in the solar or hall. Most chimneys mentioned in the leases were in side walls, but at least five were in north–south walls.[58] The latter must have been between adjoining rooms, as they could not have been in front walls without requiring support that obstructed the shop and the views of the bridge show hardly any chimneys in back walls.[59] All five, with one possible exception, were in houses on piers. The chimneys of houses over gullets presumably rested on the hammer beams.

There was no consistent placing of the privy or 'house of office', and the only requirements were presumably that it should be out of the way and that it should empty into the river. In most leases it was evidently thought unnecessary to mention the privy. Of the fifteen referred to, one was in a cellar, four were on the ground floor, five on the first floor (in one case on the leads), four on the second floor and one on the third floor. Dimensions are stated only for three (at ME11 and SE2), the largest being 5 feet square.

The gutter of the bridge's roadway was in the centre rather than at the sides,[60] and there must have been some way of conveying rainfall off the bridge. The most likely method was drains under some of the houses over the gullets. For example, in 1659 Thomas Ruck was ordered 'to take up his compter in the shopp to make cleane the sincke & to lay the boards so that the sincke may at all tymes be come to when need shall require'. In 1678 one pier had 'a gutter wanting in the head of the arch to carry the water cleare out of the street in to the river'.[61]

CHAPTER 7

Fires and rebuildings 1633–82

The fire of 1633

On 11 February 1633 the maidservant of John Briggs, a needlemaker on the principal west part (at PW3), put a tub of hot ashes under the stairs before going to bed, and by about 10 p.m. the house was on fire. The fire destroyed all the houses on the principal part and some others in St Magnus parish. A vivid description of it was left by Nehemiah Wallington, a turner who lived in Little Eastcheap:

> I here that Brigges his wife his child and maide escaped with their lives very hardly having on their bodies but their shurts and smocks, and the fire burnd so fearcely that it could not be quenched till it had burnt downe all ye houses on both sides of the way from St Magnes Church to the first open place.
>
> Att the begining of this fire as I lay in my bed and heard the sweeping of the channels and crying for watter, I arose about one of the cloke and looked downe Fish Street Hill, and did behold such a fearefull and dreadfull fire, vaunting itselfe over the topes of houses like a captaine florishing and displaying his banner and seing so much meanes and little good it did it made me thinke of that fire which the Lord threateneth against Jerusalem for the breach of his Sabbath.
>
> And allthoe there was water enough very nere, yet they could not safly come at it. But all the cundittes neere were opened and the pipes that carried watter through the streets were cutt open and the watter swept down with broomes with helpe enough, but it was the will of God it should not prvaile. And the hand of God was mor seene in this, in as much as no meanes would prosper. For the engines which are such excellent things yeet none of these did prosper for they were broken and the tide was very low, that they could gett no watter, and the pipes that were cutt yelded but littel watter. Some ladders were broke to the hurt of many, for some had their legges broke some their armes some their ribes were broke, and some lost their lives. This fire burnt fircely all night and part of the next day (for my man wase there about twelve a clocke and said he did see the furdest house on fier) till all was burnt and pulled downe to the ground, yet the timber wood and coales in the sellers could not be quenched all that weeke, till Tuseday following in the afternoone the xix of February, for I was there then my selfe and had a live coal of a fire in

my hand. Notwithstanding there were as many night and day as could labour one by another to carry away timber and brickes and tiles and rubbish cast down into litters so that on Wensday the bridge was cleared that passengers might goe over.

And this mircie of God I thought on that there was but little wind for had the wind bin as high as it was a weeke before I thinke it would have indangered the most part of the citie for in Themes Streete there is much pitch tarr rosen and oyle in their houses.'[1]

In the days before insurance the fire was a disaster for the traders affected, as well as for the Bridge House. In February, the roadway in the burnt area was widened from 15 feet to 18 feet and enclosed by boards 10½ feet high, with three refuges for foot passengers on each side (Fig. 56). This was an interim measure 'untill such time as the houses nowe burned downe shall be reedified', and the next step would have been the rebuilding of the houses.[2] At least two tenants made immediate preparations to rebuild.[3] However, Charles I had other ideas, as he was determined to make his capital more beautiful. This was reflected in the work of Inigo Jones at St Paul's Cathedral and of the Earl of Bedford in Covent Garden, and also in the continuation of James I's campaigns to ensure that all new buildings in London were brick-built and to prevent the spread of tenements around the city.[4]

Charles demanded not only that the burnt houses be not rebuilt, but also that the entire bridge be cleared of houses, 'in regard of the conveniance of passage and the uniformitie and beautie that wolde be caused thereby'. The first step was a request to the bridge wardens for a plan of the bridge and a rental of the houses on it. The plan was provided on 26 March and is almost certainly Figure 8. The bridge wardens were equally determined to prevent a considerable loss of income. The eventual compromise was that the remaining houses could stay but the burnt ones would not be rebuilt. In January 1635 Charles complained of the impeding of traffic by the narrowness of the roadway and encroachments such as 'stayers and stoopes', and made clear that he would

> never upon anie instance whatsoever give way to the rebuildinge of anie house there it beinge too great an impediment to all that passe that waye ... and because it is the only bridge over the river, belongeinge to so great and populous a citie.

Fig. 56 Detail from Hollar's Long View of London of 1647, showing the fencing put up at the north end of the bridge after the fire of 1633. The waterworks are to the left.

A commission including Inigo Jones was appointed, and in August 1635 made more detailed recommendations for the burnt area, including a roadway 20 feet wide, footpaths on each side 6 feet wide, new ribs between the piers on the east side and the filling in of the old cellars in the piers. The City estimated the cost of this as £6,142, and it was not clear how that money could be raised. In fact nothing further was done, and the temporary measures of February 1633 remained in place.[5]

The bridge estates committee did not require lessees of houses destroyed by fire to rebuild them, but in June 1634 it offered the tenants of the burnt houses an unwelcome choice: they could either continue paying rent in order to keep the option of occupying a rebuilt house in the future (if rebuilding was permitted), or they could surrender their leases and lose that option, even if they had recently paid large entry fines. Only Walter Rogers at PE1 continued to pay rent after 1634, for a house which was patched up and, in about 1644, rebuilt.[6] The surrendering of leases meant that, when the principal part was eventually rebuilt, the rebuilding was unconstrained by existing boundaries. The majority of the former occupants moved away, but many remained on the bridge: by 1634 five of the thirty-nine had moved to the south part and five to the middle part; one remained at PE1. John Sherley, goldsmith, was granted a lease of ME10 in 1639 'in consideracon of his great damage susteyned by the late great fire upon London Bridge', and in 1649 Richard Shelbury, scrivener, also a tenant in 1633, was granted leases of two new houses at the north end, partly in consideration of 'his greate losse' from the fire.[7]

The new building of 1645–49

In 1645 work at last began on filling the gap left by the fire. In February 1645 a committee of the Court of Aldermen viewed the place on the bridge where the bridge wardens proposed to build.[8] This was after the defeat of Charles I at Marston Moor, but before defeat at Naseby made his cause hopeless. Five days later Edward Jerman was appointed as surveyor to give advice 'for the better contriveing and finishing of the building to be erected upon London Bridge by the Bridgehouse carpenter'.[9] Jerman was City Carpenter from 1633 to 1657, at first jointly with his father, and was to design the Royal Exchange and many livery company halls after the Great Fire.[10] In April 1645 the bridge wardens were ordered to proceed on the basis of the model (or plan) presented by Jerman. However, in June the Aldermen considered 'two severall plotts or modells' for the building, one proposed by Jerman and one by Joseph Darvoll, who since 1627 had been the Bridge House's master carpenter of the land works (in charge of all carpentry except the tide work on the starlings). They opted for Darvoll's plan, but Jerman was to be rewarded for 'his extraordinary paines taken in the draught or modell by him presented'. In 1650 Jerman was paid £13.6s.8d. for his plan, while Darvoll was paid £3.6s.8d. for his.[11] A reasonable explanation would be that Jerman provided an elegant design, but that Darvoll, with his long experience of the bridge houses, turned it into a more practical one.

The approximate shape and appearance of the new houses is known from a print by Hollar and another less informative drawing (Figs 57, 58), but the Bridge House accounts and the lease descriptions provide a much clearer picture, including dimensions for all but three of the houses (see Fig. 59 and the

Survey).¹² They were built in three stages, working from south to north. The permission given in 1645 evidently covered ten houses, the first timber frame comprising six of them and the second frame comprising four. Permission was given in November 1647 to build three more houses, of which one was on the east side, filling the gap between the other new houses and the recently-rebuilt PE1, and two were on the west side, filling the gap there.¹³ The new houses extended from the abutment to the third pier from the north.¹⁴ As Hollar's print suggests and the leases confirm, the western ones were several feet deeper than the eastern ones, reflecting the fact that the roadway was not in the centre of the piers.

Three hammer beams were carried to the bridge in September 1645, but it was not until September 1646 that money was given to the carpenters 'at the rayseinge of the first six houses upon London bridge'. The carpenters received payments for the six houses from November 1645 to July 1647, and the plasterer was paid from August 1646 to December 1647, when the glazier was also paid. The first leases were granted in November 1647. For the next four houses, the carpenters received payments from September 1646 to December 1648. Some of these houses were leased in December 1647, before they were finished. For the last three houses, the carpenters received payments from February 1648 to March 1649, and the plasterer until August 1649. Leases were granted in June 1648 and April 1649.

Unlike on most previous occasions the Bridge House did not build the houses itself using its own labour force. Possibly it no longer had enough workmen to do so. It provided the timber, but otherwise it contracted with the carpenters and others for a fixed price. The carpenters were paid for workmanship only, including the work of carpenters, sawyers, turners and carvers.

Above: **Fig. 57** Detail from Hollar's view of London before and after the Great Fire, which included the new houses built at the north end of the bridge in 1645–49.

Left: **Fig. 58** Detail from a pencil sketch made in 1827 of a now lost painting of London in about 1660, showing the new houses of 1645–49 to the right and St Paul's Cathedral in the background.

Fig. 59 The outline of the new houses of the 1640s marked on the plan of 1633, using the dimensions in the leases (see the Survey). The houses are indicated by solid lines, the cross buildings by broken red lines and yards by broken red lines or the letter Y. The northern edge of the new building is known (Appendix 6). The southern edge is assumed here to be the southern edge of the third pier, and given the known dimensions it cannot be more than a few feet away. The exact placing of the cross buildings is an assumption. The space available means that the width of PE4, which is not recorded, becomes 21 feet and that of PW1 and 2 becomes 15 feet each. If the southernmost houses projected 4 feet beyond the third pier, PE4 would be 25 feet wide (roughly equal to the largest of the new houses) and PW1 and 2 would then each be 17 feet wide.

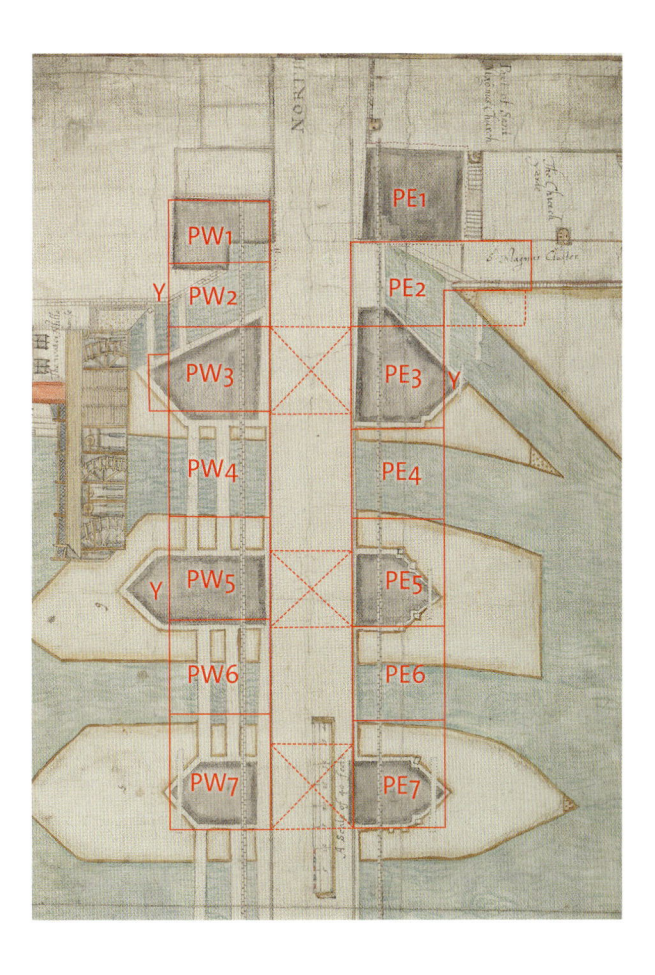

They were William Taylor and William Pilling, who built the first six houses for £600; Joseph Darvoll and William Taylor, who built the next four, also for £600; and Taylor, Darvoll and Pilling, who built the final three, for £395. Abraham Stanyon did all the plastering work, providing his own materials and receiving £617.14s.0d. for the first six houses and £776.16s.0d. for the remaining seven. Baptist Sutton was the glazier for all the houses, for a total of £73.4s.9d. A bricklayer, John Brathwaite, was employed on the last three houses, one of which was largely on the abutment rather than the bridge, and received £58.3s.5d.

The design of the new houses has been described as revolutionary, because they formed a single rectangular block and lacked the irregularity and numerous projections of earlier bridge houses.[15] In this they reflected the trend towards regularity in other London buildings, such as those of Great Queen Street and the Covent Garden piazza. Previously houses over gullets had usually been shallower than those over piers, whereas now they were even. This was probably achieved either by placing hammer beams towards the ends of the piers rather than closer to the roadway, requiring them to be much longer, or by supporting the outer edge of the new buildings by means of struts or braces resting on the hammer beams. The disadvantage of regularity, apart from extra cost, was that where the piers were longer, potential building space was sacrificed, as on the second pier on the west side.[16] The other major innovation was that the new houses left room for a wider roadway. This part of the roadway had already been widened to 18 feet after the fire of 1633, and the dimensions given in the leases, especially for rooms over the street and the leads at the south end, indicate that the new width was 20 feet. The new houses were wider than their predecessors, all but the two at the north-west end ranging from 19 feet 6 inches to 26 feet 3 inches, and most of the halls were large, that at PW7 being 25½ by 20½ feet. The houses had three and a half storeys, one less than some of their predecessors.

There were new methods of obtaining water. In December 1646 workmen were paid for advising on how water could be conveyed from the Thames into the new houses.[17] The leases and their schedules suggest that the scheme adopted involved pumping water to a cistern behind each shop, and then pumping it up again from that cistern to another in the kitchen or adjacent waterhouse or washhouse in the second storey. For example, in Francis Kirby's house (PE5), the cistern house behind the shop contained 'a leaden pipe to convey ye water into the cisterne from ye Thames' and a pump, while the second-floor kitchen contained the second cistern and 'a leaden pumpe cased with a leaden pipe which reacheth downe into the stowe cisterne behind the shopp'.[18] Pipes were also provided to convey water back into the Thames. The arrangements for water may have contributed to the placing of some of the kitchens on the first floor, as discussed later.[19] Four leases or their schedules record the privy or house of office. Two were in cellars, one was in a yard and one was in a garret. At least four houses had yards. One of these was partly on the riverbank and partly over a channel (PE2), two were on the ends of piers (PE3 and PW5), and one was on the riverbank (PW2).[20]

In some respects the planning was conservative. In particular the cross-buildings extended from first-floor level upwards. Internally, of the nine houses for which lists of rooms have survived, all but two had the kitchen on the second floor, albeit in three cases paired with a dining room. Where recorded, staircases and chimneys were at the sides.

The houses had some architectural pretensions. They had an 'Ionick story' and a 'Corynthian story', indicating classical capitals, and the former had at least two compass windows (bow windows). There was a carved cornice. As usual, the ornamentation was on the south and north ends. The king's arms and 'things belonging' were placed in front of the first six houses, and Darvoll and Taylor provided 'three flower potts for the adorning of the kings armes on the south front of the newe frame'. At the north end was the 'ballcony front', evidently the north side of the first cross building, where PE3 had a gallery with rails facing north in the first storey.[21] According to Strype, 'over the houses were stately platforms, leaded with rails and ballasters about them very commodious, and pleasant for walking, and enjoying so fine a prospect up and down the river; and some had pretty little gardens with arbors'. The remaining area south of the new houses was, he wrote, intended to be rebuilt in a similar way, 'which would have been a great glory to the Bridge, and honour to the City, the street or passage being twenty feet broad'.[22]

The new lessees were similar to those elsewhere on the bridge. On the basis of their company membership, which did not always reflect their actual trade, they were a haberdasher, a girdler, a mercer, two clothworkers, a vintner, two stationers, a scrivener, an ironmonger, a skinner and a salter. The skinner was Francis Kirby, one of the bridge wardens. The occupants in 1666 were four haberdashers, a linen draper, a woollen draper, a hosier, a silkman, a milliner, a glover, a grocer and a scrivener (one was empty).[23]

Was it all worth it? The new houses cost at least £3,260, plus the cost of the timber, making the cost of each house at least £250. In return, the Bridge House secured entry fines totalling about £2,400 and annual rent of £130, so the cost would have been recovered in not much more than seven years. The venture was therefore worthwhile financially, and would have been more so but for the destruction of the houses in the Great Fire. However, the Bridge House had to borrow heavily from the City to pay the construction costs, and by March 1649 it was seriously short of cash.[24] This may explain why the remaining gap was not filled. Steps to do so were taken in 1657, and an agreement was made with a mason to mend the cellars and stonework on the west side, but no more houses were actually built.[25] The roadway continued to be enclosed by fencing, which was periodically blown away.[26]

The Great Fire of 1666 and the sheds

The new houses were an early casualty of the Great Fire, which began on 2 September 1666. Samuel Pepys witnessed them burning on the first morning, and they can be seen alight in the best-known painting of the fire (Fig. 60).[27] Crucially, the gap in the houses prevented the fire spreading to the middle and south parts of the bridge. The Bridge House paid back half of the entry fines for the burnt houses in return for the cancellation of the leases.[28] Only two of their occupants are known to have moved to other parts of the bridge.[29] In 1667 the stonework of six cellars and one arch or rib were said to have been damaged by the fire, requiring expenditure of £1,300, and in 1682 there were still 'three peeres there which are soe very much shattered and destroyed by the late fire and still lye uncovered and open to ye weather'.[30]

As early as 4 September, when the fire was still raging, the bridge estates committee ordered that the bridge roadway be cleared and that freemen of the City be allowed to erect 'sheds' on it for carrying on their businesses. The offer was quickly taken up. The rents were usually 2s.6d or 3s. per foot, or 4s. per foot with a cellar, though by 1682 the occupants were paying 20s. per foot to the lessees. For example Edward Calcott junior, citizen and turner, had a shed 13 feet wide next to PE1, paying the Bridge House 52s. a year. Most were between 15 and 18 feet wide, like the houses which later replaced them, though one was just 8½ feet by 5½ feet.[31] They were in fact rather more than sheds, and were sometimes referred to as small tenements or as 'the New Buildings'. Many if not most were permanently occupied. A hearth tax assessment of about 1670 lists twenty-one households there, usually with two hearths each but ocasionally three or four.[32] Gervase Locke junior, citizen and mercer, stated in a petition of 1682 that he inhabited one of the sheds on the west side of the bridge, and in the poll tax assessment of 1678 he was living there with his wife, one child, two apprentices and a maid. This shed, described as a house and shop, had at least two storeys, which was probably exceptional. Often the sheds had just two or three occupants in 1678, such as Humphrey Caseby and his maid, Francis Stileman and his apprentice, and Daniel Conney and his wife.[33]

One of the bridge plots was affected by the improvements made in the City after the fire. This was the one at the extreme north-west end (PW1), fairly recently acquired and rebuilt in the 1640s. By October 1668 most of it was 'staked out' for public use, leaving only 6½ feet, which seems to have been the width of the site at the back. Comparison between the 1633 plan and later maps shows that the purpose of the staking out was to create a passage (later known as Red Cross Alley) between Bridge Street and the new 40-foot wharf stretching westwards.[34] St Magnus's church was at risk from the policy of reducing the number of churches, and according to its vestry was 'in very great danger to have been made a cole wharfe' (Fig. 61). The vestry attributed the church's rebuilding to the efforts of John Greene, haberdasher, Common Councillor and 'one of the ancients of the vestry', who lived at MW1.[35]

Cancelling the leases of the houses built in the 1640s meant that the Bridge House would have a free hand when they were eventually rebuilt. But in the immediate aftermath of the fire it probably lacked the funds to do so, and, while most of the

Fig. 60 Detail from a Dutch painting in the Museum of London showing the houses at the north end of the bridge burning during the Great Fire of 1666.

Fig. 61 The north end of the bridge after the Great Fire, with St Magnus's church in ruins (detail from Hollar's view of London after the fire).

rest of the City was being rebuilt, it would have been difficult to find contractors to do it. Indeed, it would have made little sense to undertake the relatively demanding task of rebuilding the bridge houses with their hammer beams and expensive scaffolding when there were thousands of empty sites where houses could be built more easily. The sheds therefore remained in place for about sixteen years (Figs 62, 63). When it was eventually decided to rebuild the northern part, legal action was necessary to eject the occupants of the sheds.[36]

The experience of the Finch family encapsulates most of the changes on the bridge between 1633 and 1684. Francis Finch was a hosier, occupying PE10 in 1633. He was described as

Fig. 62 Painting by Abraham Hondius of a frost fair on the Thames in 1677, with the bridge in the background. From right to left are St Mary Overy (now Southwark Cathedral), the south part of the bridge, the middle part, and the sheds on the principal part. Behind the south part can be seen the tower of St Olave's church, the parish of which included the south part of the bridge.

Captain Finch in 1648 and Major Finch in 1658, indicating service in London's Trained Bands during the civil wars, and he was a churchwarden of St Magnus in 1652 and a vestry member.[37] His house was destroyed in the fire of 1633. By 1638 he had moved to MW12, acquiring the lease in about 1649. There were two shops there, one of which he occupied himself, calling it the Dog's Head and Porridge Pot (or the Dog's Head in the Pot). In 1648 he also acquired the lease of one of the newly-built houses at the north end (PE3), which seems to have been an investment, as he let it out. It was

Fig. 63 Detail from Morgan's panorama of London in 1682, showing the sheds on the northern part of the bridge (probably much simplified) and PE1 under the tower of St Magnus's church.

burnt in 1666. Subsequently he held one of the sheds on the northern part of the bridge, again letting it out. He died in about 1677, and was succeeded at MW12 by his son William Finch, also a hosier. In 1678 William was living there with his wife, two children, two apprentices and two maids. In 1684 he was required to rebuild it so that the roadway could be widened, but chose instead to sell his interest to John Foltrop, a carpenter. He died in late 1684 or early 1685, apparently leaving only a daughter, Joyce.[38] That was the end of the Finch family on the bridge.

CHAPTER 8

Trading on the bridge

Throughout the bridge's history, all the houses on it were shop houses. Virtually no-one ever had a house on the bridge only because it was a pleasant place to live:[1] they were there because it was a good place to trade, and to understand the bridge we must examine why that was so. This chapter will therefore seek to identify the trades practised on the bridge, how these changed over time, what the advantages were of being located on the bridge and what role the bridge houses played in production and retailing in London. The bridge carried all the road traffic between London and south-east England, and its attraction may therefore seem obvious, but the shops on the bridge were not like those found around places of heavy footfall today, selling fast-food and souvenirs. Shops selling food and drink for immediate consumption were almost unknown on the bridge until the eighteenth century, and customers of the bridge shops did not buy drapery, girdles or bows on impulse because they happened to be passing a shop which sold them.

A record of the trades carried out on the bridge has been compiled in different ways for different dates, as shown in Table 3. In some cases a list of the occupants at a particular date has been used, with the trades taken either from that list or from other documents, or from both. In other cases the numbers of individuals named with their trade during a period of years have been counted, the source usually being the record of entry fines paid. The results are fairly consistent whatever the method used. The record at different dates varies in completeness, and in some years parts of the bridge are covered better than others. Up to 1606 there may be a few included who were lessees but not residents (thereafter only those clearly recorded as resident are included), and at most dates there may be a few trades that indicated membership of a company rather than the practising of that trade, as these did not always coincide. For example, in the mid-seventeenth century Gabriel Partridge (ME3) and Edmund Warnett (SE3) were both recorded as citizen and cutler, but Partridge was also described as a haberdasher, and Warnett is recorded selling draperies.[2] Members of the Girdlers' Company were almost invariably engaged in a different trade by the late seventeenth century. Moreover, what a tradesman such as a haberdasher or girdler actually sold might vary from one period to another, or even from one person to another at the same date. Once an individual had achieved the freedom of the City he could practise any trade, at least at the wholesale level, rather than just the one in which he had served his apprenticeship, and there was much overlap; for example, mercers, glovers, grocers, girdlers and others all might sell haberdashery goods. Nevertheless, the way a tradesman was described often did have some connection with the goods he or she sold.

The fourteenth and fifteenth centuries

As indicated earlier, five types of trader dominated the bridge in the late fourteenth and fifteenth centuries: haberdashers, glovers, cutlers, bowyers and fletchers (Fig. 64). These five, together with some minor but closely-related ones such as pursers and stringers, accounted for more than four-fifths of the bridge's traders in the late fourteenth century, falling only to two-thirds during the fifteenth century. Each of these trades needs to be examined in order to work out what activity was taking place on the bridge and why.

Haberdashery was the archetypal bridge trade from the late fourteenth century until the houses were removed in the eighteenth century (Fig. 65). Indeed it was the only one of the five early trades that remained important after the fifteenth century. Haberdashers sold an enormous range of goods. In the fourteenth century these included thread of various sorts; dress accessories such as combs, purses, girdles, bracelets, spectacles and looking glasses; undergarments such as shirts; hats and other headgear; writing materials including parchment and paper; items of popular piety such as rosaries; garment fastenings such as laces, points (or ties), pins and buttons; and miscellaneous small items such as thimbles and money boxes.[3] Before the mid-fourteenth century there were probably few haberdashers, as previously haberdashery goods tended to be bought either from mercers or from their makers, and haberdashers only became separate from the mercers who sold expensive cloths in the early fourteenth century, but there would probably have been similar goods being sold by people not calling themselves haberdashers. A probable example is William le Chapelier (William the hatter), who was a taxpayer in Bridge Ward, though not necessarily on the bridge, in 1292. Nevertheless, the haberdashery trade was greatly enlarged from about 1340 by the development of closer-fitting garments, which needed more fastenings, as well as by greater fashion-consciousness and by growing real wages, which helped fashions to spread down the social scale.[4]

By the late fifteenth century, the haberdashers were heavily concentrated in two areas of the City: north and east of St Paul's Cathedral and in and around London Bridge. Of the five trading groups, they were the ones who were most clearly tradesmen rather than craftsmen; in other words, they bought and sold goods but did not make them. As well as retailing, they probably sold wholesale to pedlars or chapmen and other country traders, as they certainly did later.[5]

The glovers were probably established on the bridge before the fourteenth century, as there were at least two in Bridge Ward in 1292 and two in 1319. William de Stortford left his house and shops on the bridge to his wife Margery and son William in 1288–89, and Ralph de Stortford, probably a descendant, was a glover in 1310–20 in Bridge Ward. Those elected to put into effect the ordinances for the glovers' trade agreed in 1349 included Robert de Goldesburgh, who witnessed the granting of the lease of a shop on the bridge to a glover (Thomas de Gloucestre) in 1351 and was probably the father or other relative of John Goldesburgh, a glover on the bridge in the

Table 3 Occupations on the bridge (% of all occupations recorded)

Category	1381–97	1404	1404–40	1478	1515–45	1546–75	1576	1577–1606	1633–35	1666	1682	1710–12	1743–44
Haberdashers	14	15	14	27	28	28	28	26	27	30	20	12	11
Drapers, etc.	0	0	3	0	25	14	19	18	19	16	8	4	2
Silkmen/women	0	0	1	1	0	0	0	0	5	9	6	1	0
Hosiers	0	0	1	0	0	0	0	0	10	7	10	4	5
Misc. clothing, etc.	0	0	0	0	0	0	0	0	0	0	10	4	5
Glovers	18	19	13	4	0	0	0	0	3	2	2	1	0
Leathersellers	2	0	1	0	2	3	4	5	0	0	2	3	3
Cutlers	22	19	16	12	2	4	9	5	5	2	2	1	6
Girdlers	0	2	3	8	1	1	4	5	6	2	0	0	0
Goldsmiths/jewellers	2	6	5	4	0	0	2	3	0	0	2	0	3
Metalworkers	2	0	0	3	2	1	0	4	0	7	10	4	3
Pinmakers/needlemakers	0	0	1	1	1	0	0	0	2	0	2	7	11
Spurriers	2	6	4	3	1	0	0	0	0	0	0	0	0
Bowyers	16	9	10	17	10	7	5	1	0	0	0	0	0
Fletchers	14	17	15	9	6	1	2	1	0	0	0	0	0
Armourers, etc.	4	4	4	1	0	0	0	0	0	0	0	0	0
Grocers	2	0	3	6	19	33	21	16	8	2	2	0	2
Vintners	0	0	0	0	0	4	5	4	5	0	0	3	0
Misc. durables	0	0	1	0	0	0	0	0	0	5	10	15	16
Stationers/booksellers	0	0	0	0	0	1	0	1	2	5	8	12	8
Barbers/apothecaries/surgeons	0	0	3	0	0	1	0	0	2	4	4	5	2
Victuallers, etc.	0	2	1	0	0	0	0	0	0	2	2	5	9
Misc.	2	2	3	4	3	3	2	9	8	11	2	16	16
Total number	50	53	160	77	108	76	57	76	63	56	51	73	64

The figures are percentages of all occupations recorded in each year or period. In each year or period, no individual is included more than once even if mentioned several times. The individuals counted in 1404 are also included in 1404–40. Figures for 1682 are for the middle and south parts only, excluding the sheds on the north part. One unidentified trade has been omitted in 1381 and six in 1404–40. Figures may not add up to 100 due to rounding.

Haberdashers includes pointmakers (1 in 1404–40), cappers (1 in 1404–40, 1 in 1515–45), milliners (1 in 1633, 1 in 1666, 1 in 1743–44), hatters (3 in 1743–44).

Drapers, etc. includes merchant taylors (13 in 1515–45, 6 in 1546–75, 6 in 1576, 8 in 1577–1606, 1 in 1666), clothworkers (2 in 1546–75, 3 in 1576, 3 in 1577–1606, 4 in 1633), mercers (11 in 1515–45, 1 in 1546–75, 1 in 1577–1606, 3 in 1633, 1 in 1666, 1 in 1682), yarnmen (1 in 1666), worsted shop (1 in 1710–12).

Misc. clothing and adornment: 3 bodice sellers (one a bodice and whalebone seller), 2 salesmen 1682; whalebone merchant, glass necklace maker, periwig maker 1710–12; necklace maker, peruke maker, hair merchant 1743–44.

Glovers includes pursers (2 in 1381–97, 2 in 1404, 4 in 1404–40).

Leathersellers includes skinners (1 in 1381–97, 1 in 1576, 3 in 1577–1606), fellmongers (1 in 1404–40).

Cutlers includes sheathers (3 in 1381–97, 2 in 1404, 3 in 1404–40).

Goldsmiths/jewellers includes broochmakers (1 in 1404, 2 in 1404–40), silversmiths (1 in 1743–44).

Metalworkers: ironmonger 1381–97; pewterer 1478; 2 pewterers 1515–45; coppersmith 1546–75; 2 pewterers, founder 1577–1606; 2 pewterers, tinman, ironmonger 1666; 3 ironmongers, 2 pewterers 1682; pewterer, tinman, brasier 1710–12; pewterer, tinman 1743–44.

Bowyers includes stringers (1 in 1381–97, 1 in 1404, 4 in 1404–40).

Armourers, etc. includes furbers (1 in 1381–97), chapmakers (1 in 1381–97, 1 in 1404, 2 in 1404–40).

Grocers includes pepperers (1 in 1381–97), waxchandlers (1 in 1515–45).

Vintners includes distillers (1 in 1633, 1 in 1710–12), strong water shop (1 in 1710–12).

Misc. durables: bottlemaker, horner 1404–40; combmaker, glassman, boxmaker 1666; 3 trunkmakers, looking glass maker, watchmaker 1682; boxmaker, 2 trunkmakers, brushmaker, combmaker, watchmaker, clockmaker, scale maker, instrument maker, spectacle maker 1710–12; boxmaker, 2 brushmakers, 2 clockmakers, 2 scale makers, mathematical instrument maker, spectacle maker 1743–44.

Stationers/booksellers includes music shops (2 in 1710–12, 1 in 1743–44).

Victuallers, etc. includes cooks (1 in 1404, 1 in 1404–40, 1 in 1710–12), pastry cooks (1 in 1710–12, 2 in 1743–44), coffee house/coffeemen (1 in 1710–12, 3 in 1743–44).

Misc.: mason 1381–97; chaplain 1404; 3 clerks/chaplains, fishmonger 1404–40; tallow chandler, cobbler, sergeant 1478; cordwainer, sergeant, footman 1515–45; scrivener, marbler 1546–75; scrivener 1576; 3 fishmongers, painter-stainer, scrivener, salter, waterbailiff 1577–1606; 2 shoemakers/cordwainers, salter, scrivener, fishmonger 1633; salter, scrivener, shoemaker, sempster 1666; drysalter 1682; scrivener, shoemaker, hempshop, flaxman, perfumer, painter, 4 slopshops 1710–12; cork cutter, hop merchant, perfumer, painter, merchant, fishmonger, snuffmaker, turner, 2 blue shops 1743–44.

Sources:

1381–97: LMA, CLA/007/FN/01/018 and 019.

1404: BHR, 001 (printed in Harding, pp. 38–43); some trades added from earlier and later rentals and accounts.

1404–40: BHR, 001 and 002.

1478: BHR, 060; trades not stated in 1478 have been added from other years.

1515–45: BHR, 005 to 007.

1546–75: BHR, 007 to 009.

1576: lessees – BHR, 009; trades – ibid.; BHJ, A; TNA, E 179/145/225, m. 86 (see http://socrates.berkeley.edu/~ahnelson/SUBSIDY/252k.html) [accessed 11 April 2018].

1577–1606: BHJ, A; BHR, 009 and 010.

1633–35: principal part – British Library, Sloane MS 1457, pp. 93–94; other parts, occupants from LMA, CLC/W/GE/001/MS03461/001, 1635 list, trades from CCLD and TNA, PROB 11.

1666: Matthew Davies et al. (eds), *London and Middlesex 1666 hearth tax*, British Record Society hearth tax series 9.2 (2014), p. 702; TNA, E 179/258/4; BHJ, 001; CCLD; TNA, PROB 11.

1682: LMA, CLA/007/EM/06/04, pp. 116–25; a few missing trades from the following: CCLD; TNA, PROB 4 and 11; LMA, CLA/002/02/01/1990.

1710–12: LMA, CLA/007/FN/09/001; some other occupants identified using 1711 land tax with TNA, PROB 11.

1743–45: BHJ, 008; BHP, 008; LMA, COL/CCS/CO/06/004; TNA, online catalogue.

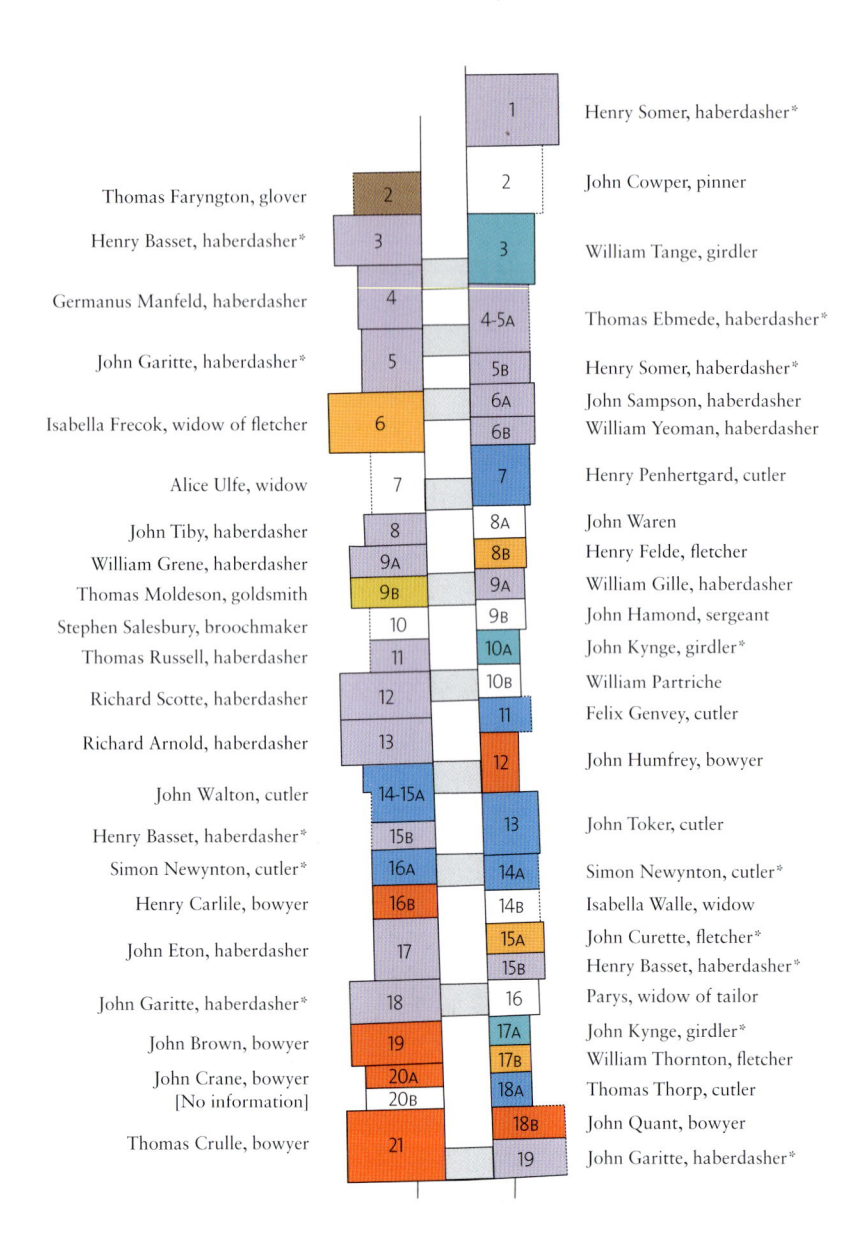

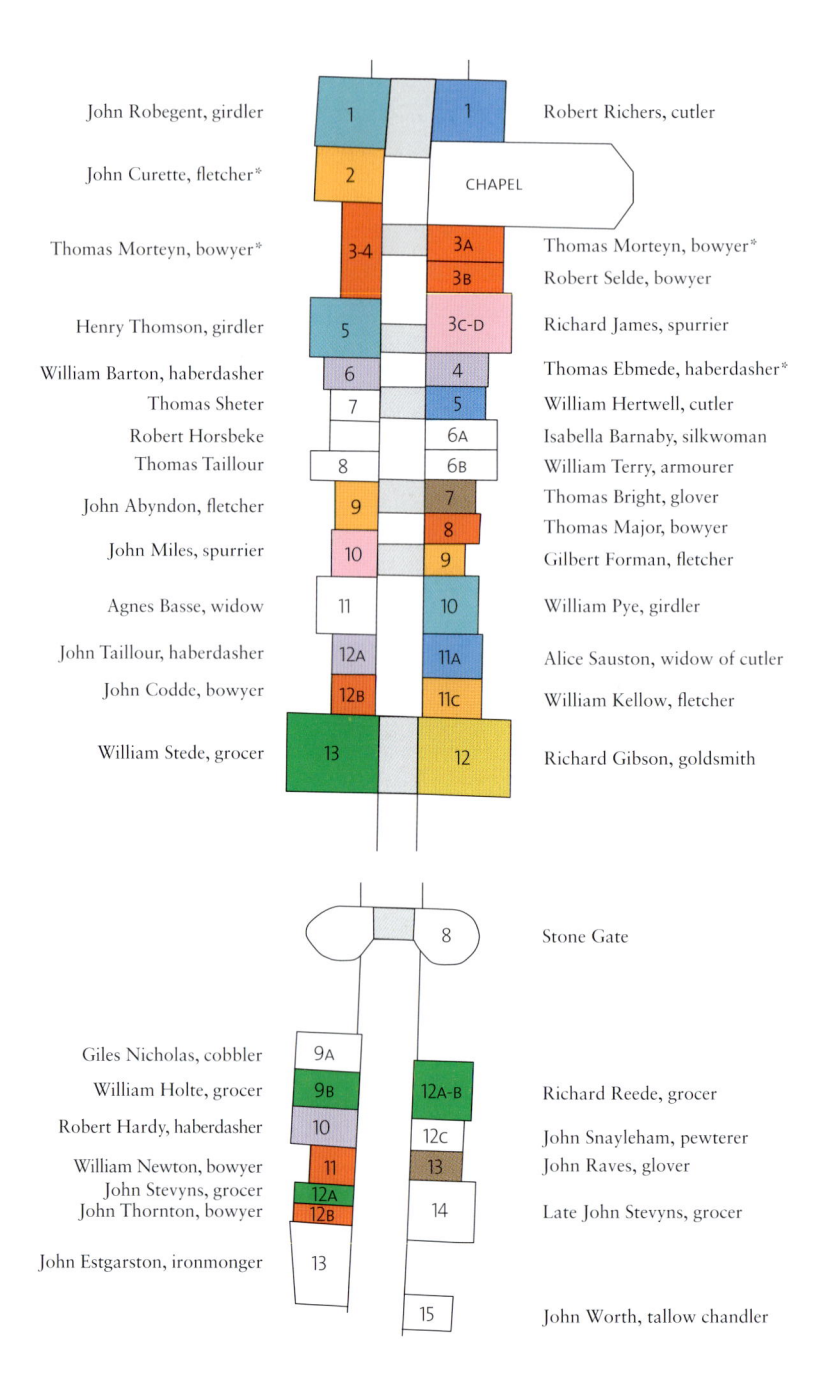

84 LONDON BRIDGE AND ITS HOUSES, c. 1209–1761

West side (south to north):

- Thomas Faryngton, glover — 2
- Henry Basset, haberdasher* — 3
- Germanus Manfeld, haberdasher — 4
- John Garitte, haberdasher* — 5
- Isabella Frecok, widow of fletcher — 6
- Alice Ulfe, widow — 7
- John Tiby, haberdasher — 8
- William Grene, haberdasher — 9A
- Thomas Moldeson, goldsmith — 9B
- Stephen Salesbury, broochmaker — 10
- Thomas Russell, haberdasher — 11
- Richard Scotte, haberdasher — 12
- Richard Arnold, haberdasher — 13
- John Walton, cutler — 14–15A
- Henry Basset, haberdasher* — 15B
- Simon Newynton, cutler* — 16A
- Henry Carlile, bowyer — 16B
- John Eton, haberdasher — 17
- John Garitte, haberdasher* — 18
- John Brown, bowyer — 19
- John Crane, bowyer — 20A
- [No information] — 20B
- Thomas Crulle, bowyer — 21

East side (south to north):

- 1 — Henry Somer, haberdasher*
- 2 — John Cowper, pinner
- 3 — William Tange, girdler
- 4–5A — Thomas Ebmede, haberdasher*
- 5B — Henry Somer, haberdasher*
- 6A — John Sampson, haberdasher
- 6B — William Yeoman, haberdasher
- 7 — Henry Penhertgard, cutler
- 8A — John Waren
- 8B — Henry Felde, fletcher
- 9A — William Gille, haberdasher
- 9B — John Hamond, sergeant
- 10A — John Kynge, girdler*
- 10B — William Partriche
- 11 — Felix Genvey, cutler
- 12 — John Humfrey, bowyer
- 13 — John Toker, cutler
- 14A — Simon Newynton, cutler*
- 14B — Isabella Walle, widow
- 15A — John Curette, fletcher*
- 15B — Henry Basset, haberdasher*
- 16 — Parys, widow of tailor
- 17A — John Kynge, girdler*
- 17B — William Thornton, fletcher
- 18A — Thomas Thorp, cutler
- 18B — John Quant, bowyer
- 19 — John Garitte, haberdasher*

Second section, west side:

- John Robegent, girdler — 1
- John Curette, fletcher* — 2
- Thomas Morteyn, bowyer* — 3-4
- Henry Thomson, girdler — 5
- William Barton, haberdasher — 6
- Thomas Sheter — 7
- Robert Horsbeke
- Thomas Taillour — 8
- John Abyndon, fletcher — 9
- John Miles, spurrier — 10
- Agnes Basse, widow — 11
- John Taillour, haberdasher — 12A
- John Codde, bowyer — 12B
- William Stede, grocer — 13

Second section, east side:

- 1 — Robert Richers, cutler
- CHAPEL
- 3A — Thomas Morteyn, bowyer*
- 3B — Robert Selde, bowyer
- 3C-D — Richard James, spurrier
- 4 — Thomas Ebmede, haberdasher*
- 5 — William Hertwell, cutler
- 6A — Isabella Barnaby, silkwoman
- 6B — William Terry, armourer
- 7 — Thomas Bright, glover
- 8 — Thomas Major, bowyer
- 9 — Gilbert Forman, fletcher
- 10 — William Pye, girdler
- 11A — Alice Sauston, widow of cutler
- 11C — William Kellow, fletcher
- 12 — Richard Gibson, goldsmith

Third section:

- 8 — Stone Gate

- Giles Nicholas, cobbler — 9A
- William Holte, grocer — 9B
- Robert Hardy, haberdasher — 10
- William Newton, bowyer — 11
- John Stevyns, grocer — 12A
- John Thornton, bowyer — 12B
- John Estgarston, ironmonger — 13

- 12A-B — Richard Reede, grocer
- 12C — John Snayleham, pewterer
- 13 — John Raves, glover
- 14 — Late John Stevyns, grocer
- 15 — John Worth, tallow chandler

Left: **Fig. 64** Tenants on the bridge in 1478. In most cases these are likely to have been occupants, but eight held two or more houses that were not adjacent; their names are asterisked here. Several occupations missing in the 1478 rental have been added from other rentals or the accounts. Houses are shown the same size as in 1633. The drawbridge area, then without houses, is omitted (Source: BHR, 060, rentals).

mid-1390s (at PE6B and PW11).[6] In the late fourteenth and early fifteenth centuries there were also usually several people selling purses on the bridge, and the pursers were certainly established early: in 1310 Robert de Borham, a purser, was sworn to keep the gate on the bridge, and three pursers or pouchmakers paid tax in Bridge Ward in 1319. They included Ralph Gandre, whose probable descendant, Thomas Gandre, was a keeper of the stone gate in 1357 and was a purser on the bridge by 1372 (at PE14A by 1404).[7] Probably the glovers and pursers did not confine themselves to selling gloves and purses.

The glovers were the first of the five early trades to decline significantly. One reason was an influx of country people making gloves in the suburbs and not acquiring the freedom of the City, as leases of the bridge houses were almost certainly granted only to freemen. Another was that glovers increasingly relied on haberdashers to market their wares. The companies of glovers and pursers, both said to be too decayed to survive on their own, amalgamated in 1498 and were absorbed into the Leathersellers' Company in 1502.[8] There may have been just as many gloves being sold on the bridge, but it was no longer glovers selling them.

Cutlers made or sold edged weapons and tools. This is the only one of the five early trades that can be proved to have been present on the bridge in the late thirteenth century, in the person of Simon le Cotiler and others. Often a bladesmith made the blade, a hafter made the handle, a sheather made the sheath and the cutler put these together and sold the finished article. There were sheathers on the bridge as well as cutlers. The City's cutlers were concentrated in three areas: by the conduit in Cheapside, around the River Fleet and on London Bridge, the first of these being the most important. At least four fifteenth-century Masters of the Cutlers' Company traded on the bridge: John Amell senior in 1459–60 (PE8B and 9A), Henry Penhertgart in 1472–73 (PE7), William Hertwell in 1489–90 and 1495–96 (ME5) and Simon Newenton in 1492–93 and 1498–99 (PW16A).[9] The reason why the cutlers largely disappeared from the bridge in the sixteenth century is unknown.[10] It may have been simply an increased preference for other parts of the City rather than any decline in the trade or change in the persons selling cutlery items.

Bowyers made bows, such as crossbows and longbows, fletchers made arrows and stringers made strings for bows. From 1285 every freeholder in England with land worth between 40s. and 100s. a year was expected to keep in his house a sword, a knife and bows and arrows, and from 1363 all able-bodied men were required to practise archery. There seem to have been few bowyers in London in 1300 (only one is recorded before that date), but their numbers increased in the early fourteenth century, mainly through immigration from bow-making centres such as Bristol and Chester.[11] The numbers of fletchers and stringers are likely to have risen and fallen with those of the bowyers. Both bowyers and fletchers were strongly clustered in the fifteenth century in three parts of the City: the Ludgate area, around Aldermanbury and on London Bridge.[12]

Until 1371 some people made both bows and arrows, but thereafter they were required to choose one trade or the other, which a few resisted, such as Robert Verne, later recorded living on the bridge. In 1371 he promised to be a bowyer only, but in September 1375 he was found to be practising both trades, and promised to be a fletcher only. By October he had broken his promise and the Mayor fined him and ordered him to be a bowyer. Nevertheless, in 1386 he was Master or Warden of the Fletchers' Company, along with Stephen Sethere or Sedere (later at PW5A).[13] Four fifteenth-century Masters or Wardens of the Fletchers' Company were traders on the bridge: John Turner or Tournor in 1418 and 1428 (MW1), John Halle in 1420 (SE1), Richard Otehill in 1420 and 1431 (later at PW15B) and Walter Takeneswell in 1424 (ME3B).[14] Henry Yonge was Master of the Longbowstringmakers' Company in 1416 (SE2B).[15] Wardens of the Bowyers' Company are not well recorded, but they included William Sertayn in 1394 (SE2A), Robert Crull in 1416 and 1439 (SW3–4), and possibly Stephen Santon in 1429 (SE2A).[16]

Firearms began to replace longbows with the arrival of the arquebus from Germany in 1517 and the musket from Spain in 1536. Archery continued as a sport, and as late as 1637 the government was trying to enforce the archery laws, but the declining military importance of archery is faithfully reflected in the declining numbers of bowyers and fletchers on the bridge in the sixteenth century. They did, however, include four Makers of the King's Bows, or Queen's Bows, from 1512 to 1581: Henry Pikeman (ME11C, then MW4–5), William Buckstead (MW4–5 and ME5), William Pikeman (son of Henry, not recorded in the rentals) and John Pikeman (MW5). The last fletcher, William Reynolds at PW19, was Master of the Fletchers' Company in 1587–88 and was described as the Queen's Fletcher. He died in 1597. He may also have been involved in making pikes, as his will refers to 'greate doinges' with John Hayborne, the Queen's pikemaker and to accounts between them. He left 40s. to the Fletchers' Company 'to meete and make mery at my buryall'.[17] The tenancy of the last bowyer, Richard Odye, ended in 1602.

Only a few other trades are worth mentioning before the sixteenth century. There were several armourers and spurriers, and also a furber (Thomas Langstone up to 1385), whose role was to repair weapons. In fact the furbers were one of the bridge's earliest recorded trades: Anselm the furbisher upon London Bridge was recorded in 1300 and 1310 (in the latter year being sworn to keep the gate on the bridge), and Reginald le Fourbour of London Bridge was mentioned in a will of 1348.[18] There were a few goldsmiths or jewellers. In the fifteenth century there were several girdlers, who made belts using leather, metal or linen, and a slowly rising number of grocers, who were to be significant in the following century.

There were always some female tenants on the bridge (six in 1404), and probably most of these were widows continuing their husband's trade. Indeed they were sometimes described simply as so-and-so's wife, even though in the period before 1440, unlike later, tenancies were often explicitly granted to a husband and wife rather than just to the husband. However, several women in the fifteenth century acquired a lease for themselves rather than taking it over from a dead husband. The most notable example was Isabella Barnaby, who was a silkwoman at ME6A from 1430 until her death in 1478. The trade in silk was then an entirely female one.[19] Unfortunately nothing more is known about her. Other examples of women who did not succeed a dead husband are Alice Bray, daughter of Richard Bray, at PW10 in 1411 ('being a maid'; she seems to have married in 1417, when she and her husband became joint tenants),[20] Agnes Babyngton, a linendraper at ME10B from 1417 to 1419, and Alice Assheby, a spurrier at MW12B from 1428 onwards. A wider range of occupations was open to women in London in this period than in the following century.[21]

Now we can draw some conclusions about the trades on the bridge and the advantages of being located there. The first is that the goods sold on the bridge were not convenience ones which were bought frequently, such as bread. Shop selling these items tended to be widely distributed because people were not willing to travel far to obtain them. Instead, the items sold were what geographers call 'shopping goods' or 'comparison goods', which were bought only occasionally and for which customers would travel to a specialist trading area.[22] The emphasis on 'shopping goods' is the most important and continuous distinguishing feature of the bridge's shops.

Despite the heavy footfall, food and drink were not sold on the bridge, except specialist items traded by grocers. The only victualler in 1404–40 was a cook at SW13B, which was on the bridge abutment rather than the bridge. This may have been a deliberate policy, as in 1320 five retailers of ale on the bridge were ordered to stop selling it there.[23] Indeed there may have been a deliberate policy from early in the bridge's history of reserving the shops for relatively prestigious trades, as was sometimes the case with inhabited bridges in other cities.[24] After 1320, apart from the Sun tavern mentioned in 1493, there is no evidence of alehouses on the bridge until one was created in 1581 in a new cellar between the principal and middle parts.[25] When sheds were erected after the Great Fire, their lessees were forbidden to sub-let them to victuallers or sellers of beer.[26]

Shops selling 'shopping goods' were and are usually in major commercial thoroughfares, and those in the same trade tend to cluster together because purchasers compare items in different shops. If, for example, Ludgate or London Bridge is the recognised place to buy bows and arrows, a shop selling them somewhere else is likely to be at a disadvantage. There can also be other benefits, such as co-location with related trades and access to business information. How a cluster comes together in the first place, including the possible role of official policy, is unclear, but London Bridge certainly had such clusters by the fourteenth century. Also, it has been argued that up to the eighteenth century the aim of most retail promotion, for example through handbills, shop front or reputation, was to bring the customer to the shop, rather than to inform them about particular goods; the shop then provided expertise about types and qualities of goods and had the ability to supply them.[27] On that basis we can reach our second conclusion, that London Bridge was an excellent trading location: it had established clusters of businesses, its constant traffic made its shops highly visible, and it was a prestigious location, being one of London's most notable structures. There is a little evidence of clustering *within* the bridge: in 1478, for example, the haberdashers were most numerous in the northern half of the principal part, which the high rents suggest was the best trading position, and the bowyers were clustered on both sides of the Square (Fig. 64).

A third conclusion is that the traders on the bridge were predominantly sellers rather than makers of goods. Defoe was later to distinguish between those engaged in handicrafts, such as smiths, shoemakers and carpenters, who made the goods they sold, and trading men, who did not: 'such are, whether wholesale or retail, our grocers, mercers, linen and woollen drapers, Blackwell-hall factors, tobacconists, haberdashers, whether of hats or small wares, glovers, hosiers, milliners, booksellers, stationers, and all other shopkeepers, who do not actually work upon, make, or manufacture, the goods they sell'.[28] Defoe's list is close to being a summary of the trades on the bridge, at least for the seventeenth century. For the fourteenth and fifteenth centuries, the haberdashers were clearly sellers rather than makers. It is harder to be certain about the others, but in some cases, such as fletchers and at least some cutlers, they tended to assemble goods manufactured by others.

Arrow-making, for example, involved three processes, which were carried out on piecework as a cottage industry.[29] None of the main trades on the bridge involved extensive use of fire or bringing large quantities of heavy materials onto the bridge, and this too may have been a deliberate policy of the Bridge House; certainly it was hostile later to trades requiring ovens or furnaces.[30] Also, the small size of the bridge shops would have made some crafts difficult to carry out there. Manufacturing requiring little space, such as gloving, may have taken place on the bridge, but undoubtedly the dominant activity was selling items made elsewhere.

A fourth conclusion is that the shops on the bridge were an important part of London retailing. The major trades there usually formed one of only two or three clusters which accounted for most of that trade throughout the City. The bridge was one of London's four or five main streets for fashionable shopping,[31] though it largely lacked the most luxurious trades, notably those of the goldsmiths and jewellers. That many of the customers came from the City specifically to the bridge shops rather than being on their way between London and south-east England is indicated by the fact that rents were far higher in the northern half of the principal part than elsewhere on the bridge (Table 1).

In fact we can go further and suggest that the bridge shops were increasingly important to London in this period. That is what the changes in rents seem to indicate (Appendix 5). In Cheapside, rents (corrected for inflation) declined from 1300 to about 1420, reflecting among other things the impact of the Black Death, and were then fairly stable until about 1550, after which they rose rapidly. The pattern of rents on the bridge was very different. There (again corrected for inflation) rents fell from 1358 to about 1420, but less sharply than in Cheapside, and were rising again by 1460, continuing to do so until at least the 1530s. There were rarely more than one or two of the bridge houses unlet. Part of the reason for rising rents was that more of the bridge was prime commercial territory, especially the southern part of the principal part. In 1538 rents per foot of frontage, compared with the level on the northern half of the principal part, were 84% on the southern half of the principal part (67% in 1358), 56% on the middle part (50% in 1358), and 52% on the southern part (45% in 1358). Rising rents underlay the improvement in the Bridge House's finances which made possible the rebuilding of so many of the houses between 1477 and 1548. Of course the rebuilding also contributed to the increased rents.

The sixteenth and seventeenth centuries

Apart from haberdashery, all of the five main trades just discussed had declined almost to nothing by the end of the sixteenth century. The gap was filled largely in three ways: by even more haberdashers, by traders selling textiles and by grocers. Stow in 1603 regarded mercers and haberdashers as typical of the bridge. London's haberdashers multiplied rapidly in the sixteenth century, probably reflecting both the growth of London and growing demand from the gentry and the middling sort, as well as the involvement of some in overseas trade. By the 1590s their livery company was second in size only to the Merchant Taylors.[32] Several of the bridge's inhabitants became Wardens of the Haberdashers' Company in the late sixteenth and seventeenth centuries, though none seem to have reached the higher rank of Master.[33]

Drapers, mercers, merchant taylors and clothworkers

Fig. 65 Woodcut of a haberdasher's shop in about 1680, showing a customer, the shopkeeper and a chapman.

became prominent on the bridge in the early sixteenth century. Undoubtedly textiles had previously been sold there by haberdashers and others, but the change in occupations seems too great to be explained simply by traders being described differently. In 1561 the Mercers' Company, questioned about silk prices, replied that the company contained few retailers of silk, which was sold instead by merchant taylors, haberdashers, clothworkers and grocers, who were concentrated in three areas: London Bridge, Cheapside and the end of Wood Street and Milk Street.[34] In the seventeenth century the textile dealers on the bridge were joined by hosiers (a largely new trade of the seventeenth century) and silkmen (no longer a female trade from the sixteenth century).[35] One of the merchant taylors, Simon Lowe, who held PE6 from 1536 until his death in 1578 and was living there in 1576, became Warden of the Merchant Taylors' Company in 1549–50 and was an MP in 1553–54.[36]

Grocers became numerous on the bridge fairly suddenly in the early sixteenth century and largely disappeared almost as suddenly in the early to mid-seventeenth century. Grocers originally traded in peppers and spices, and there was a pepperer on the bridge in the 1390s (by the staples at the London end).[37] In fact, grocers handled a much wider range of goods, including most imports from the Iberian peninsula and the Mediterranean, and almost anything traded in bulk and sold by weight. They had an important role in the cloth trade, exporting cloth and importing raw materials such as dyes. They are hard to define because there was no restriction on what a wholesaler traded in, and little in practice on retailers, so grocers sold an extremely wide range of goods and other sorts of trader sold grocery goods. But in the fifteenth century three types of goods accounted for about four-fifths of the grocers' activity. One was metals, especially imported iron and steel and tin from Cornwall, though they probably had only a minority stake in this business. A second was dyes, together with miscellaneous items such as alum, soap, wax and oil. A third was spices, though even this did not belong exclusively to the grocers. In effect, the grocers were general merchants, though they could usually be relied on to keep spices.[38] The Grocers' Company included the apothecaries until 1617, when they were allowed to form a separate company, which is probably why apothecaries are recorded on the bridge only after that date.[39]

The reason for the sudden and temporary prominence of grocers on the bridge is unclear. They probably shared in the trade in textiles on the bridge,[40] and they may have offered a wide range of goods, largely new to the bridge, which would later be sold by more specialized traders, such as metal wares, dyes, wines and apothecaries' goods. There may have been more grocers' shops in London as a whole, reflecting the increased reluctance of grocers in the sixteenth century to travel to fairs and markets and an expectation that country people would come to them in London.[41] This raises the possibility that change in the trades on the bridge merely followed trends in London shopping rather than indicating any change in the bridge's role. Grenade in 1578 referred to the numerous goldsmiths and money-changers of Cheapside and the 'magnificent shops' there selling silk but also to 'the mercers, haberdashers, ironmongers, grocers, apothecaries etc'; there were cutlers and linen drapers as well. In Lombard Street there were twenty goldsmiths' shops but also 'hosiers, drapers, mercers, booksellers, apothecaries, haberdashers etc'.[42] The bridge's trades were similar to these, apart from having few, if any, goldsmiths and (as yet) no booksellers.

The mid-sixteenth century may have been the peak in the bridge's importance to London shopping. Rents probably kept up with those in Cheapside to the 1570s, but subsequently, while still rising in real terms, they fell well behind (Appendix 5). This presumably reflected judgements by tradesmen about how valuable the bridge was as a location for their businesses, though why the bridge might have become a less valued location is unknown.

The bridge was too narrow for street traders to be tolerated, though such trading was probably hard to prevent. In 1617, for example, Humfrey Searel was imprisoned for selling apples in the street on the bridge. In 1694 the Court of Aldermen was informed of

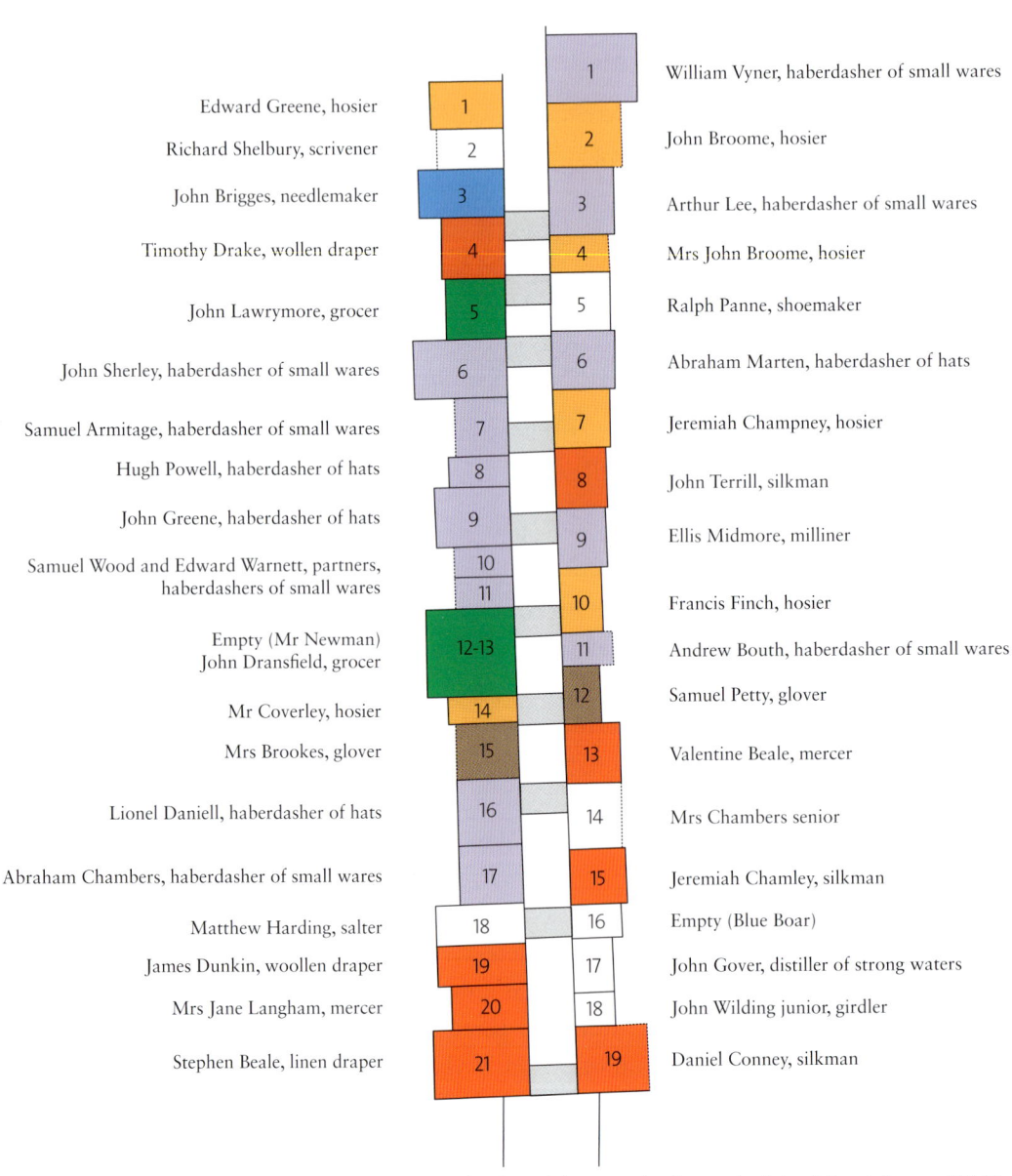

West side	No.	No.	East side
Edward Greene, hosier	1	1	William Vyner, haberdasher of small wares
Richard Shelbury, scrivener	2	2	John Broome, hosier
John Brigges, needlemaker	3	3	Arthur Lee, haberdasher of small wares
Timothy Drake, wollen draper	4	4	Mrs John Broome, hosier
John Lawrymore, grocer	5	5	Ralph Panne, shoemaker
John Sherley, haberdasher of small wares	6	6	Abraham Marten, haberdasher of hats
Samuel Armitage, haberdasher of small wares	7	7	Jeremiah Champney, hosier
Hugh Powell, haberdasher of hats	8	8	John Terrill, silkman
John Greene, haberdasher of hats	9	9	Ellis Midmore, milliner
Samuel Wood and Edward Warnett, partners, haberdashers of small wares	10, 11	10	Francis Finch, hosier
Empty (Mr Newman) John Dransfield, grocer	12-13	11	Andrew Bouth, haberdasher of small wares
Mr Coverley, hosier	14	12	Samuel Petty, glover
Mrs Brookes, glover	15	13	Valentine Beale, mercer
Lionel Daniell, haberdasher of hats	16	14	Mrs Chambers senior
Abraham Chambers, haberdasher of small wares	17	15	Jeremiah Chamley, silkman
Matthew Harding, salter	18	16	Empty (Blue Boar)
James Dunkin, woollen draper	19	17	John Gover, distiller of strong waters
Mrs Jane Langham, mercer	20	18	John Wilding junior, girdler
Stephen Beale, linen draper	21	19	Daniel Conney, silkman

Fig. 66 Occupants of the principal part in 1633. The fire of that year broke out in John Briggs's house (PW3) (Source: British Library, Sloane MS 1457, pp. 93–94).

Fig. 67 Trade token of Edward Muns, citizen and draper, of the Sugar Loaf on London Bridge (SW10), 1668. Muns was the son of a draper, born in about 1615, and was lessee at SW9 from 1644 to 1676, though by 1664 James Goldham, his former apprentice, seems to have been in charge there, still trading under the sign of the Sugar Loaf.

diverse idle vagrant persons ballad singers pickpocketts & others frequenting London Bridge and parts thereabouts who under shewe and pretence of selling ginger bread apples oranges ballads and other knack's doe use certain tricks & devices to drawe croudes of people togeather to the end to pick pocketts & committ other cheats and disorders.[43]

However, a woman selling apples was being tolerated at the stocks, where there were no houses, in 1682, and until at least the 1530s stalls were allowed on the bridge during Southwark Fair, probably in the wider section south of the stone gate.[44]

Bridge customers

Who did the traders on the bridge sell to? As already indicated, many of their customers would have been Londoners, and the continuing high rents on the northern part of the bridge confirm this. There would have been Southwark customers too, such as those engaged in cloth finishing purchasing items such as dyes.[45] But a significant part of the trade was evidently with chapmen, who travelled around villages with a pack, and country shopkeepers, especially those from the south-eastern counties. The bridge's booksellers, who were great advertisers, make this particularly clear. For example, John Back at the Black Boy stated in 1686 that he 'furnisheth any countrey-chapmen, with all sorts of books, ballads, and all other stationery-wares at reasonable rates'.[46] Indeed one bridge trader, John Shakemaple at the Anchor (SE2), though described as a citizen and grocer, apparently served the minority of chapmen who had horses with some of the tools of their trade, as his stock in 1680 included ropes and cord, cart saddletrees, whips, 'ruggs for horses', packthread, sacking, girt web and horse bells.[47] Ralph Bodman, a trunkmaker at ME11 in 1675–82, called his shop the Pedlar and Pack, and the shop had borne that name at least since 1619.[48] The goods sold by chapmen were similar to those of the haberdashers, though they also included textiles, ready-made clothes and small books.[49] The bridge could hardly have been a better shopping street for chapmen if it had been deliberately planned for them.

As for where customers came from, examples include William Oliver, a Salisbury chapman, buying from girdlers and a grocer of London Bridge in the 1610s; Robert Streete, who 'hath sought to gett his liveing by buying and selling in Darking' in Surrey, purchasing from a haberdasher, a grocer and a mercer on the bridge in the 1630s; Edmund Warnett, cutler (SE4), selling goods to a draper of Warbleton in Sussex in the 1640s; James Dunkin, draper (MW11), supplying a chapman of Rye in the mid-seventeenth century; Michael Cadman, a Rye mercer, buying from a hosier and a 'shopkeeper' of London Bridge in the 1710s (though larger quantities from tradesmen elsewhere in Southwark and London); William Appleby, a Gravesend shopkeeper, buying woollen and linen goods, brandy and stockings from a linen draper and a hosier on the bridge in the 1720s; James Bishop, a haberdasher of hats and goldsmith in Maidstone, purchasing from a hatter on the bridge in the 1740s; and Thomas Durnford, a pinmaker (PE2–3), selling goods to a tradesman in or near Sandwich in the 1750s.[50] Debts owed to Thomas Ruck, a haberdasher at ME5, in 1673 were from people in Canterbury (three), Ashford (two), Sandwich, Margate, Sheerness, Cranbrook, Tenterden, Goudhurst and 'Botton', all in Kent, Hellingly, Rudgwick and Burwash, all in Sussex, and Croydon and Wandsworth, both in Surrey, together with three in London, one in Sudbury (Suffolk) and five in New England.[51]

The most comprehensive example of the customers of a bridge tradesman relates to James Reynolds, a haberdasher of small wares, in 1721. He had traded at the southern part of ME3 from 1715 or earlier, and by 1721 was bankrupt, which resulted in an inventory being drawn up of his assets. His stock included thread and twist, whipcord, writing paper, pins, needles, buttons, tape, lace, ink and ink powder, filleting, ribbons, stomachers, worsted, spectacles, buckram, tobacco and many other items, with a total value of £495. His main creditors were Josias Weld of London Bridge, a silkman (SE7), and John Waller of Shoreditch, a weaver. One hundred and thirty-three debtors to Reynolds are named at identifiable places, of whom thirty-one were in London, including eight on the bridge. Most of the rest were in south-east England, especially in Kent (Fig. 68).[52]

However, Reynolds's customers contrast with those of William Giles, another haberdasher, at the Hat and Feather (SE13) in 1684. Thirty-three of his debtors were from named places, and twenty-eight, usually described as merchants, were not. The debtors were from many parts of England, as well as Caernarvon in Wales, but there were fourteen in East

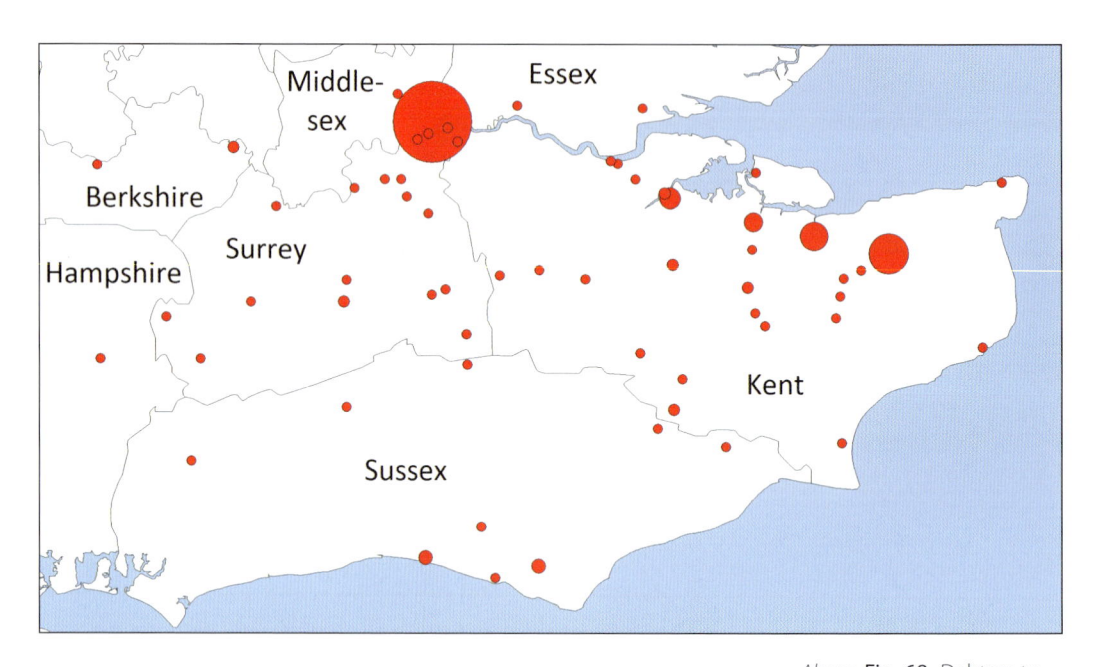

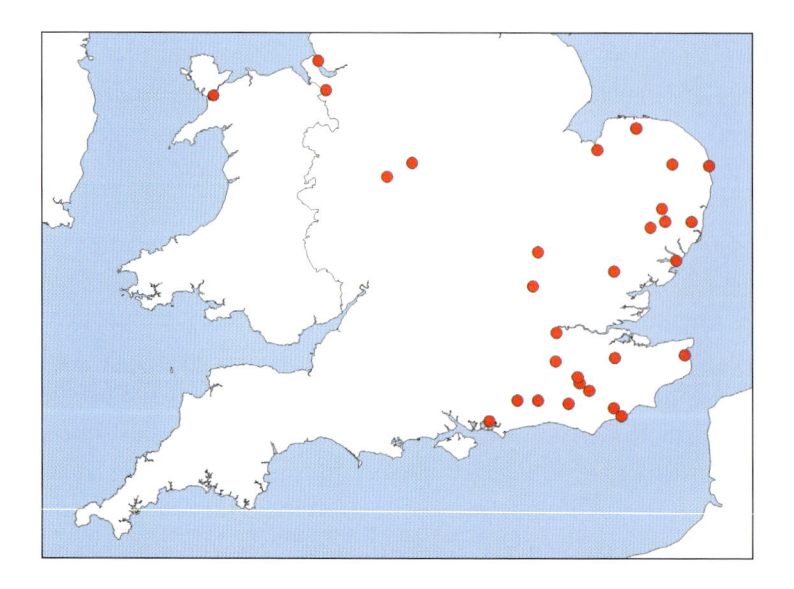

Above: **Fig. 68** Debtors to James Reynolds, haberdasher of London Bridge, 1720. 130 debtors are covered here. There was also one debtor at each of Stony Stratford, Newport Pagnell (both Buckinghamshire) and Mells (Somerset). Some locations were not stated, and fourteen debtors were at unidentifiable places (Source: TNA, C 104/263, bundle 18).

Left: **Fig. 69** Debtors to William Giles, haberdasher of London Bridge, 1684. Thirty-two debtors at named places are covered (Source: TNA, PROB 4/2773).

Anglia and eleven in the three south-eastern counties (Fig. 69). Among the eleven largest debtors from named places, owing from £46 to £176, seven were in East Anglia.[53] Evidently different traders on the bridge had different clienteles, but the fragmentary evidence does suggest that the bridge shops had a particular role in serving chapmen and other tradesmen of the south-eastern counties.

Booksellers

A trade which was not especially numerous but is particularly well recorded was that of the booksellers, who were also publishers. The first seems to have been Thomas Gosson, who was a bookseller in the St Paul's area from 1579 and had a shop on the bridge, adjoining the stone gate, from 1595 until his death not later than 1600. This was probably in a shed put up next to the gate in 1551, where Gosson's son later traded; it can be seen in Norden's view (Fig. 113). The business passed to Gosson's widow Alice in 1600–01 and then to his son Henry from 1601 to at least 1640. As well as the shop on the bridge, Henry Gosson also had one in Paternoster Row (previously his father's) until at least 1609, and in 1613 was living in Catherine Wheel Alley rather than on the bridge. Like most booksellers on the bridge Gosson sold cheap popular writings. Such works included ballads, broadsides, newsbooks, novels and histories, romances, jest books, pious works and almanacs. He was lessee of the shed (described later as 'a shedd converted to a shopp') from 1612. By 1630, and probably long before that, he also held the east part of the gate. In that year he agreed to rebuild the shed, but after a new frame had been prepared and 'begunne to be erected', the king's commissioners (presumably those charged with preventing dwellings on new sites in London) ordered that it be taken down. In 1631 he was allowed to make an opening through the stone wall of the gate into the shed. Henry Gosson remained the lessee until 1646, and, although the lease passed to Joseph Gosson, the premises were occupied by another bookseller, Nicholas Gamage. By 1648 they were known as the Three Bibles. In 1650 the shed was rebuilt, one foot longer and wider. Gamage held the lease from 1650 to 1654, by which time there was an 'outward shop' in the shed, 15 feet 4 inches long, and an inner one on the first floor of the tower, 12 feet in diameter. From 1654 the premises were apparently no longer used for bookselling.[54]

Other booksellers on the bridge in the first half of the seventeenth century were John Spencer in 1625 and Stephen Pernell, near the gate, in 1633–35, but in neither case is their exact place of business known. In 1630 Spencer acquired the rights to works including Thomas Middleton's *A mad world my masters* and Ben Jonson's *Alchemist*. He was later librarian of Sion College.[55]

While the Three Bibles premises ceased for a time to be used for bookselling, the business itself may have continued on a different part of the bridge, though the only evidence is use of the same name. Charles Tyus or Tias was selling books at ME7 by 1656 (Fig. 51). His shop was recorded from 1657 to 1664 as the Three Bibles, though in 1660, the year of Charles II's Restoration, as the King's Arms. Like Gosson, Tyus specialized in popular works such as ballads and chapbooks. His inventory records books both at a warehouse in Tooley Street and at his house on the bridge, where they could be found in great quantities not just in the shop but also in the garret, the little chamber over the street, the hall, the chamber within the hall and even over the stairs. There was a printing press at the shop, though valued at only 5s. In all there were just under 10,000 books, together with reams of printed pages sufficient to make up another 80,000.[56]

The business passed on Tyus's death in 1664 to his widow Sarah and then to Thomas Passinger, who had been Tyus's apprentice since 1657 and became Sarah's second husband. By 1682 it had moved to MW1, but in 1684 the rebuilding of the middle part forced it to move again, and it is next recorded at PE14. Passinger advertised that at his shop 'English and Irish chapmen … may be well-furnished, and have good penniworths'. He was one of the 'Ballad Partners' who dominated the ballad and chapbook trade. On his death in 1687/88 he left half his stock to Sarah and half to his brother John and his apprentice Thomas Passinger, who was also his nephew. The latter was also to receive 'all my copyes and parts of copyes and bookes and copper plates and things relating thereunto', together with

> all my share in the ballad warehouse of all the stocke and copyes of books and ballads which I now have in partnership with Mr William Thackerye in a warehouse in Pye Corner.

The business was continued by Sarah, who was living there in 1690 with three servants, and on her death in 1692 by the nephew, Thomas, who was there until at least 1695.[57] The next owner was Ebenezer Tracy from 1695 to 1719. He published ballads, chapbooks and nautical manuals, and also owned a patent medicine called the Balsam of Chili. (He was challenged over the Balsam of Chili by John Stuart, stationer at MW1, who called his shop the Old Three Bibles, or the Three Bibles and Ink Bottles, evidently relying on the fact that the Three Bibles had traded in the previous building on the site.) Ebenezer was succeeded by his sons Henry Tracy in 1718–24 and John Tracy in 1722–24 (Fig. 70), but it was widow Tracy who was recorded in the land tax at PE14 in 1722 and then at PW19 in 1724 and, as widow Tracy and son, in 1727.[58] There is no further evidence of the business.

Although there seems to have been no continuity, the Gossons' former premises were used as a bookshop by Thomas Parkhurst from about 1667 to 1678 and then by Joseph Collier from 1679 to 1700. In 1678 Collier was the only person living on the premises and was described as 'bookseller and

Fig. 70 The sign of the Three Bibles bookshop, as printed in a book catalogue of 1722.

journeyman to Mr Parkehurst'. The shop was known as the Golden Bible or the Bible, though possibly in 1679–80 as the Angel. Parkhurst operated it in addition to his shop in Cheapside, and published theological books. He was described by Dunton, one of his apprentices, as the most 'eminent Presbyterian bookseller in London', who had 'printed more practical books than any other that can be named in London'. He remained in business elsewhere until 1711, and was Master of the Stationers' Company in 1703. Collier had also been one of Parkhurst's apprentices, and according to Dunton, 'He has a great deal of learning, a discerning judgement, is pleasant in his conversation, and sincere in his piety'. In 1690 he was living at the Golden Bible with his wife, two children and a maid. The last evidence of him there is from 1700, and by 1705 the premises were occupied by a tinman. Collier was Treasurer of the Stationers' Company from 1702 to 1724.[59]

Five other bookshops were established on the bridge from 1671 to 1699, three of them fairly short-lived. First, there was Thomas Taylor's, described as next door to the Beehive in 1671 and at the Hand and Bible in the 'New Buildings' (the sheds on the northern part) in 1673–76. He dealt chiefly in theology.[60] Taylor presumably left when the sheds were removed at the end of 1682, though there are later references to a Hand and Bible under Elizabeth Smith in 1691 and John Vousden in 1694, the latter at PW2.[61] Secondly, John Williamson was at the Sun and Bible (possibly also in the New Buildings) in 1670–78, where he was succeeded, probably only briefly, by Stephen Foster in 1679–80. John Gilbertson was bookseller at the Sun and Bible in 1689 (at PE10), as was Henry Green in 1705, but no more is known of it.[62] Thirdly, Arthur Bettesworth was at the Red Lion (in or near SE5) from 1699 to 1715, publishing mainly religious works. He moved in 1715 to Paternoster Row.[63]

Fourthly, Charles Passinger sold books in 1678–82 at the Seven Stars in the New Buildings.[64] He was living there in 1678 with his wife, an apprentice and a maid. The apprentice was Joseph or Josiah Blare, who in 1683 established a bookshop nearby called the Looking Glass, by 1690 at PE6. His speciality was chapbooks, and he advertised that 'He furnisheth country chap-men or others, with all sorts of history books, small books, or ballads'. This popular literature made him very rich, and his estate amounted in 1707 to £3,493, mostly held in financial instruments such as bank bills and East India Company bonds. His stock consisted of 31,000 books in the shop and printed pages sufficient to make up another 51,000 or so, together valued at £191.[65] On his death in 1706 the business passed briefly to his widow Elizabeth (long enough to spark a lawsuit over infringement of the Stationers' Company's patent for almanacs), and then to what were apparently partnerships, including Thomas Norris (*c.* 1707–26), F. Hodges (1710), James Hodges (1720–57), Edward Midwinter (1721–30), Thomas Harris (1741–45) and Stanley Crowder, who had been James Hodges' apprentice (1755–60). It kept the Looking Glass name to the end, but in about 1730 moved to the middle part and then in about 1739 off the bridge to Bridge Street, where it was described as 'facing St. Magnus Church, near London-Bridge' and 'over against St. Magnus Church'. As well as chap books and penny histories, Hodges and Norris published more serious works, such as ones on navigation and popular science. Norris was described as 'a very rich bookseller on London Bridge, whose country seat was at Holloway'. James Hodges was later town clerk of the City, and was knighted in 1758. In 1760, although its premises were not demolished, Crowder moved the business to Paternoster Row.[66]

Fifthly, John Back, who was from Hinxhill in Kent and

an apprentice of Thomas Passinger in 1675–82, set up on his own in 1682 at the sign of the Black Boy 'near the draw bridge'. By 1690 he was at PE20, living there with his wife and a maidservant. He too dealt mainly in chapbooks and ballads. In about 1696 he was appointed bookseller to the Society of Kentish Men. He died in 1703, and was succeeded as a bookseller by Matthew Hotham from 1704 to 1725.[67]

Not all the bridge's booksellers sold cheap popular literature, but that was clearly the bridge's speciality. Nearly all the publishers of such works were in two areas: at London Bridge, with five in the 1680s, and around Smithfield Market. In both areas they were well placed to serve the chapmen, who carried their cheap books throughout an increasingly literate kingdom.[68] Blare's book stock on its own amounted to one for every forty-four families in the kingdom.[69] In some cases the bridge shop was part of a larger enterprise. Tyus, for example, apparently printed at the shop on the bridge, but kept much of his stock in a Southwark warehouse, and some of the others had another bookshop elsewhere.

By 1711 there were two establishments on the bridge described as a 'musick shop'. Russell Gatcliffe, about whom nothing is known, was at PW15 from about 1707 to 1716,[70] and Elizabeth Miller was at ME4. The latter was the Violin and Hautboy (sometimes the Golden Violin), founded by her husband John in 1690 or earlier. He published music and sold both music and musical instruments. Elizabeth ran the shop from John's death in 1707 to her own in or about 1739. Her nephew Samuel Weaver, already living with her, took over the shop. His name appears on a collection of sonatas for violincello by Merci published in about 1745. By the time of his death in that year his shop goods had been seized by his landlord for debt, and only a few musical instruments were left.[71] In addition to the bookshops and music shops, there were several printsellers on the bridge in the 1740s and 1750s, such as William Herbert (Fig. 82).[72]

From the 1680s to the 1750s

The trades on the bridge were changing significantly again from the late seventeenth century and this raises several questions. Did the bridge remain a place for 'shopping goods' rather than convenience goods, for retailing rather than making things, and for clusters of shops selling similar specialist products? And, whatever the answer to that question, did it remain as attractive a place for doing business? The grocers had almost entirely disappeared by the mid-seventeenth century. The proportion of haberdashers, for so long the mainstay of the bridge, and the dealers in cloth and clothing declined significantly from 1666 to 1744, from 66% to 23%. In 1710–12 they included a periwig maker, a glass necklace maker and a whalebone merchant, a trade closely linked with bodice-making, and there were also four slopshops, selling ready-made clothing. However, as in other periods, a change in the descriptions of traders did not necessarily mean a change in the goods sold.

New arrivals filled the gaps. One was metalworkers or dealers in metal goods of various kinds, rising from 4% in 1666 to 23% in 1743–44. They included cutlers, pewterers, tinmen, goldsmiths, pinmakers and needlemakers (Fig. 73). The latter two became the most notable component, amounting to 11% in 1743–44 (four pinmakers and three needlemakers), compared with none in 1666. An example is James Price (MW2), who bought a business of pinmaking and buying and selling of brass wire from John James of the Sun on London Bridge for £100

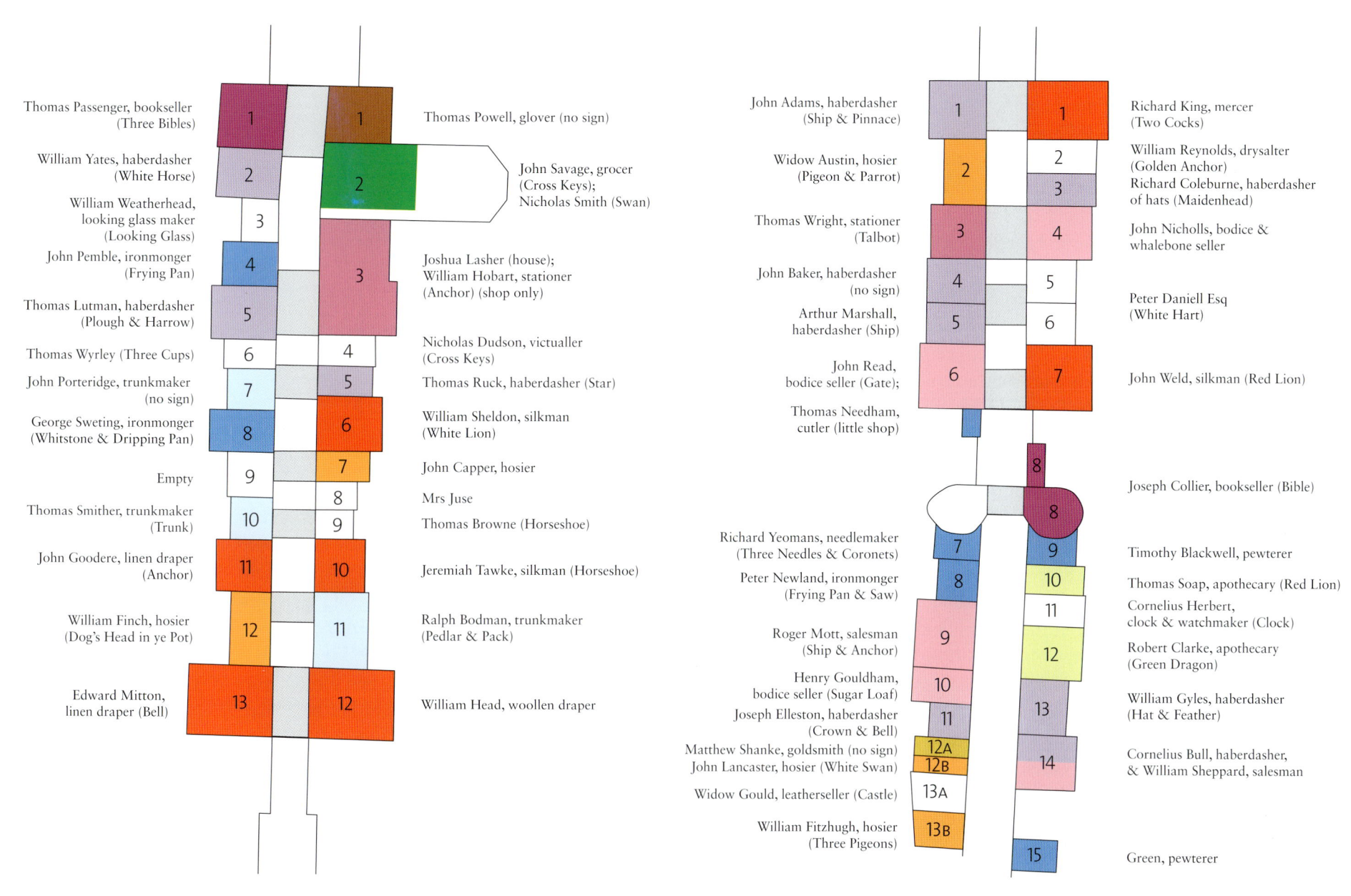

Fig. 71 Occupants of the middle part (left) and south part (right) in 1682, as recorded in the Bridge House view (or inspection) of 11 January 1682. A few occupations have been added where known from other sources, and several signs from the views of 1675–78. Not every shop had a sign; two listed in 1682 as not doing so had signs recorded shortly before (Thomas Powell at the King's Arms and John Porteridge at the Three Cranes) (Source: BHV 2).

in 1694. He died in 1722, when all his goods were granted to a creditor, Richard Durnford, another pinmaker on the bridge. Price's trade goods included brass wire, 'drawn wire', pin heads, shafts, pin metal, red and white pins, country pins, pins in papers and packets and brass knitting needles, totalling £386, though apparently no tools. Price's son, also James, continued a pinmaking business on the bridge until at least 1744.[73] Richard Durnford senior and junior were pinmakers on the bridge by 1710, at PE3 and PE20. Richard junior had shares in a brass wire manufactory at Byfleet in Surrey. Robert Campbell in his analysis of London trades in 1747 described pinmaking as 'but a poor business', in which journeymen earned no more than common labourers, but the Durnfords prospered: by 1717 they were lessees of eight houses on the bridge, they aquired other property elsewhere in London, and in 1754 John and Thomas Durnford, sons of Richard senior, were still at work on the bridge (at PE2–3).[74]

Among the needlemakers, John Souch at the Golden Salmon and Spectacles (SE3) was selling sailmakers' needles, fish hooks and other equipment for fishing in 1730. Francis Rusk and Richard Fowler at the Salmon and Spectacles were supplying sail-needles to the Navy in 1728–33, though what connection they had with Souch is unknown.[75] In the 1750s Coles Child (PW17) was supplying not just needles but a huge range of small items, ranging from buttons to toys, many of which were haberdashers' wares, and indeed he was recorded in the 1740s both as a needlemaker and a haberdasher.[76] Pins and needles were themselves haberdashers' wares, so the arrival of pinmaking and needlemaking businesses was in part an increase in specialization.

Another significant new category was durable goods not previously sold on the bridge. Sellers of these had begun to

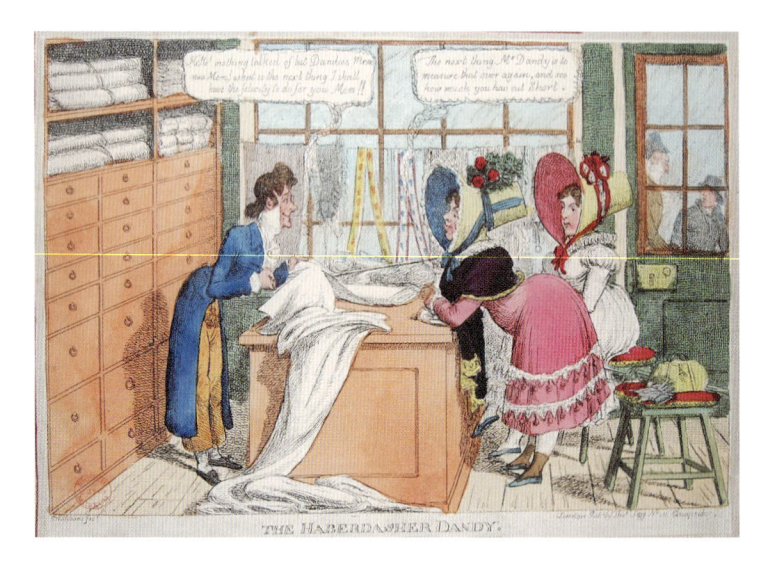

Fig. 72 Satirical print of a haberdasher's shop in about 1818.

appear by 1666, and in 1682 included three trunkmakers, a looking-glass maker and a watchmaker. In 1743–44 they included a boxmaker, two brushmakers, a spectacle maker, two clockmakers, two scale makers and a mathematical instrument maker. Trade cards sometimes indicate the range of goods they sold: in the 1690s Samuel Grover, surgical instrument maker at the Sceptre and Hart (PW9 and then ME9; Fig. 74), was selling 'all sorts of chirurgeons instruments the best sort of razors penknives scissers & launcetts' (and might earlier have been described as a cutler); in about 1700 James Tallman (ME5) was selling 'all sorts of scales, weights, beams and stilliards and gold scales'; and in the 1750s John Grant, brushmaker, was selling 'all sorts of ship & house brushes, brooms, mops & hair sives', together with painters' brushes and turners' goods (Fig. 75), Robert Vincent, scale maker at the Hand and Scales (SW13B), was selling scales and weights for diamonds and gold coins, scales and weights for grocers, assay scales, steelyards and brass

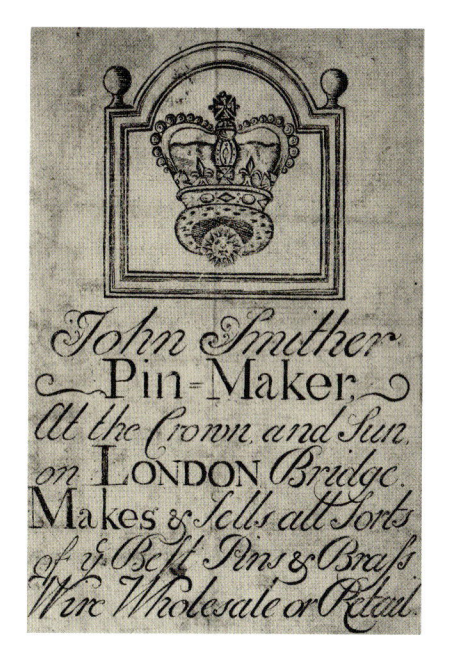

Left: **Fig. 73** Trade card of John Smithers, pinmaker. He lived at PE9 from about 1737, and was succeeded by his widow there until 1759.

Middle: **Fig. 74** Trade card of Samuel Grover, surgical instrument maker. He was trading on the north-west part of the bridge by 1693, but by 1695 was at ME9, living there with his wife, a son, two daughters and an apprentice. On his death in about 1707 he was succeeded there by his widow until at least 1724.

Right: **Fig. 75** Trade card of John Grant, brushmaker, of about 1750. He traded at one of the new buildings of the 1740s. He had succeeded to the business of Gerrard Pitham, who had taken a lease of SE11 in 1716. Grant also ran a public house in the premises. When they were demolished in about 1760 he moved to Leadenhall Street.

cocks, and Christopher Stedman, mathematical instrument maker at the Globe (SE5), was selling 'all sorts of mathematical instruments for sea or land, gauging, surveying, measuring, geometry, navigation, arithmetick &c. wholesale or retail'.[77]

Booksellers were also more prominent on the bridge from the 1670s, and so were stationers, the latter dealing in items previously sold by haberdashers. An example is Charles Walkden at PW5, whose stock at his death in 1722 included an immense variety of papers, together with wallpaper, pocket and quarto books, parchment, slates, quills, inkhorns, ink and ink powder, totalling £351.[78] He was succeeded in the same premises by Richard Walkden, whose trade card in the 1730s offered all sorts of accomptants & shop-keepers books, ye greatest variety of paper-hangings for rooms, & all other sorts of stationary wares, wholesale or retail at the lowest prices. Where may be had Bibles, Common Prayers, Testaments, Psalters &c. N.B. He is also the maker of the fine British ink-powder for making black writing ink which is universally allowed to excell all others whatsoever yet made & is of the greatest convenience for country shopkeepers to make their own ink to sell again, as likewise for merchants & sea captains.[79]

One of the largest stationery businesses was that of James Brooke, established at SW1 by 1705, based later at the chapel house, and taken over after his death in 1750 by his great-nephews Thomas Wright (Fig. 76) and William Gill. Brooke had paper mills at Maidstone and Boxley in Kent.[80] As for the increased proportion of miscellaneous trades, the two 'blue shops' of 1743-44, selling dyes, had precedents, as there had usually been a salter on the bridge from the 1580s onwards, but some of the others did not, such as the perfumer and the snuffmaker.

One of the most revealing changes may have been the rising number of sellers of food and drink on the bridge. Apart from the alehouse in a cellar from 1581 to 1685, there were no alehouses until John Wilding's Cross Keys was established by 1658 at ME4, probably moving in the 1680s to ME10, where there was a Cross Keys alehouse in 1743.[81] In 1710–12 there were two cooks, a victualler and two coffee houses, in addition to any sellers of food and drink in the single-storey shops that replaced the Square in the 1680s.[82] The first coffee house seems to have been Hamett's 'at the gate'. It is first recorded as such in 1702, but Henry Foot Hamett was living at or near SE3 in 1690 and Susanne Hamett, widow, succeeded him there until

about 1709. The London Bridge Coffee House is recorded in 1702, and Mr Needham's Old London coffee house (PE9) and one run by Mr Dickins in 1711–12.[83] The bridge estates committee remained hostile to pastry cooks because of their ovens, but seems to have become more relaxed about victuallers.

Inventories from the late seventeenth and eighteenth centuries give some idea of the stocks held on the bridge. The most valuable ones recorded were the silk belonging to John Sheldon and his partner at ME6 in 1662, amounting to £3,000, and the fabrics of Edward Pitt, citizen and leatherseller, at

Fig. 76 Portrait of Thomas Wright (1722-98). Wright was the son of a pastry cook and street cleaner. He worked for Richard Walkden, stationer, at PW5, becoming his apprentice from 1738 to 1745. By 1748 he was a master stationer in partnership with his brother-in-law William Gill, and in 1750 they took over their great-uncle's stationery business in the chapel house. In 1759/60 the business moved to Abchurch Lane. Wright was later Master of the Stationers' Company (1777), an Alderman (1778) and Lord Mayor (1786), leaving in 1798 a fortune estimated at £400,000.

Nonsuch House in 1677, totalling £1,550. Three haberdashers, Thomas Ruck in 1673 and William Giles and Cornelius Bull, both in 1684, had stock worth £176, £386 and £576 respectively, and that of Jeremy Tawke, a silkman, totalled £400 in 1682. Two apothecaries had smaller stocks – Robert Clarke in 1693 a two-thirds share worth £100 and Thomas Soper in 1694 £43. John Shakemaple's goods for horses in 1678 were valued at £75. Other examples noted above are the £191 of Josiah Blare, bookseller, in 1707, the £386 of James Price, pinmaker, in 1722, and the £351 of Charles Walkden, stationer, in 1722.[84]

The bridge remained in the eighteenth century a place for shopping goods rather than convenience goods, and indeed many of the same types of goods were sold as in the fourteenth century. It also remained a place for retailers or wholesalers rather than makers, but there are occasional indications of things being made on the bridge. In 1659 the Bridge House viewers found a forge in a garret, and in 1682 at the house of Matthew Shanke, goldsmith (SW12), they encountered 'a furnace for melting there silver &c lately made in ye back part of ye shop with a [*illegible*] funnell without licence and dangerous'. The inventory of Timothy Blackwell, a pewterer at SE9 in 1679, lists working tools in his shop. Among the apothecaries, Robert Clarke in 1693 had a 'distill house' in a garret at SE12, and Thomas Soper in 1694 had three stills in a garret at SE10, together with equipment such as a powdering tub. After Isaac Putham leased a newly-built house in 1747, he converted the ground floor into a coffee room and used some of the upper parts as a tailor's workshop.[85] Trade cards sometimes stated that traders on the bridge both made and sold things, such as Edward Butlin, maker of paper hangings, and Samuel Grover, surgical instrument maker, both in about 1690; James Howard, necklace maker at the Hand and Beads, and Richard Walkden, stationer and maker of ink powder, both in or about 1735; and John Grant, brushmaker, Basil Denn junior, goldsmith and jeweller, Walter Wilkins, breeches maker, Churcher and Christie, leathersellers and breeches makers, Robert Vincent, scale maker, and Christopher Stedman, mathematical instrument maker, all in the 1750s, though this may not always have meant that the making of goods was carried out on the bridge.[86] Evidently some manufacturing did take place on the bridge, but the main reason for locating a business there must always have been the marketing opportunities, and probably most businesses there confined themselves to retailing and wholesaling.

By the 1740s the bridge's trades were no longer so clearly clusters of similar businesses. Probably a greater range of goods was sold, including items such as necklaces, perfumes, mathematical instruments, clocks, music and prints, and the traders themselves tended to be more specialised, or at least to have a more specialised designation. The bridge seems no longer to have been a place for fine fabrics, and some relatively humdrum items were sold, such as pins and brushes. The increased number of victuallers and coffeemen may also indicate that the shops were less valued for retailing, though there continued to be some prestigious trades. There is a hint that the bridge became a place to buy cheaply, in Pennant's remark much later that 'Most of the houses were tenanted by pin or needle makers, and oeconomical ladies were wont to drive from the St. James's end of the town, to make cheap purchases', though this is not enough evidence to characterise the bridge as 'a downmarket area'.[87]

Part of this may have reflected a wider trend towards greater specialisation, but it is also likely that the growth of the West

End and the development of high-class shops there made the bridge less important to London shopping in the eighteenth century.[88] Although the evidence for rents on the bridge is patchy and ambiguous in this period, it does suggest that the bridge lost ground against other shopping areas. Rents there seem to have been roughly static in real terms in the century from 1653 (Appendix 5). In the eighteenth century the ageing building stock on the bridge may have contributed to that situation. Unfortunately the only comparative information readily available is from a small group of houses in Leadenhall Street – not a major shopping street – where rents increased about 50% in real terms in the same period. But the evidence of rents and changing trades is consistent with a slow decline in the bridge's role in London shopping. Static rents were potentially threatening to the future of the bridge houses, as they were relatively expensive to build and maintain and imposed a cost on the City by preventing the bridge being widened.

CHAPTER 9

Families and community

Bridge families

There were no bridge dynasties spanning numerous generations, though more continuity would probably be visible if we could trace the transfer of properties through marriage.[1] Many individuals and families remained only a short time on the bridge, until better opportunities elsewhere, a higher bidder for their shop, bankruptcy or death removed them. Even those who remained longer tended to move from one house to another, and there are even a few examples of the swapping of houses on the bridge.[2] An example of a family who stayed longer is the Mogers. William Moger, a haberdasher (though described as a mercer in 1402), surrendered a property on the bridge and acquired two others there in 1396–97. In 1404 he held ME3C, where he was succeeded by his widow Katherine in 1419–21.[3] William Moger junior, also a haberdasher, held ME11A in 1418, and was succeeded there by his widow Juliana in 1419. Thomas Moger, another haberdasher, was lessee of PE14A from 1416 to 1462, being succeeded there by John Moger in 1463–66. Another Thomas Moger, a bowyer, was at ME7 and then ME8 from 1465 to about 1500.

Another example is the Crull family. Robert Crull, a bowyer, was lessee of SW4 at least from 1404 to 1421, combining it with SW3 in the latter year. He was one of the Wardens of the Bowyers' Company in 1416 and 1439.[4] When the rentals begin again in 1460, the lessee of the combined property was Richard Crull. Another Crull, Thomas, also a bowyer, held SW1 by 1460, and continued to do so until it was burnt in 1471. He seems then to have moved to PW21B, adding PW21A to it in or about 1475. His widow Alice succeeded him there until about 1500. John Crull, a bowyer, held SW2 in 1468–69. Thomas Crull was one of the bridge wardens in 1538,[5] and was probably the Master Crull who held ME1 in the 1540s. There is no subsequent record of the Crull family on the bridge.

In the sixteenth and seventeenth centuries, one of the longer-lasting families was the Chapmans – successively John Chapman senior and junior and Samuel Chapman. They held and probably occupied a single property, SE9, for the century from 1542 to 1642. Little is known about them, except that John Chapman junior was a merchant taylor. The Langhams also occupied a single property, PW20, from 1564 to 1633. The first lessee was John Langham, a scrivener (at least by company), who was certainly occupying the property in 1576. He was succeeded in or about 1609 by his widow Mary; in 1619 by their son Benjamin Langham, who had been apprenticed to a grocer; in 1625 by John Langham, probably Benjamin's brother; in 1630 by Mary Langham; and in 1631 by Jane Langham, who was a mercer.[6] The house was burnt in 1633, and the Langham family evidently moved away. A single generation on the bridge was more typical. For example, Timothy Richbell, one of two sons of a yeoman of Bromley in Kent, leased SE4 from 1609, calling it the Golden Bell and trading as a grocer. He was nearly ejected in 1631 in a dispute over a new lease, for 'the affronte and indignite' offered to the bridge estates committee. In 1634 he sold his land in Bromley, went abroad, probably to Ireland, and was declared bankrupt. William Richbell, probably his brother, was at SE7 from 1613 to 1625.[7]

A more prominent family was the Osbolstons, who were haberdashers and from 1592 also lessees of the wheelage. The wheelage was the tolls on carts crossing the bridge, from which citizens of London and perhaps others were exempt.[8] Lambert Osbolston held MW2 from 1590 to 1608, and also SW1, which was the wheelage house, from 1592 to 1619. He was a member of the Haberdashers' Company, but was also described as a scrivener. He was clerk of St Thomas's Hospital from 1577 and its rent collector by 1591, and was under-renter and clerk of the Haberdashers' Company from 1582 or earlier to 1602. He may have overreached himself, as he ended his life in a debtors' prison, discharged from both clerkships.[9] His deputy, William Apjohn, a mercer, succeeded him at the wheelage house. But his son, Robert Osbolston, was deputy to Apjohn and clearly became prosperous, holding leases of four bridge houses at various times, including the chapel house and the wheelage house. He became rent-gatherer to the Bridge House by 1627 and to the Chamber of London by 1638, and acquired the bridge tolls in 1654, for an entry fine of £615 and rent of £87.10s.0d. per year. His son later estimated that the tolls yielded £100 a year clear profit, though his main income seems to have been £550 a year profit from his lease of the lighthouses of North and South Foreland in Kent. He too was a haberdasher, at least by company, though he was also described as a linen draper. He was a Warden of the Haberdashers' Company twice and a Common Councilman of the City in 1661–64. He married into the Nethersoll family, of Kent and ME11.[10] On his death in 1669 Robert was succeeded as collector of the wheelage by his eldest son, William, who belonged to the Mercers' Company. He held the wheelage and wheelage house from 1671 to 1678, and was living there in the latter year with two men (probably the toll collectors). The lease passed into other hands in that year. He died in 1679, leaving bequests of many thousands of pounds and mentioning five servants.[11]

Another example is the Ruck family. The first Thomas Ruck, described as a scrivener, was the son of a merchant of Cranbrook, Kent. He was lessee of MW7 from 1602 to 1618, and his widow succeeded him there until 1624. The second Thomas Ruck was a haberdasher (though by company a girdler), occupying ME5, the Star, from at least 1634, and acquiring the lease of it in 1653 (Fig. 53). He was a churchwarden of St Magnus in 1655. He died in 1672, and was succeeded by his son, the third Thomas, another haberdasher, who inherited both the lease of ME5 and land in Tipperary.[12] In 1678 he was living at ME5 with his wife, one child, his mother and a maidservant. When required to rebuild it in 1684, he sold it to Robert Browne, tyler and brickmaker, and bought from

FAMILIES AND COMMUNITY   105

Figs 77–78 Portraits of William Daniel, haberdasher (d.1678), and his second wife Mary (d.1681). They lived at SE5–6 and at Clapham.

Browne the lease of three houses newly-built by Browne at the north end (PE16–18). By 1689 Ruck was living in one of the three new houses, together with his wife, three children and a maidservant. He remained there until about 1712 and held the three houses until 1718.[13]

One family rose into the first rank of City society. Lionel Daniel was a haberdasher of hats at PW16 from 1625 or earlier until the house was burnt in 1633. His son William had been apprenticed to him in 1616 and in 1624 set up himself as a haberdasher at SE5; later he was described as a beavermaker. He added SE6 in 1645 and had largely rebuilt the combined property by 1650. He was a Warden of the Haberdashers' Company twice, was a Common Councilman of the City on several occasions and was elected an Alderman, though as he was a Dissenter he was unable to serve, so he paid a fine instead. From 1641 until his death in 1678 he also had a house in Clapham, as well as property in London, Southwark and Essex. He and his wife are almost the only bridge inhabitants of whom portraits have been located (Figs 77, 78). William's son Peter Daniel was a merchant, and was living at SE5–6 by 1676. In 1678 his household on the bridge consisted of himself, his wife Elizabeth, five children, an apprentice, a journeyman, five maidservants and one manservant (the only one on the bridge). In contrast to his father he was a Tory. He was an Alderman from 1682 to his death in 1700, was twice Master of the Haberdashers' Company, was knighted in 1684, was an MP in 1685–87 and was one of the City grandees to whom Charles II committed the control of the City's estate in the 1680s. He was heavily involved in the widening of the bridge's roadway in the 1680s, being on the committee appointed to implement it and acquiring and then selling leases at the northern end. He sold the lease of SE5–6 and moved away when it was rebuilt in the mid-1680s.[14]

Peter Daniel was an unusual figure in the bridge's history. Many of the bridge's residents were wealthy, but they were retailers and wholesalers rather than merchants, and virtually none reached the rank of Alderman or master of one of the greater livery companies. The hearth tax records of 1664–66 (Appendix 4) indicate that, while the Daniels had eleven hearths or chimneys, only five other bridge households had more than six hearths. The averages were 4.8 on the south part, 4.2 on the middle part, 5.6 on the principal part, and 4.7 overall. This was fewer than the London-wide averages for merchants (8.0) and drapers (6.8), but similar to those for haberdashers (5.3), textile workers (4.2) and metalworkers (4.2).[15]

An example of a family from the late seventeenth and eighteenth centuries is the Harberts. Cornelius Harbert senior, a clockmaker and watchmaker, was baptised at St Olave Southwark in 1645 and was an apprentice from 1659 to 1668. He was occupying SE11 by 1677, his sign being the Clock and later the Dial (Figs. 79-81). In 1678 he was living there with his wife, two children, two apprentices and a maidservant. He bid unsuccessfully for one of the building leases at the north end of the bridge in 1682. In 1697 he acquired the lease of SE11, and on his death in 1710 was succeeded there by his widow Elizabeth, who left owing rent. Cornelius Harbert junior, also a clockmaker and watchmaker, was born in about 1676 and apprenticed to his father in 1691. He was Master of the Clockmakers' Company in 1727. He was occupying ME11 by 1705, but in 1715 acquired the lease of SW7 and moved there, remaining there until the fire of 1725 and the decision that it should not be rebuilt. He moved to SE4, and later, in 1749, leased one of the new houses at the north end (the third from the north). He died in 1751. He was succeeded at the house leased in 1749 by his daughter-in-law Margaret Herbert or Harbert, though it is William Herbert who is recorded in the rental. William Herbert was a seller of prints and maps. He moved almost immdiately to another of the new houses (the third from the south), calling it the Golden Globe, and remained there until the house was demolished in 1759 (Figs 82, 101).[16]

A family who cannot, unfortunately, be shown to have lived on the bridge is that of William Hewett, a wealthy clothworker. In about 1536, as recorded much later, his daughter Anne was

Figs 79–81 A watch made by the first Cornelius Harbert in about 1670. It was two inches in diameter.

FAMILIES AND COMMUNITY   107

1720, based on Osborne family tradition.[17] Unfortunately Hewett never appears in the rentals of bridge houses, though it is conceivable that he was a sub-tenant. The Bridge House accounts refer to £15 paid to Hewett 'for service done by hym in Bryttayne, and for rendrynge [surrendering?] a grannte made unto hym of a housse upon London Bridge, nowe lett unto Olyffe Burr coppersmythe, late the housse of Thomas Burvylde grocer' (SW9), but this was in 1561 and does not provide evidence of Hewett living on the bridge.[18]

The bridge population in the late seventeenth century

Only in the late seventeenth century can we obtain a view of the bridge's inhabitants as a whole, including the women of the bridge. This is thanks to unusual taxes – the poll tax and the marriage tax – and the lists they generated. They vary in completeness, the record for the marriage tax of 1695 being the most comprehensive, followed by the poll tax of 1678.[19] In 1678, with five houses omitted, there were 300 people recorded living on the middle and south parts of the bridge, together with another fifty-two in the sheds on the northern part, who are not included in the analysis here (Fig. 83).[20] As well as wives and children, but only in three cases a member of a third generation, most households contained one or two apprentices and a maidservant. The 300 were fifty-five householders (including three widows), forty-one wives of householders, seventy-six children, fifty-three apprentices, seven journeymen or 'men', fifty-six female servants, one male servant, six lodgers and five others. The average number of people per household was 5.5, not far from the 5.1 in households

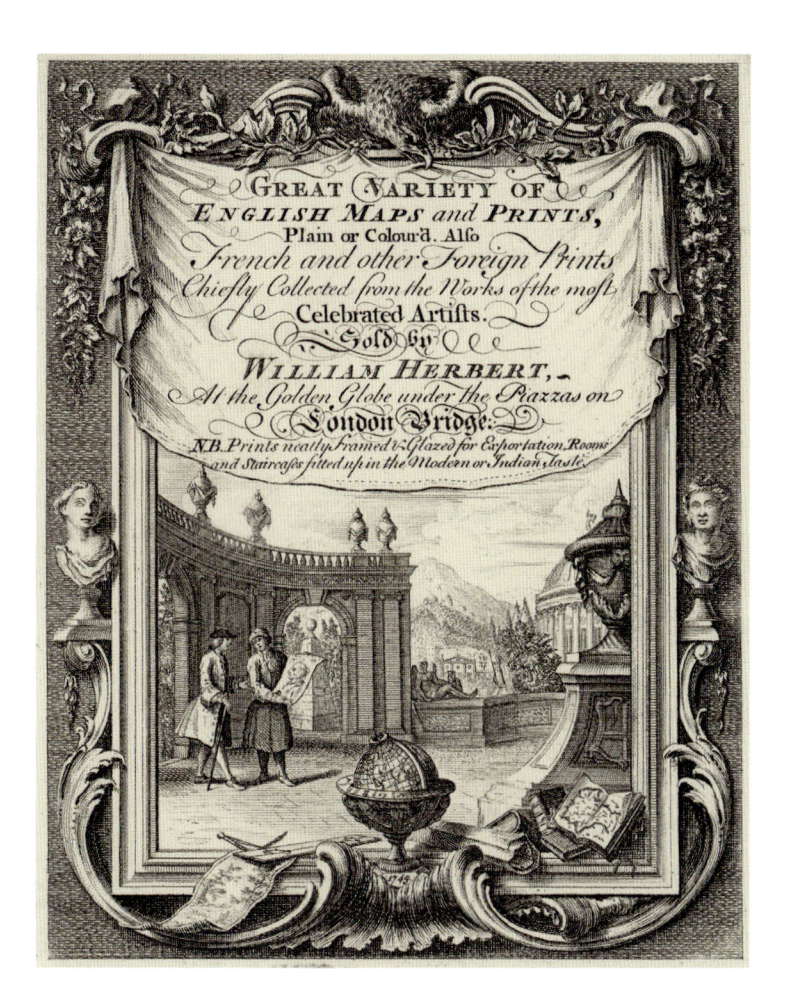

Fig. 82 Trade card of William Herbert, printseller at the Golden Globe, which was the third from the south of the new houses built in the 1740s.

playing at a window, lost her balance and fell into the river. Hewett's apprentice, Edward Osborne, showing great courage, jumped into the water and rescued her. When wealthy suitors later began to request Anne's hand in marriage, Hewett said 'Osborne saved her and Osborne should enjoy her'. The marriage took place in 1562. Both Hewett and Osborne later became Lord Mayor. The story was recounted by Strype in

108 LONDON BRIDGE AND ITS HOUSES, c. 1209–1761

Robert Ince, wife, 2 children, apprentice (John Shepard)

Thomas Thorpe, wife, child, maid (Grace Jenkins); Samuel Curle, wife, child, maid (Jane Elsey)

William Yates (haberdasher), 2 apprentices (Robert Kirke, John Yate), 2 maids (Jane Tayler, Jane Roofe)

Edward Living, wife, 2 apprentices (Samuel Smith, Francis Buckingham), maid (Joanna Bedwood)

John Pemble (ironmonger), wife, child, apprentice (Joseph Scott), maid (Mary Davis)

Thomas Luttman (haberdasher), wife, apprentice (Edward Hill), maid (Mary Harrington)

Thomas Worley, wife, child, 2 apprentices (Joshua Camberback, Daniel Rust)

John Portresse (trunkmaker), wife, 2 children, apprentice (James Lawrence), journeyman (Richard Wall)

Elizabeth Hill (widow of ironmonger), 5 children, apprentice (George Sweeting), maid (Helena Johnson)

[Thomas Smither, trunkmaker]

[Empty]

George Ligoe, wife, 2 children, apprentice (John Goodhew), 2 maids (Mary Horton, Elizabeth [blank])

William Finch (hosier), wife, 2 children, 2 apprentices (John Lancaster, Robert Boarne), 2 maids (Ann Parton, Elizabeth Boarne); Hannah Richardson; Cicely Greene

Edward Mitton (linendraper), wife, apprentice (Richard Barton), maid (Mary Higgins), partner Thomas Wood

Thomas Powell (glover), wife, 3 children, apprentice (Joseph Safford), maid (Susanna Stratton)

John Savage (grocer), wife, maid (Mary Horne), lodger Mr Wimborne & daughter; Nicholas Smith, wife, child, apprentice (Robert Downes), maid (Elizabeth Ayers)

Joshua Lasher, wife, 4 children; John Blower, apprentice (John Bayley)

John Wilding (victualler), wife, grandchild, maid (Jane Barnes)

Thomas Ruck (haberdasher), wife, child, mother Hanna Ruck, maid (Ann Wollat)

William Sheldon (silkman), wife, 2 children, 2 apprentices (Daniel Harwill, John Cater), 2 maids (Mary Willin, Mary Fuse)

Thomas Passinger (bookseller), wife, child, 2 apprentices (John Back, Charles Davison), maid (Elizabeth Sancroft)

[Empty]

Thomas Browne, wife, 2 apprentices (Mary Bradway, Bridget Eunuch)

[Mrs Hayward]

Ralph Bodman (trunkmaker), wife, 2 apprentices (John Arundell, John Mitchell), maid, 2 apprentices (Sarah Ray, Mary Taylor)

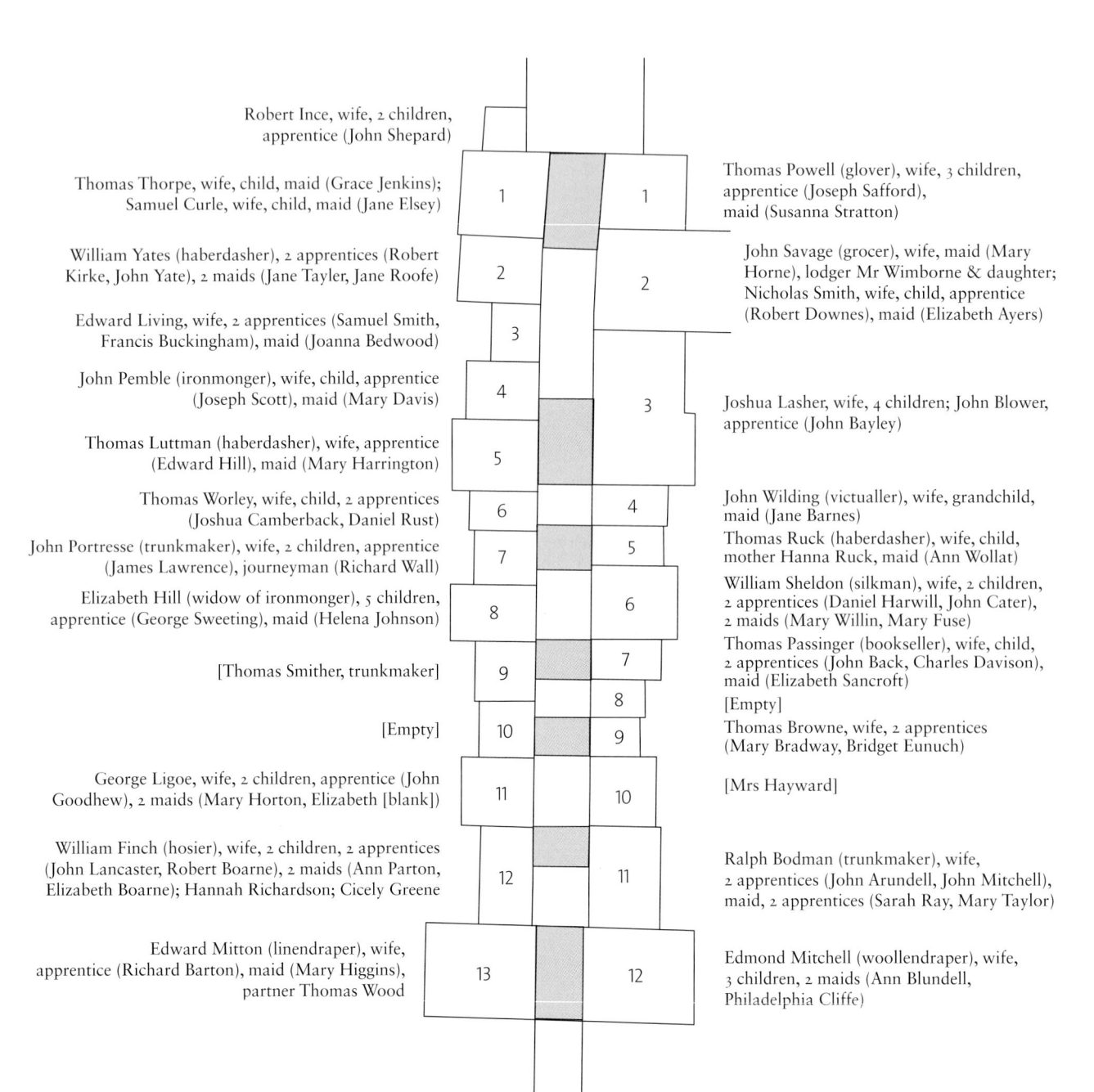

Edmond Mitchell (woollendraper), wife, 3 children, 2 maids (Ann Blundell, Philadelphia Cliffe)

Fig. 83 Residents of the middle part of the bridge in 1678, from the poll tax assessment. Names are spelled as in the assessment. Occupations have been taken from other sources (chiefly the 1666 hearth tax and BHV 2). Householders missing from the list have been added from BHV 2 and are in square brackets. Robert Ince held a small shop on the north side of MW1 (Sources: LMA, COL/CHD/LA/03/067/003; BHV 2).

within the City's walls in 1692.[21] A typical household was that of Thomas Wright, a stationer, at the Dog (SW3), with his wife, four children, two apprentices and a maidservant. An example of a household headed by a woman is that of Jane Austin, hosier at the Pigeon and Parrot (SW2), with a child, an apprentice and a maidservant. Two households each had two female apprentices: Thomas Browne, whose occupation is unknown, at ME9 and Ralph Bodman, trunkmaker, at ME11. Most households had one maidservant, but seven had none, eight had two and one had five (that of Peter Daniel). There were few lodgers, probably because the leases forbade 'inmates' and at least at this time there were regular views or inspections of the bridge houses.

By the time of the marriage tax of 1695, there were again houses along the full length of the bridge. Five hundred and fifty-one inhabitants are listed, of whom 241 were on the northern part, 170 on the middle part and 140 on the south part.[22] They comprised 101 householders (including nine women), eighty-four wives of householders, sixty-seven sons, eighty-seven daughters, seventy-five male servants (probably all of whom were apprentices), eighty-two female servants, forty-seven lodgers and eight others. Average household size was 5.5, as in 1678, though it was higher on the middle part (6.3) and lower on the south part (4.5). Little is known about household size in earlier centuries, but if the size was similar in the late fourteenth century, when the number of houses on the bridge was at its maximum of up to 140, the bridge's population would have been almost 800.

There were almost equal numbers of men and women on the bridge – 51% and 49 % respectively in 1678 and 47% and 53% in 1695. Of the women in 1695, 3% were householders, 29% were wives of householders, 30% were daughters, 28% were servants and 11% were lodgers and others. Elizabeth Dawling, widow, on the middle west part, had a household of four, including Charles Dawling, probably her son, a male servant and a female servant. Elizabeth Stephens, widow, at PW3, had a household of seven, including a son, three daughters, a male servant and a female servant. As in 1678, most households had a female servant, but seven had more than one and twenty-nine had none. About twenty-six households contained one or more lodgers. The largest household in 1695 was that of William Motham, haberdasher at the Anchor (PE2), with eleven members, comprising himself, his wife, four sons, two daughters, two male servants and one female servant.

The bridge's residents may have been relatively unscathed by the deadliest disease of the seventeenth century. According to Dr E. Barnard, who claimed to have the information from an apothecary on the bridge, only two of them died from the plague in 1665.[23] Certainly the bridge houses must have had a constant change of air, unlike many of the City's alleys. Unfortunately Barnard's proposition is impossible to verify, as we have a list of the bridge's householders in that year but not of all its residents. Few if any of the householders' names appear in the burial registers of St Magnus and St Olave in the plague months of 1665, but some of the bridge's inhabitants did die in that period, such as two sons and two daughters of John Wilding (ME4), and members of the families of Thomas Dobson (MW11) and Nathaniel Lasher (ME8).[24]

Community

The bridge's inhabitants were certainly capable of collective action, for example when petitioning for better terms for repairs, better lighting on the bridge or improved traffic management.²⁵ How this was organised is unknown. Before the Reformation there was a religious fraternity of St Thomas the Martyr, based in the bridge chapel, which was amalgamated at some time after 1343 with the fraternity of *Salve Regina* based at St Magnus, and that might have facilitated collective action, although its membership was probably not confined to residents of the bridge.²⁶ Collective action could not easily have been organised through a parish vestry, as the bridge was divided between two parishes. A more likely route is the ward meeting, as Bridge Ward included the whole of the bridge, albeit with other areas too. Equally, the inhabitants could simply have held a meeting at a nearby tavern on the infrequent occasions when there was a problem common to all of them.

On the day-to-day level, there were clearly many links between bridge inhabitants, based on friendship, neighbourliness, family ties and commercial relationships. Whether there were stronger ties than between any other group of people living in close proximity is impossible to assess, but the fact that the bridge was a linear community rather than one with neighbours all around may have made it so. Wills and other documents provide occasional glimpses of these relationships. For example, Anthony Scalticke, fishmonger (MW3), referred in his will of 1638 to his loving cousin, Ralph Harrison (MW10), and his loving friends, Hugh Powell (ME9) and Richard Wilding (MW4).²⁷ In 1663 Edmond Walcott, haberdasher (SE3), appointed as overseers of his will his friends Robert Osbolston (SW1 etc.), William Daniel (SE5–6), Peter Daniel (ditto), John Worger (SE4), Thomas Soper (SE10) and Henry Murchard (not recorded on the bridge).²⁸ Samuel Armitage's will of 1636 must reflect relationships developed before the principal part was burnt in 1633. He had been a girdler by company but by trade a haberdasher of small wares at PW7. He appointed as executors his friends Arthur Lee (PE3) and Edward Taylor (not recorded on the bridge), and referred to his sister Williamot, the wife of Edward Williamot (PE5), his sister and neice Susanna and Elizabeth Chambers, probably of the family of William Chambers (PW7), to whom Armitage had been a servant, his friend John Gover the elder (PE17) and his 'antient neighbors' Hugh Powell (ME9) and Anthony Scalticke (MW3). Armitage had married Margaret, the widow of William Clayton, one of the original tenants of Nonsuch House, and was briefly a tenant there himself in 1597–98. His widow Joan later married Laurence Warkman (MW5).²⁹ These examples suggest that relationships were closest within each part of the bridge, rather than spanning the bridge as a whole.

In 1607 Edmund Nicholson, grocer at PW12–13 since 1590, sold his grocery business to Avery Dranfeild and Robert Phipps for £2,700. They moved into PW12–13. The money was handed to Thomas Foxhall, John Busbridge (PW21) and Arthur Lee (PE3) in trust for Nicholson's daughter Margaret, 'being his only child and one whome he always most entirely loved and respected'. He had great confidence in his trustees 'for theire integrity honest faythfull and upright dealing towards him and the said Margaret'. He was also keen that Margaret should not marry young, because she was small and her mother, who had been larger and stronger, had died in childbirth; in particular he refused to let her marry John Chambers, girdler, probably the tenant of that name at PE11. Nicholson died soon afterwards. The trustees were soon receiving offers of £300 or £400 from gentlemen and others for the hand of a girl with such a fortune. According to the other trustees, Arthur Lee first rejected the suggestion that the three trustees should agree on a husband they all approved of because it was too early, and then agreed to let Chambers marry her when she was only a few days over the age of sixteen. Sadly, she died in childbirth before reaching the age of eighteen.[30] No doubt stories showing close relationships between the bridge's families could be multiplied, but most of that interaction is lost to us.

From the seventeenth century onwards there are examples of bridge inhabitants having a suburban retreat, though there is also a single fifteenth-century example: the will of John Amell, cutler (PE8–9A), of 1473 refers to his chamber at Walworth. William Daniel had a house at Clapham in 1641–78. Edward Munns, draper, and possibly Thomas Powell, glover, also had houses in Clapham, and Edmond Walcott, haberdasher, had a little chamber in the same parish in 1668. Inventories record the unnamed partner of John Sheldon, silkman, occupying a house at Streatham in 1661, Gervase Locke, mercer, in 1688 and Robert Clarke, apothecary, in 1693 each occupying houses at Camberwell, and James Price, pinmaker, occupying a house in Gravel Lane in 1722. Thomas Norris, bookseller, had a 'country seat' at Holloway in about 1720.[31] Probably it was becoming more common for traders on the bridge to have a suburban retreat, reflecting trends elsewhere in the City, which was slowly being given over more thoroughly to commerce and less to domestic life. There were also some who lived nearby rather than on the bridge, such as the stationer Thomas Wright in Southwark in the 1750s.[32] These trends may have encompassed only a minority of the bridge's inhabitants, but they must have begun to change the character of life there, reducing the interaction between neighbours.

CHAPTER 10

The great rebuilding of 1683–96

Between 1683 and 1696 almost all the houses were rebuilt and the bridge was transformed (Fig. 84). The process began at the northern end, which since 1666 had been occupied only by temporary buildings.

The northern end

By the late 1670s the bridge estates committee was receiving requests from people wanting to build on the northern part of the bridge.[1] What may have held up rebuilding was that the bridge's stonework needed to be repaired first. Eventually, in May 1682, it was decided that the sheds should go by Christmas 1682, the stonework should be repaired by 25 March 1683 and contractors should complete new buildings there by Christmas 1683.[2]

This time the Bridge House was not to have any direct involvement in the building, apart from repairing the stonework. Instead, plots would be let out on building leases, just like any other building sites. This was not quite unprecedented on the bridge, as there are a few examples from the 1640s and 1650s (Table 2), but it was unprecedented on this scale. Evidently the bridge estates committee believed it could ensure the quality of the new houses by enforcing detailed requirements, such as the size of the timbers used. There was then the question of whether the leases should be to one or more major builders or to people who might live in the new properties. A paper among the committee's records favoured the latter option, noting that it would be easier to rebuild after another fire if the risk had been spread, any bankruptcies would have less impact and higher rents could be charged:

> particular persons who have occasion to dwell in their respective tenements which they now petition for may afford to give the City a better rate than generall undertakers who build to lett out againe for advantage.[3]

The committee decided that each pier and adjoining gullet should be let to a single contractor.[4] This resulted in blocks from 47 to 54 feet long (Figs 85–87). It meant that each hammer beam would be the responsibility of a single lessee, which was important as the lessees were to pay for all repairs, including repairs to hammer beams. The committee was successful in

Right: **Fig. 84** Nicholls's print of both sides of the bridge in 1711, showing almost exclusively houses built between 1683 and 1696. Note that Nicholls has one too few piers under the middle part and one too many under the drawbridge houses.

THE GREAT REBUILDING OF 1683–96   113

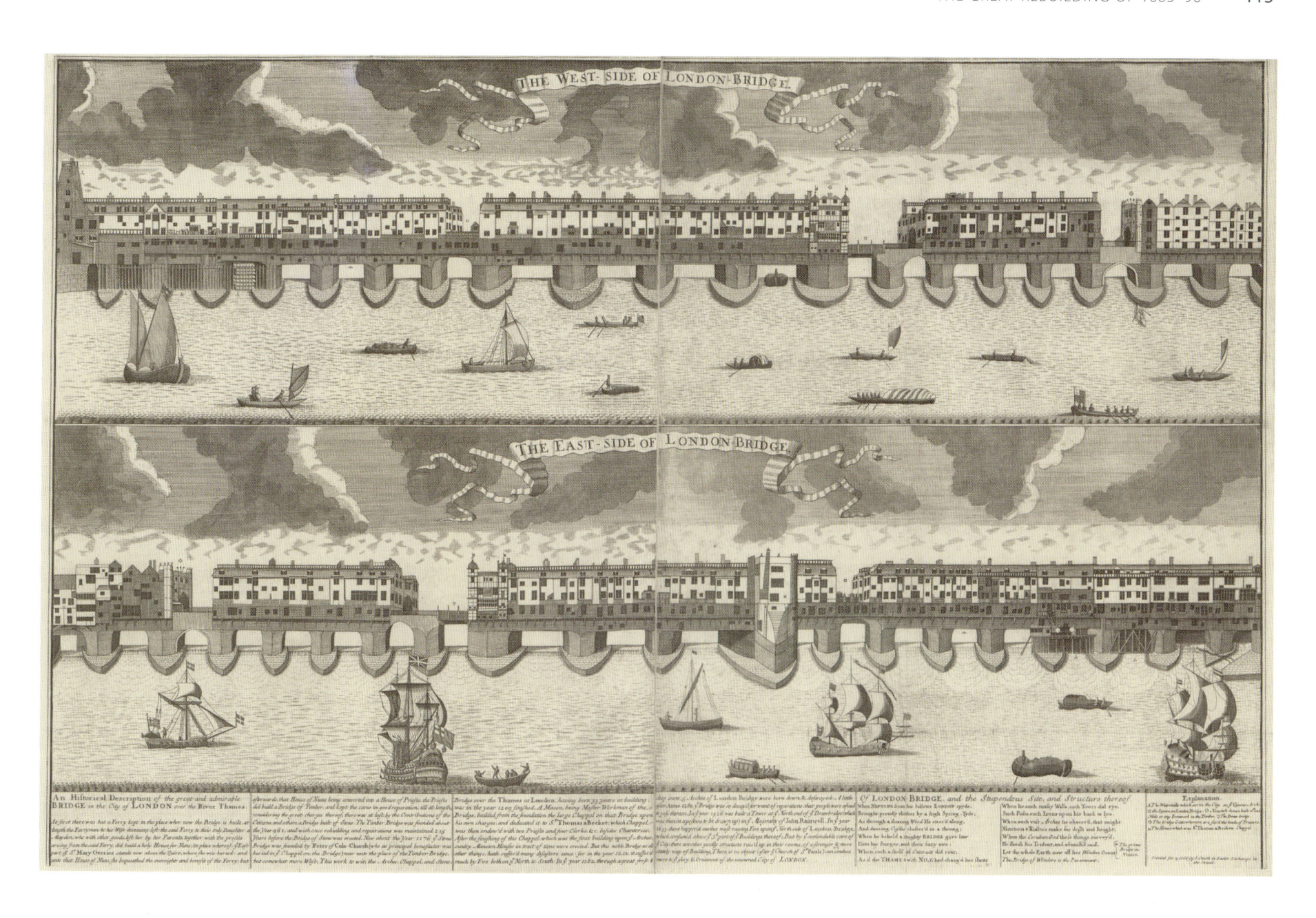

114 LONDON BRIDGE AND ITS HOUSES, c. 1209–1761

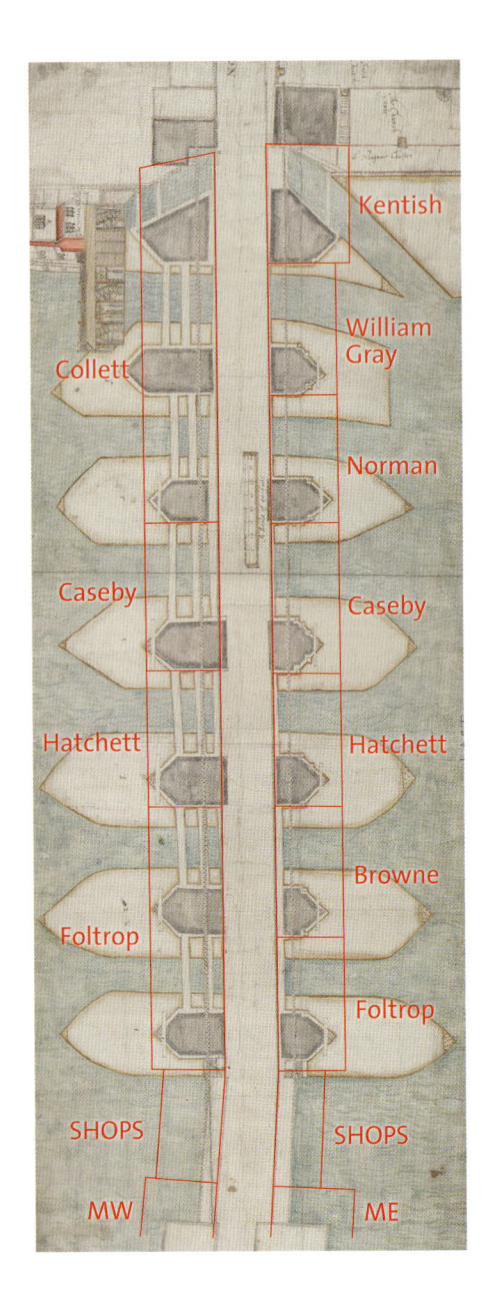

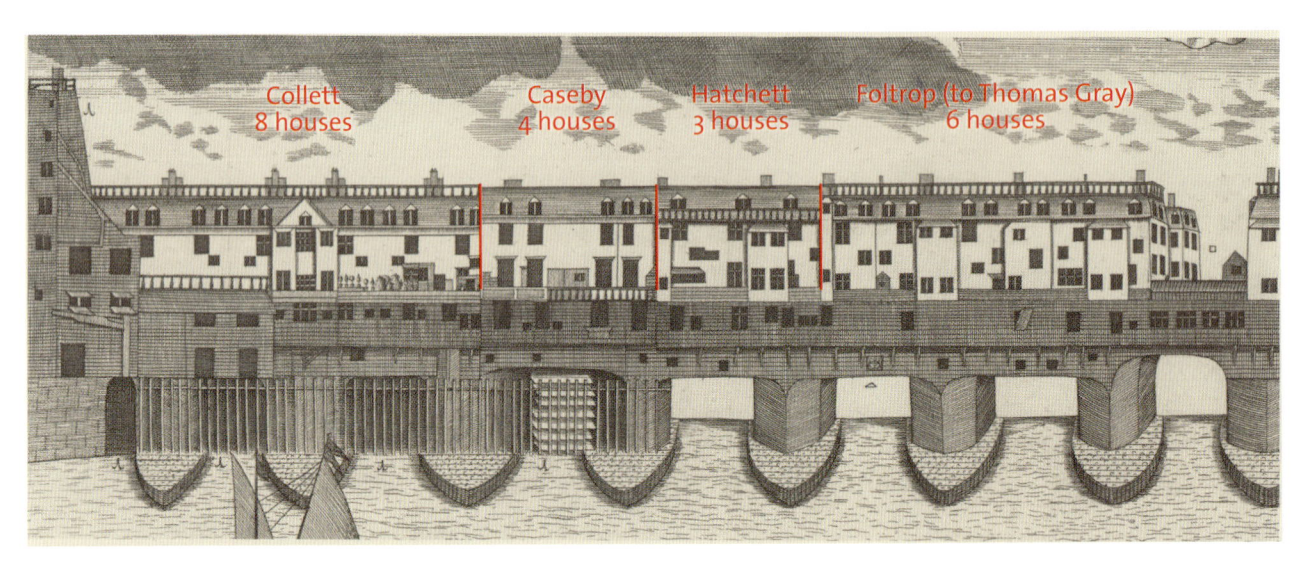

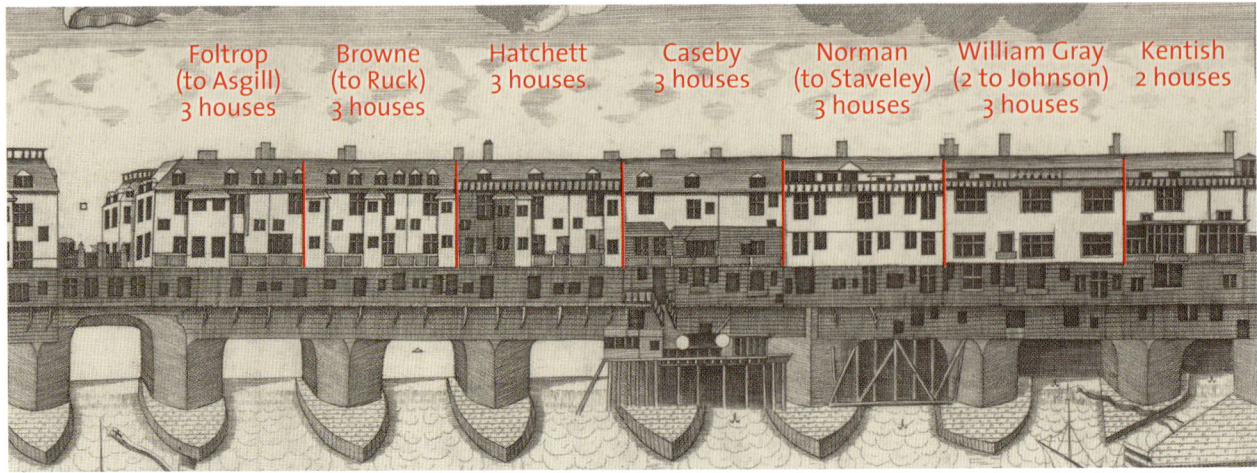

Left: **Fig. 85** Plots leased on the northern part of the bridge in 1683, marked on the plan of 1633. Plot depth is assumed to have been 28 feet throughout on the west side, and on the east side 26 feet except for Kentish's houses (31 feet) (Sources: BHP, 003, 1684, abstract of all the leases; CCLD, 02595 and 02600; for plot depths, see text).

Above: **Figs 86–87** Details from Nicholls's print of 1711, showing the west side (above) and east side (below) of the northern part of the bridge with the lessees of 1683 (and in some cases those they sold to) named.

attracting competing bids, and the blocks were distributed among eight different lessees. None of the builders seem to have occupied the new houses, and several people who did live on the bridge made unsuccessful bids, such as Gervase Locke, mercer, who had lived in one of the sheds, and Cornelius Harbert, clockmaker.[5]

As with most London building projects, the builders were a mixture of investors and building tradesmen, and many of the latter transferred the completed houses to others as soon as possible. Four of the five building tradesmen were carpenters: John Foltrop, who was a major London builder, William Gray, who was master carpenter to the Bridge House, Richard Norman and Thomas Kentish. The fifth was Robert Browne, a bricklayer. Those from other trades were Humphrey Caseby, merchant, Thomas Collett, citizen and vintner, and Thomas Hatchett, citizen and merchant taylor. Collett and Hatchett had both previously been lessees (but not occupants) of sheds on the bridge, and Caseby had occupied one of the sheds. Caseby employed Thomas Bigg, a carpenter, to do the actual building, but took a close interest in what was done and was there every day – annoyingly for Bigg, who complained that Caseby kept changing his mind. Those who bought groups of houses from their builders were Thomas Gray, merchant, John Johnson and Henry Asgill, both citizens and painter stainers, Babington Staveley, citizen and merchant taylor, and Thomas Ruck, citizen and girdler (and occupant of ME5). All the leases were granted in 1683.[6]

Several instructions were given for the new houses. First, they were to leave room for a roadway 20 feet wide and were not to encroach on it. Secondly, the timbers were to be of the sizes or 'scantlings' specified. Thirdly, the houses were to be 'uniforme upright & without jetties'. This was a common provision in building agreements of the late seventeenth century, ruling out irregular projections, but it was not a guarantee of regular facades. Fourthly, all were to have three and a half storeys, the ground, first and second storeys being 10 feet, 9½ feet and 8½ feet high respectively, with garrets above. Fifthly, the buildings on the first, third, fifth and seventh piers were to be 'tyed over' – in other words to have cross buildings. These were to be confined to the second storey and above.[7] So there were still to be cross buildings, but unlike in the 1640s they would be only on every other pier and would not begin in the first storey. Collett, Hatchett and Caseby petitioned in 1683 against having to erect cross buildings at all, arguing that

> the said building over will very much incommode and darken the said buildings and (which to your petitioners is an argument above all other) may (in case of fire) endanger the ruine of the whole bridge.

Nevertheless, Collett's lease provided for cross buildings to be erected, and later writers testify to their existence.[8]

As in the 1640s, the new buildings were to have a consistent back line further out from the roadway than before (Fig. 85), but this was neither in the articles of agreement nor set out in writing anywhere else. Only for some properties is the depth recorded. On the west side that of seven houses was 29 feet, while it was 27 feet in two other cases and 31 feet in one. On the east side, PE2 and 3 were 31 feet deep, compared with 26 feet at PE6. 26 feet seems more likely for the rest of the eastern houses, especially as their successors in the 1740s were 26½ to 27 feet deep.[9] Whatever the exact measurements, the new houses were much deeper than their predecessors of the 1640s, by about 3 to 4 feet on each side. On the west side this took them to the ends of the piers; on the east side it took them well beyond the piers (Fig. 85). As discussed earlier, the two ways of achieving this were either by placing hammer beams between the ends of the piers rather than closer to the roadway, requiring much longer beams, or by supporting the outer edge of the new buildings by means of struts or braces resting on the hammer beams. Later views suggest that both measures were adopted for all the new houses of the 1680s (Fig. 88). One result was that the timberwork supporting the houses began at a lower level than before and the tops of the bridge's arches were concealed from view.

Whereas the new houses of the 1640s had had a unified and much admired design, those of the 1680s were mere speculative dwellings of no architectural merit. Whatever the degree of uniformity at the front, there was very little at the back, and the different groups of houses can easily be distinguished on Nicholls's view of the bridge in 1711. Most had windows irregularly spaced, and placed differently from their neighbours. Some had balustrades at rooftop level, some had them below the garret storey, some had them at first-floor balcony level and some had none. Many houses had projections at the back, presumably containing staircases or closets.

The building process was not entirely smooth, mainly because the Bridge House was nine months or a year late in repairing the stonework, and then a further quarter of the year was lost because of a harsh winter.[10] Both Hatchett and Caseby were ordered to remedy hearths and chimneys that were creating a fire risk.[11] Caseby fell out with his builder, Thomas Bigg, over delays, extra work and one or more of the houses 'sagging'. Bigg blamed Caseby for the latter, for ignoring advice not to place six chimneys in the middle of the hammer beams and for not adding the proposed hanging cellars under

Fig. 88 Detail from Samuel Scott's painting of the bridge in about 1750 (Fig. 98), showing the timbers supporting houses on the middle east part and several props or 'shoars' resting on the starlings.

two of the houses, which he thought would have prevented sagging. He argued that costs had been increased by building with half storeys, like the other new houses, instead of knee rafters (what this meant is unclear), and also by changes such as the addition of balconies to the three eastern houses. Bigg was to receive £655 for the four houses on the west side, but believed he deserved £810 because of the extra work, and £575 for the three houses on the east side.[12]

By 1745 most of the houses of the 1680s on the east side were in such poor condition that they had to be demolished, including Caseby's three. Caseby claimed in 1684 that some of his houses were 'soe badly framed yt they are extreamly sunke & doe daily sinke more & more', and the bridge estates committee refused to make his leases up to the usual sixty-one years. His houses on both sides were causing concern in 1724–25, when they had to be shored up, and even the western ones, though not demolished in 1745, had valuations far below those of their neighbours because of their bad condition.[13] Caseby's houses were a special case, but Fig. 85 suggests a reason why the fifteen houses on the southern part of the east side had to be demolished in 1745 while nearby houses built at the same time survived: it is simply that they extended much further back from the piers, increasing the risk of sagging.

Whatever the problems stored up for the future, the rebuilding of the northern part of the bridge was a great success in the short term. Without any call on the Bridge House's limited funds, other than for repairs to the stonework, forty-one new houses had been erected, yielding £855 in entry fines and £380 a year in rent.[14] This undoubtedly emboldened the City in dealing with the rest of the bridge.

Growing traffic and the keep-right rule

What prompted the rebuilding of most of the rest of the bridge was the desire to widen the roadway. There was apparently little concern about its width when Nonsuch House was built in the 1570s, as the arch underneath it was only 12 feet 5 inches wide, significantly narrower than most of the roadway. But London's population was already growing rapidly: from perhaps 120,000 in 1550 to 200,000 in 1600, 375,000 in 1650 and 490,000 in 1700.[15] This undoubtedly led to increased traffic on the bridge. After the fire of 1633, Charles I sought to widen the roadway in the burnt area to 20 feet, with a footway 6 feet wide on each side. Although nothing came of that, the City did widen it from 15 feet to 18 feet and create refuges on each side for pedestrians, to reduce the danger they faced from carts and from 'beasts made wilde and furious through the indiscreete and violent usage of theire drivers'.[16] The new building of 1645–49 allowed for a roadway 20 feet wide. There clearly was greater concern about its width in the 1630s and 1640s, but not yet about its height, as the new houses had cross buildings at first-floor level. In 1658 inhabitants of the bridge complained about 'the irregular passeinge' of coaches and carts 'and the standinge of costermongers & other loose people there', which hindered passage and thereby damaged their businesses.[17]

In 1670 there began a policy which was to have significant consequences. This was to confine wheeled traffic in each direction to one side of the road in order to improve its flow (Fig. 89). Much has been made of the fact that the first explicit keep-left rule was established on London Bridge in 1722. What has escaped notice is that this began much earlier as a keep-right rule. As set out in 1675, carts entering the city were to keep to the east side and those leaving it to the west side. Two beadles were to attend daily to direct carts to the correct side of the road.[18] The rules of the road reflect the fact that most people

Right: **Fig. 89**
Reconstruction drawing by Peter Jackson of traffic on the bridge after the keep-left rule was established in 1722, with a beadle directing drivers to the left.

are right-handed and that this generates different preferences according to the form of transport. Drivers of teams who walk or ride beside their horses proceed on the team's left controlling it with a whip in the right hand, and prefer to be on the right side of the road so as to be able to protect their team. Postilions riding on the horses have the same preference. But if a team is being driven from the vehicle, the driver sits on the right with the whip in the right hand, and prefers to drive on the left, which makes it easier to judge the distance from oncoming vehicles. Right-handed horse-riders mount from the left, and so they ride on the left.[19]

The change to keeping left in 1722 was perhaps because too many people had found the keep-right rule disagreeable and defied it, or because of the increasing importance of coaches, which were driven from the vehicle, unlike waggons. The new rule was subsequently incorporated in the Act of 1756 under which the bridge was widened, and later it was applied to all roads by the Highways Act of 1835. In 1722 the Bridge House was required to provide a third man to help direct traffic, and Edward George fulfilled this role from 1723 until his death in 1753. He worked from 6 a.m. to 9 p.m. in summer and 8 a.m. to 7 p.m. in winter, apart from an hour for dinner at 12 noon.[20] Despite the attempts at traffic management, not much could be achieved without rebuilding the houses and widening the roadway.

The middle part and the drawbridge houses

In the end the widening of the middle part and the drawbridge area was achieved by the simple expedient of indicting the lessees for nuisances obstructing passage, specifically the fronts of the buildings encroaching on the roadway and the cross buildings at first-floor level. The new hostility to first-floor cross buildings perhaps reflected the growing use of coaches, though even a well-loaded waggon could fall foul of a cross building only 10 feet above the road. In December 1683 the indictments of the houses on the middle part were referred to a committee to negotiate with the lessees, and in January 1684 the committee met them at the Hoop Tavern on Fish Street Hill. It reported that they were generally willing to comply on reasonable terms, either by removing the offending parts of their houses or by surrendering their interests. The committee favoured buying out the existing lessees, pulling down all the old buildings and replacing them with 'faire substantiall uniforme houses'. It had secured a proposal for doing so from two of the carpenters involved in rebuilding the northern end of the bridge, Thomas Kentish and William Gray. In return for a sixty-one-year lease of the middle part (except Nonsuch House, the chapel house and ME1) and ground rents kept at the old level of £89.10s.0d., they would pay up to £3,000 to the City for purchasing the existing interests and would build new houses there similar to those at the northern end. This was agreed by the Court of Aldermen, but a fortnight later there had been a change of plan, perhaps because the proposal was too harsh towards existing lessees. Instead the lessees were offered the value of their interest or, if they were willing to rebuild, the making up of their leases to sixty-one years. They were to make proposals by 10 March or be prosecuted.[21]

Some agreed to surrender their interest. John Greene, for example, at MW1 noted that rebuilding would cost at least £500, 'he being in very ill circumstances to undertake it haveing left of all business in the City and is retired into the country for his health's sake'. He agreed to accept £40 a year for the rest of

THE GREAT REBUILDING OF 1683-96 | 119

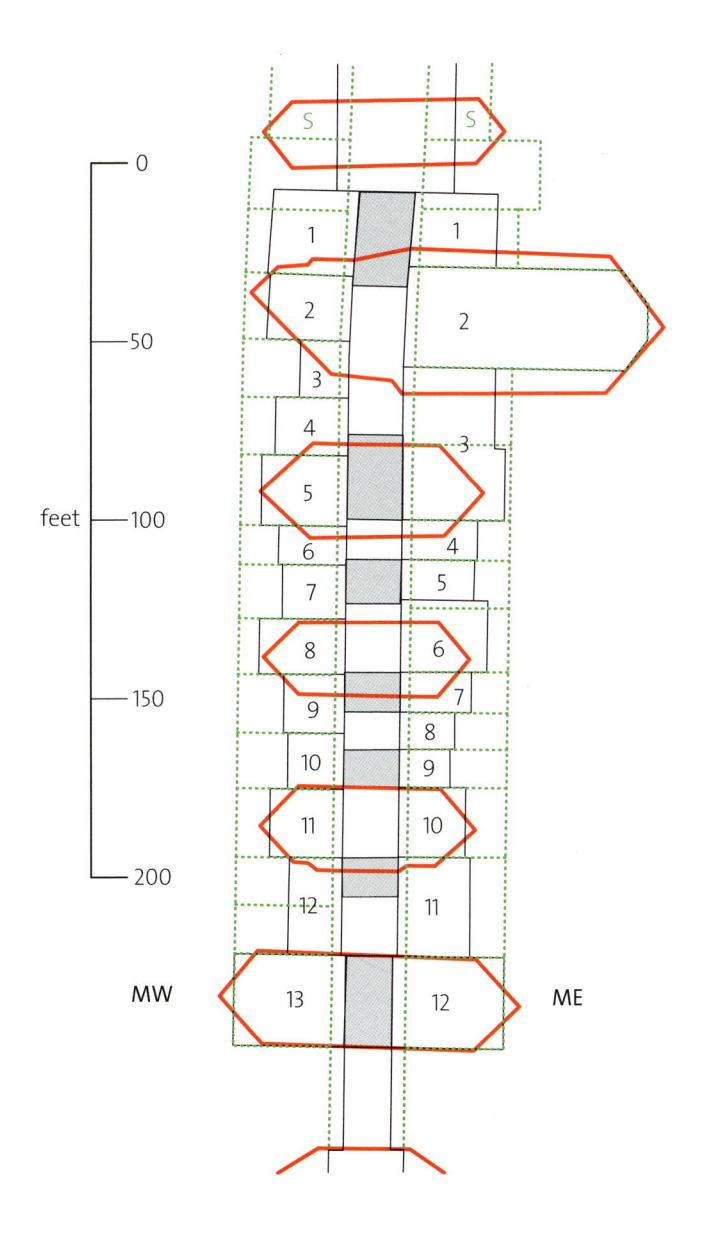

Fig. 90 Plan of the middle part with the layout of the 1680s shown in green and overlaid on the earlier layout, indicating how much further the houses now extended beyond the ends of the piers. 'S' marks the single-storey shops built in the 1680s. The changed boundary between ME5 and 6 is shown. The depth of 28 feet seems to relate to the ground-floor shops and to the projecting bays, between which were balconies and walls set slightly less far back.

his term. Simon Leeson at ME4 'offers to build or to take £200 for interest & it is not worth £100'; eventually he rebuilt. Most agreed to rebuild, and some did so themselves, but just over half the properties passed into the hands of building tradesmen.[22]

Building agreements were made in mid-1684, and had provisions similar to those for the northern houses. The new houses were to have their fronts and backs 'upright' without projecting jetties, balconies or closets unless approved. Storeys were to have the same heights as at the northern end, and there was to be a platform of lead above the garrets with rails and banisters, 12 feet from east to west. The hammer beams were to be larger in cross-section (20 by 18 inches) than those under the northern houses, which may indicate that there were already problems there. Within three months of demolition, the Bridge House was to make 'such new corbells or other beareings of stoneworke' as the builders proposed, and the rebuilding was to be completed in June 1685.[23] The depth of the new houses was to be determined by the Aldermen or their appointees, and there seems to have been a consistent depth of 28 feet on both sides, except around the chapel house (Fig. 90).[24] At ME10–11 building was stopped by the bridge estates committee in 1684 when the builder used timbers smaller than required.[25]

Nonsuch House was to be kept, indicating the admiration still felt for it. However, its fronts were to be set back on both sides of the street and the first-storey rooms over the street were to be removed (Fig. 91). John Foltrop was paid £182.10s.0d. in November 1685 for doing this, including 'beautifying the outside thereof'. He received a further £31.18s.0d. for brickwork on its north side.[26] The chapel house was also to be kept, but its lessee was to set back the front so that the roadway was 20 feet wide. The drawbridge was widened to 20 feet in 1685.[27]

Like at the north end, the Bridge House failed to make the

changes to the stonework within the time promised. Worse, some of the work was defective, affecting MW2 to 8. According to Richard Norman, the carpenter who rebuilt MW2–4,

> when your peticoners said houses were raised thereon the said stone worke broke in peices and your peticoner was forced to prop up his houses untill the said stone worke was taken downe and brought up againe namely from the 8th of October 1685 untill May 1687. [This] did not only putt your peticoner to £100 charges in propping his houses and removing his chimneys but alsoe brought a great discredit and ill name on his said houses soe that the said houses which otherwise would have lett for £40 a yeare apeice and fine your peticoner now profers for £30 a yeare and can gett noe tenant.

He estimated his loss at £600.[28] The 'shoors' by which the houses were propped up were probably timbers resting on the starlings, as Norman and others feared that if repairs were not completed by winter and there was a frost, 'the ice would cutt the shoors away, and tumble downe your petitioners houses' (see Fig. 88). In June 1686 six houses were said to be in danger of falling, and John Oliver, one of the City's surveyors, advised removing their chimneys to lessen the weight, which was done. Andrew Dandy, whose houses (MW7–8) had been rebuilt by his uncle less than thirty years before, estimated that the whole process of rebuilding them again had cost him £576.[29]

The new houses were somewhat more regular externally than those at the northern end, with a consistent balustrade at roof level. The regularity concealed the fact that the medieval boundaries between the plots had largely survived (Figs 90, 92). One boundary was certainly altered by the builders: ME5, rebuilt by Robert Browne, was widened from 10 feet 10 inches to 13 feet 1 inch, while ME6, rebuilt by Richard Norman, correspondingly decreased in width from 20 feet 4 inches to 17 feet 9 inches.[30] Possibly there were other adjustments where a single builder had brought together adjacent properties.[31] Otherwise existing boundaries were perpetuated.

Fig. 91 Detail from a drawing of the bridge, apparently based on Scott's painting. It shows Nonsuch House as altered in the 1680s, with the passage under it two storeys high. The house had evidently retained one of the original round-headed ground-floor windows, and the four-light windows and pilasters in the first and second storeys were probably also original.

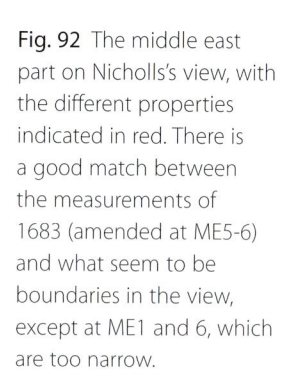

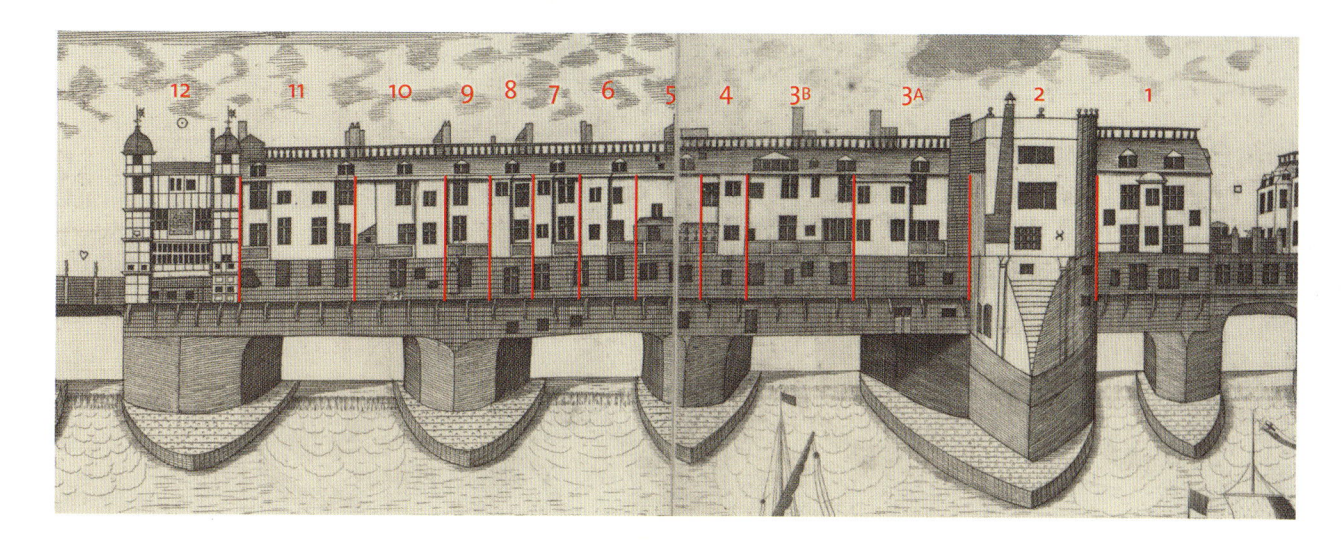

Fig. 92 The middle east part on Nicholls's view, with the different properties indicated in red. There is a good match between the measurements of 1683 (amended at ME5-6) and what seem to be boundaries in the view, except at ME1 and 6, which are too narrow.

The building agreements had no provisions about cross buildings or 'tye overs', and this had to be sorted out later. In 1684 Edmund Clarke at MW2 was allowed to rebuild the cross building there. By 1688 Andrew Dandy had been required to add a 'cross building or tye over' at MW7–8, 'for the strengthneing of the buildings on both sides & preservacon of the stone worke'.[32] In 1693 three new tie-overs were ordered in the middle part, apparently in response to problems with some of the new houses. The one at ME3 was just 7 feet 8 inches wide, suggesting that its main purpose was structural rather than to provide extra space. In return for consenting to it, the lessee there was allowed the use of half of its lower floor and the whole of its upper floor.[33]

Surprisingly, in view of the recent experience of fire, the firebreak provided by the Square was eliminated. The northernmost houses of the middle part were allowed to extend 12 feet further north than before (the lease of ME1 indicates that the actual extension was 14½ feet), and the remaining space was filled by a row of single-storey shops on each side. These prompted a petition from lessees and inhabitants on the bridge, who pointed out that the Square had been a safeguard in case of fire, 'and a great conveniency in such cases for playing of engines'. Also,

> such shopps will in all probability be inhabited by poore people who may not onely prove chargeable to ye parish but haveing noe chimneys in their said shopps may occasion much danger by burning of charcole.[34]

The shops were nevertheless built. On the west side, Thomas Gray put up six shops and a warehouse behind them, stretching 40 feet from north to south and 24 feet from east to west. On the east side John Foltrop built four shops. They had a frontage of 40 feet, were 18 feet deep and had flat roofs of lead. (Their lessees were forbidden to turn the roofs into gardens without providing extra support.)[35] When it was proposed to renew the leases of the shops in 1744, inhabitants of St Magnus parish put forward objections similar to those of sixty years earlier, noting that the occupants of the

> sheds or low buildings ... have generally been indigent people & such as deal in gingerbread & drams [spirits], and other mean business, and have frequently become chargeable to the said parish.[36]

The shops meant the end of the alehouse kept by Henry Thurston in a cellar by the Square. It was known in 1678–85 as the Bunch of Grapes, but was described in 1684 as the Sussex House. Thurston stated that

> haveing lived soe many yeares in the premisses [he] hath now through his great industry and good carriage amongst the neighbourhood setled himselfe in his trade the only support of himselfe and family

and asked to be left where he was or to be provided with new premises in the same place. He sold out in 1685 to John Foltrop, but, perhaps by agreement with Foltrop, obtained new premises on the north-west part of the bridge, where he was living in 1689 with his wife, a child, a servant and a maidservant.[37]

Rebuilding the drawbridge houses began to be considered in November 1684. John Tutty at SW5 suggested that he might simply cut back the front of his house as he did not have a first-floor cross building (his part of the cross building was the second floor upwards); he was threatened with indictment if he did not rebuild.[38] Building agreements were made in late 1685 and early 1686 and leases or extensions to leases were granted in 1686. As elsewhere, the changes to the stonework seem to have been delayed.[39] No building tradesmen were involved here, except John Foltrop at SE4–7. Nathaniel Blagrave, who had to rebuild the wheelage house (SW1), noted that rebuilding was likely to cost him £300 and would add only about £9 a year to the rent of £36 a year he was already receiving.[40] Lucy Phillips (SE2) complained that her house had lost some of its depth at both ends because of the widening of the roadway and the uniform back line, that its rent had fallen from £30 a year to £20, and that rebuilding and loss of rent for several years had cost her almost £200.[41] As on the middle part of the bridge, the existing boundaries between houses were largely retained. No one seems to have expressed regret about the loss of the house with many windows. Nothing is recorded about cross buildings, but there were arches over the roadway at both ends of the block (Figs 84, 93).

Of the thirty-nine householders on the middle part and in the drawbridge houses in 1682, only thirteen were still on

Fig. 93 The south end of the drawbridge houses in 1749 – detail from the panorama of London by Samuel and Nathaniel Buck.

Fig. 94 The bridge seen from the south-west – view published by John Bowles in 1723–24.

the bridge in 1689: eight on the middle part (only one in the same location), two on the south part (both in their former location) and three on the north part, together with the widow of another.[42]

South of the stone gate

Widening the street south of the stone gate was less urgent because it was relatively wide already and had no cross buildings. The committee for widening was instructed in July 1685 to consider whether the buildings on the west side outside the gate encroached on the street, suggesting that rebuilding just one side was being considered. By April 1687 negotiations had begun with the tenants on both sides,[43] but the only action taken on the east side was that Francis Wilkinson rebuilt SE14 by 1690. Perhaps his house had projected further into the roadway than the others there. Later he said he had been encouraged to rebuild 'as an example to others (which soon after had its effect)'.[44]

On the west side the main problem was Evan Evans, who occupied a house just south of those belonging to the Bridge House. It projected 5 feet into the roadway at the junction of Tooley Street and the bridge approach (see Fig. 114). He was a salesman and a draper, and was a contractor supplying clothing to the army. When the committee called him before them in December 1696 and offered to purchase a nearby lease and provide him with accommodation equal to what he currently enjoyed, he replied 'Purchas the leases first & then I will talk with you'. In March 1697 the committee called him in again with the same offer, and his reply, as recorded, was 'There he lived & there he expected to live and to the like effect'. The committee responded by adding a new clause to a parliamentary bill about road repairs, entitling the City to acquire properties at the south end of the bridge. Evans, with seventeen years remaining on his lease, had rebuilt the premises, and demanded £3,000. The City's counter-offer was £1,000. The outcome is not recorded, but the City certainly succeeded in acquiring the property and setting it back.[45]

Meanwhile it was decided in 1693 that the houses on the west side should be set back 5 feet. This was a problem for some of them because they backed onto the Bear Tavern, and so could not compensate at the back for ground lost at the front. It was agreed instead that first storeys could jetty out 2 feet in front. The plan on John Foltrop's lease of SW12–13 shows jettying 2 feet 6 inches deep. New leases were agreed in 1694 and 1695, and again made up terms to sixty-one years.[46] Foltrop seems to have been the only building tradesman involved. At the back the new houses were simple gabled structures with more regular windows than those of the bridge's other new buildings (Fig. 84). From 1696 almost the only houses on the bridge dating back before the 1680s were those on the east side south of the stone gate.

The City's approach to widening the roadway was undoubtedly harsh towards existing lessees, but it was a triumph in securing a wider roadway fairly quickly at little immediate cost. And the rebuilt bridge had its admirers: Strype said in 1720 that 'now it is the most stately bridge in the whole world', with 'a pile of such building as cannot be paralleled upon any bridge in the world'.[47]

The new houses

Thomas Gray acquired six houses on the north-west part of the bridge built by Foltrop in 1683, each about 16 feet wide, and a list of their fixtures from 1739 gives us their plan. On the ground floor were shops, all but one of them with shutters and several of them with a screen dividing the front shop from a back shop or counting house. On the first floor were two rooms, of which one was the kitchen and the other, when named, was a dining room or parlour (probably with similar functions whatever the name). In the cases where that room was not named, it was simply 'one pare of stairs forward', indicating that it was at the front or street side, while the kitchen was at the back or river side. On the second floor were two more rooms, and there were garrets above. The only 'necessary house' mentioned was in one of the kitchens.[48]

The basic plan of Gray's houses – ground-floor shop, dining room and kitchen on the first floor, two chambers on the second floor, and garrets – was probably common to all the new houses of the 1680s, with only minor variations (Fig. 95). It was certainly common to the houses covered by the six inventories available, from 1688 to 1722, apart from an additional closet in two of them.[49] In two of the inventories the kitchen had the most valuable contents, but, apart from kitchens, the rooms most expensively furnished were the dining room in three cases and the second-floor chamber forwards (on the street side) in three, identifying that room as the main bedroom. Three of the dining rooms had beds in

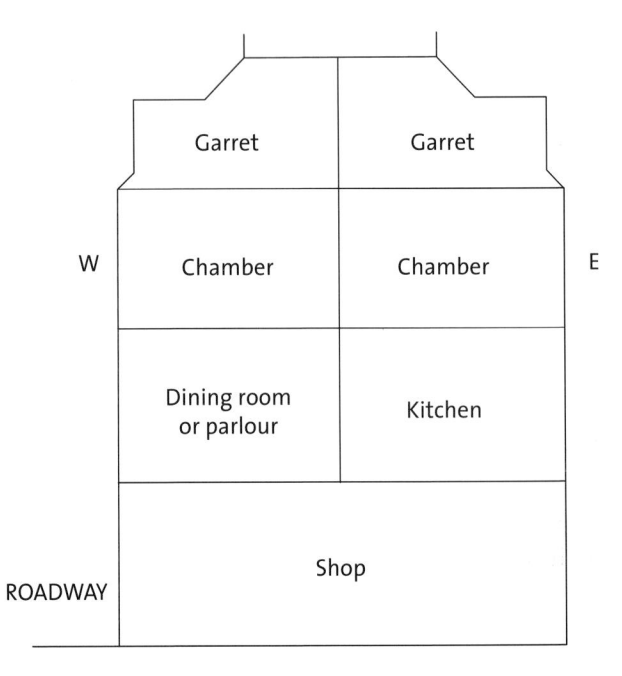

Fig. 95 Reconstructed cross section of one of the houses built on the bridge in the 1680s, based on evidence discussed in the text. It might also have had a cellar.

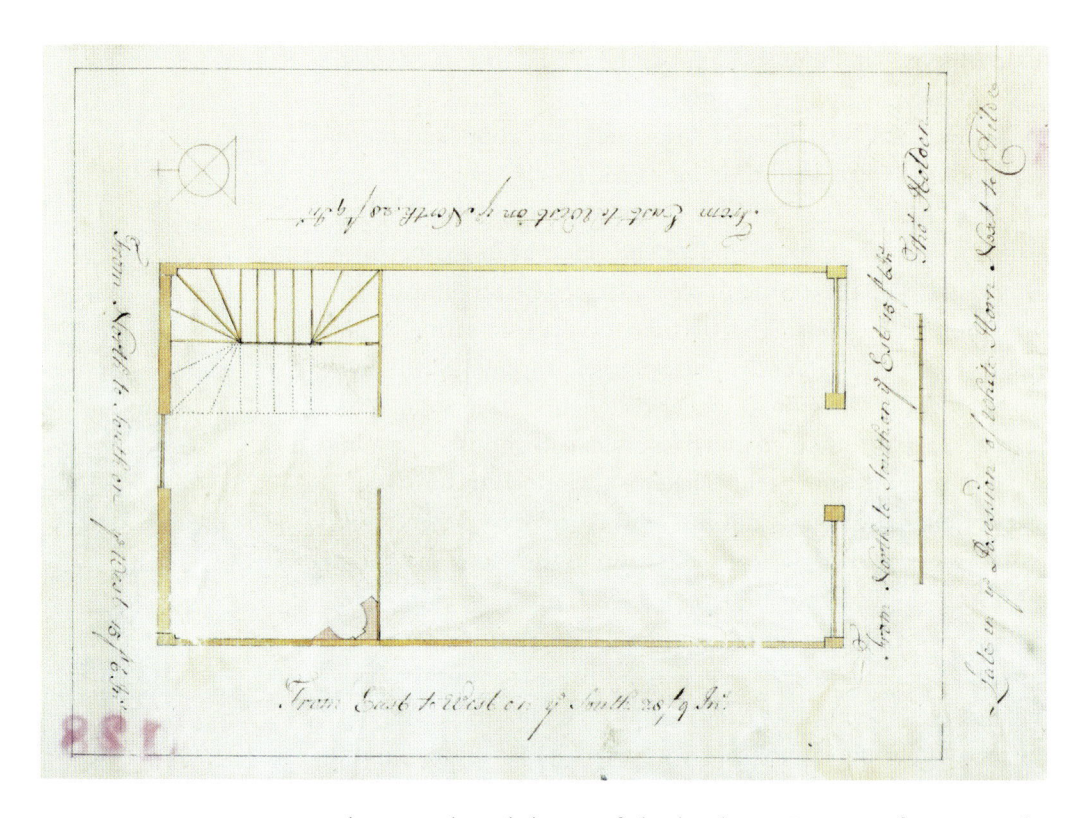

Fig. 96 Ground-floor plan from about 1743 showing PW18, built by John Foltrop in about 1683. Some of the other lease plans of the 1740s show a single room on the ground floor.

them, and so did one of the kitchens. By way of an example, Gervase Locke in 1688, at PE2, had the usual large range of haberdashery goods (especially hats) in the shop; a first-floor kitchen with a table and seven chairs; a first-floor dining room with a round table, thirteen cane chairs, three turkey-work chairs and a couch; a chamber over the kitchen; a closet and a chamber over the dining room, the chamber having the most valuable furnishings of any room, such as chests of drawers of olive wood; and above the second floor a little upper chamber and an upper chamber next to the street. Locke also had a house in Camberwell with kitchen, parlour, two chambers and washhouse. His goods totalled £1,357, including £488 in cash, together with £3,000 of debts owed to him, though his own debts to others are not recorded.[50]

The major innovations in the seventeenth century were to have the kitchen on the first floor instead of the second and the new ways of obtaining water. These seem to have been connected. The new houses built in the 1640s obtained water by pumping it up rather than winching it up in buckets, and from the 1670s piped water was available. In 1671 the City granted to Joseph Ayloffe the right to supply water from the waterworks at the north end of the bridge via pipes to houses on the bridge and in Southwark in return for a third of the profits, and some of the bridge houses certainly took advantage of this.[51] Whether pumps were still needed to convey that water to upper storeys is unknown.

In the 1640s, all but two of the new houses had their lower cistern in a cistern house behind the shop, or in one case in the ground-floor entry. The two exceptions were the only houses known to have had first-floor kitchens: PE2, where the lower cistern was in the yard, and PW3, where it was in the cellar.[52] The impact of a cistern being in the yard is unclear, but a cistern in the cellar would have meant water having to be pumped up three storeys if the kitchen was on the second floor. That was impossible: because of atmospheric pressure, water cannot be pumped up beyond 32 feet even if there is a perfect vacuum, and in practice the limit is 20 to 25 feet.[53] At PW3, either there was some reason for placing the cistern in the cellar and therefore the kitchen had to be on the first floor, or there was some reason for placing the kitchen on the first floor and therefore the cistern could be out of the way in the cellar. In both of the houses with first-floor kitchens, the hall was on the same floor, presumably on the street side and so without a view. ME6, rebuilt in about 1650, had a similar water system, with 'two cisternes & two pumpes & pipes downe into the Thames', and possibly for a similar reason had a first-floor kitchen, but in this case the hall was placed on the second floor instead of the first.[54] Both kitchen and hall could thus be on the river side of the house, but the hall was in a less convenient place. The new houses of the 1680s followed what had been done in two houses in the 1640s: both kitchen and hall on the first floor, but consequently a hall or dining room without a view. They could presumably have been arranged like the majority of the houses of the 1640s, with two sets of pumps and cisterns and second-floor kitchens. The fact that they were not suggests that the disadvantage which must have existed under any water supply system of having to convey water to the second floor was no longer offset by the hall's importance as a place for entertaining and displaying status. This suggests in turn that, like the rest of the City, the bridge was acquiring a more purely commercial and less domestic character. The increasing tendency of the bridge's inhabitants to acquire country retreats may have contributed to this.

Nevertheless, several inventories provide a picture of elegant living on the bridge in the eighteenth century. In 1722, Charles Walkden, a stationer at PW5, had a shop on the ground floor; a staircase with sixteen pictures and twenty-four prints; a first-floor kitchen; a first-floor dining room with several tables, eight cane chairs, yellow harrateen window curtains and eighteen pictures; a second-floor chamber forwards, evidently the best bedroom, containing a bed with blue china drapery, seven cane chairs, a Dutch table, an inlaid chamber table and stuff window curtains; a second-floor chamber backwards, containing a bed with green china drapery, a walnut chamber table, green stuff window curtains and other items; and two garrets, one containing a bed with blue print drapery and eight silk cushions. The household goods totalled £105 (including £25 in ready money), the shop goods £351, debts received £417, hopeful debts £607 and desperate debts £600, and there was a house in Pall Mall mortgaged for £520.[55]

Daniel Mitchell in 1757 lived in one of the new houses of the 1740s, the second from the north end. He was in partnership with Daniel Pope as a haberdasher, sharing both trading stock and household goods. The partnership had a second shop in the Borough, evidently much larger, though the living accommodation there was smaller (kitchen, dining room and chamber) and it contained much less than half of the household goods. The shop on the bridge had sash windows in front with 27 panes of crown glass, and inside were three counters, three sliding sashes with 'drawers & holes round the shop', five shop stools, candlesticks and a sconce in a gilt frame. The combined stock of both shops amounted to £1,185, comprising a huge range of hats and caps, handkerchiefs, hatbands, trimmings, lace, earrings, gloves, fans, stomachers, ribbons, watch strings and silk purses. On the first floor were the kitchen and the dining room, the latter having a mahogany dining table, a wainscot dining table, four matted chairs, four other chairs, a mahogany claw table, a mirror in a walnut and gilt frame, blue and white linen window curtains and a bed and bolster, together worth £14, the highest value of any room. On the second floor were three chambers (the only difference from the houses of the 1680s); all had four-poster beds, one with blue china drapery, one with green china drapery and one with linen drapery, and there were several pieces of walnut furniture. Above were garrets. There was an eight-day clock on the staircase. All rooms had window curtains, and most had pictures and prints on the walls.[56] It was still possible to live well on the bridge in the 1750s.

CHAPTER 11

From the fire of 1725 to the removal of the houses

The fire of 1725

On the night of 8 September 1725, a fire which began in Tooley Street, Southwark, spread to the bridge and destroyed all the houses as far as the stone gate – eight on the west side and seven on the east – as well as damaging the gate. In that fire most of the bridge's remaining pre-1680s buildings perished. All but three of the houses were insured against fire.[1] All the lessees were willing to rebuild, apart from Anne Vane (SW8), who could not afford it. Rents had risen more on this part of the bridge than on the others (Appendix 5), suggesting that its value as a commercial location had increased, and this probably contributed to the willingness to rebuild. In return the tenants asked for their leases to be extended, and also that hammer beams be provided for the houses over gullets. The bridge estates committee noted that the leases of the eastern houses made it responsible for the hammer beams, whereas those of the western houses, which were more recent, did not. However, it agreed to provide hammer beams for the western houses too, in order to encourage rebuilding and so that 'there may be good substantiall and lasting foundacons for such buildings beyond the terms of years such tennants may have therein'. The houses on the west side were to be rebuilt as they had been before, with the same scantlings, storeys and regularity, and the ones on the east side were to be rebuilt like those on the west, unless they were required to be rebuilt in brick. This potentially applied to those which were not actually on the bridge, and SE15 was certainly rebuilt in brick. Rebuilding was to be completed within two years, and tenants were obliged to obtain insurance. One of the lessees who had not been insured, Gerrard Pitham at SE11, estimated that rebuilding would cost him £300.[2]

All the houses were rebuilt except the four nearest the stone gate – two on each side. The committee first delayed their rebuilding while it decided what to do about widening the gate, and required the surrender of the leases. When it eventually advertised the sites in 1730 and 1731 there were no acceptable bids, so it decided to keep the space empty in case of fire. A wall was to be built on each side, at least 6½ feet high,

> as well to guard the inhabitants from the weather as also to prevent stopping up and incumbring the passage by persons getting up and looking over the same, which in other parts of the bridge is found very inconvenient.[3]

However, despite the concern about fire, it could not resist putting the space to remunerative use, and by 1733 there was a single-storey room with a cellar under it on each side. By 1741 the eastern one was occupied by a pewterer and the western one had been converted into a coffee room by William Kinleside, an apothecary.[4]

The opportunity was also taken in 1727 to improve the approach to the bridge, previously 'very steep and incomodious' – presumably rising towards the stone gate. John Cocker's house directly opposite Tooley Street had formerly been 2½ feet above the pavement and was now to be 3 feet above, and the new buildings and the adjoining roadway were to be set at the same level. Also, action was at last taken to widen the roadway at the stone gate, as discussed earlier, increasing its width to 18 feet.[5]

The falling in of leases in the 1740s

The leases granted in the 1680s were almost all for sixty-one years, and that meant that most of the leases of the bridge houses would expire together in the mid-1740s. This ought to have been a financial windfall for the Bridge House, with large entry fines from new leases, and to an extent it was, but the ending of the leases also threw up problems that were to call into doubt the very existence of the bridge houses.[6] Evidently something had changed since the houses south of the stone gate were rebuilt without problems after 1725.

There was certainly increasing hostility towards houses on bridges in the eighteenth century, both in England and elsewhere in Europe. More people now shared Charles I's view that removing the houses from London Bridge would make it both more beautiful and more convenient. James Ralph argued in 1734 that 'nothing can be more ridiculous than [a bridge] incumber'd with houses from end to end'. Nicholas Hawksmoor in 1736 considered it absurd to build a bridge and then impede the passage with houses and thereby destroy the benefit the bridge was meant to provide.[7] Moreover, London Bridge was losing its monopoly. A bridge was opened at Putney in 1729, with a roadway 19 feet wide and a footway 4 feet wide, and parliamentary approval was given for a bridge at Westminster in 1736, though it was not opened until 1750. Westminster Bridge had a roadway 30 feet wide, with a footway 6 feet wide on each side.[8] Neither of these bridges had houses on them. As London's population grew, and as more houses were built south of the river, London Bridge must have become increasingly congested. In 1722 inhabitants in and near the bridge claimed that the number of country vehicles using the bridge had more than doubled in seven years, that the street-keepers were negligent and that there were 'stopps' on the bridge three or four times a day causing coaches to be held up for an hour or more, with consequent damage to trade on the bridge.[9] Without removing or rebuilding the houses, the bridge's roadway could not be widened beyond 20 feet. Also, as it was more expensive to build and maintain houses on a bridge than on dry land, the bridge needed to remain an advantageous location for businesses if the greater cost was to be worthwhile, and it may have been in gradual decline as a trading location. On the other hand, the houses made a considerable contribution to the Bridge House's finances, and this was regarded as essential for maintaining the bridge. As the Bridge House had largely transferred the cost of rebuilding and repairs to its lessees, income from the houses went straight into its balance sheet. Removing the houses was to prove highly controversial.

For the landlord, the first step for leases which were about to end was to view the properties, find out what rents were currently being paid, decide whether they needed to be rebuilt or, if not, what fines and rents could be levied, and advertise them for letting or rebuilding. The views of 1742–43 had mixed results. Although the approaching expiry of the leases must have discouraged expenditure on repairs, all the houses on the west side of the north end and the six northernmost ones on the east side were in good repair or even 'very good repair'. The others on the east side needed to be rebuilt. In the middle part, everything on the west side apart from Nonsuch House needed to be rebuilt and about half of those on the east side (ME6–11).[10] Re-letting the buildings in good repair was a simple matter. They were let individually, and the leases were mostly obtained by the occupants. Substantial entry fines were paid, almost all from £50 to £115. In total, the twenty-seven re-let houses on the northern part of the bridge yielded £2,370 (£88 per house), almost all of it in 1744, together with £166 in annual rent.[11]

The bridge estates committee intended to use any rebuilding to improve the passage over the bridge. This was to be achieved by setting back the ground floors of the new buildings, leaving room for a covered pedestrian walkway or 'piazza'. The loss of ground-floor space would be compensated for by replacing each three existing houses by just two new ones. The plan was devised by George Dance, who became the City's Clerk of the Works in 1735.[12] For it to be implemented in full, all the bridge houses would need to be rebuilt or significantly altered.

Unfortunately there were no bidders for the building leases.[13] The market for leases of existing houses remained reasonably healthy, but building new houses speculatively was evidently less attractive. Dance's plan must have contributed to this, as it made each house significantly more expensive. Also, it was reported that insurance companies were refusing to provide insurance for houses on the bridge. The bridge estates committee planned to investigate the matter, including meeting the directors of the Sun Fire Office, but nothing further is recorded.[14] The offer of building leases also coincided with a severe slump in the London property market, the low point being in 1744, at least partly reflecting the falling in of many of the long leases granted for rebuilding after the Great Fire.[15]

One response to the lack of bidders was to look more carefully at whether rebuilding was really necessary. Those who viewed the fourteen houses on the middle west part in July 1744 reported as follows:

> We do find that the same are repairable and at no very great expence, saving at an empty house of Mrs Timewell's the hammer beam there and a brace at the next lock being defective. We are of opinion that a new hammer beam should be added to support the old one and a new brace put up at the said lock. And the said fourteen houses should be published to be let for one & twenty years.[16]

The new houses of 1745

Re-letting was not an option for the fifteen houses on the east side of the north end. Already in 1743, Gerrard Pitham, a brushmaker, who held three of them (formerly Caseby's), had pointed out that they were 'considerably sunk from an upright and lean towards the Thames'; he had had to move out of them himself to another house on the bridge. By 1745 all fifteen were said to be so ruinous that they were in danger of falling and needed to be demolished.[17]

The committee decided to revert to an earlier practice, followed in the 1640s, and to have the houses built by a contractor for a fixed price. There were to be ten houses in place of the existing fifteen. Five bids were received, ranging from £3,780 to £4,253, and the lowest was accepted. It amounted to £378 per house, much less than the £500 which Dance had said was likely, and which he had supported by an itemised costing.[18] The successful bidder was Thomas Reynolds, a carpenter of Basinghall Street. Under the articles of agreement of April 1745, Reynolds was to build according to Dance's plans (Fig. 97). The scantlings of the timbers were specified, including hammer beams 14 by 14 inches (much smaller than in the 1680s) and girders under the shop floors 14 by 12 inches (two under each shop, lying east to west). The shop storey was to be 8 feet 10 inches high, the first and second storeys each 10 feet high and the attic storey 7 feet high. At the back of the attic storey there was to be a 'flat' (or lead) instead of a room, and there was also to be a flat over the room at the front, together with balustrades at front and back (see Fig. 29). Privies were to be provided in the cellars. The woodwork and stucco outside was to be painted a stone colour.[19] No cross buildings were included. Dance's plan indicates a depth of about 26½ or 27 feet, probably much like the previous houses. When it was discovered that the single-storey shops facing the Square were supported by the same hammer beam as one of the houses Reynolds was to demolish, the shops were pulled down too

and not replaced.[20] The new houses were to be finished by 24 June 1746, but in fact were still unfinished in September 1746, when Reynolds said the reason was 'the trusses having given way'. They were eventually advertised in April 1747, when almost complete.[21] They were probably London's last major timber construction, though they included some brickwork in the cellars, walls and pillars. The hammer beams used may have been inadequate, as the new houses were reported ten years later to have sunk 1½ feet.[22]

As on previous occasions, building strained the Bridge House's finances, though the entry fines from existing houses must have helped considerably. The usual remedy, borrowing from the City, was not possible because the City had serious financial problems of its own. One remedy adopted may have been to spend less on repairs.[23] A more serious problem was that the completion of the new houses coincided with the slump in the property market. Only a few offers were made for the new houses. In May 1747, four were let, for entry fines totalling £220 and rents ranging from £12 to £23. Christopher and Francis Hurd, who were haberdashers, took the southernmost two houses. John Grant, a distiller, took one house after undertaking not to use it for distilling; in fact he traded there as a brushmaker and publican. Isaac Putham took the fourth house from the south. As his widow Anne later explained, he

> converted the lower room into a coffee room & kept the upper part as being light & convenient for his business as a taylors work shop and was in great hopes of thriving.

Unfortunately he died soon afterwards, leaving her in 'very indigent circumstances'; she said she was 'between seventy and eighty years of age, very infirm, and not worth twenty shillings

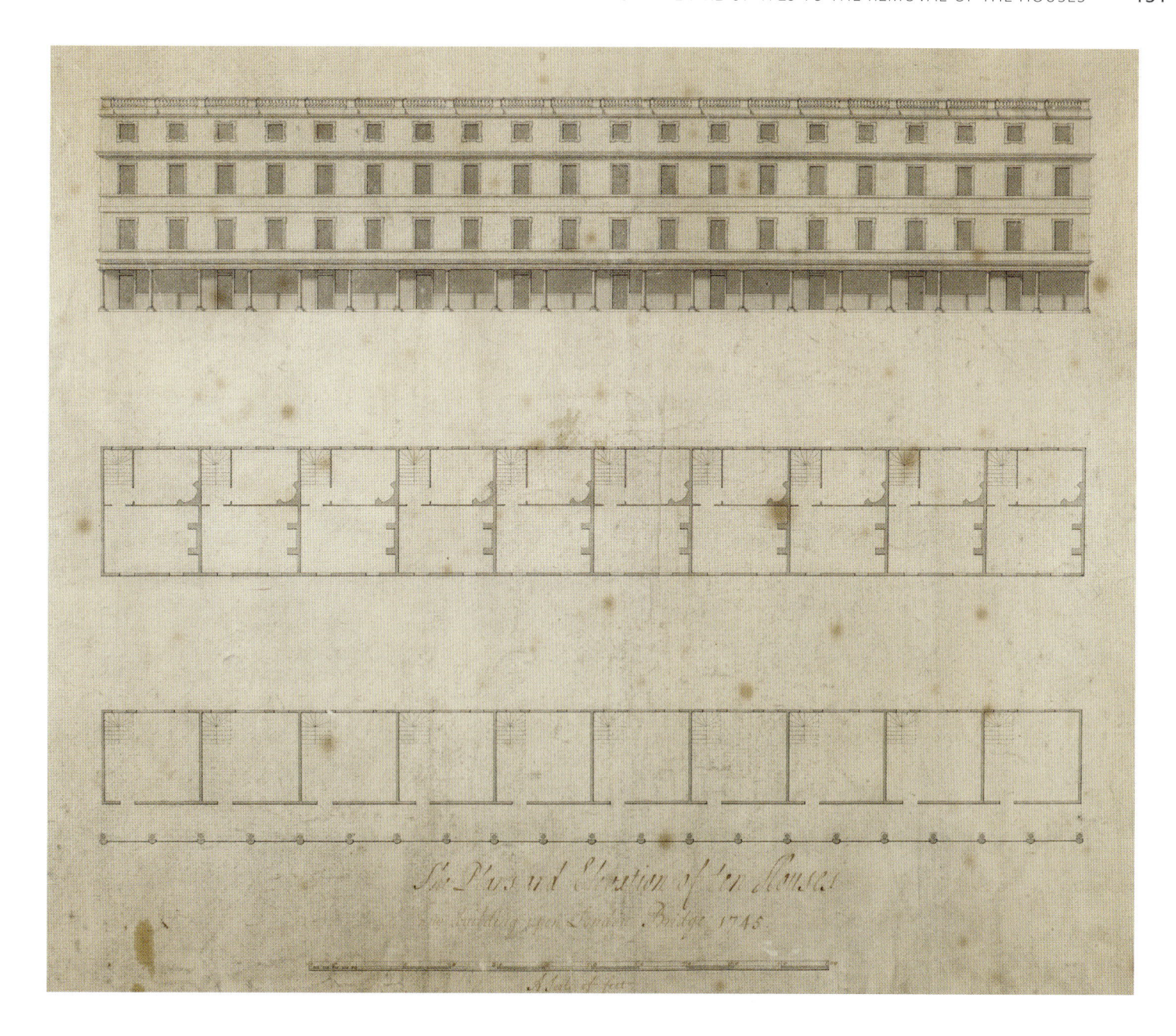

Fig. 97 George Dance's plan and elevation of the ten new houses built on the east side of the bridge in 1745, showing the covered walkway.

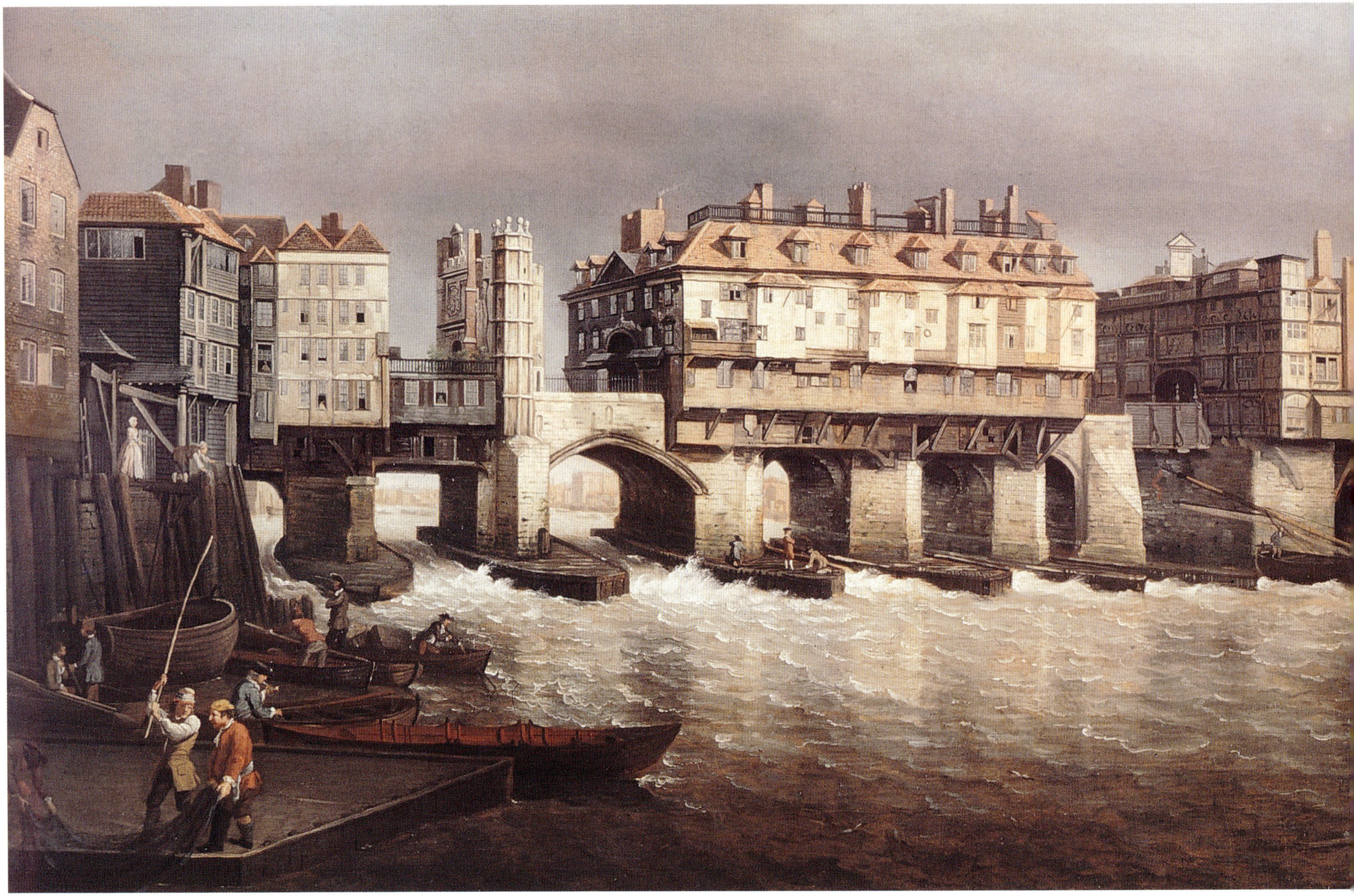

FROM THE FIRE OF 1725 TO THE REMOVAL OF THE HOUSES   133

Fig. 98 Samuel Scott's view of the east side of the bridge in about 1750. It includes the row of new houses built in the 1740s on the right, and the single-storey building that had replaced houses next to the stone gate on the left.

Fig. 99 Canaletto's drawing of the west side of the bridge in about 1750, with the waterworks and the tower of Saint Magnus's church on the left.

Fig. 100 Detail from an engraving by Bowles looking from Fish Street Hill southwards towards St Magnus and London Bridge in about 1750. The furthest coach is passing the new houses of the 1740s on the bridge, and beyond is the first of the 'tie-overs' on the middle part. The artist has exaggerated the width of the street.

in the world'. Her rent had to be reduced and she was made a tenant at will.[24]

The other houses were only very slowly filled, the last being let in April 1750. Several prospective tenants were rejected as unsuitable. William Ellgott's offer was rejected because he was a pastry cook and the committee 'would not lett the house to any of that trade in regard to the oven', reflecting the fire risk, even though Dance advised that as the house was on a pier it would be safe. The committee told William Deakin, who 'intended to keep a cook's shop & sell strong beer', that it would not let the house to a publican. By late 1747 prospective tenants must have been aware of the committee's weak bargaining position, and no entry fines were paid for any of the remaining six houses, which was probably unprecedented. The rents ranged from £16 to £20.[25] The new houses were a failure in financial terms: an outlay of at least £3,980 and income of only £220 in entry fines and £173 a year in rent.[26]

Managing the existing houses

As for the houses on the middle part, many of them in poor repair, the committee decided in 1746 to advertise them on building leases, but meanwhile to allow the existing occupants to remain as tenants at will provided they agreed that they would leave on three months' notice. The same policy was applied to much of the south end, and by 1754 thirty-five of the bridge houses were held by tenants at will.[27] This was a deliberate policy rather than a sign that only people who could not afford an entry fine wanted the houses. It kept options open, and it was financially beneficial for the Bridge House.[28] Although no entry fines were received for those properties, the rents paid by the occupants as sub-tenants to the lessees had been much higher than the rents the lessees themselves had paid, and those higher rents now flowed directly to the Bridge House. Rents from leaseholders declined steadily from 1743, but with the rents from tenants at will the total rent increased from £625 in 1743–44 to £781 in 1749–50 and £822 in 1752–53. Requests from the tenants to reduce the rents were rejected, except in a few cases for houses out of repair.[29] Of course this policy left the Bridge House with the risk of properties being left empty and the responsibility for repairs. However, some tenants agreed to carry out repairs in return for lower rents or rent holidays. For example Mr Christie agreed to repair in return for his rent being reduced from £15 to £10, and John Dawling near the stone gate agreed to repair his chimneys, leads and ceilings in return for remission of a year's rent of £20. William Akers at the Cross Keys alehouse had a leaking roof and floors 'almost ready to fall into the Thames', but agreed to remedy this himself in return for £4 of rent being abated. The committee warned leaseholders about their obligation to repair, noting that some of the houses 'are scarcely tenantable by reason of the tyling being so bad it rains in'. Some apparently serious defects could be remedied without a huge outlay, such as a defective hammer beam which Dance estimated could be put right for about £20.[30] A few large entry fines were still being received, notably £316 for the chapel house in 1747, and the property market recovered, reaching a peak in 1753.[31]

What then are we to make of George Dance's estimate from 1754 that the leased properties required repairs costing £4,025 and those occupied by tenants at will required repairs costing £7,238? The works proposed by Dance were extremely thorough, and the exercise looks like part of a campaign to have the houses removed. What was needed to enable the houses to be let and occupied was certainly far less, as Dance's own estimates for necessary repairs indicate. For example, in 1750 Richard Richardson's house required work on cellar floors, tiling, leadwork, rails and banisters and plastering and painting, costing £35 (1754 estimate £237), and in 1753 Mr Thorpe's chimney, railings and leads needed £18 spent on them (1754 estimate £199).[32]

The bridge houses presented the City with a difficult situation in the 1750s, but not yet a desperate one. The City still had choices, and was not forced to remove the houses by structural or financial problems. A sustainable situation had been achieved for the short term; whether it was sustainable in the longer term depended on whether there would eventually be bidders willing to invest in new houses or major works on the existing ones. Inability to insure the bridge houses against fire would not have helped.

Removing the houses

Probably the main significance of the difficulties of the late 1740s and 1750s was political rather than economic, in that, combined with the threat from Westminster Bridge, they tipped the balance in favour of those who wanted to pull down the houses and widen the passage over London Bridge. Opponents of the houses could point to the lack of bidders for building leases, the poor return on the ten new houses, the poor state of some of the other houses, and the possibility that the bridge houses would become a drain on the Bridge House's finances rather than a vital support.

After Westminster Bridge opened in 1750, two proposals for bridges were pushed forward in the City: one to widen London Bridge and one to build a new bridge at the Fleet Ditch (now Blackfriars Bridge). It was a period of increasing hostility to obstacles, including not just the narrow London Bridge but also the City gates, all but one of which were removed in 1760. Both bridge proposals were controversial. The Blackfriars one was narrowly passed in the Common Council in December 1753, narrowly avoided repeal in February 1754 and resulted in a bill being presented to Parliament in 1756. The bridge was built in 1760–69. A motion for a committee to consider making London Bridge 'more open and commodious to passengers' was narrowly defeated in the Common Council in December 1754, by eighty-six votes to eighty-two (despite a majority of Aldermen supporting it), and in 1756 it was noted that the Council had twice rejected such a motion.[33]

In fact the Common Council never approved the removal of the houses, and instead it was bypassed. A bill with that purpose was presented to Parliament ostensibly by 'divers merchants, tradesmen, citizens, and inhabitants of the City of London, and Borough of Southwark' and of Surrey, Kent and Sussex, claiming that the passage over it was 'very narrow, inconvenient, and dangerous'. Questioned about the opposition of the Common Council, James Hodges, one of the bill's

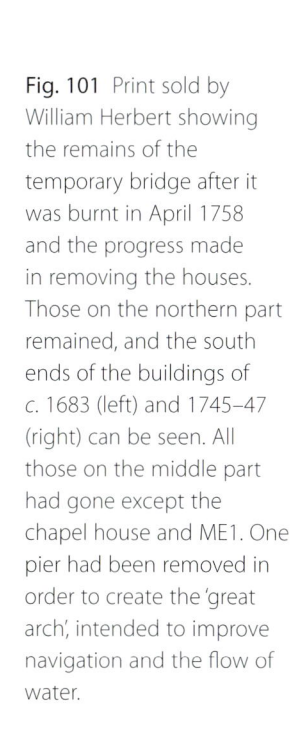

Fig. 101 Print sold by William Herbert showing the remains of the temporary bridge after it was burnt in April 1758 and the progress made in removing the houses. Those on the northern part remained, and the south ends of the buildings of c. 1683 (left) and 1745–47 (right) can be seen. All those on the middle part had gone except the chapel house and ME1. One pier had been removed in order to create the 'great arch', intended to improve navigation and the flow of water.

Fig. 102 Print by William Daniell showing the bridge widened and without houses in 1804. The larger arch had replaced two of the earlier arches.

supporters, stated that it would be 'odious' to think that the City would oppose a measure so evidently for the public good. The House of Commons accepted the promoters' case. On 5 May 1756 the Common Council observed that what it described as private persons had applied for a bill to widen the bridge and agreed to petition against it by 100 votes to 92. The arguments against the bill were not just the great expense but that it was subversive of property, that an absolute necessity was required to destroy such property, the hazard of altering an ancient structure and the destruction of one of the City's most ancient gates. On 11 May the Council received a petition against the proposal from sixty-one individuals or firms

Fig. 103 Print by E.W. Cooke of the south end of the bridge in about 1830, showing the bridge as widened. The starlings remained, but the outer parts of the piers had been cut down to a level only a few feet above the starlings. Under the middle of the first arch on the left can be seen the vaulting springing from the southern abutment (partly rediscovered in 1984).

occupying houses on the bridge saying it would be hard to establish their trades elsewhere. Some petitioned individually: William Urlwyn, who had taken a seven-year lease in 1752, said that having to leave would

> in a great measure be his undoing having gained since his occupying the premises a comfortable livelyhood for himself & aged wife which your petitioner cannot at his time of life expect to find in any other part of the town.

Henry Barber, a cutler, with a wife and seven children to support, complained that he would 'be driven to a new neighbourhood and must look out for a new sett of customers', with the risk of poverty if he failed. The opponents were too late. On 27 May the bill received Royal Assent, and a committee was appointed to execute it.[34] However close-fought the battle over the houses was in 1754–56, it is hard to see that the City would long have remained content with its main bridge being only 20 feet wide. The difficulties over rebuilding and letting the houses may simply have accelerated an almost inevitable decision.

The Act empowered the City to purchase all the interests in the houses and remove them and to widen the bridge to 45 feet, including two footways each 7 feet wide. Buying out lessees and sub-lessees was expected to cost £13,916.[35] The committee at first proceeded cautiously, and in June 1756 commissioned Henry Flitcroft to examine whether removing the houses would endanger the fabric of the bridge. Evidently he gave a satisfactory answer, as notices to quit began to be issued in the same month, and in March 1757 the committee decided that all the buildings on the bridge (except those south of the stone gate on the east side) should be removed as soon as possible.[36] By then demolitions had already begun. The houses were cleared in three campaigns: the middle part and the drawbridge houses, except the chapel house and ME1, at the start of 1757; the north-east part, the chapel house and ME1 and the western houses south of the stone gate in early 1760 (though a few of the north-east houses went in 1758); and the north-west part and the eastern houses south of the stone gate in spring 1761. SW10 may have been the last to go, as rent was paid on it up to Midsummer 1761.[37] A temporary wooden bridge put up to maintain the passage was destroyed by fire in April 1758 (Fig. 101).

Some of the bridge's occupants relocated their businesses nearby, while others moved further away. For example, Walter

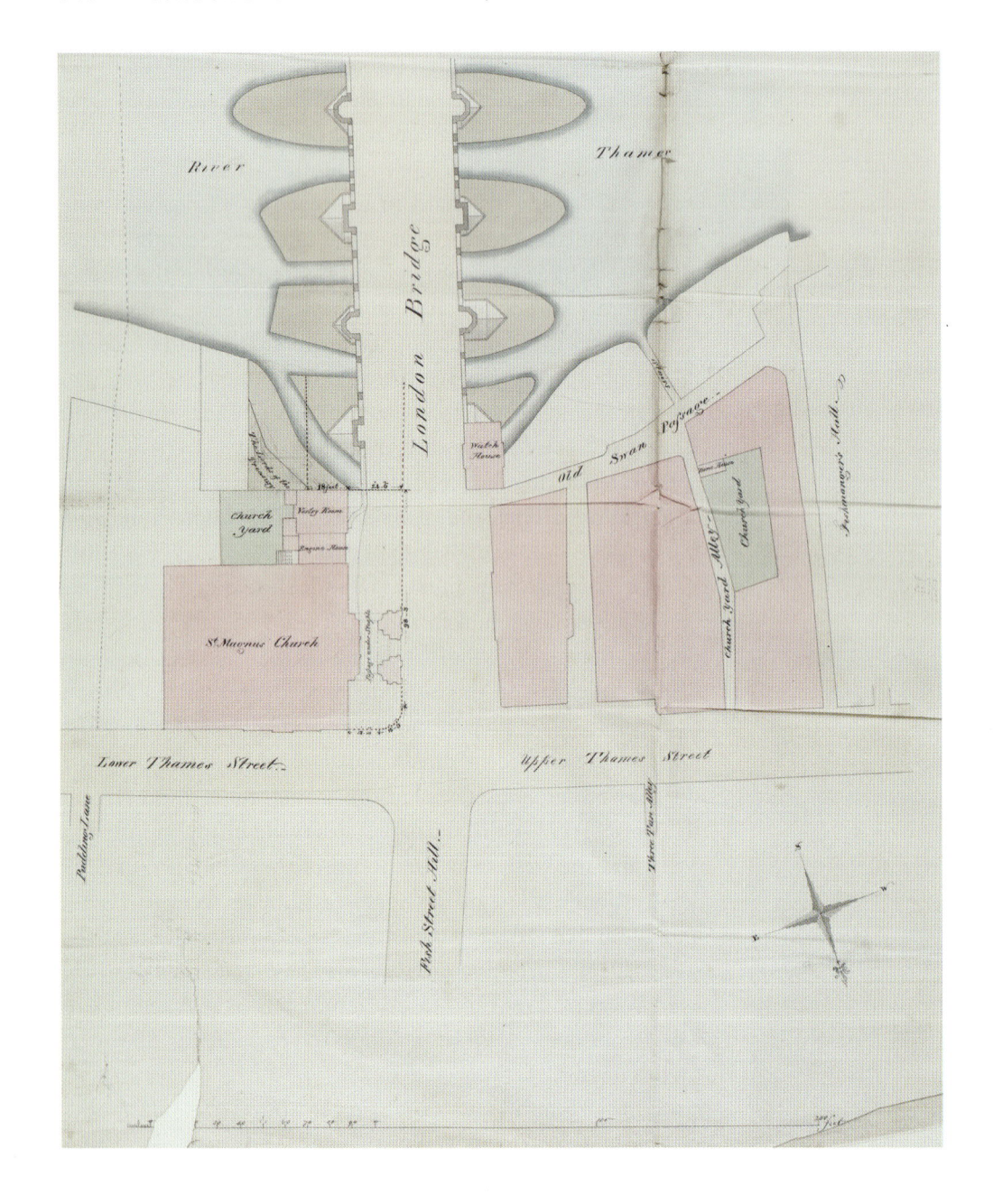

Left: **Fig. 104** Plan drawn for St Magnus parish in 1826, showing the widened bridge and the footway under the church's tower. North is at the bottom. The parish's detached churchyard further west (shown here in Church Yard Alley) was to be taken for the approach to the new bridge, and in return the parish successfully requested part of the approach to the old bridge, which it still holds today.

Above: **Fig. 105** Drawing by George Shepherd of St Magnus and the northern end of the widened bridge in 1811.

FROM THE FIRE OF 1725 TO THE REMOVAL OF THE HOUSES   141

Fig. 106 E.W. Cooke's view of the old London Bridge being demolished in January 1832, looking north, with the new bridge on the left and St Magnus directly ahead. The present bridge is on the site of the new bridge of 1824–31.

Watkins, breeches maker, moved to Change Alley, Cornhill; John Howard, necklace maker, to Fish Street Hill; William Herbert, printseller, to Leadenhall Street; Christopher Stedman, mathematical instrument maker, also to Leadenhall Street; Robert Vincent, scale maker, apparently to the northern end of the Borough; Wright and Gill, stationers, to Abchurch Lane; and Coles Child, needlemaker, to Upper Thames Street. Probably the longest survivor of any of the bridge's businesses was that established by Charles Walkden. Richard Walkden had moved it to Lower Thames Street by 1763, and it eventually became Cooper, Dennison and Walkden, remaining in business until 1981.[38]

Once the houses had gone, the bridge was widened to 45 feet (Fig. 102). Where the piers projected beyond the new width they were cut down to just above the level of the starlings (Fig. 103). At the north end, one of the new footways passed underneath the tower of St Magnus's church (Figs 104, 105). After more than 500 years, the bridge stood clear without any buildings on it, and continued to serve London for almost seventy years more. The Bridge House's finances flourished rather than suffered,[39] probably because of building on its land in Southwark. But the way the bridge had been constructed, with numerous piers protected by starlings, meant that maintenance continued to be expensive and navigation continued to be obstructed.

Eventually, in 1823 an Act was passed for building a new bridge. This was designed by John Rennie, with just five arches, and was constructed between 1824 and 1831, slightly west of the old one. The old bridge was demolished in 1831–32, with work to remove the starlings continuing into 1834 (Fig. 106).[40] The structure on which so many generations had lived, worked and loved over so many centuries vanished without leaving any visible trace, and an important part of London's history was erased.

Survey of the houses on London Bridge, 1604–83

Introduction

Most of the information below is from leases granted by the City.[1] Which properties they relate to has usually been determined using the rentals. The individuals named after the date are those to whom the lease was granted.[2] The lease descriptions have been calendared, usually omitting 'length' and 'breadth' (which identify only the longer and shorter sides respectively) and the ubiquitous 'or thereabouts'. 'Compting house' has been changed to 'counting house'. Storeys are not explicitly stated in the leases, and '(G)', '(1)', '(2)' and so on have been added here. The new houses of 1645–49 have been placed at the end because their plots were different from those of the previous houses on that part of the bridge.

Whether houses were over a pier or a gullet or both is shown by the reconstructed plan of the bridge (Fig. 14). Dates of building are derived from evidence discussed in the text (see Table 2). For numbers of hearths, see Appendix 4; gaps have been filled from a list of 1672–73.[3] Measurements in 1683 are from the list compiled in that year (Fig. 11), covering the middle part and the drawbridge houses.[4] They are exterior dimensions, whereas the leases provide interior dimensions, though party walls were reckoned to be only about 6 inches thick.[5] The 1683 list identifies cross buildings on that part of the bridge, but they are firmly linked to particular houses only for the east side; their assignment here to houses on the west side is deduced from their location. Cross buildings on the principal part in 1358 are identified from the rental of that year;[6] there were usually cross buildings in the same places in the seventeenth century, but not always. Cross buildings belonging to the new houses of 1645–49 are identified from the leases themselves.

Note that measurements were probably between the furthest points of a room, making some storeys seem more spacious than they were, that small rooms such as waterhouses were apparently omitted in many cases, that rooms were sometimes over the street without this being mentioned, and that successive leases indicate that rooms said to have been the same length and breadth as the one below often in fact had slightly different dimensions (e.g. where there was jettying).[7] Where the lease does not state which measurements were the width and which the depth, the width of the house was usually the distance that is repeated frequently and consistently.

It is often hard to reconcile the lease descriptions with the houses in the views, especially as regards the number of storeys. This may sometimes be because the relationship between windows and storeys is unclear, or because of changes made between the dates of the view and the lease. Many second-floor waterhouses can be seen, but virtually no hanging cellars (except at ME3 in the Norden view) or first-floor balconies (except at PW6 and 9 in the Pepys view). For the accuracy of the views, see Appendix 2.

Principal east

See Fig. 107. For likely widths of houses for which no lease has survived, see Appendix 1.

PE1

Adjoined St Magnus church (see Appendix 6 and Figs 8, 63); on the bridge abutment rather than on the bridge. Rebuilt c. 1572, c. 1644 and c. 1668, on the latter occasion in brick.[8] In 1725 it was noted that the depth at ground-floor level was only 20'9", and that 32' was the depth at first-floor level.[9] No list of rooms found. Seven hearths in 1666.

1644 (William Viner, citizen and goldsmith): length 32', including 11'3" over part of cloister of St Magnus; breadth 22'5".[10]

PE2

Straddled the first gullet, and its ground floor was partly over St Magnus's cloister (see Appendix 6). No list of rooms or measurements found.

PE3

Over a pier. Split into two tenements in 1544, which the lease of 1606 required Arthur Lee to convert back into one. No list of rooms found. PE3B had a hautpas in 1358.

1606 (Arthur Lee, citizen and girdler; late occupied by Edward Young and widow Wall and now Arthur Lee):

Fig. 107 The principal east part in Norden's view of 1597–98 (Fig. 1), with house numbers and dates of building added. The houses on this part of the bridge are difficult to identify, so exact distances have been marked in red (assuming the correct point has been identified as the edge of PE2 on the right) and the view has been interpreted by outlining likely houses in green. Later measurements indicate that Norden placed some of the piers too far north, especially the second to fifth from the north end.

from street to Thames, besides counting house, 22½′; along streetside 22½′.[11]

PE4
Over a gullet. No list of rooms or measurements found.

PE5
Largely over a gullet. The property listed in 1358 which was later split into PE4 and PE5A (the latter merging with PE5B) had a hautpas in 1358.

1611 (Edward Williamot, citizen and mercer): (G) shop 21′ × 19′; (1) hall over shop, 19½′ × 14′; chamber behind hall towards street, 9′ square; buttery behind hall, 10′ × 4½′; lead before hall window towards Thames, 18′ × 6′; (2) chamber over part of hall, 17½′ × 10′; kitchen with a buttery behind kitchen over other part of hall, 24′ × 8½′; (3) chamber over last chamber, 19′ × 10′; (4) garret over all the house, 24′ × 10′.[12]

PE6
Largely over a pier. There was expenditure on 'mendynge and makynge newe' this house in 1538.[13] *PE6A had a hautpas in 1358.*

1615 (Anthony Stapleton, citizen and haberdasher)

[*document damaged*]: cellar 16′ × 9′; (G) shop, 21′ × 20′; (1) hall over shop towards Thames, [*gap*], breadth 15′; chamber towards street, 12′ × 10′; chamber towards south, 8½′ × 5′; (2) [kitchen] over part of hall, 15½′ × 7′; little waterhouse towards Thames, 6′ × 5′; chamber behind kitchen, [*gap*], breadth 10′; little chamber towards street, 10′ × 7′; little buttery, 10′ × 5′; (?3) [chamber], 13′ × 10′; chamber on south, 13′ × 10′; chamber towards street, length 14′, breadth [*gap*]; (4) garret 29′ × 10′.[14]

PE7

Over a gullet. PE7B had a hautpas in 1358.

1623 (Jeremy Champney, citizen and clothworker): hanging cellar, 20′ × 9′; (G) shop, 20′ × 19′; (1) hall over shop, 19½′ square; chimney and little closet over passage or entry, 11′ × 3′; lead eastward of hall, 12½′ × 4½′; (2) chamber over part of hall, 8′ × 6′; kitchen over other part of hall and lead, 25′ × 9′; staircase 6′ × 5′; (3) chamber over kitchen, 19′ × 13′; little room adjoining chamber last aforesaid, 14′ × 5½′; (4) garret over all.[15]

PE8

Largely over a pier. There was a 'new augmentation' of Wright's house in August–September 1621, including a new hammer beam.[16]

1622 (Robert Wright, citizen and mercer): cellar, 16′ × 7′; (G) shop, along street with the entry 20′, breadth 18′; (1) chamber over part of shop, 14′ × 10′; hall over other part of shop, 20′ × 10′; little lead on east end of hall; (2) kitchen over said chamber, length with waterhouse and stairs 16′, breadth 10′, with buttery at upper end thereof; chamber over hall of same length and breadth; (3) two garrets over chamber and kitchen of same length and breadth.[17]

PE9

Over a gullet. PE9A had a hautpas in 1358.

1630 (Ellis Midmore, citizen and clothworker): hanging cellar 7′ square; one other cellar, 17′ × 8′; (G) shop with entry, 20½′ × 17′; (1) chamber wainscoted throughout over part of shop, 21½′ × 9′; hall wainscoted throughout over part of shop and entry, 24′ × 10′; (2) kitchen over hall, 23′ × 11′; chamber thereunto adjoining, 24′ × 11′; chamber at north-west end of kitchen, 10′ × 7′; (3) two chambers over kitchen of same length and breadth; chamber adjoining said two chambers, 24′ × 11′; (4) two garrets and 'a leade to walke in'.[18]

PE10

Over a pier and a gullet. The shop seems to be too small for the rooms above it.

1615 (Edmond Leaver, citizen and cutler): (G) shop, 21½′ × 14½′; (1) hall over part of shop, 22½′ × 14½′; chamber over other part of shop, 10′ × 6′; (2) kitchen over part of hall, 21′ × 12′; chamber behind kitchen, 21½′ × 11′; (3) chamber over last chamber, 21′ × 11′; chamber over kitchen, 21′ × 11′; (4) two little garrets over all.[19]

PE11

Over a pier. No list of rooms or measurements found.

PE12

Over a gullet. Built 1477. PE12B had a hautpas in 1358. See Fig. 55.

1625 (William Hooke; occupied by Edwin Gryffen, citizen and leatherseller): shop with an entry, north–south 19½′, east–west 12½′; little cellar under shop; counting house, 4′ square; staircase, north–south 5½′, east–west 5′; (1) hall over part of shop and entry, north–south 10′, east–west 17½′; chamber over part of shop, east–west 20½′, north–south 10′; (2) kitchen over hall, east–west 21′, north–south 10½′; chamber with an entry adjoining kitchen, east–west 17′, north–south 10′; (3) chamber over said chamber, east–west 17′, north–south 10½′; two little chambers more, east–west 22′, north–south 10′; (4) garret over said two little chambers of same length and breadth.[20]

PE13

Over a pier and a gullet. Built 1477.

1611 (Thomas Hickman, citizen and haberdasher): cellar, 8′ × 6′; (G) shop, 20′ × 19′; (1) hall over part of shop, 15′ × 9′; parlour next to hall over other part of shop, 21′ × 10′; little lead towards Thames eastward, length 12′, breadth 4′ in one part, 3′ in the other; (2) kitchen, 12′ × 8′; chamber next to street, 20′ × 12′; (3) chamber over part of last chamber, 18′ × 10′; chamber over kitchen, 21′ × 10′; (4) one garret over all, 16′ square.[21]

1631 (Samuel Armitage, citizen and girdler; occupied by Valentine Beale, citizen and merchant taylor): cellar, 8′ × 6′; (G) shop, with entry 3′ broad, 20′ × 19½′; (1) 'a little walkinge leade upon the first storie'; hall wainscoted throughout with wainscot settles, 15′ × 10′; parlour wainscoted in like manner, 20′ × 10′; (2) chamber over part of hall and parlour wainscoted throughout, length 20′, breadth at north end 15′ and south end 12′; kitchen 12′ × 8′, passage 7′ square; (3) chamber 11′ × 9′; chamber on same floor, 18½′ × 10′; (4) two garrets.[22]

PE14

Over a pier and a gullet. Built 1477. No list of rooms or measurements found. PE14A had a hautpas in 1358.

PE15

Over a pier and a gullet. Built 1526–29.

1605 (Thomas Turner, citizen and girdler): shop, 22′ × 18′; little hanging cellar; (1) hall and chamber over shop, length with stairs 21′, breadth 16′; (2) chamber, 12½′ × 12′; kitchen, 16′ × 6′; (3) two garrets.[23]

PE16

Over a pier. Built 1526–29. Had a hautpas in 1358; in 1616 its share of the cross building was only half of the second floor; see Fig. 110.

1616 (William Charlton, citizen and merchant taylor): cellar, 23′ × 7′; (G) shop, 18′ × 11½′; (1) room over shop, 18′ × 11½′; (2) chamber over part of last room, 14′ × 11½′; kitchen over other part of said room, 13′ × 11½′; (3) little garret over all, 12′ × 11½′.[24]

PE17

Largely over a gullet. Built 1526–29.

1632 (John Gover the elder, citizen and girdler): hanging cellar, 18′ × 6′; (G) entry with house of office, 18′ × 3′; shop, 15′ × 14½′; counting house at east end of shop; (1) hall wainscoted throughout with settles, 16½′ × 15½′; (2) chamber over hall, 16½′ by 8½′; kitchen, 16½′ × 8½′; (3) two chambers over said kitchen and chamber which is over hall; (4) two garrets over said two chambers.[25]

PE18

Over a gullet. Built 1526–29.

1612 (Rice Gray, citizen and haberdasher): (G) shop, 14′ × 10′10″; (1) hall, 17′ × 10′; (2) kitchen, length with staircase 12′, breadth 10′; chamber on same floor, 10′ × 9′; (3) chamber over kitchen with a chimney, 19′ × 10′; little jetty at end of it, 10′ × 4′; (4) small garret over all.[26]

PE19

Largely over a pier. Built 1526–29. No list of rooms or measurements found. Had a hautpas in 1358.

Principal west

See Figs. 108, 109. For likely widths of houses for which no lease has survived, see Appendix 1.

PW1

This was an addition to the Bridge House estate, and was largely on the bridge abutment (see Appendix 6 and Fig. 8). It had three parts: a small cellar over the first gullet, first recorded in 1598; a house partly above it, purchased in 1620; and a cellar under the rest of the house, purchased in or about 1628; all rebuilt in 1630–31. No list of rooms or measurements found, except for the last-mentioned cellar.

1628: cellar under tenement occupied by John Brooke, east–west 24′4″, breadth at east end 11′ and at west end from stone wall there 15½′.[27]

PW2

Over a gullet. No list of rooms or measurements found.

PW3

Over a pier. Built 1596.

1617 (Elizabeth Butler, widow): cellar, 27′ × 17′; (G) shop, length 29′, breadth with staircase on street side 16′ and towards Thames 15½′; (1) hall over part of shop towards Thames, 22′ × 16½′; parlour towards street with staircase over other part of shop, 16′ × 14′; (2) kitchen over hall towards Thames, 16′ × 15′; buttery behind kitchen northwards, 17′ × 8′; house of office behind buttery; chamber over parlour, 16′ × 7′; (3) chamber over kitchen, 23′ × 16′; chamber over chamber which is over parlour, 16′ × 15′; (4) two garrets over all, 26′ × 20′; lead over all, 16′ × 6′.[28]

PW4

Over a pier and a gullet. Built 1535–36. PW4A had a hautpas in 1358. The jetty over the street referred to in the lease was almost certainly part of a cross building.

1617 (Richard Willcoxe, citizen and haberdasher): cellar, north–south 38′ [*sic*], breadth 9′; (G) shop, east–west 22′, breadth 21′ 'with a little nooke being taken out of the square there' being 8′ × 4′; (1) hall over part of shop towards Thames, east–west 21′, breadth 18′; chamber over other part of shop, east–west 12′, breadth 10′; buttery behind hall towards street, 10′ × 6′; (2) kitchen over hall towards Thames, 14′ square; chamber behind kitchen towards street, north–south 21′, breadth 11′ with jetty over street 6′ long; (3) chamber over kitchen towards Thames, 15′ × 12′; chamber over last chamber towards street, north–south 21′, breadth 16′; (4) chamber over chamber which is over kitchen, north–south 10′, breadth with staircase 9′; chamber adjoining thereunto towards street, north–south 21′, breadth 18′; (5) two little garrets over all.[29]

PW5

Over a pier and a gullet. Built 1535–36. PW5A had a hautpas in 1358.

1631 (Henry Chamberlin, citizen and merchant taylor): (G) shop, 21′ × 20′ with a staircase; (1) hall over shop wainscoted throughout, 18′ square; chamber behind hall, 20′ × 8′; little room adjoining said chamber, 10′ × 6′; (2) kitchen over hall with a buttery in it, 16′ square with a staircase; little chamber, 11½′ × 10′; little chamber, 15′ × 9′; waterhouse, 5′ × 4′; (3) four little garrets over said rooms, 32′ × 19′.[30]

PW6

Over a pier and a gullet. Built 1463. The Pepys view shows the lead or balcony, windows with gothic arches and elaborate chimneys. PW6A had a hautpas in 1358.

1614 (Mary Sherley, widow): cellar, 17′ square; little waterhouse 'standing upon the peir of the arch', 10′ × 8′;

Fig. 108 The principal west part in the Pepys view, with house numbers and dates of building added. Several houses appear very narrow because the perspective means they are partly hidden behind their neighbour.

(G) shop, east–west 32′, breadth with staircase 20′4″; (1) hall over part of shop, 20′4″ × 13½′; lead over Thames, 20′ × 6′; chamber behind hall, 19′ × 10′; (2) kitchen over hall, 14′ × 13′; little room behind kitchen, 20′ × 6′; chamber behind kitchen towards street, length with staircase and entry 20′, breadth 10′; chamber towards south, 16′ × 10′; (3) chamber over last chamber, 14′ × 11′; chamber towards north, 16′ × 9′; little room over street, 10′ × 6′; (4) garret towards west, 16′ × 15′.[31]

PW7
Over a gullet. No list of rooms or measurements found. PW7B had a hautpas in 1358.

PW8
Largely over a pier. Coal would have been winched up to the coal-hole.

1615 (Hugh Powell, citizen and haberdasher): cellar, 6′ × 5′; (G) shop, 21′ × 10′; (1) hall over part of shop towards Thames, 14′ × 10′; little room next to hall towards street,

Fig. 109 The principal west part in Norden's view from the west in 1600, showing the towers at the south end and those further north, as well as the alehouse between the principal and middle parts. The houses were not as regular at the back as they are shown here.

9′ square; (2) kitchen over hall, 14′ × 10′; chamber next to kitchen towards street, 9′ square; (3) chamber towards street, 11½′ × 9′; chamber over kitchen, 19′ × 10′; (4) garret towards Thames, 20′ × 10′; garret towards street, length with a coal-hole 14′, breadth 9′.[32]

PW9

Over a pier and a gullet. Repaired and enlarged in 1523.[33] The Pepys view shows the gallery or balcony. PW9B had a hautpas in 1358.

1631 (John Greene, citizen and haberdasher): cellar, 16′ × 12′; (G) shop, length 26′, breadth with entry and staircase 20′; counting house at west end of shop, 4½′ square; (1) hall over part of shop wainscoted throughout, 20′ × 13′; leaded gallery adjoining thereunto, 15′ × 5′; chamber over part of shop and bridge way, length 14′, breadth at north end 7′ and south end 14′; (2) kitchen paved with freestone, length 26′, breadth with chimney, staircase and waterhouse 9′; little chamber at end of kitchen, 9′ × 8½′; room adjoining kitchen wainscoted throughout, 18′ × 8½′; chamber at end of same, 10′ × 8½′; (3) chamber in third storey with chimneys, staircase and passage, 19′ square; two rooms at end of same, 19′ × 11′; (4) two garrets.[34]

PW10

Over a gullet. Built 1531–32. No list of rooms or measurements found.

PW11

Over a gullet. Built 1531–32. No list of rooms or measurements found.

PW12–13

PW12 was over a pier and PW13 over both pier and gullet. Built 1531–32. Described in the 1631 lease as two tenements now made into one, but evidently still two dwellings separately occupied. The position of 'Mr Newman' in the list of occupants in 1633 (Fig. 66) indicates that the first house was PW12 and the second PW13. On the ground floor, PW12 had the whole shop and PW13 only an entry. The descriptions are hard to interpret, but if the last-mentioned kitchen and chamber of PW12 were on the third floor, and one of the second-floor chambers of PW13 was within the footprint of PW12, the two houses were respectively about 11½′ wide by 40′ deep (possibly including a cross building) and 19′ wide by 30′ deep. However, this is difficult to reconcile with the Pepys view. Norden's view from the west shows two towers on the river side (Figs 45, 109), but these do not appear in the Pepys view. PW12 had a hautpas in 1358, not shared with the house opposite.

1631 (John Milton, citizen and scrivener): two houses now made into one:
(A) (late occupied by William Newnham, citizen and grocer): shop, 31½′ × 25′; cellar, 28′ × 10′; entry, 31′ × 3′; staircase, 10½′ × 6′; (1) hall over part of shop, 18½′ × 11½′; chamber over fore part of shop, wainscoted throughout, 15½′ × 11′; (2 & ?3) chamber with chimney over hall, wainscoted throughout, 18½′ × 11½′; kitchen with chimney, 19′ × 11½′; chamber behind kitchen, 21′ × 11½′.
(B) (late occupied by Edmund Phippes): other part of aforesaid cellar, 28′ × 9′; (G) entry with staircase, 28′ × 3′; (1) hall wainscoted throughout with passage, 19′ × 18′; two little butteries, 11½′ × 7′; chamber towards street, wainscoted, 19½′ × 12′; (2) kitchen with staircase and little buttery, 19′ × 17½′; chamber forward behind said kitchen, wainscoted throughout, 20′ × 12½′; chamber adjoining said chamber, 21′ × 11′; passage, 16′ × 7½′; (3) chamber over kitchen, 19′ × 11½′; chamber backward, 15′ × 9½′; one other chamber, 15′ × 9′; gallery

with a lead, 13′ × 9′; waterhouse, 5′ × 3′; little shed, 3′ square.[35]

PW14
Over a gullet. Built 1592. Had a hautpas in 1358, which the dimensions of Calverley's first-floor chamber suggest was 11½′ wide in the seventeenth century. See Fig. 55.

1631 (John Calverley, citizen and merchant taylor): (G) shop, 24′ × 8½′; counting house and house of office at end of same; (1) hall over part of said shop, 19′ × 9′; chamber at end of same eastward, 11½′ square; (2) chamber over that, 17′ × 9½′; kitchen on same floor, length 15′, breadth with chimney 7′; (3) two rooms and a lead over said kitchen and last-mentioned chamber; (4) garret over them.[36]

PW15
Over a pier and a gullet. Built 1592. No list of rooms or measurements found. It was twice as wide as PW14, and PW14 and 15 together were known as 'the red house'.[37]

PW16
Over a pier and a gullet. A storey with a garret was added in 1501.[38] The little room 'made into the shopp' was probably the structure with a gabled roof on the end of the pier in the Pepys view. PW16A had a hautpas in 1358.

1613 (John Earle, citizen and merchant taylor): cellar, 19′ × 15½′; (G) shop, 22½′ × 22′; little room 'which is made into the shopp' towards the west, 12½′ × 8′; (1) hall towards stairs over part of shop with chimney and entry, 22½′ × 11½′; chamber over other part of shop towards street, 13½′ × 11½′; room over other part of shop, 16′ × 11′; (2) chamber over hall towards Thames, length with stairs, chimney and entry 11½′, breadth 22½′ [*sic*]; (3) garret over last chamber towards Thames containing length and breadth of said chamber; (2) kitchen behind last room towards street with chimney and oven, 12′ square; little buttery behind kitchen, 12′ × 4′; chamber on south side of kitchen, 14′ × 11½′; (3) one garret over last chamber of same length and breadth.[39]

PW17
Largely over a gullet. Built 1526–29.

1612 (William Boorne, citizen and vintner): hanging cellar, 15½′ × 5½′; (G) shop, length 21½′, breadth with the stairs 19½′; (1) hall over part of shop towards Thames, length with chimney 19½′, breadth 12½′; chamber next to hall over other part of shop, length with chimney and entry 19½′, breadth 13′; (2) chamber over last chamber, length with staircase and chimney 19½′, breadth 14½′; kitchen over hall towards Thames, length with chimney and oven 19½′, breadth 12′; waterhouse 4′ × 3′; (3) chamber with little room next to it, length with staircase 19½′, breadth 13′; chamber next to Thames, length with chimney 19½′, breadth 14½′; (4) two garrets over all.[40]

PW18
Over a pier. Built 1526–29. Had a hautpas in 1358. In 1615 it had the whole of the first floor of the cross building and half of the second, and its garret extended over part of PE16; see Fig. 110.

1615 (William Hutchenson of Newport, Essex, mercer; occupied by Francis Arnold): cellar, 24′ × 14′; (G) shop, 30′9″ × 14′; (1) hall over part of shop towards Thames, 21′ × 15′; chamber over other part of shop towards street, length with staircase 24′, breadth 11′; (2) kitchen and buttery over part of hall towards Thames, 20′ × 15′; chamber behind kitchen towards street, 17′ × 15′; (3) one [*illegible*] divided into three rooms, 46′ × 15′.[41]

PW19
Largely over a gullet. Built 1526–29.

1613 (Thomas Champney, citizen and clothworker): hanging cellar, 13′ × 6′; another hanging cellar towards Thames, 13½′ × 5′; (G) shop, length with staircase 31½′, breadth 13½′; (1) hall over shop, 25′ × 13½′; little room behind hall, 6′ × 4½′; (2) kitchen over part of hall, length 13½′, breadth with waterhouse and chimney 12′; chamber behind kitchen over part of hall, 16′ × 13½′; chamber behind last chamber next to street, 6′ × 5′; (3) chamber over kitchen, 16′ × 13½′; chamber behind last

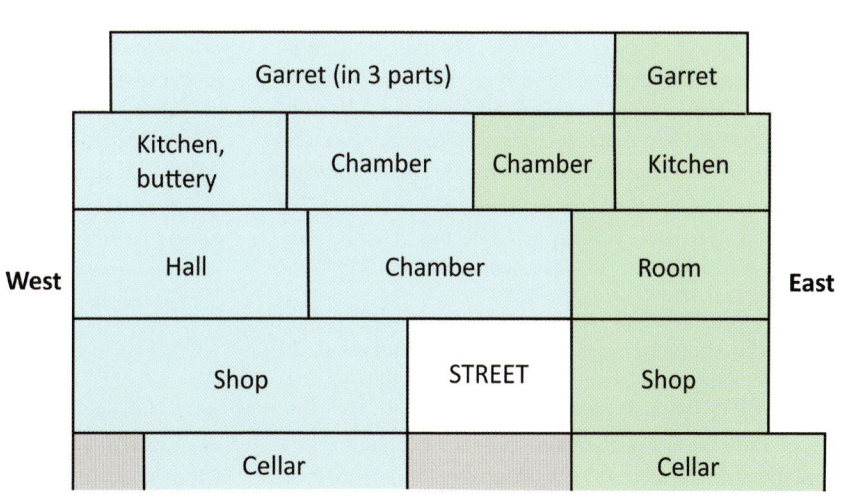

Fig. 110 Cross section of PE16 and PW18, based on leases of the 1610s, showing the unusual arrangement of the cross-building.

chamber towards street, 13½' × 13'; little buttery behind last chamber towards east, 8' × 5½'; (4) one garret over all last two chambers.[42]

PW20

Over a gullet. Built 1526–29. The description from 1630 omits the garrets.

1610 (Mary Langham, widow): cellar under shop, 12' × 6'; (G) shop, 21½' × 14'; little back room towards west behind shop, 14' × 10'; (1) hall over shop, east–west 26', breadth 14'; (2) kitchen and chamber over hall, 25' × 14'; (3) two chambers over kitchen and last chamber, together 26' × 14'; (4) one garret over all of length and breadth of last chambers.[43]

1630 (Jane Langham, widow): hanging cellar, 12' × 5'; one other cellar 12' × 4'; (G) shop, 20' × 14'; warehouse at end thereof, 10' × 6½'; (1) hall wainscoted throughout, 23½' × 16'9"; (2) chamber over part of hall wainscoted, 17' × 13'; kitchen at end of same chamber, 11' × 10'; (3) two chambers over aforesaid chamber and kitchen, together 27' × 14'.[44]

PW21

Largely over a pier. Built 1526–29. The plan seems to be: ground floor, 34' by about 20'; first, 28' by 22' (perhaps with a balcony or 'lead'); second, 32' by about 24'; third, 35' by 10' and garret 32' by about 10' (see Fig. 54). This indicates jettying southward, which the Pepys view confirms. This house and PE19 had towers flanking the roadway (Fig. 109). PW21B had a hautpas in 1358; this may have been transferred to PE19 in the rebuilding of 1526–29.

1615 (John Busbridge, citizen and skinner): cellar, 22' × 14½'; (G) shop, 19' × 17'; warehouse behind shop, 20' × 17'; (1) room or chamber over part of shop towards street, 22' × 13'; hall over back part of shop, 22' × 15'; (2) chamber over last chamber, 24½' × 13'; chamber over hall towards Thames, 19' × 9'; little closet in last chamber over Thames, 5' × 4'; kitchen over part of hall, 24' × 10'; (3) chamber over kitchen, 18' × 10'; one long garret divided into four rooms, two of them containing 10' apiece in length and 8' apiece in breadth, the other two containing 6' square; one other room towards Thames, 17' × 10'; one lead round about the house, 28' × 3'.[45]

Alehouse

Created in the eighth pier from the north as an alehouse in 1581. Ceased to be an alehouse in 1685.[46]

1653 (John Greene, citizen and haberdasher): cellar or vault heretofore used as an alehouse, containing 'one roome coming downe from ye streete', 20' × 7½'; one room with chimney behind said room towards Thames, 20' × 8'; one other little room or buttery, 8' × 6'.[47]

Middle east

See Fig. 111.

ME1

Largely over a gullet. Built 1539–41. The location of the cant window on the second floor indicates that the tower shown by Norden was beside the roadway rather than on the house's north-east corner, forming part of a pair of towers like those on the north side of the Square (see also MW1). It is not clear in Norden's view how this house was supported, but it may have been built on part of the Square, where the superstructure of the bridge was wider, and also benefited from the greater length of the chapel pier. Six hearths in 1666.

1654 (Michael Webb, citizen and mercer): (G) shop, east–west 25', breadth on street side with staircase 19'4"; cellar on same floor [*sic*], length 11', breadth with bulk of stairs 8'; (1) hall over shop besides chimney and 'cant window', north–south 13', breadth being wainscoted 13'; parlour on north end of shop besides closet wainscoted, north–south 14'; little room on south side of parlour besides a house of office on south-east corner, 14' × 7'; leads on north side of parlour, east–west 10', breadth 5'; (2) two chambers on a floor over hall and part of Mr John Green's house [MW1], together east–west 26', breadth besides the 'cannt window' and chimney 14'; kitchen north–south with the entry besides chimney 14'; waterhouse on south-east corner, 6'6" × 5'; (3) three other chambers over last two chambers and kitchen of same length and breadth; leads on north side, east–west 32'6", breadth 5'.[48]

1683: Front 20'7"; depth 24'8"; cross building 26'8" wide.

ME2

The chapel house. Over a pier. Upper parts built 1553. In the late eighteenth or early nineteenth century the cellar was said to be 65' (including 3' under the street) by 20'6", and 14' high.[49] Six hearths in 1666, but this may be an incomplete record; in lists of c. 1670 there were two houses, one with five hearths and one with three.[50] See Figs 26–29.

1627 (Robert Osbolston, citizen and haberdasher; late occupied by Henry Bury, citizen and salter): shop, length 36', breadth with entry 24'; warehouse backward, 24' square; counting house of deal in warehouse; 'a great large cellar', 64' × 24'; warehouse under part of cellar, 19' square; (1) entry leading into hall, 12' square; hall, 30' × 23'; two little counting houses on south side of hall; little parlour, 13' × 10'; dark parlour towards street, 14' × 13'; little counting house in parlour; kitchen, 22' × 11'; little buttery, 9' × 8'; coal-house, 7' square; (2) gallery leading into fair chamber over hall, 39' × 11'; chamber towards street, 21' × 12'; chamber on left side of gallery, 18' × 16'; little room adjoining said chamber, 12' × 8'; fair chamber over hall, 23' × 22'; counting house in same; chamber adjoining to that, 14' × 12'; little closet in said chamber; (3) five chambers with an

SURVEY OF LONDON BRIDGE'S HOUSES, 1604–83　151

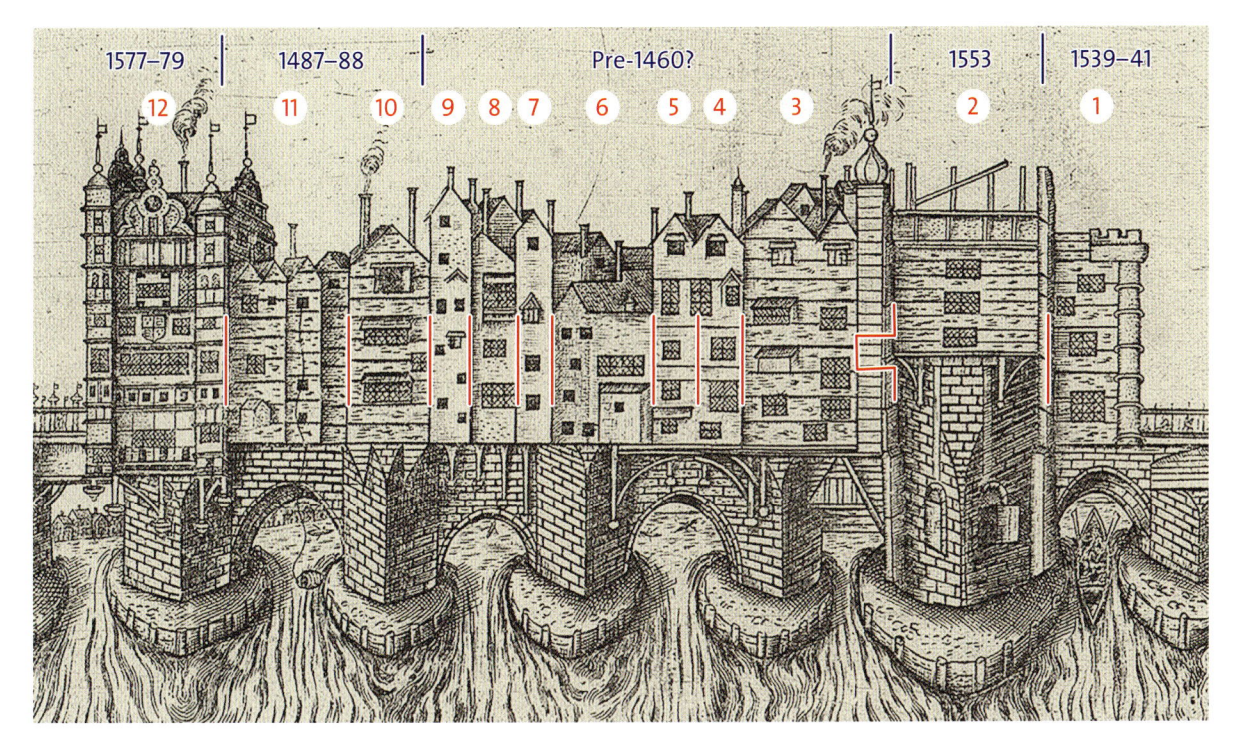

Fig. 111 The middle east part in Norden's view of 1597–98, with house numbers and dates of building added. ME2's staircase projected in front of ME3. The dividing line between ME4 and 5 as indicated by the measurements of 1683 cuts across one of the windows in the view. The most serious inaccuracy in the view is the shape of ME2 and the widths of ME2 and 3.

entry over aforesaid gallery and rooms, 70′ × 19′; large lead over all, 76′ × 24′.[51]

The schedule to the lease of 1627 refers to a false floor in the further part of the lower cellar at the east end on the north side, 26′ × 8½′; 'the great hall with the settles benches and skreene there'; and the chamber over the hall with windows north and south and chimney west.

1653 (Robert Osbolston, citizen and haberdasher): three cellars, east–west 65′, breadth 25′; (G) shop all over said cellars of same length and breadth; (1) hall partly wainscoted, kitchen, two chambers and passage room all on a floor over shop of same length and breadth besides jetties; (2) seven rooms over them of same length and breadth besides jetties; (3) six rooms over them of same length and breadth, with a large lead over all the rooms of same length and breadth.[52]

1683: Front 27′10½″.

1686 (after setting back of front): front north–south from out to out 28′ feet, depth east–west from out to out 65′9″ on ground floor.[53]

ME3

Over piers and a gullet. Under a lease of 1597 Thomas Greene was to add a storey.[54] The ground floor ended on the north side at the stone wall of ME2, but the upper storeys extended 14″ over that wall.[55] Usually consisted of two houses, at least from the 1670s. Six hearths in 1666, but that may have been only one of two houses.

1653 (Gabriel Partridge, citizen and cutler): cellar, 'beinge tryangular in the stone peere', north–south 20′, breadth 12′; one great hanging cellar eastward, north–south 28′, breadth 10′; one other hanging cellar, north–south 23′, breadth 4′3″; (G) shop, east–west 30′7″, breadth 19′9″; one other shop on north side of said shop, east–west 26′6″ besides counting house eastward, breadth 23′ with staircase; (1) hall partly wainscoted partly over said north-side shop and partly over street, north–south 22′, breadth 18′; little buttery adjoining south end of hall, 8′ square; parlour wainscoted throughout behind hall towards Thames, east–west 19′8″, north–south 13′ besides chimney on south side and buttery on north side; chamber wainscoted throughout on south side of parlour, east–west 19′ besides the little dining room, house of office and counting house all towards Thames, breadth 17′6″ with the staircase; chamber wainscoted throughout on south-west corner of last-mentioned chamber, east–west 12′6″, breadth 10′6″; (2) chamber over hall of same length and breadth; entry and larder at south end of last chamber; chamber on same floor over parlour of same length and breadth besides a little buttery northward and the staircase; kitchen paved on south side of last-mentioned chamber, north–south 18′ with staircase and passage room, breadth 17′ besides the chimney, waterhouse, leads and house of office; (3) two garret chambers, one low garret, passage room, counting house, chamber and another kitchen in fourth storey; (4) large garret over last-mentioned passage room, counting house, chamber and kitchen.[56]

1683: Front 43′; depth 30′2″; cross building 24′6″ wide.

ME4

Over a pier and a gullet. In 1593 the tenant, James Lusher, was ordered to show what right he had to a cellar under an adjoining house,[57] and the tenants in 1622–53 evidently had a hanging cellar under ME5. Three hearths in 1666.

1622 (William Rudd, citizen and girdler, late occupied by James Lusher, citizen and haberdasher): hanging cellar, 21′ × 5′; (G) shop, 20′ × 11′; little counting house, 4′ square; (1) hall, length 24′, width with staircase 10′4″; (2) kitchen over part of hall, 19′4″ × 10′4″; chamber over other part of hall, 6½′ × 10′4″; (3) chamber over last chamber of same length and breadth; chamber over kitchen, 13′ × 10½′; waterhouse, 4′ square; (4) two garrets over all, 24′10″ × 10′4″.[58]

1653 (Simon Leeson, citizen and barber chirurgeon; occupied by John Wilding, citizen and haberdasher): hanging cellar, north–south 20′, breadth 5′; (G) shop over cellar, east–west 21½′, breadth 10′8″; little counting house at east end; (1) hall wainscoted over shop, east–west 25′, breadth 10′8″; (2) kitchen and little chamber on a floor over hall of same length and breadth; (3) two chambers over kitchen and chamber of same length and breadth; (4) two garrets over them of same length and breadth.[59]

1683: Front 10′10″; depth 22′4″.

ME5

Over a gullet. As in 1358, this house had the whole of a cross building instead of sharing it with the opposite house. Three hearths in 1666. See Fig. 53.

1653 (Thomas Rucke, citizen and girdler): (G) shop, east–west 21½′, breadth 10′9″; (1) hall wainscoted throughout over shop, east–west 25′4″, breadth with chimney and staircase 10′9″; room wainscoted throughout adjoining on same floor, north–south 12′9″, breadth 9′10″; (2) buttery, kitchen and little garret all on a floor over hall and room, of same length and breadth with the staircase; (3) two chambers over buttery and kitchen, east–west 27′, breadth 10′9″; (4) two garrets over them.[60]

1683: Front 10′10″; depth 21′6″; cross building 13′ wide.

ME6

Over a pier and a gullet. To be rebuilt with four storeys under the lease of 1649, so the description of 1653 is of the new house. Seven hearths in 1666.

1649 (Abraham Gardiner, citizen and fishmonger): platform, east–west 24½′, north–south 20½′.[61]

1653 (Abraham Gardiner, citizen and fishmonger): cellar, north–south 18′10″ besides coal-hole northward, breadth 14′8″; (G) shop over cellar, east–west 24′7″ besides counting house on south-east end, breadth with staircase and entry 20′3″; (1) chamber and kitchen on a floor over shop, together east–west 27′7″ besides a leaded gallery and two little counting houses on each end thereof, breadth with staircase and chimneys 20′3″; (2) chamber and hall over chamber and kitchen, together east–west 28′7″ besides two counting houses eastward, breadth 20′3″; (3) two chambers on a floor over them, east–west 29′ besides two counting houses eastward, breadth 20′3″; (4) garret chamber over them of same length and breadth.[62]

1683: Front 20′4″; depth 25′2″.

ME7

Over a pier and a gullet. Under a lease of 1593 Miles Troughton was to enlarge the property, spending £20. Three hearths in 1666. See Figs 12, 51.

1649 (Lawrence Warkman, citizen and vintner; occupied by Daniel Stockwell, citizen and haberdasher): cellar, 10′ × 2½′; (G) shop, 18′ × 10′; (1) hall over shop wainscoted, 20′ × 10′; little room on same floor over street, 10½′ × 7′; (2) kitchen, 17′ × 9′; room over street, 10′ × 9′; (3) chamber over kitchen, 20′ × 9′; chamber over room which is over street, 9½′ × 7′; (4) little low garret.[63]

1683: Front 11′ (rear 10′10″);[64] depth 21′; cross building 11′4″ wide.

ME8

Over a gullet. The upper storeys appear to have been described out of order.[65] Two hearths in 1666.

1631 (John Lardine, citizen and barber chirurgeon): hanging cellar, 10′ × 5′; (G) shop, 19½′ × 10′; (1) chamber over shop, 17′ × 10′; (3?) chamber in third storey, length 19′, breadth with chimney 9′; (2?) kitchen paved with freestone and chamber at west end of same.[66]

1683: Front 10′5″; depth 15′.

ME9

Over a gullet. Three hearths in 1666. See Fig. 52.

1632 (Roger Daniel, citizen and leatherseller): (G) shop, 15′ × 10½′; (1) hall wainscoted over shop, 15′ × 10½′; little room on same floor over street, 10½′ × 7′; (2) kitchen over hall, 15′ × 10½′; chamber on same floor, 10½′ × 8′; (3) chamber over kitchen, 20′ × 10½′; (4) little low garret over it.[67]

1653 (Alice Powell, widow): hanging cellar, 13′9″ × 5′; (G) shop, east–west 15′, breadth 10′9″; (1) hall wainscoted partly over shop and partly over street, east–west 22′, breadth 10′9″; (2) kitchen and chamber over hall, together of same length and breadth besides a little waterhouse eastward; (3) chamber over said kitchen and chamber of same length and breadth; (4) garret over that.[68]

1683: Front 10′8½″; depth 15′; cross building 10′9″ wide.

ME10

Over a pier. Built 1487–88. The two descriptions show that a storey was added between 1616 and 1653. There is no obvious explanation for the second chamber on the second floor in 1616. The cross building recorded in 1683 in fact belonged to ME11. Four hearths in 1666.

1616 (Susan Maye, widow; late occupied by Zelderhaes Wood): cellar, north–south 15′, east–west 12′; (G) shop with an entry, north–south 19½′, east–west 19′; (1) hall over shop eastward, north–south 20′, east–west 11′; room westward over shop, 19′ × 10½′; (2) chamber over last room, 19½′ × 11½′; kitchen with little buttery over hall, 19½′ × 11′; chamber towards street, 19½′ × 11′; (3) two little garrets over all, north–south 19½′, east–west 24′.[69]

1653 (Thomas Hall, citizen and mercer): cellar, 18′ × 13′; (G) shop over cellar, 19′3″ square; (1) hall wainscoted and buttery over shop of same length and breadth besides jetties; (2) kitchen, chamber and waterhouse over hall and buttery of same length and breadth besides jetties; (3) two chambers over them of same length and breadth; (4) one garret over them.[70]

1683: Front 19′2″; depth 19′6″; cross building 12′2″ wide [actually belonged to ME11].

ME11

Largely over a gullet. Built 1487–88. The cross building recorded in 1683 at ME10 in fact belonged to this house, and was apparently 14½ feet long. Four hearths in 1666.

1623 (William Nethersoll, citizen and cutler): (G) shop, 27′ × 14′, with a little closet 4′ square; (1) hall over part of shop, 16′ × 11′; buttery over passage there, 13′ × 5′; chamber over other part of shop, 21′ × 14′; (2) chamber over hall and passage, 22′ × 12′, with a little house of office there 5′ square; kitchen behind chamber last aforesaid, 20′ × 14′, with a little waterhouse there 3′ square; (3) two little garrets over all, 25′ × 17′.[71]

1657 (Alice Nethersoll, widow): hanging cellar; (G) shop next to street, from out to out with entry and staircase 27′3″, breadth 21′; (1) hall and parlour on a floor over shop and entry containing same length and breadth; little room near adjoining [over street in 1639 lease], 14½′ × 5′; (2) chamber and kitchen on a floor over hall and parlour of same length and breadth; little room adjoining there [over room over street in 1639 lease], 14½′ × 5′; leads with staircase, 14½′ × 6′; (3) two garrets over chamber and kitchen of same length and breadth.[72]

1683: Front 27′5″; depth 21′3″ [see ME 10 for cross building].

ME12

Eastern part of Nonsuch House. Over a pier. Built 1577–79. By 1647 the Williamots had converted a first-floor room next to the hall into a kitchen (in addition to 'the greate kitchen'), and were ordered to convert it back 'to its first condicion or otherwise to take up the pavement thereof'.[73] Six hearths in 1666. See Figs 47–50.

1642 (Susan Williamot of Chester and Samuel Williamot, citizen and mercer of London; occupied by Samuel Browne, citizen and cutler): cellar, 23′ × 18′; (G) shop, 31′ × 25′; little counting house adjoining shop, 5½′; (1) washhouse over street, 12′ × 7′; chamber on same floor over street of same length and breadth; hall over shop, 19′ × 13′ besides chimney and staircase; parlour on same floor, length 22′, breadth besides two studies adjoining 16½′; (2) two chambers over washhouse and chamber over street of same length and breadth; chamber over hall of same length and breadth; kitchen and chamber over parlour, besides the waterhouse and closet, together of same length and breadth as parlour; (3) two chambers over the two chambers over street of same length and breadth; three garrets, buttery and two closets over said chambers; (4) leads over said garrets 31′ × 12′ besides two turrets; garret over street, 14′ × 7′.[74]

1683: Front 25′6″; depth 32′2″; cross building 25′6″ wide.

Middle west

See Fig. 112.

MW1

Largely over a gullet. Built 1539–41. See the Pepys view for the 'nooke' of 1653. The schedule to the 1653 lease refers to a parlour on the second floor. The position of the compass windows on the second and third floors indicates that the tower on the north side was next to the roadway (see also ME1). By 1678 there was a little shop on the north side of this house,[75] and this seems to have been the little chamber north-west of the shop, with a garret chamber over, in 1653, evidently added between 1639 and 1653. Under a sub-lease of 1678 Thomas Passinger was to build 'a roome upon the upper leades'.[76] Six hearths in 1666.

1639 (John Greene, citizen and haberdasher): cellar, 13′ × 5′; (G) shop, 24′ × 21½′; (1) chamber wainscoted towards street and over part of shop, 14′ × 10′; hall towards Thames and over other part of shop, 18′ square; leaded gallery westward 11′ × 7′; (2) chamber over chamber before mentioned, 14′ × 9′; little chamber behind same, 10′ × 6′; kitchen over hall, 18′ × 9′; little washhouse behind said kitchen, 9′ × 8′; (3) chamber wainscoted, 19′ × 9′; room over kitchen westward, 18′ × 10′; (?4) chamber, 14′ × 12′; lead northward, 24′ × 6′.[77]

1653 (John Greene, citizen and haberdasher): cellar, north–south 18′, breadth 5′ besides a coal-hole; (G) shop, east–west 25′, breadth with entry and staircase at east end 21′9″ and west end 21′2″, 'with a nooke at ye south west corner thereof under part of Mr Clarks howse' [MW2]; little chamber on north-west side of shop, north–south 13′3″, breadth with bulk of staircase 12′2″; (1) chamber wainscoted partly over street and partly over shop, north–south 15′4″, breadth 10′5″; hall wainscoted on same floor over other part of shop towards Thames, 18′ square besides staircase and window; leaded gallery

154 LONDON BRIDGE AND ITS HOUSES, c. 1209–1761

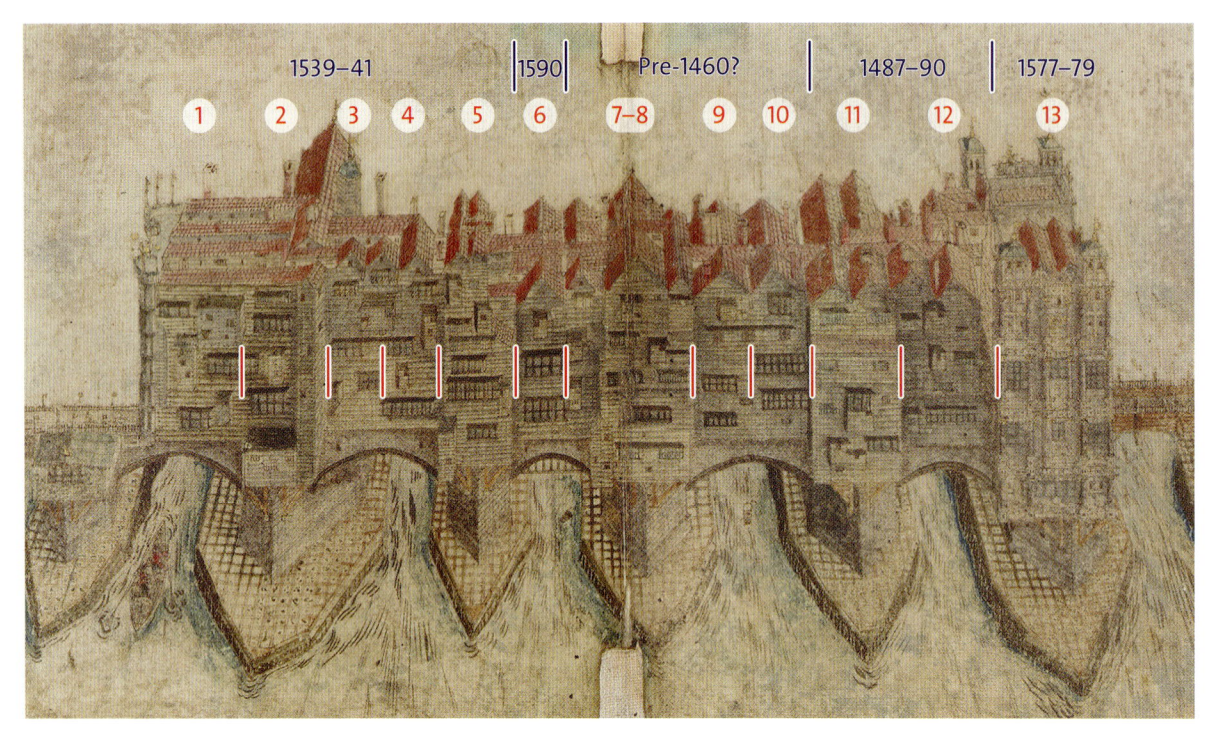

Fig. 112 The middle west part in the Pepys view, with house numbers and dates of building added.

westward 11′ × 7′; garret chamber over first-mentioned chamber of same length and breadth; (2) chamber and little room adjoining both over street chamber, together north–south 21′ besides the compass window, breadth 10′; kitchen on same floor over hall, north–south 19′ besides staircase, breadth 10′ besides waterhouse; (3) chamber over kitchen, east–west 14′10″, breadth at west end 13′4″ besides staircase, and east end 11′9″; little chamber on same floor, length 12′9″, breadth 7′9″ besides the compass window; (4) garret chamber and two roofs and two gutters over them, a lead northward, east–west 24′8″, breadth 9′.[78]

1683: Front 23′9″; depth 25′2″; cross building 26′8″ wide [shared with MW2].

MW2

Over a pier. Built 1539–41. The Pepys view shows a protruding tower, which can also be seen in Norden's view from the west (Fig. 109). Six hearths in 1666.

1639 (Edmund Clarke, citizen and clothworker): cellar, 18′ × 8′; (G) shop, 24′ × 18′; (1) chamber over street behind hall, 13½′ × 10′; hall over shop westward, 18′ × 17½′; (2) chamber over chamber which is over street, 13′ × 11½′; chamber over part of hall, 14′ × 10′; kitchen over other part of hall with the entry, 16′ × 10′; waterhouse, 5′ square; (3) chamber over last-mentioned chamber and kitchen with the entry, 15′ [?] × 18′; chamber, 13′ × 11′.[79]

1653 (Edmund Clarke, citizen and clothworker): cellar, north–south from out to out 25′, breadth 8′; (G) shop over cellar, east–west 25′, breadth 18′ with entry and staircase; (1) hall wainscoted throughout over shop, with a pair of leads and staircase westwards, together of same length and breadth; chamber on same floor eastward over street, east–west 13½′, breadth 11′; (2) chamber and kitchen on a floor over hall, together east–west 21′ besides staircase and waterhouse, breadth 18′; chamber on same floor over said chamber which is over street, of same length and breadth; (3) two chambers over said kitchen and two chambers, together of same length and breadth; (4) one garret.[80]

1683: Front 18′1½″; depth 24′3″; cross building [see MW1].

MW3

Over a pier and a gullet. Built 1539–41. Had a gable on the east side in 1667.[81] Three hearths in 1666.

1631 (Anthony Scaltike, citizen and fishmonger): hanging cellar, 11′ × 5′; (G) shop with staircase, 15′ × 12′; counting house at end of same, 5½′ square; (1) hall wainscoted throughout, 15′ × 12′; (2) kitchen paved with freestone over part of hall, 9′ × 7½′; buttery at north-west part thereof paved in like manner; chamber over other part of hall and staircase, 15′ × 9′; (3) two chambers over last-mentioned chamber and kitchen; (4) one little garret.[82]

1653 (Abraham Gardiner, citizen and fishmonger; occupied by Anne Scaltcke, widow): hanging cellar, 11′ × 5′; (G) shop with staircase over cellar, 15′ × 12′; counting house at the end of it, 5½′ square; (1) hall wainscoted throughout over shop, with the staircase 15′ × 12′; (2) chamber, kitchen and buttery all on a floor over hall, together of same length and breadth besides jetties; (3) two chambers and one closet on a floor over said chamber, kitchen and buttery, together of same length and breadth; (4) one garret over them; reserved out of the lease to Anne Scalticke the two last mentioned chambers and one closet on a floor, which rooms she now dwells in and is to enjoy for life rent-free.[83]

1683: Front 15′8″; depth 14′6″.

MW4
Largely over a gullet. Built 1539–41. The lease descriptions suggest it did not share in the cross building attached to ME3, though the descriptions for ME3 and MW5 seem not to account for the whole cross building. The 1653 lease omits the garret. Apparently enlarged backwards by 1683. Three hearths in 1666.

1612 (Jeremy Smith, citizen and haberdasher): cellar, 9′ × 4½′; (1) shop, towards street 15′ × 12′; (1) hall over shop, length 16′, breadth 15′ with stairs and chimney; (2) kitchen over part of hall, 15′ × 9′; chamber next to kitchen, 15′ × 8½′; (3) two rooms over kitchen and last chamber, 17½′ × 15′; (4) 'a nooke rome' over last two rooms.[84]

1633 (Richard Wildeinge, citizen and girdler): (G) shop, 14½′ square; (1) hall over shop wainscoted throughout, length 16′, breadth with chimney 15′; (2) kitchen, 10′ × 9′; chamber adjoining kitchen, 12′ × 8½′; (3) chamber over kitchen and last-mentioned chamber, 20′ × 16½′; (4) garret over same.[85]

1653 (Abraham Gardiner, citizen and fishmonger; occupied by Edward Smith, haberdasher): cellar, 9′ × 5′; (G) shop, north–south 15½′, breadth 14′ besides staircase; (1) hall wainscoted over shop of same length and breadth; (2) kitchen and little chamber on a floor over hall, of same length and breadth; (3) chamber with partition in it over kitchen and chamber, of same length and breadth.[86]

1683: Front 15′7″; depth 21′.

MW5
Over a pier. Built 1539–41. There is no obvious explanation for the discrepancies in the dimensions in the two descriptions.

1652 (Lawrence Warkman, citizen and vintner): cellar, north–south 'within the biggnes of a piere' 20′, breadth 10½′; (G) shop, east–west with counting house and staircase 27½′, breadth 20′; (1) hall wainscoted, length 20′, breadth at south end 10′10″, at north end 6′; leads with counting house and house of office, together 20′ × 5½′; (2) kitchen with rooms eastward, 26′ × 19′, with a buttery; waterhouse, 7′ × 4′; (3) chamber wainscoted over part of said rooms, length with chimney 20′, breadth 12′; chamber on same floor, 20′ × 10′; a lead on same floor; (4) two garrets over same rooms.[87]

1653 (Lawrence Warkman, citizen and vintner): cellar, north–south from out to out 20′, breadth 15′; (G) shop over cellar, east–west with counting house and staircase 25′, breadth 20′ with the entry, staircase and part of counting house; (1) hall wainscoted throughout over shop, north–south 20′, breadth 15′; leads with counting house, house of office and part of staircase on west side of hall, together 20′ × 5′; two little warehouses on east side of hall, together north–south 20′, breadth 6′ besides little room eastward over street, 10′7″ × 4′8″; (2) kitchen, buttery and two chambers over hall and warehouses of same length and breadth besides waterhouse and staircase; (3) chamber wainscoted throughout and one other chamber on same floor over them of same length and breadth besides leads and staircase; (4) two garrets over them.[88]

1683: Front 20′; depth 24′9″; cross building 24′6″ wide [shared with MW4?].

MW6
Largely over a gullet. Built 1590. Had a gable next to the street in 1659, which was to be plastered.[89] Three hearths in 1666.

1656 (Joyce Midmore, widow): hanging cellar, 8′4″ by 5′3″; (G) shop, length 18′9″, breadth 10′3″ besides staircase and counting house; (1) hall over shop wainscoted throughout with settles, 20′ × 10′3″; (2) kitchen over part of hall, length 13½′ besides waterhouse and staircase, breadth 10′ with chimney; chamber at east end of same, 10′ square; (3) chamber over same wainscoted throughout, 23′ × 10′; (4) garret over same.[90]

1683: Front 10′7″; depth 19′8″.

MW7–8
MW7 over a gullet, MW8 over a pier. Three houses from 1358 to 1523, when the central one was divided between the other two; the remaining two were under the same ownership from 1531 and were at some stage merged. Part of the ground floor was a separate shop from 1613 to 1625 (let to William Turpin), and so was not included in the lease of 1613, though the later leases do include it.[91] MW7 adjoined a cross building but had no share of it, which may explain why it had a 'darke chamber' and a 'voyd rome'. The combined premises were to be rebuilt with 3½ storeys under the lease of 1655. The new houses had six hearths and five hearths in 1666.

1613 (Thomas Rucke, citizen and scrivener): hanging cellar, 26′ × 6′; (G) shop, length with entry 20′, breadth 12½′; counting house behind shop, 7′ × 5½′; (1) hall over part of shop, length with entry leading into other rooms 15′, breadth 12′; chamber over other part of shop, 20′ × 15′; little dark chamber behind hall towards street, 15′ × 9′; (2) kitchen over hall, 13′ × 9′; little void room towards north, 9′ × 8′; chamber behind kitchen towards street, 15′ × 9′; chamber towards north, 19′ × 15′; (3) three little rooms over kitchen and two chambers; reserved out of the lease to William Turpin, the stool of office in the hanging cellar and access to it.[92]

1633 (George Hunte, citizen and grocer): cellar, 14′ × 7′; (G) shop, length with entry 30′, breadth 17′; little wainscoted room towards Thames, length 13′, breadth besides chimney 10½′; (1) wainscoted room over shop, length 19′ with chimney, breadth 13′; room adjoining on same floor, 15′ × 12½′; (?2) kitchen, length with waterhouse 15′, breadth 9½′; room adjoining kitchen, 10′ × 9½′; room towards street on same floor, 15′ × 11′; chamber adjoining, length 19′, breadth 12½′ with chimney and house of office; (3) two garrets, 24′ × 14′9″.[93]

1655 (William Latham, citizen and draper; occupied by Thomas Kidder): cellar, 15′ × 8′; (G) two shops partly over cellar, north–south towards street 31′, breadth 17′ besides staircase and counting houses westward; (1) several rooms over said shop and counting house of same length and breadth; (2) several rooms over them of same length and breadth; (3) garrets over them.[94]

1683: Front 30′8″; depth 19′1″ and 25′.

MW9
Over a pier and a gullet. Probably two households with two hearths and one hearth in 1666. See Figs. 12, 51.

1631 (Rowland Witherall, citizen and clothworker): cellar, 8′ × 7′; (G) shop with staircase, 15½′ square; (1) hall with wainscot press at north-west end being in part wainscoted, 14′ × 12′; room at end of same, 11′ × 8′; (2) kitchen paved with freestone in third storey, 20′ × 7½′; chamber at end of same, 9½′ square; (3) two garrets.[95]

1653 (Martha Charlton, widow): cellar, 9′ × 7½′; (G) shop, north–south from out to out 15′10″, breadth 15½′ besides a little counting house westward; (1) hall wainscoted partly over shop and partly over street, east–west 23′9″, breadth at west end 14′8″ and at east end 11′; (2) kitchen paved with freestone in third storey, length 20′, breadth 7½′ besides staircase; chamber at east end thereof, north–south 11′, breadth 9′; (3) two garrets over them.[96]

1683: Front 16′1″; depth 17′10″; cross building 11′4″ wide.

MW10
Over a gullet. Under the lease of 1640 Sarah Gardner was to add a storey. A 'new substantiall joyst' had to be added to support the kitchen partition in 1667.[97] Four hearths in 1666. See Fig. 17.

1640 (Sarah Gardner, widow; occupied by Raphe Harrison, citizen and cordwainer): (G) shop, 16′ square; (1) hall over shop, east–west 24′, breadth 18′; (2) three little garrets over hall, 20′ square.[98]

1659 (Ralph Harrison, citizen and cordwainer): (G) shop, east–west 16′9″, breadth with staircase and counting house 15′6″; (1) hall wainscoted over shop of same length and breadth besides jetty westward and jetty eastward over street, which contains in breadth 5′ besides the staircase; (2) two chambers and kitchen as they were then divided [*sic*] with staircase of same length besides waterhouse, breadth 20′6″; (3) garret chamber of same length and breadth; (4) cockloft over same.[99]

1683: Front 15′6″; depth 16′6″; cross building 10′9″ wide.

MW11
Over a pier. Built 1489–90. A post had to be added in the hall to support the kitchen partition in 1656.[100] Four hearths in 1666.

1655 (Richard English, citizen and merchant taylor; occupied by James Dunkyn): cellar 16½′ × 10′; (G) shop, 21′ × 19′3″; (1) hall wainscoted throughout and buttery over shop, length 22′, breadth 19′ with staircase and chimney; (2) kitchen paved with freestone and two chambers over hall and buttery; buttery on south side of said kitchen, 9½′ × 3′3″; (3) over kitchen, two low garrets, a chamber adjoining and (4) a garret over same.[101]

1683: Front 19′6″; depth 21′.

MW12
Largely over a gullet. Built 1489–90. Five hearths and two hearths in 1666 (four and three hearths in 1674).[102]

1653 (Francis Finch, citizen and clothworker): hanging cellar, north–south 20′6″, breadth 3′; (G) two shops, together north–south with staircase 27′, breadth 15′3″ besides staircase; (1) hall and parlour wainscoted throughout over shops, length together 27′, breadth 17′6″; buttery at east end of parlour over street, 14½′ × 6′; (2) kitchen and chamber on a floor over hall and parlour, 27′ × 17′6″; little chamber over buttery; (3) two chambers and kitchen over them of same length and breadth; (4) two garrets over them of same length and breadth.[103]

1683: Front 27′5″; depth 16′; cross building 12′2″ wide.

MW13
Western part of Nonsuch House. Over a pier. Built 1577–79. Eight hearths in 1666. See Figs 47–50.

1653 (Jane Weedon, widow): cellar, east–west within the walls 25′, north–south 17½′; (G) shop over cellar, east–west 31′9″, 25′ on street side; (1) two halls on a floor wainscoted over shop, of same length besides staircase and jetties and of same breadth, with one other staircase and chimneys; two chambers on same floor over street, together north–south besides gallery over drawbridge 25′; (2) two chambers wainscoted, kitchen and two other chambers all on a floor over halls and street chambers of same length and breadth; (3) three garret chambers, kitchen and two other chambers all on a floor over them, of same length and breadth; (4) one garret with leads and turrets.[104]

1683: Front 25′6″; depth 32′2″; cross building 25′6″ wide.

SURVEY OF LONDON BRIDGE'S HOUSES, 1604–83

South-east

See Figs 113–15.

SE1

Largely over a pier. Built 1495–96. The Pepys view shows a shallow bow, presumably consisting of windows, in the north facade. Five hearths in c. 1665.

1639 (Philip Tilles, citizen and clothworker): cellar, east–west 20′, breadth at west end 15′; (G) shop, length 30′, breadth besides part of staircase 18½′; (1) hall wainscoted over east part of shop, length 18′, breadth besides chimney 14′; leads and little room, together 18′ × 6′; little buttery at end of chimney, 5′ square; parlour wainscoted over street, 19′ × 14′; (2) kitchen, 19½′ × 14′; waterhouse, 7′ × 5½′; buttery over said buttery of same length and breadth; chamber over parlour of same length and breadth; (3) four garrets over said kitchen and chamber besides the narrow leads on north side.[105]

1683: Front 21′11″; depth 30′9″; cross building 18′7″ wide.

SE2

Largely over a gullet. Probably built 1507–08; first appears in the rental in 1510. It was described in 1687 as having been before its recent demolition 'a good part thereof but lately new built', which is otherwise undocumented.[106] Six hearths in c. 1665.

1608 (Henry Woodfall, citizen and haberdasher): cellar, 18′ × 9′; (1) shop, east–west with counting house and pair of stairs 24′, breadth 12′; (1) hall over shop, east–west 20′, breadth 12′ with chimney and buttery towards Thames eastward; 'one windowe of glasse', 3′ × 5½′; (2) kitchen over part of hall towards east, 12′ × 8′; chamber over other part of hall towards street and adjoining kitchen, 13′ × 12′; (3) two garrets, one over chamber and other over kitchen.[107]

1649 (Anne Woodfall, widow, and Henry Phillips, citizen and haberdasher): hanging cellar, 20′ × 9′; (G) shop over same, east–west 25′, breadth 12′; house of office at end of shop, 4′ × 3½′; (1) hall over shop wainscoted throughout, 23′ × 12′; house of office, 5½′ × 3½′; (2) kitchen and chamber over hall of same length and breadth, which chamber is wainscoted throughout; (3) two garret chambers.[108]

1683: Front 12′5″; depth 25′6″.

SE3

Over a gullet. Probably built 1507–08; first appears in the rental in 1510. Under a lease of 1631, Robert Osbolston was required to enlarge the house towards the Thames;[109] hence the increased depth of the shop in 1653. In 1684 the first-floor jetty projected 1′6″ towards the street and was 9′10″ up from roadway level.[110] Four hearths in c. 1665.

1618 (Joseph Negoose, citizen and draper): (G) shop, east–west 20′, breadth 12′; (1) hall over part of shop towards Thames eastward, 12′ square; chamber next to hall over other part of shop, north–south 12′, breadth 8′; (2) chamber over said chamber towards street, north–south 12′, length 13′; kitchen over hall, north–south 12′, breadth 10′; (3) garret over all, 24′ × 12′.[111]

1653 (William Walcott and Edmond Walcott, citizens and haberdashers): (G) shop, east–west 25′, breadth 12′;

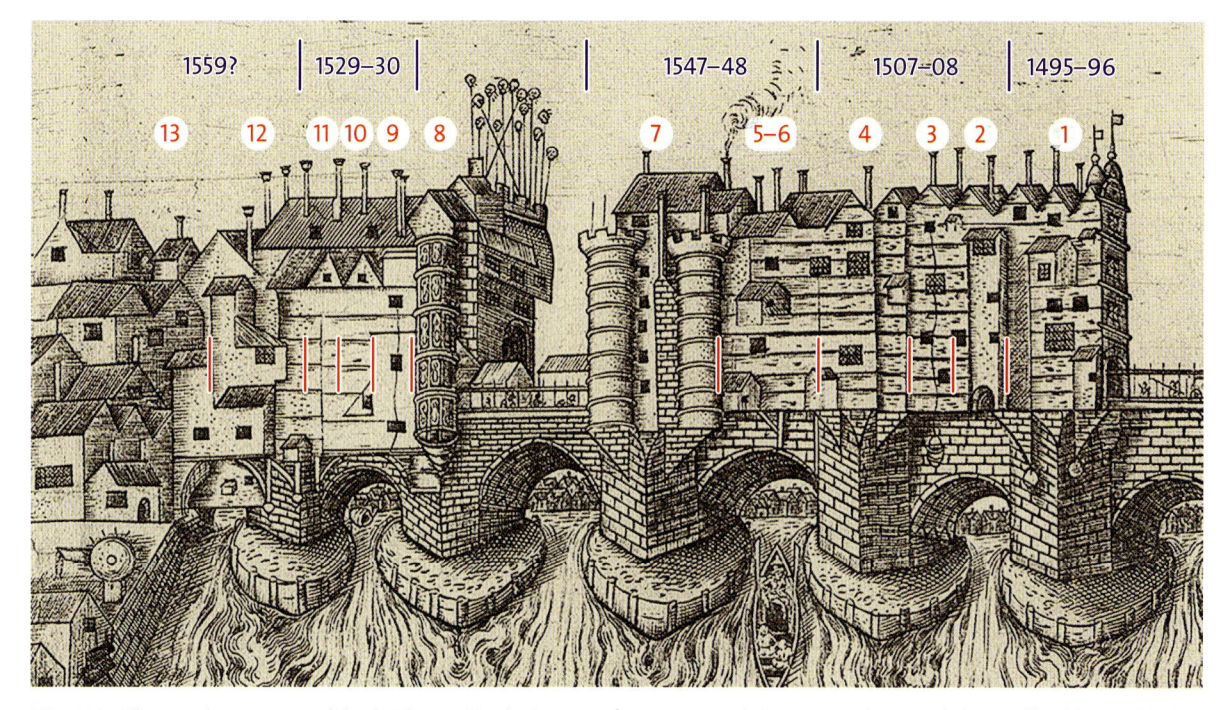

Fig. 113 The south-east part of the bridge in Norden's view of 1597–98, with house numbers and dates of building added. Norden makes SE7 too wide, at the expense of SE5–6.

(1) hall wainscoted throughout over shop of same length and breadth with staircase and presses besides jetties; (2) kitchen paved with freestone and chamber over hall of same length and breadth besides jetties; (3) two garrets over them of same length and breadth.[112]

1683: Front 12′1″; depth 25′6″.

SE4

Over a pier. Probably built 1507–08; first appears in the rental in 1510. Under a proposed lease in 1629 Timothy Richbell was to spend £20 enlarging the shop, but he claimed he had never agreed it, and, 'for the affronte and indignite offered unto this court', the committee decided to eject him when his existing lease expired; after agreement was reached, the new lease of 1633 said nothing about enlargement.[113] The depth stated in 1683 was less than that in the leases. Five hearths in 1672–73.

1633 (Timothy Richbell, citizen and grocer): cellar with house of office, 16′ × 12′; (G) shop, length 25½′, breadth with entry 18′; (1) hall wainscoted throughout next to Thames on part of shop, length 18′, breadth with chimney and staircase 17′; chamber wainscoted throughout behind hall over other part of shop, length 18′, breadth with chimney 12′; (2) kitchen next to Thames, 11′ × 9′; little room next to kitchen, length 18′, breadth with staircase 8′; little buttery in same room, 5′ square; chamber behind kitchen and last room with chimney, 18′ × 15′; (3) garret over kitchen, 18′ × 11′; garret over last chamber, 18′× 9′; garret next to last garret, 18′ × 10′.[114]

1651 (Edmund Warnett, citizen and cutler; occupied by William Younge): cellar, north–south 14′4″ between the walls besides house of office, breadth east–west between the walls 14′; (G) shop, out to out east–west 26½′, breadth with the entry 19½′; (1) hall wainscoted throughout next to Thames over part of shop, north–south out to out 19½′, breadth with chimney and staircase 18′; chamber wainscoted throughout behind hall over other part of shop, north–south out to out 19½′, breadth with chimneys 15′ besides little counting house over Thames; (2) kitchen next to Thames over hall, north–south 19½′, breadth 12′ besides chimney, buttery, waterhouse and staircase; chamber behind kitchen on same floor, 19½′ × 14′; (3) four small garrets, passage room and house of office over kitchen and chamber.[115]

1683: Front 19′7″; depth 25′3″; cross building 20′ wide.

SE5–6

Largely over a gullet. Built 1547–48. Each house in 1649 had a first-floor room in the cross building extending the full width of the street, but nothing in the upper floors of the cross building, which belonged to SW4 and 5. In 1650 Daniel's great expense in rebuilding part of his house was described as not required by his lease but encouraged by the bridge estates committee.[116] The lease of 1653 must record the rebuilt house. Eleven hearths in c. 1665.

1649 (William Daniel, citizen and haberdasher): two houses:
(A) hanging cellar between the arches; (G) shop, length 17′, breadth 15½′ towards street; counting house at end of same, 4′ square; staircase 6′ square; (1) hall with wainscot settles, length 19′, breadth with chimney 15′; chamber at end of same over the bridge way, 12′ × 6½′; (2) kitchen, 15′ × 8′; chamber thereunto adjoining, 15′ × 12′; (3) two garrets.
(B) (G) shop, 17′ × 15½′; counting house at north-east corner of same, 7′ × 4′; staircase, 5′ square; (1) hall with a wainscot press, 19′ × 15′; little chamber at end of hall over bridge way, 11′9″ by 6′9″, wainscoted throughout; (2) kitchen, 14′ × 13′; chamber behind kitchen, 15½′ × 12′; (3) chamber over last chamber, 13½′ × 10′; (4) garrets over same.[117]

1653 (William Daniel, citizen and haberdasher): two hanging cellars, together north–south 32′2″, breadth 8½′; (G) two shops, together north–south 32′2″, breadth 19′ besides staircases and counting houses on east side; (1) two halls partly wainscoted both on a floor over shops, of same length and breadth besides jetty; two little chambers on same floor over street way, together length 14′, breadth 12′ besides staircase; (2) kitchen, dining room and two chambers all on a floor over the two halls, of same length and breadth besides jetties eastward; (3) kitchen and three chambers all on a floor over said kitchen, dining room and two chambers, of same length and breadth besides jetties; two little buteries westward; (4) two fair chambers on a floor over last-mentioned kitchen and three chambers, of same length and breadth with a lead besides two little counting houses; (5) two garrets over them.[118]

1683: Front 32′5½″; depth 14′1″; cross building 14′6″ wide.

SE7

Eastern part of the house with many windows. Largely over a pier. Built 1547–48. The two storeys at the top, not matched at the western house, are clearly shown in Hollar's view (Fig. 117). In 1678–82 the house had an additional small shop on its south side.[119] Six hearths in c. 1665.

1653 (Thomas Arnold, citizen and clothworker): cellar upon the stone pier, east–west 20′, breadth 15′; (G) shop, east–west 25′, breadth 20′ besides entry, staircase and window; two little counting houses at east end of shop; (1) hall and parlour both wainscoted on a floor over shop, east–west 27′2″, breadth 20′ besides staircase and windows; little chamber on same floor over street way, north–south 12′7″ besides counting house eastward, breadth 6′; little buttery at north end thereof, 7′5″ × 4′4″; (2) two chambers and kitchen on a floor over hall, parlour and little chamber, of same length and breadth besides staircase and window and buttery eastward; (3) four rooms over them of same length and breadth; (4) two garret chambers over them of same length and breadth with the leads; (5) two low garrets over them.[120]

1683: Front 22′8″; depth 25′8″; cross building 13′ wide.

SE8

Part of the stone gate. Over a pier. The opening of a doorway between the shed and the gate was permitted in 1631. Under a lease of 1650 the shed was to be enlarged by one foot.[121] Three hearths in c. 1665. See Fig. 34.

1630 (Henry Gosson, citizen and stationer): shed converted to a shop, one part whereof eastward is 14½′ × 7′, other part southward is 6′3″ square; part of bridge gate, containing cellar, 12′ over [sic]; hall of same size between circumference; staircase, breadth 6′; three rooms of same size one over another; little washhouse at end of uppermost room eastward.[122]

1654 (Thomas Heath, citizen and clothworker; occupied by John Meadowes): one outward shop into the street, length 15′4″; cellar; (G) kitchen over cellar; (1) inner shop over that; (2) hall over that; (3) chamber over that; (4) chamber over that with a closet and leads.[123]

SE9

Over a gullet. Built 1529–30. In 1667 the house of office was to be boarded to prevent rain getting into the kitchen.[124] Four hearths in 1672–73.

1651 (George Nash, citizen and merchant taylor; occupied by Timothy Blackwell, citizen and pewterer): (G) shop, length 19′9″, breadth 14′ with staircase and 'the bulke of the gate wall'; (1) hall partly wainscoted over shop, 20′9″ × 14′; (2) kitchen and chamber over hall on a floor, of same length and breadth; (3) chamber wainscoted with leads, of same length and breadth; (4) low garret over same.[125]

SE10

Over a gullet. Built 1529–30. Described as a small tenement of three rooms in 1617; it was to be enlarged by the tenant, Henry Allen, and a hammer beam was to be provided by the Bridge House 'if the said hammer beame may be convenientlye laid'. In 1628 Allen was said to have

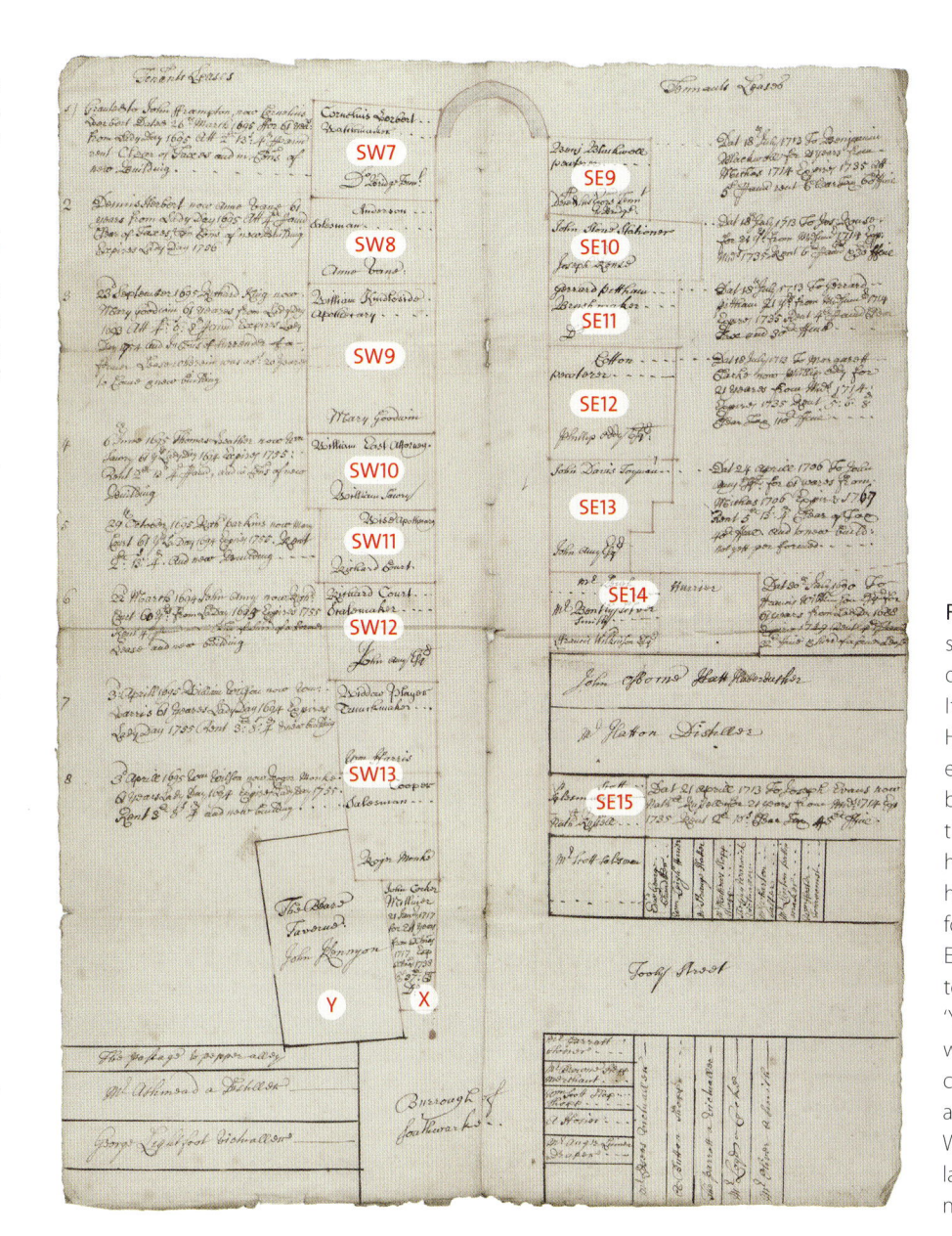

Fig. 114 Plan of the area south of the stone gate, drawn after the fire of 1725. It is not to scale. Bridge House properties are edged in red, and others in black. The numbers used in the Survey for the bridge houses have been added here in red. 'X' is the plot formerly occupied by Evan Evans, as reduced in order to widen the road in 1696. 'Y' is the Bear Tavern. The walls of the Bear Tavern's cellar were found during an excavation in 1984 (see Watson, p. 142, where the labels place the Bear too far north).

Fig. 115 Houses on the east side south of the stone gate in Nicholls's view of 1711, with house numbers added. The two storeys added by Robert Clarke to SE12 after 1654 can be clearly seen.

leads over it, formed part of SE12 in 1712 and apparently in 1653.[130] *Extra storeys had been added by 1712.*[131] *Five hearths in* c. *1665.*

1653 (Margery Pernell, widow; occupied by Christopher Danbrooke): (G) shop, east–west 23′4″ besides little house of office, breadth 11′3″; (1) hall wainscoted over fore part of shop, 16′ × 11′3″; (2) chamber and kitchen over hall, of same length and breadth besides a jetty forwards towards street and a jetty eastward 4½′ and a little waterhouse; (3) garret.[132]

SE12

Over a pier and a gullet, partly supported by a hammer beam.[133] *Probably built 1559. Robert Clarke added two storeys after obtaining his lease in 1653. A room in SE11 belonged to this house in 1712, with the leads over it, and was evidently the little room or parlour listed in the leases.*[134] *Five hearths in* c. *1665.*

1634 (Francis Norton, citizen and haberdasher): cellar, 10′ square; (G) shop over cellar, length 20½′, breadth with staircase 18′; (1) hall over shop wainscoted, 23½′ × 18′; little room wainscoted on same floor, 11½′ × 10′; (2) chamber partly over hall, 18′ × 11′, with little counting house at south-west end; kitchen on same floor, length 18′, breadth 14½′ with the staircase; (3) two rooms over said kitchen and chamber of same length and breadth; (4) lead over part of last-mentioned rooms, 14½′ × 4′; room adjoining leads, 20½′ × 10′; (2) another little lead over little wainscoted room before recited, 11′ × 9′.[135]

1653 (Robert Clarke, citizen and apothecary): cellar, east–west 13′, breadth 10′; (G) shop over cellar, east–west 23′2″, breadth 19′2″; (1) hall wainscoted throughout over shop, of same length and breadth besides a jetty towards street; little parlour wainscoted on same floor at north-east corner of hall, east–west 13½′, breadth 10½′; (2) chamber and kitchen over hall of same length and breadth; pair of leads over little parlour of same length

spent £160 rebuilding the back part of his dwelling.[126] *Four hearths in* c. *1665.*

1639 (Henry Allen, citizen and fishmonger): cellar, 20′ × 6½′; (G) shop, length 21½′, breadth 10½′ with the staircase; (1) hall, wainscoted half-way, over shop, of same length and breadth; (2) chamber wainscoted over part of hall, length 10′ (besides the room for a press), breadth 8½′; kitchen, length 13′, breadth besides chimney and staircase 7½′; (3) room over kitchen and chamber, length 23½′, breadth 7½′ besides chimney and staircase; (4) one garret.[127]

1653 (Nathaniel Allen, citizen and fishmonger): hanging cellar, north–south 22′8″, breadth 7′10″; (G) shop, east–west 22′3″, breadth 10′7″; (1) hall half-wainscoted over shop of same length and breadth besides jetties; (2) chamber and kitchen over hall of same length and breadth besides jetty; (3) two chambers wainscoted over said chamber and kitchen of same length and breadth; (4) one garret.[128]

SE11

Over a pier and a gullet, partly supported by a hammer beam.[129] *Built 1529–30. A room on the first floor, with the* and breadth; (3) two garret chambers over chamber and kitchen of same length and breadth; (4) garret and leads partly over them.[136]

SE13

Over a gullet and the bridge abutment. Probably built 1559. Three hearths in c. 1665.

1653 (Edmond Goodenough, citizen and merchant taylor): hanging cellar under east part of house, north–south 28′ besides staircase and coal-house, breadth 9′; (G) shop with entry and staircase, north–south 19′11″, breadth besides little counting house at north-east corner 18′ from out to out; (1) hall wainscoted and little chamber on same floor eastward over said shop, together north–south 19′11″, breadth 19′6″ with staircase besides little closet at north-east corner; (2) chamber and kitchen on a floor over hall and chamber, of same length and breadth besides little closet westward and jetty in kitchen eastward; (3) two garrets and leads over them.[137]

SE14

On the bridge abutment. The lease description is hard to interpret. It could indicate a house about 26′ wide, the front being occupied by a shop 19′8″ wide and a passage about 6′ wide at the front (not mentioned in the description) leading to the back shop and the hall. In 1678 one sub-tenant had a shop forwards and a house backwards, while the other had a house of which the fore part lay over the shop forwards, suggesting that the links were between the fore shop and the back part of the hall and between the back shop and the fore part of the hall.[138] However, the plan of c. 1725 shows a narrow and deep property (Fig. 114). Apparently two houses, with four hearths and five hearths, in c. 1665.

1659 (Mary Ward, widow): (G) fore shop, now divided, north–south 19′8″, breadth towards street 11′10″ [*sic*]; back shop, now divided, north–south 26′, breadth 11′7″; (1) fore part of hall wainscoted over shop, north–south towards street, 19′8″, breadth 11′7″ besides jetties; back part of hall, length with chimney 13′3″, breadth 11′2″; passage into hall, length with staircase and house of office 13′6″, breadth 11′7″; (2) chamber, kitchen and washhouse on a floor over hall and passage, of same length and breadth; (3) two garrets over same.[139]

SE15

On the bridge abutment, and detached from the other bridge houses (see Fig. 114). Built 1486. Five hearths in c. 1665.

1653 (John Ducey, citizen and draper; occupied by John Bateman, citizen and pewterer): cellar, east–west from out to out 16′2″, breadth 11′10″; (G) shop over cellar of same length and breadth; (1) hall over shop of same length and breadth besides jetty towards street; (2) chamber wainscoted over hall of same length and breadth besides a jetty; (3) chamber wainscoted over that of same length and breadth; (4) chamber wainscoted over that of same length and breadth; (5) garret over that.[140]

South-west

See Figs 114, 116–18.

SW1

The wheelage house, held by the lessee of the wheelage, or tolls. Largely over a pier. Probably built 1507–08; first appears in the rental in 1511. The Pepys view shows a shallow bow, presumably consisting of windows, in the north facade. The street frontage stated in 1683 was almost 4′ longer than that in the lease of 1654. With SW2, twelve hearths in c. 1665; separately, seven hearths in 1672–73.

1654 (Robert Osbolston, citizen and haberdasher): cellar, north–south 15′6″ between wall and wall, east–west 15′ in middle; (G) shop, east–west 22′8″ out and out, north–south 18′4″; (1) hall over shop wainscoted, north–south 18′4″, east–west 12′3″; parlour on same floor wainscoted, north–south 18′4″, breadth 17′5″ with buttery and chimneys; (2) kitchen over hall, 18′4″ × 14′5″; chamber over parlour, 18′4″ × 14′5″; (3) four garret chambers over kitchen and chambers.[141]

1683: Front 22′2″; depth 22′; cross building 18′7″ wide.

SW2

Largely over a gullet. Probably built 1507–08; first appears in the rental in 1511. Five hearths in 1672–73.

1653 (Matthew Sheppard, citizen and grocer; occupied by Robert Osbolston): hanging cellar, 20′ × 8′; (G) shop divided, length 24′, breadth with little counting house and staircase 16′; (1) hall wainscoted over part of shop, length 17′, breadth with staircase and chimney 12′; (2) kitchen over hall, length with chimney 16′, breadth with washhouse 9′; little chamber at east end of kitchen, 12′ × 8′; (3) two garrets over kitchen and little chamber, 17′ × 12′; (1) parlour over north part of shop, wainscoted throughout, length 23′, breadth with staircase 9′; (2) kitchen over parlour, 10′ × 8½′; chamber at east end of kitchen, 12′ square; lead at west end of same, 6′ × 5′; (3) two garrets over kitchen and chamber, 10′ × 19½′.[142]

1683: Front 24′9″; depth 16′.

SW3

Over a pier. Built 1495–96. Its cross building can be seen in Fig. 44. One hearth in c. 1665; three hearths in 1672–73.

1654 (Joan Wood, widow): cellar, 18′ square; (G) shop, 21′ × 19½′; little counting house behind shop, 6½′ square; (1) hall over shop wainscoted, length 19½′ with staircase and chimney, breadth with chimney 16′7″; chamber over street wainscoted on same floor, of same length north–south, breadth 11′4″; (2) kitchen with washhouse and dining room, east–west 21′, breadth both

Fig. 116. The south-west part of the bridge in the 1881 redrawing of the Pepys view, with house numbers and dates of building added. The 1881 version is used here because of its greater clarity; for the original, see Fig. 2. The least good fit with the 1683 measurements is SW3, which is too wide in the view. The building on the right with a large gable at right angles to the bridge houses must be the Bear Tavern.

together 19′; chamber over chamber that is over street, of same length and breadth as said chamber; (3) two garret chambers over kitchen and chamber; two garret chambers over chambers over street.[143]

1683: Front 19′9″; depth 21′; cross building 20′ wide.

SW4

Largely over a gullet. Built 1547–48. Had the second floor upwards of the cross building, but nothing on the first floor. Four hearths in c. 1665.

1631 (John Clarke, citizen and vintner): hanging cellar, 14½′ × 8½′; (G) shop, 16½′ × 15½′; little counting house, 4′ square; (1) hall over shop wainscoted in part, 18½′ × 12½′; (2) kitchen over hall, 13′ × 12′; little room behind kitchen, 14′ × 9′; chamber over bridge way, 10′ × 7′; (3) chamber over aforesaid kitchen, 13½′ × 9½′; garret over street, 12½′ × 9½′; little buttery over street, 6′ × 4′; (4) low garret over room over kitchen; leads, 8½′ × 7′.[144]

1653 (John Clarke, citizen and vintner): hanging cellar, 11′ × 8½′; (G) shop, east–west 18½′ besides staircase and little counting house, north–south 16′; (1) hall wainscoted over shop, 20′ × 16′; (2) kitchen over hall, 16′ × 14′; waterhouse at end thereof, 7½′ × 2½′; chamber over street way, 11½′ × 7½′; chamber on same floor, 16′ × 12′; (3) two chambers over them of same length and breadth; (4) two garretts over them and a lead over staircase, 8′ × 7′.[145]

1683: Front 16′2″; depth 23′6″; cross building 14′6″ wide [shared with SW5].

SW5

Largely over a gullet. Built 1547–48. Had the second floor upwards of the cross building, at least in 1657, but nothing on the first floor. Successive leases show the enlargement of the house backwards. Five hearths in c. 1665.

1604 (Mary Leather, widow): shop, 18′ × 16′; little counting house behind shop, 8′ × 4′; little hanging cellar under shop, 9′ × 7′; (1) hall over shop with chimney, 18′ × 16′; (2) chamber and kitchen over hall of same length and breadth; (3) garret divided in two over chamber and kitchen.[146]

1622 (Henry Elyott, citizen and cutler) [as in 1604, but the shop 21′ × 16′].[147]

1657 (Samuel Dannold, citizen and vintner): hanging cellar; (G) shop, length with staircase 23′, breadth 16′4″; (1) hall over shop wainscoted round, length 22′, breadth 16′4″ with chimney; leads adjoining to hall, 11′8″ × 4′2″; (2) kitchen over hall, length 16′4″, breadth with chimney and staircase 14½′; chamber on same floor, length 16′4″, breadth with chimney 12′; chamber over street, 10′ × 7′; (3) chamber over said chamber over street of same length and breadth; chamber over kitchen and chamber, length 20′, breadth with chimney and staircase 16′4″; leads adjoining said chamber, 9′ × 6′; (4) two garrets over said chamber of same length and breadth; two leads adjoining said garrets, 9′ × 8½′; garret over chamber over street of same length and breadth.[148]

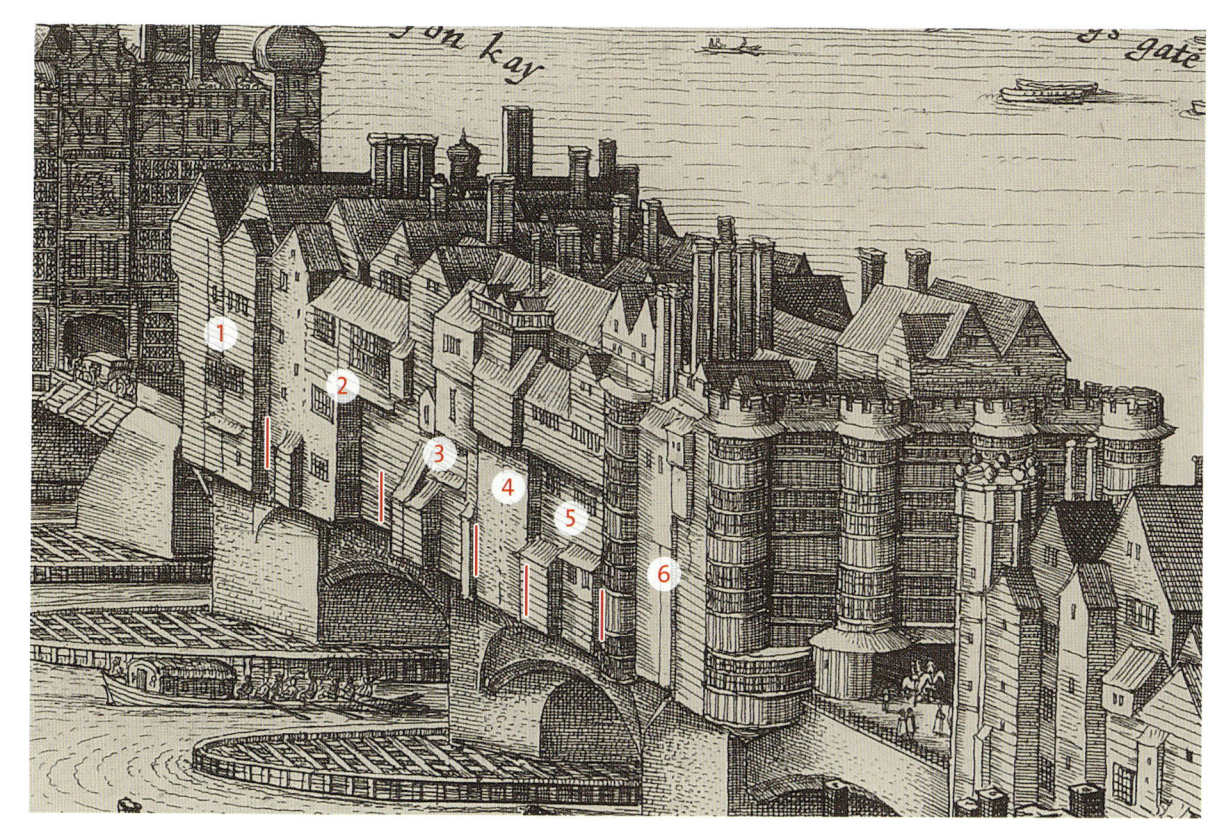

Fig. 117 The drawbridge houses in Hollar's Long View of 1647, with house numbers added. The dimensions of 1683 correspond fairly well to boundaries shown in the view, except between SW2 and 3, but how accurately the buildings are depicted is uncertain; see Appendix 2.

1683: Front 16′3″; depth 23′6″; cross building [see SW4].

SW6

Western part of the house with many windows. Largely over a pier. Built 1547–48. Five hearths in c. 1665. See Figs. 117, 118.

1634 (John Blancher, citizen and draper): cellar, 20′ × 16′; (G) shop over cellar, length 24′, breadth besides staircase 18½′; two counting houses at west end of same; (1) room over street, 13′ × 6′; parlour over shop eastward, length 18′ with chimney, breadth 14′; hall wainscoted adjoining on same floor, length 18′, breadth besides chimney and staircase 11′; (2) chamber over room which is over street, of same length and breadth; chamber over parlour of same length and breadth; kitchen on same floor, 18′ × 11′; (3) garret over aforesaid rooms of same length and breadth; leads, 32′ × 5′.[149]

1653 (Samuel Yate, citizen and mercer): cellar, 22′1″ × 16′3″; (G) shop over cellar, east–west 25′, breadth besides staircase and window southward 20′; two counting houses on west end of same; (1) room over street way, north–south 13′, breadth 6′; parlour and hall wainscoted throughout both on a floor over shop and adjoining room over street way, together east–west 27′ besides staircase and little counting house both westward, breadth 20′; (2) three chambers and kitchen all on a floor over said room, parlour and hall, together of same length and breadth besides part of waterhouse and staircase; (3) three garret chambers over them of same length and breadth; leads east–west 25′ × 5′; leads north–south 15′ × 5′.[150]

1683: Front 22′8″; depth 25′; cross building 13′ wide.

Stone gate

The west side of the stone gate contained a dwelling occupied by the beadle of Bridge Ward. See Fig. 34.

SW7

Over a gullet. Built 1504. Enlarged c. 1597.[151] Three hearths in c. 1665.

1653 (Henry Gray, citizen and salter; occupied by Thomas Pengfeild): (G) shop, east–west 17′, breadth beside street 13′, at west end 11′ [*illegible*]″, at middle 8′; (1) one [*illegible*] over shop of same length and breadth; (2) chamber over that of same length and breadth; (3) chamber over that of same length and breadth; (4) garret chamber over them.[152]

SW8

Over a gullet. Built 1610. Three hearths in c. 1665.

1654 (Stephen Phillips, citizen and fishmonger): (G) shop, east–west 17′2″ from out to out besides staircases, breadth 15′2″; (1) hall over shop in part wainscoted, east–west 18′, breadth with chimney 15′2″; (2) kitchen paved with freestone and one chamber at end of same,

Fig. 118 Nonsuch House and the drawbridge houses in Morgan's panorama of 1682, with house numbers added.

both on a floor over hall, of same length and breadth; (3) two chambers on a floor over kitchen and chamber of same length and breadth; (4) one low garret over them.[153]

SW9

Over a pier and a gullet. In 1620 Rice Gray's lease was extended 'in consideracon of new building the lower storey and setting the whole house upright, and putting in strong oken tymber on the west part of the house'; according to the lease itself, what setting upright meant was to 'settle strengthen & sett uprighte all and everie the principall supporters posts & rafters' and anything else defective.[154] *Four hearths in c. 1665.*

1607 (Thomas Elwood, citizen and draper): (G) shop, length 24', breadth towards north 12' and towards south 18' 'with a litle nooke over the peere'; (1) hall with stairs, 14' × 11'; chamber, 14' × 11' with a little room over the nook; (2) kitchen, 16' × 12'; chamber over hall towards street, 15' × 12'; room behind same, 13' × 10'; (3) garret over all.[155]

1653 (Edmond Mountjoy of Weatherfield, Essex, gentleman; occupied by Henry Amey and William Angell): cellar, north–south 14', breadth 10'10"; (G) two shops, together north–south 25'2", breadth with staircase 23' besides counting house westward; (1) hall and parlour wainscoted and little chamber all on a floor over said shops, together of same length and breadth; (2) kitchen, chamber and waterhouse all on a floor over said hall, parlour and chamber, together of same length and breadth; (3) two garrets over them.[156]

1693 (after rebuilding): two tenements, north–south 25'3"; depth 22' plus 2' 'on their brest somers' in front [i.e. jettied out 2'].[157]

SW10

Largely over a gullet. To be rebuilt from the ground by Munnes or Muns under the lease of 1644;[158] *the lease of 1650* refers to 'his extraordinary great charges in the substantiall newe building of the tenement hereafter demised', so it records his new building. Four hearths in 1672–73.

1650 (Edward Munnes, citizen and draper): cellar, 18' × 10'; (G) shop, length 19'10" besides staircase and counting house, breadth 12'8"; (1) hall over shop; (2) kitchen and little chamber over hall; (3) chamber over that; (4) garret.[159]

1694 (after rebuilding): north–south 12'8"; east–west on shop floor 22', plus additional 2½' above.[160]

SW11

On the bridge abutment. Three hearths in c. 1665.

1650 (Thomas Ward, citizen and draper; occupied by Thomas Brett): (G) shop, length 13', breadth 12' besides staircase and little buttery; (1) chamber wainscoted over shop, 13½' × 12'; little room wainscoted adjoining said chamber, 7½' × 6½'; (2) kitchen, length 14', breadth with chimney and staircase 12½'; chamber adjoining kitchen, 11' × 8'; (3) chamber wainscoted over said kitchen and chamber of same length and breadth; (4) garret, 11' × 8'.[161]

1695 (after rebuilding): front 12'9"; depth 20'.[162]

SW12

On the bridge abutment. The lease of 1616 required Wilding to spend £40 on 'new buildeing of part of the sayd messuage or tenement for the enlargement therof'. Under a lease of 1646 Thomas Ward was to add a storey, but in 1649 he was granted a new lease because he had in fact rebuilt it from the ground floor four storeys high.[163]

1616 (Zabulon Wildeinge, citizen and fishmonger): cellar, 21' × 9'; (G) shop, 21' × 13'; (1) chamber over shop, 21' × 13½'; (2) chamber over part of last chamber, 13' × 12'; kitchen over other part of chamber, 13½' × 8'; (3) two little garrets within the roof.[164]

SW13

On the bridge abutment. Under a lease of 1627 Edward Pierse was required to rebuild the lower storey and make other repairs.[165] Usually divided into two houses. No list of rooms found. Three hearths and four hearths in c. 1665.

1648 (Mary Pierse, widow; occupied by Randall Ellis and William Fitzhugh): length north–south 26'8" besides a counting house 3' square, breadth at north end 22'2" and south end 18½'.[166]

The new houses of 1645–49

See Figs 57–59.

PE2

Straddled the first gullet. Six hearths in 1666.

1653 (Francis Kirby, citizen and skinner; occupied by John Child, citizen and clothworker): cellar, east–west 20', breadth 18'; (G) shop, north–south 19'7" with the entry besides the staircase, breadth 19'; warehouse behind shop eastward, east–west 21', breadth 11'8"; one yard or balcony compassed with rails and banisters on south side of warehouse, east–west 19'7", breadth 7½'; (1) hall and kitchen over shop and warehouse, together of same length and breadth besides staircase and jetties; (2) two chambers on a floor over hall and kitchen, together of same length and breadth besides staircase and jetties; (3) two garret chambers, a passage room and two leads east–west over them.[167]

PE3

Over a pier. Had a cross building. Seven hearths in 1666.

1661 (sub-lease from Francis Finch, citizen and clothworker, to Edmond Pyke, citizen and haberdasher): cellar, east–west 25', breadth 19'; (G) shop with entry and stairs, north–south 24'8" out to out, breadth 22'; little yard on east side of shop paved with freestone with house of office at [*gap*]; (1) hall over part of shop, north–south 19'4" besides little buttery at north end and another at south end, breadth 15'8" between the walls; chamber on same floor partly over shop and partly over street, north–south 20'5" with the entry or passage, breadth 15'; gallery leaded with rails and banisters at north end of said chamber; (2) kitchen, buttery and chamber on a floor over hall and chamber, of same length and breadth; (3) two chambers with closets over kitchen, buttery and chamber, besides two little leads and garret.[168]

PE4

Over a gullet. No list of rooms or measurements found.[169] Five hearths in 1666.

PE5

Over a pier and a gullet. Had a cross building. Five hearths in 1666.

1653 (Francis Kirby, citizen and skinner; occupied by William Fitzherbert, citizen and fishmonger): cellar, east–west 17' in middle, breadth 14' besides staircase and house of office; (G) shop, north–south 25' with staircase, waterhouse and counting house, breadth 21'5"; (1) hall over shop and a little chamber at west end thereof, partly over street, together east–west 31'8", breadth 17'9" besides chimney and staircase; (2) kitchen, little dining room, buttery and chamber all on a floor over hall and chamber, together of same length and breadth besides chimney and staircase; (3) three garret chambers over them of same length and breadth, with two leads east–west.[170]

PE6

Over a gullet. Five hearths in 1666.

1653 (Nicholas Smyth, citizen and haberdasher; occupied by Thomas Hobbs): cellar, north–south 23'4", breadth

10′; (G) shop with staircase and waterhouse, north–south 22′7″, breadth 21′6″; (1) hall, buttery and little counting house on a floor over them, which with the staircase are of same length and breadth besides jetties; (2) kitchen, little parlour, chamber, little room at head of stairs, all on a floor over them, of same length and breadth besides jetties; (3) several garret chambers and two leads over them.[171]

PE7
Over a pier and a gullet. Had a cross building. Six hearths in 1666.

1653 (Robert Burrow, citizen and stationer): cellar, 17′4″ × 14′; (G) shop with staircase, waterhouse and counting house, north–south 25′4″, breadth 21′9″; (1) hall over shop, east–west 22′, breadth 19′4″ besides staircase and chimney; chamber over street way, north–south 20′, breadth 10′; (2) kitchen, dining room and chamber all on a floor over hall and chamber, of same length and breadth besides staircase and little waterhouse in kitchen eastward; (3) three garret chambers over them of same length and breadth, with the leads and one low garret.[172]

PW1
Largely on the bridge abutment. No list of rooms or measurements found. Five hearths in 1666.

PW2
Straddled the first gullet. Had a back yard.[173] No list of rooms or measurements found. Five hearths in 1666.

PW3
Over a pier. Had a cross building. Six hearths in 1666.

1653 (Nicholas Smyth, citizen and haberdasher): cellar, east–west 21′6″, breadth 18′7″; another cellar adjoining, east–west 12′, breadth 7′; (G) shop over cellars, east–west 24′9″, breadth 19′6″ with staircase; counting house on west side of shop, north–south 13½′, breadth 5′; (2) hall, kitchen, buttery and staircase all on a floor over shop and over street way, together east–west 34′3″, breadth 20′4″; lead at north end of hall, 10′ × 3½′; (2) two chambers on a floor over hall, kitchen, buttery and stairs, which are together with staircase and chimneys of same length and breadth besides jetties; (3) two garret chambers over them of same length and breadth; (?4) two leads north and west and two garrets over them of same length and breadth.[174]

PW4
Largely over a gullet. No list of rooms found. Six hearths in 1666.

1657 (Thomas Hollier, citizen and barber chirurgeon): north–south from out to out with the entry and staircase 25′1″; east–west from out to out 24′3″.[175]

PW5
Over a pier and a gullet. Had a cross building. Lasher had added dormer windows without permission by 1656.[176] Five hearths in 1666.

1653 (Joshua Lasher, citizen and girdler): cellar, east–west 29′, breadth 13′; (G) shop over cellar with staircase, waterhouse and counting house, 24′ square; paved yard beyond shop westward, 19′6″ × 10′; (1) hall over shop, staircase, waterhouse and counting house, with the staircase and counting house of same length and breadth besides jetties; chamber at east end of hall over street, north–south 18′6″, breadth 9′; (2) kitchen, narrow dining room and chamber on a floor over hall, staircase and counting house, together of same length and breadth with a kitchen belonging to Master Pitt's house; (3) several garret chambers and two leads over them.[177]

PW6
Largely over a gullet. Five hearths in 1666.

1653 (William Kenton, citizen and vintner): hanging cellar, north–south 22′3″, breadth 11′; (G) shop with staircase, cistern house and counting house, together east–west 24′2″, breadth 22′3″; (1) hall with staircase and buttery all over said shop, staircase, cistern house and counting house, together of same length and breadth besides jetties and besides little study at south-west corner of hall which is east–west 7′4″ and breadth 6′1″; (2) kitchen and two chambers with other necessary rooms over hall, staircase, buttery and little study, together of same length and breadth besides jetties; (3) three garrets, east–west with the leads of same length and breadth.[178]

PW7
Over a pier and a gullet. Had a cross building. Five hearths in 1666.

1653 (Jeremy Tawke, citizen and clothworker; occupied by John Coney and Gabriel Partridge): cellar, east–west 20′9″, breadth 13′10″ besides a room under waterhouse and staircase; (G) shop with staircase, cistern house and counting house all on a floor over cellar, north–south 26′3″, breadth 24½′; (1) hall over shop, east–west 25½′, breadth 20½′ besides staircase and chimney; chamber at east end of hall over street way, 20′ × 9′3″; (2) chamber, kitchen and dining room all on a floor over hall and the chamber that is over street, together of same length and breadth besides staircase and kitchen chimney; (3) three garret chambers over them; leads, east–west 35′, north–south 25′, breadth throughout 4½′.[179]

APPENDIX 1

Reconstructing the plan of London Bridge

This appendix explains how the plan of the bridge and its houses (Fig. 14) has been reconstructed. The aim has been to show them just before the fire of 1633.

Piers

Labelye's plan of the piers and starlings in 1746 has been used as the base map (Fig. 9). There is no reason to believe that the piers were significantly altered in the preceding century and a half, and the piers shown by Labelye correspond reasonably well with those on the 1633 plan (Fig. 8), except that on the latter those of the principal part are at right angles to the roadway and on Labelye's they are not.

Roadway

The roadway did not proceed in a precisely straight line from one end of the bridge to the other, as the 1633 plan makes clear. For the northern end, the best guide to its position is the 1633 plan, but that shows a roadway intended to be 20 feet wide instead of the 15 feet before the fire. It is assumed here that towards the south the planned widening was entirely on the west side, as there would have been no reason to widen it eastwards and thereby render it even more out of alignment with the roadway through the middle part. This is consistent with the house depths there, such as the 34 feet at PW21, ensuring that no house (or none whose dimensions are known) projected too far beyond a pier. But towards the north, the location of the arch over the second gullet, discovered in 1921, indicates that the planned widening there was on the east side.[1] There is no evidence showing at what point the earlier course of the roadway reached the western edge of the planned one, nor on whether it was a consistent 15 feet wide. In the reconstruction it is assumed to be consistently 15 feet wide, to proceed in a straight line from seventh pier to the third, and then to follow the west side of the planned roadway. This works well for the relationship between house depths and piers and for the roadway avoiding cellars (shown in black on the 1633 plan). Also, it places the roadway more at right angles to the piers than it would be if the trajectory planned in 1633 were followed.

The 1633 plan shows that the roadway swerved between the principal and middle parts. Both the 1633 plan and the dimensions of the ground taken from the chapel house to widen the roadway in the mid-1680s[2] indicate that the roadway there was not quite at right angles to the chapel house. South of the chapel house as far as the stone gate it is assumed to have been straight and across the centre of the piers on which Nonsuch House and the stone gate stood, based on the equal size of those two structures on each side of the roadway. South of the stone gate, the roadway seems to have swung a little to the west, as Rocque's map of c. 1745 and a plan showing the stone gate suggest.[3] However, the location of the springers on the east side of the southernmost arch at its junction with the bridge abutment, excavated in 1984, indicate that the change of direction was only slight.[4] The roadway then continued in a straight line to an awkward junction with Borough High Street and Tooley Street (see Fig. 114).

The width of the roadway is based on evidence discussed in the text. Here it is given a standard width of 15 feet, except south of the stone gate (17–18½ feet), at Nonsuch House and the drawbridge (12½ feet) and at the stone gate (13 feet). The 1633 plan suggests that it may have widened slightly from the first pier at the north end northwards, but no adjustment is made for that here. The width of the Square (33 feet) is taken from the 1633 plan.

Houses: middle and south parts

For the middle part and the drawbridge houses, the best guide is the measurements of 1683. The position of the houses in relation to the piers has been determined as follows. For the middle part, the north and south sides of Nonsuch House coincided with the north and south edges of a pier, or almost so, providing a fixed point. There is no such fixed point for the drawbridge houses, and they are assumed here to have projected beyond the two outermost piers equally at each end. Several lease descriptions record houses being enlarged backwards before 1683, and house depths in earlier leases have been used instead of those stated in 1683 in the following cases: ME3 (northern part), ME7, MW4, 7 and 9, SE3 and SW4 and 5 (all less deep than in 1683); ME8, MW8 and SE5 and 6 (all deeper). Depths are less reliable than widths because there were probably inconsistencies in the recording of projecting rooms or staircases. Cross buildings have been placed on the reconstruction following the document of 1683, except that the lease descriptions for ME10 and ME11 indicate a cross building at ME11 rather than at ME10 (see the Survey).

The area south of the stone gate has been reconstructed using the lease descriptions, with some help from the plan of *c.* 1725 (Fig. 114). The north and south edges of the stone gate correspond to the north and south edges of the second pier from the south end, providing a fixed point. As the reconstruction here relies on internal measurements of rooms, 6 inches has been added to each house for party walls.[5]

Houses: principal part

The main guide for the principal part has been the lease descriptions, though they have not survived for all the properties and in a few cases it is not clear which dimension was the street frontage. The following other information is available:

(i) The northern limit of the houses was the south wall of St Magnus's church on the east side and the northern edge of the grey structure marked on the 1633 plan by red dots on the west side (see Appendix 6).

(ii) Norden's view (but not the Pepys view) indicates that the southern limit of the houses was south of the seventh pier but not quite as far south as the edge of the starling. (The Pepys view is assumed to be wrong because it makes PW21 too narrow.)

(iii) The length of the east and west sides, indicated mainly by the leases granted in 1683, was 363½ feet and 351½ feet respectively.[6] This matches the limits just identified.

(iv) The cross buildings are likely to have been in the same places in 1358 and *c.* 1633, and those on the east and west sides must correspond to each other, except in the one case where the whole cross building belonged to a house on one side. The seventeenth-century leases indicate a north-south width of about 10½ feet.[7]

(v) Large cellars, with an east-west dimension over 12 feet, must (unless shared) correspond to piers and hanging cellars must correspond to gullets.

(vi) A house incorporating one of the 1358 plots is likely to be about 10½ feet wide, and a house incorporating two such plots is likely to be about 21 feet wide,[8] though this cannot necessarily be relied on, especially where groups of houses had subsequently been rebuilt together.

(vii) The Bridge House accounts record that PE14A was over the fifth pier from the north end and PE7–8 and PE12–13 were over gullets.[9] PE9 must also have been over a gullet.[10]

(viii) PW15 was described as being twice the width of PW14.[11]

The evidence for the width of individual properties is given in the table to the nearest 6 inches.

The reconstruction of the principal part is less exact than that of the rest of the bridge, but is unlikely to be far wrong. The cross buildings match on the two sides, and large cellars correspond to houses on piers while hanging cellars or the absence of cellars correspond to houses over gullets. Boundaries on opposite sides often matched each other approximately, and perhaps in reality did so exactly.

APPENDIX 1: RECONSTRUCTING THE PLAN OF LONDON BRIDGE

No.	Width (feet and inches)	Evidence
PW1	15 ft 6 in	Dimensions of cellar
PW2	c. 14 ft	PW2 and 3 are 3 houses in 1358
PW3	16 ft	Lease
PW4	21 ft	Lease
PW5	20 ft	Lease
PW6	20 ft 6 in	Lease
PW7	c. 20 ft	2 houses in 1358
PW8	10 ft	Lease
PW9	20 ft	Lease
PW10	10 ft	1 house in 1358
PW11	10 ft	1 house in 1358
PW12-13	c. 30 ft 6 in	Lease
PW14	c. 9 ft	Lease
PW15	c. 19 ft	Twice the width of PW14; 2 houses in 1358
PW16	22 ft 6 in	Lease
PW17	19 ft 6 in	Lease
PW18	14 ft	Lease
PW19	13 ft 6 in	Lease
PW20	14 ft	Lease
PW21	22 ft	Lease
Party walls	10 ft 6 in	
Total	351 ft 6 in	

No.	Width (feet and inches)	Evidence
PE1	22 ft 6 in	Lease
PE2	c. 22 ft	2 houses in 1358
PE3	22 ft 6 in	Lease
PE4	c. 12 ft 6 in	PE3 to 5 are 5 houses in 1358
PE5	c. 19 ft 6 in	Lease
PE6	c. 20 ft	Lease
PE7	c. 19 ft 6 in	Lease
PE8	20 ft	Lease
PE9	20 ft 6 in	Lease
PE10	21 ft 6 in	Lease
PE11	c. 11 ft	1 house in 1358
PE12	19 ft 6 in	Lease
PE13	20 ft	Lease
PE14	c. 21 ft 6 in	2 houses in 1358
PE15	c. 19 ft	Lease
PE16	11 ft 6 in	Lease
PE17	c. 18 ft	Lease
PE18	11 ft	Lease
PE19	22 ft	Equality with PW21; PE18 and 19 were 3 houses in 1358
Party walls	9 ft 6 in	
Total	363 ft 6 in	

APPENDIX 2

The reliability of the views of the bridge

Norden's view of 1597 (Fig. 1)

Norden usually clearly distinguished each house from the next, which makes it easy to compare the width of the houses in his view with the measurements made in 1683, as shown in the table opposite. The widths are almost always accurate to within a few feet, except that he made notable buildings (SE7, ME12 and ME2) too wide, in two of these cases at the expense of the immediate neighbour. The degree of accuracy is less clear on the principal part because of his awkward handling of perspective. Norden is also generally accurate as regards the widths of the arches when compared with Labelye's plan and measured from the point of each pier to the next. In the sixteen cases where Labelye showed the arch wider or narrower than the average for the bridge, it is also correspondingly wider or narrower than the average in thirteen cases in Norden's view, though Norden's piers in the principal part (especially the second to fifth from the north) are too far to the north.

Whether Norden correctly shows numbers of storeys is less clear, though that may be because the relationship of windows and storeys is often uncertain, because windows may not always be shown accurately, or because houses were enlarged after 1597. Numbers of storeys do sometimes match, most clearly at PE8 and ME5, and in several more cases they would match if the garrets were very low and lacked windows facing the river. The discrepancies are greatest at PE15 to 19, where Norden shows a fairly consistent height, apart from the lower PE18, whereas in the leases PE17 and 18 had one more storey than PE15 and 16.

The Pepys view (Fig. 2)

In the Pepys view it is harder to determine where one house ends and the next begins, but comparison with the 1683 measurements indicates that this view, too, is fairly accurate as regards the width of houses, again subject to a discrepancy of a few feet, as shown in the table. It does not make important buildings wider. It seems, however, to be a little less accurate on the principal part, even when the perspective has been allowed for. In particular, MW18 is too wide and MW21 too narrow, in the latter case because its south side should extend beyond the edge of the pier. Also, PE19 and 20 are too deeply recessed relative to PE18 and 21. The Pepys view is less accurate than Norden on the width of piers. In the thirteen cases where the piers are visible in the view and were wider or narrower than the average, the view shows them correspondingly wider or narrower only in seven of those cases.

As for numbers of storeys, these often correspond reasonably well to the leases, especially if garrets were small, but there are several cases of houses apparently having more storeys than the leases indicate (PE13, PE18, MW10 – unless the hall was higher than a normal storey – and SW3). There is no sign of the towers shown at PW12–13 in Norden's view from the west, though the one at PW9 does seem to be there, with a plain tiled roof and perhaps containing a staircase. The Pepys view sometimes provides a good match with information in the leases, such as the first-floor balconies or leads at PW6 and 9, the little room west of the shop at PW16, the jettying southwards at PW21, the 'nook' under MW2, the counting house, house of office and waterhouse at MW5 (all projecting in the view), and several projecting counting houses and waterhouses.

Hollar's Long View of 1647 (Fig. 10)

Hollar seems to show correctly the house with many windows, which corresponds fairly well to the building in Morgan's panorama (Fig. 118). It is difficult to make any sense of the houses he shows on the middle part, which may be partly due to the perspective. The drawbridge houses have approximately the right widths, but they have too few windows in the lower storeys and correspond too little to the houses in the Pepys view; on the other hand in some respects they do correspond to the leases, with the second floor jettied out partly at SW2 and wholly at SW3 to 5. Hollar's Nonsuch House is not convincing, as it is too tall and has bands of windows across most of the facade and onion domes on the towers that are not corroborated in other drawings (see especially Figs 47 and 91), except in Bowles's print (Fig. 94).

Morgan's panorama of 1682 (Figs 63, 118)

Like other creators of panoramas, Morgan had to simplify, as he seems to have done with the sheds at the north end. His middle part (not reproduced here) is as hard to interpret as Hollar's, with too few windows in the lower storeys. The drawbridge houses are reasonably accurate as regards widths, but generally have too few storeys. Where Morgan is most valuable is in showing the house with many windows and Nonsuch House, apparently accurately. The latter in particular has two round-headed windows on the ground floor on the west side, and the upper windows are consistent with those in Scott's view (Figs 91, 98).

NORDEN			PEPYS		
House	1683 width (feet)	Norden width (feet)	House	1683 width (feet)	Pepys width (feet)
SE7	22.7	27.3	MW1	23.8	23.3
SE5-6	32.5	24.8	MW2	18.1	20.5
SE4	19.6	21.9	MW3-4	31.3	30.0
SE2-3	24.5	23.7	MW5	20.0	18.1
SE1	21.9	23.5	MW6	10.6	13.5
			MW7-8	30.7	30.6
ME12	25.5	31.5	MW9	16.1	14.7
ME11	27.4	27.1	MW10	15.5	14.7
ME10	19.2	18.3	MW11	19.5	22.1
ME9	10.7	9.7	MW12	27.4	23.8
ME8	10.4	10.3	MW13	25.5	27.2
ME7	11.0	8.0			
ME6	20.3	22.3	SW1	22.2	21.5
ME4-5	21.7	21.2	SW2	24.8	22.2
ME3	43.0	32.1	SW3	19.8	25.7
ME2	27.9	38.9	SW4-5	32.4	30.6
ME1	20.6	18.3	SW6	22.7	21.9

Eighteenth-century views

For the houses, the most reliable views are those of Nicholls and Scott (Figs 84, 98). Nicholls appears to get distances right, and the detail seems convincing. However, he puts one too many piers under the middle part and one too few under the drawbridge houses. Nicholls and Scott agree closely on the windows and other features of the drawbridge houses, but Scott seems to have compressed the houses on the middle part. Canaletto is accurate as regards the outlines of the buildings, but does not provide much detail (Fig. 99). Samuel and Nathaniel Buck's panorama of 1749 (not reproduced here except the detail at Fig. 93) is reasonably accurate, except that they omit the pier between Nonsuch House and the drawbridge houses, make the houses of the middle part extend too far north and have implausibly high roofs at the north end. Bowles's view of 1722 is also reasonably accurate (Fig. 94), but the houses are made too tall and narrow, the projections at the back of the houses are ignored and Nonsuch House is given an implausible set of windows.

APPENDIX 3

Tracing the bridge houses back to 1358

Tracing the houses back from the seventeenth century to 1460 is relatively straightforward. There are annual lists of lessees (not quite annual in the late fifteenth and early sixteenth centuries), set out in house by house order for each part of the bridge on each side. Occasionally a house is out of order, for example being placed at the end of the part, but they usually returned to their proper place after a few years. In the 1620s the order of ME4 and 5 was reversed because the same man held both ME3 and ME5 and so they were listed together, and this persisted in the rentals until the houses were removed, but that was exceptional; the correct order in that case is indicated by other documents, such as the list of measurements of 1683. Complicated things could happen, such as a house being divided and added to its two neighbours, or a man leasing a second house, moving there and disposing of the first, but in most such cases the rents stated make it possible to work out what had happened.

Before 1460 there is a rental of 1404 which was updated to 1421,[12] but then there is a gap. Fortunately entry fines are recorded up to 1440, usually naming the previous lessee,[13] and sometimes the person who paid the entry fine was still there in 1460. Also, from 1421 to 1440 the Bridge House clerks were using a numbering system for the houses, so that, for example, on the principal east part, the houses were numbered from north to south from 1 principal east to 34 principal east (e.g. 'xv tenementi principalis orientalis'), and similarly in the middle and south parts; on the west side of the bridge the numbering was from south to north in each part. The other clue is the rents, which were often the same in 1421 and 1460. It has therefore been possible to link the properties listed in 1404–21 and in 1460.

There remains the gap between 1358 and 1404. In 1358 a different numbering system was in use, from south to north within each part on each side. The drawbridge houses, added after 1358, were numbered separately, and ME1 was numbered within the principal part. The 1358 rental provides only the number and the rent. However, as the rent had rarely changed by 1404, and both rentals are in house by house order, there is no difficulty in linking the houses of 1358 with those of 1404, and therefore also with those of the seventeenth century.

The results are set out in the table below. An asterisk in the first column indicates a 'hautpas' in 1358. The drawbridge houses are omitted because, having been twice destroyed, there was no continuity between those of 1358 and the seventeenth century.

APPENDIX 3: TRACING THE BRIDGE HOUSES BACK TO 1358

1358 (original numbering)	Seventeenth century (numbered as in Fig. 14)	Date of merging	Width (seventeenth century)	Original width of each house	Observations
Between the staples of the bridge and the stone gate on the east side					
1st	SE15		11 ft 10 in	11 ft 10 in	
2nd, 3rd	SE14	1420	19 ft 8 in (?)	9 ft 10 in (?)	Uncertain width; see the Survey
4th	SE13		19 ft 11 in	9 ft 9¼ in	Boundary assumed to have been altered, possibly on rebuilding in 1559
5th–7th	SE12	By 1460; *c.* 1504	19 ft 2 in		
8th–10th	SE9–SE11		31 ft 10 in	10 ft 6⅔ in	Gone by 1460; rebuilt later[i]
House in gate	SE8				
Between the staples of the bridge and the stone gate on the west side					
1st, 2nd	SW13	1605	26 ft 8 in	13 ft 4 in	[ii]
3rd, 4th	SW12	1523	13 ft	13 ft	Assumed to have been split into two before 1358
5th	SW11		12 ft 9 in	12 ft 9 in	
6th	SW10		12 ft 8 in	12 ft 8 in	
7th, 8th	SW9	1484	25 ft 3 in	12 ft 7½ in	
9th, 10th	SW7, SW8		*c.* 25 ft 2 in	*c.* 12 ft 7 in	Gone by 1460; rebuilt later[i]
Mansion in gate					
Between the drawbridge and the chapel on the east side					
1st–4th	ME11, ME12	By 1404; 1462; 1524	52 ft 11 in	*c.* 9 ft (?)	[iii]
5th, 6th	ME10	1420	19 ft 2 in	9 ft 7 in	
7th*	ME9		10 ft 8½ in	10 ft 8½ in	
8th	ME8		10 ft 5 in	10 ft 5 in	
9th*	ME7		11 ft	11 ft	
10th, 11th	ME6	*c.* 1501	20 ft 4 in	10 ft 2 in	
12th*	ME5		10 ft 10 in	10 ft 10 in	
13th	ME4		10 ft 10 in	10 ft 10 in	
14th*, 15th, 16th, 17th*	ME3	By 1404; *c.*1511; 1519	43 ft	10 ft 9 in	
Between the drawbridge and the chapel on the west side					
1st–5th	MW12, MW13	By 1421; *c.* 1475; *c.* 1501	52 ft 11 in	*c.* 9 ft (?)	[iv]
6th, 7th	MW11	By 1404	19 ft 6 in	9 ft 9 in	

1358 (original numbering)	Seventeenth century (numbered as in Fig. 14)	Date of merging	Width (seventeenth century)	Original width of each house	Observations
8th*, 9th	MW10	1427	15 ft 6 in	10 ft 6⅓ in	Boundary assumed to have been altered
10th*	MW9		16 ft 1 in		
11th, part of 12th	MW8	1523 (division of 12th); 1532 (merger of 11th to 13th)	30 ft 8 in	10 ft 2⅔ in	
Part of 12th, 13th	MW7				
14th	MW6		10 ft 7 in	10 ft 7 in	
15th*	MW5		20 ft	10 ft	Two plots assumed to have been merged by 1358
16th	MW4		15 ft 7 in	10 ft 5 in	Boundary assumed to have been altered, possibly on rebuilding in 1539–41
17th, 18th*	MW3	By 1404	15 ft 8 in		
19th	MW2		18 ft 1½ in	9 ft 0¾ in	Two plots assumed to have been merged by 1358; described as two tenements in 1460
20th	MW1		23 ft 9 in	c. 11 ft 10½ in	Combined with new (post-1358) house listed under principal west

Between the chapel and the staples of the bridge towards London on the east side

1358 (original numbering)	Seventeenth century	Date of merging	Width (seventeenth century)	Original width of each house	Observations
1st	ME1		20 ft 7 in		House of 1358 assumed to have been extended southwards
2nd*–4th	PE18, PE19	c. 1505			Boundaries altered upon rebuilding in 1526–29[v]
5th, 6th	PE17	c. 1501	c. 18 ft	c. 9 ft	Possibly altered 1526–29
7th*	PE16		11 ft 6 in	11 ft 6 in	Possibly altered 1526–29
8th, 9th	PE15	c. 1501	c. 20 ft	c. 10 ft	
10th, 11th*	PE14	1484			
12th, 13th	PE13	1474	20 ft	10 ft	
14th*, 15th	PE12	By 1404	19 ft 6 in	9 ft 9 in	
16th	PE11				
17th, 18th	PE10	1517	21 ft 6 in	10 ft 9 in	
19th, 20th*	PE9	1549	20 ft 6 in	10 ft 3 in	
21st, 22nd	PE8	1484	20 ft	10 ft	
23rd*, 24th	PE7	1426	c. 19 ft 6 in	c. 9 ft 9 in	
25th, 26th*	PE6	1539	c. 20 ft	c. 10 ft	
27th, part of 28th*	PE5	1557	c. 19 ft 6 in		Boundaries assumed to have been altered
Part of 28th	PE4				
29th, 30th*, 31st	PE3	By 1404; 1463	22 ft 6 in		

1358 (original numbering)	Seventeenth century (numbered as in Fig. 14)	Date of merging	Width (seventeenth century)	Original width of each house	Observations
32nd, 33rd	PE2	1461			
34th, 35th	PE1	1409	22 ft 5 in	11 ft 2½ in	

Between the chapel and the staples of the bridge towards London on the west side

1358 (original numbering)	Seventeenth century (numbered as in Fig. 14)	Date of merging	Width (seventeenth century)	Original width of each house	Observations
1st*, 2nd	PW21	1476	20 ft	10 ft	
3rd, 4th	PW20	1505	14 ft		
5th	PW19		13 ft 6 in	10 ft 4½ in	Boundaries assumed to have been altered upon rebuilding in 1526–29
6th*	PW18		14 ft		
7th, 8th	PW17	1478	19 ft 6 in	9 ft 9 in	
9th, 10th*	PW16	1511	22 ft 6 in	11 ft 3 in	
11th, 12th	PW15	1522	c. 20 ft	c. 10 ft	
13th*	PW14		c. 9 ft	c. 9 ft	
14th, 15th	PW13	By 1460	c. 19 ft	c. 9 ft 6 in	
16th*	PW12		11 ft 6 in	11 ft 6 in	
17th	PW11				
18th	PW10				
19th*, 20th	PW9	c. 1501	20 ft	10 ft	
21st	PW8		10 ft	10 ft	
22nd*, 23rd	PW7	1434			
24th, 25th*	PW6	1411	20 ft 4 in	10 ft 2 in	
26th, 27th*	PW5	1466	20 ft 6 in	10 ft 3 in	
28th, 29th*	PW4	1473	21 ft	10 ft 6 in	
30th, 31st	PW3	By 1461	16 ft		Boundary assumed to have been altered
32nd	PW2				

[i] The houses next to the stone gate had curving north walls because of the shape of the gate. The seventeenth-century widths of SE9 and SW7 are taken here as 10 feet.
[ii] Combined 1404–96; split 1502–1605; combined 1605–1707; split 1707 onward.
[iii] Four houses in 1358; the same in 1404 (two of them merged), but also one new one; in 1462 the four houses have become two, and the rent of the new house has increased from 26s.8d. to 66s.8d., presumably reflecting the building of the new drawbridge tower, but exactly what the new tower consisted of and how it related to the existing houses is unclear. The drawbridge tower is assumed here to be 17 feet wide, leaving 36 feet 1 inch for the four earlier houses.
[iv] Unlike on the east side, no new house appears here in 1404, and three of the plots of 1358 are held by the lessee of the stone house in the drawbridge tower by 1475. The drawbridge tower is assumed to be 17 feet wide and to incorporate one of the houses of 1358.
[v] The rent of PE18 (incorporating two houses of 1358) stayed almost the same after rebuilding, while that of PE19 (incorporating one) more than trebled.

APPENDIX 4

The hearth tax of 1664–66

House No.	Name and assessment	Evidence for location
St Magnus, London Bridge west side		
PW1	John Johnson linendraper 5	Fire Court (see Appendix 6)
PW2	James Vyner haberdasher 5	Ward list
PW3	Nicholas Smith hosier 6	Lessee
PW4	Thomas Weaver haberdasher 6	Ward list
PW5	Joshua Lusher haberdasher 5	Lessee
PW6	Richard Clegate silkman 5	Ward list
PW7	Robert Barton woollendraper 5	Ward list
MW1	John Greene haberdasher 6	Lessee
MW2	John Greene draper 6	BHV 1
MW3	Robert Roundtree glassman 3	
MW4	Edward Smith haberdasher 3	
MW5	St Cleere Raymant 3	Lessee 1669; BHV 2
MW6	Thomas Man combmaker 3	Ward list
MW7	Edward Greene haberdasher 6	Ward list
MW8	John Hill ironmonger 5	BHV 1 & 2
MW9?	Robert Warkeman haberdasher 2	
MW9?	Thomas Dobson yarnman 1	
MW10	Robert Harrison shoemaker 4	Ralph Harrison lessee
MW11*	Edward Austin hosier 4	Ward list
MW12	Sarah Britt sempster 2	BHV 2

House No.	Name and assessment	Evidence for location
MW12	Francis Finch hosier 5	Lessee
MW13	Edward Pitt linendraper 8	BHV 1 & 2
St Magnus, London Bridge east side		
ME12	Thomas Buckham silkman 6	Ward list
ME11	Richard Love draper 4	Ward list
ME10	William Howard silkman 4	BHV 2
ME9	Richard Hilliard boxmaker 3	BHV 2
ME8	Nathaniel Lasher haberdasher 2	
ME7	Thomas Passinger bookseller 3	BHV 2
ME6	William Sheldon silkman 7	Lessee
ME5	Thomas Ruck haberdasher 3	Lessee
ME4	John Welding victualler 3	BHV 1 & 2
ME3	Gabriel Partridge haberdasher 6	Lessee
ME2	[blank] Clearke salter empty 6	Ward list – Nathaniel Clerke
ME1	Michael Webb mercer 6	Lessee
PE7	Thomas Powell glover 6	
PE6	Daniel Stockwood milliner 5	
PE5	John Cheshire grocer 5	
PE4	Thomas Wood haberdasher 5	
PE3	[blank] Greene empty 7	

House No.	Name and assessment	Evidence for location
PE2	James Peters scrivener 6	
PE1	Anne Vyner haberdasher 7	Lessee
St Olave		
SW13B*	Nathaniel Smith [hosier] 3	BHV 2
SW13A*	William Fitzhughs [hosier] 4	BHV 2
SW12*	George Walker 2 houses 8	BHV 2
SW11*	Thomas Knight 3	
SW10*	James Houldinge [Goldham?] 4	BHV 2
SW9	Henry Amie [merchant taylor] 4	Sub-tenant in 1653 lease
SW8	Thomas Dixson 3	BHV 2
SW7	Thomas Yardley 3	BHV 2
SW6	Henry Randolph 5	
SW5	James Holden 5	1672–73 list; ward list
SW4	James Roe 4	1672–73 list; ward list
SW3	Thomas Wright [stationer] 1	Lessee 1669; BHV 2
SW1–2	William Osburton [mercer] 12	Robert Osbolston lessee of SW1; BHV 2

House No.	Name and assessment	Evidence for location
East side of the bridge		
SE1	Ralph Kinge 5 [mercer]	BHV 2
SE2	George Legge 6	1672–73 list
SE3	Edward Skailes [haberdasher] 4	BHV 2
SE5–6	Peter Daniel & William Daniel [haberdasher] 11	Lessee
SE7	John Weld [silkman] 6	BHV 2
SE8	Thomas Purchas [Parkhurst, bookseller] 3	BHV 2
SE10	Thomas Soper [apothecary] 4	BHV 2
SE11	Nicholas Harreson [tinman] 5	BHV 2
SE12	Robert Clarke [apothecary] 5	Lessee
SE13	Thomas Pettit 3	BHV 2
SE14A	Henry Golding 4	BHV 2
SE14B	John Brooke 5	BHV 2
	[Two taxpayers in houses not owned by the Bridge House omitted]	
SE15	John Bateman [pewterer] 5	BHV 1 & 2

Sources: Matthew Davies *et al.* (eds), *London and Middlesex 1666 hearth tax*, British Record Society hearth tax series 9.2 (2014), p. 702; TNA, E 179/258/4. For added occupations, see notes to Table 3.

Note: Asterisks indicate that the order in the original document has been altered. The assessments relate to 1666 for the principal and middle parts, and to an unknown date from 1664 to 1666 for the south part. The 1666 list includes under 'London Bridge' some households in Bridge Street, which are omitted here. Locations have been identified mainly from the rentals (BHR) and from records of views (BHV). Where those do not help, the hearth tax list of 1672–73 for St Olave's parish (TNA, E 179/188/504) and ward lists (LMA, CLC/W/GE/001/MS03461/002) have been used; their order, though it cannot be wholly relied on, is largely house by house.

APPENDIX 5

Rents on the bridge

The purpose of this appendix is not to provide an index of rents but simply to obtain some indication of the rising and falling of rents, as far as possible compared with other areas, so as to learn something about the fortunes of the bridge as a shopping area. Any such exercise has a large margin of error. Rents were (and are) affected by the size of the building and its plot, its age and state of repair, the length of the lease and where the responsibility lay for repairs. Also, rents were revised only when a new lease was agreed, which might be after twenty-one years or longer. Figures also need to be adjusted for inflation, and that has a large impact on the results, though not on comparisons with other areas.

Entry fines were a complicating factor, as the total paid was both the entry fine and the rent, and a large fine might compensate for a small rent. The fine might also be affected by whether an earlier unexpired lease was surrendered. As discussed in the text, entry fines up to the 1540s were fairly small – usually about a year's rent – and are ignored here. From the 1540s fines began to rise sharply, while rents rose only slowly, so different methods of analysis are then needed.

1358–1550

In this period there is plentiful information about rents, and several comparisons can be made: with other Bridge House estates and with part of Cheapside.[14] The Bridge House estates chosen were those at Old Change, Paternoster Row and St Dionis parish, because these were reasonably large holdings (though far smaller than the estate on the bridge itself) and were little changed during the period covered.[15] The Phelps-Hopkins index

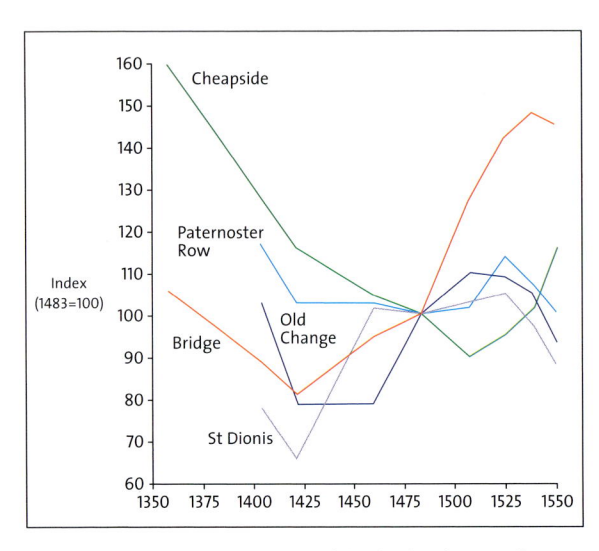

Fig. 119 Graph showing rents of the bridge houses from 1358 to 1550, together with rents of other Bridge House properties and in Cheapside.

of builders' wage rates in southern England has been used to correct for inflation.[16] (Using Clark's index of agricultural workers' wages would make little difference to the results.)[17] The results are shown in Figure 119 and discussed in the text.[18]

1550–1759

Three types of information are available for parts of the bridge at particular dates.

(i) Entry fines and rents paid to the Bridge House. There is a full record for the mid-1650s, but, as the leases granted then were generally for sixty-one years and were subsequently extended to compensate for rebuilding, there is little more until the 1740s. The entry fines have been converted into their equivalent in annual rent.[19] As the leases of *c.* 1653 usually involved the surrender of an existing lease with many years to run, the fines may not have reflected the full value.

(ii) 'Improved rents'. These were apparently the full rents an occupant would be expected to pay. A list of 'neat improv'd rents' used to calculate compensation in 1759 presumably records improved rents net of ground rent.[20]

(iii) Rents actually being paid by the occupants. These were usually ascertained when a lease was about to expire, or when a lease was succeeded by a tenancy at will. A record of rental values assessed for the land tax in 1753 seems to reflect these actual rents.

There are three main problems here:

(i) Comparing rents of different types creates a risk that like is not being compared with like. Also, the burden of repairs was increasingly transferred to lessees, and rents or entry fines would otherwise have risen more.[21]

(ii) The bridge houses were almost all rebuilt in the 1680s, so they were old buildings and often in need of repair by the 1740s, which will have depressed the rents. Also, rents were often depressed towards the end of long leases, and were probably even more so once the future of the houses was uncertain. In 1742 the rents being paid for PW17–22 were said to have fallen from about £150 seven years earlier to £101 because the leases were close to expiry.[22] Several houses in bad repair (PW10–13 and MW7–8) depressed the figures for those parts of the bridge in the 1740s and 1750s.

(iii) Comparing rents at specific dates rather than by means of annual series creates a risk of them being influenced by short-term factors, such as the slump in London rents in the mid-1740s.

Here, rents will be compared for the same groups of buildings or the same parts of the bridge at different dates, as follows. The figures relating to the whole or most of the bridge are those of 1550 (ground rents), c. 1653 (entry fines and ground rents),[23] and 1753 (the land tax figures).[24]

(1) The whole of the middle and south parts in 1550, c. 1653, 1753.
(2) 14 houses[25] for which leases were renewed in the 1570s (in order to make comparison with the Leadenhall Street figures possible): 1550, 1570s (entry fines and ground rents),[26] c. 1653, 1753.
(3) PW2–21 in 1550, 1742–43 (actual rents),[27] 1744–45 (entry fines and ground rents),[28] 1753, 1759 (estimated annual rents to determine compensation).[29]
(4) Houses south of the stone gate in 1550, c. 1653, 1725 (ground rents and improved rents),[30] 1753. These houses were all rebuilt after the fire of 1725, so were relatively new in the 1740s and 1750s.
(5) MW2–12 and ME3–11 in 1550, 1638 (actual rents assessed for tithe),[31] c. 1653, 1684 (ground rents and improved rents),[32] 1753. Unfortunately this series swings wildly (index figures of 420 in 1638, 114 in c. 1653, 313 in 1684, 96 in 1753), so it is not included in Fig. 119.

Comparisons can be made with rents in Cheapside 1500–1670[33] and on Rochester Bridge's estate in Leadenhall Street 1577–1760.[34] All figures have been corrected for inflation, as before 1550.

The figures are set out in Figure 120. Conclusions need to be drawn cautiously, as there are several figures which look anomalous (PW2–21 in 1744–45 and the middle part throughout). The table prompts two main conclusions. First, rents of the houses south of the stone gate rose much more than those elsewhere, for which there are two plausible explanations: that their rents were increased by the growth of Southwark, and that many of the houses, previously small, were enlarged in the seventeenth century. The higher rents could explain why there was no shortage of people willing to rebuild them in 1725. Secondly, rents rose much slower on the bridge than in Cheapside from 1550 to c. 1653 (with the possible exception of the first few decades of that period) and slower than in Leadenhall Street from the 1570s to the 1750s. In the century from c. 1653 they may have done little more than kept pace with inflation.

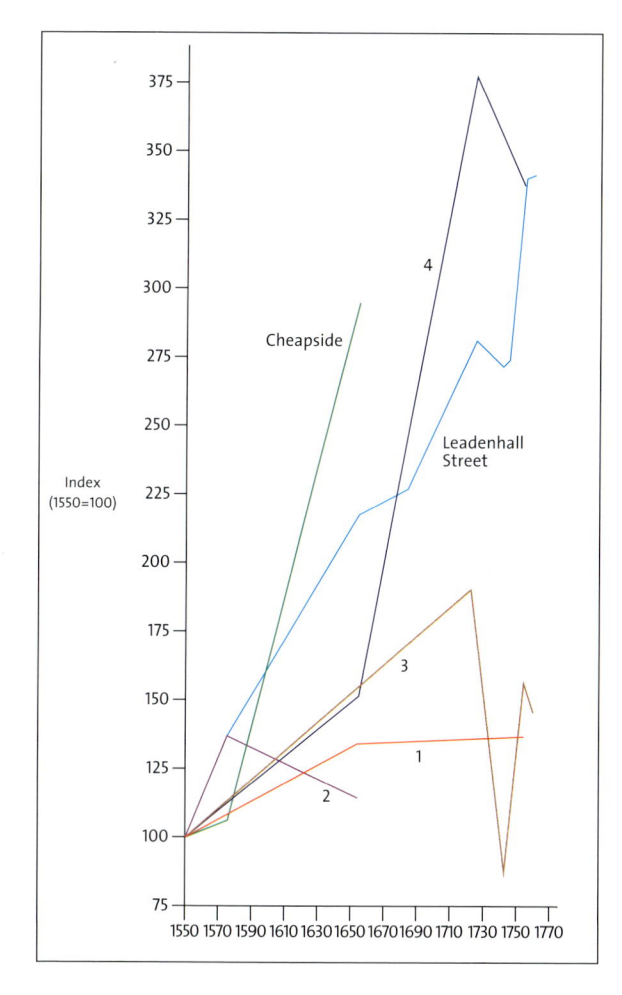

Fig. 120 Graph showing rents of the bridge houses from 1550 to 1759, together with rents in Cheapside and Leadenhall Street. Group 1 is the whole of the middle and south parts; 2 is fourteen properties on the middle and south parts for which there is evidence in the 1570s; 3 is PW2 to 21; 4 is the properties south of the stone gate. For Leadenhall Street, rents are indexed from 136 in c. 1575, corresponding to the level of rents of group 2.

APPENDIX 6

The northern end of the bridge

The purpose of this appendix is to explain the topography of the northern end of the bridge and to identify the northern limit of the bridge houses.

East side

The most northerly house regarded as being on the bridge (PE1) was described in 1534 and 1688 as adjoining St Magnus's church.[35] The south wall of St Magnus seems to have been retained after the Great Fire,[36] though the westernmost part of it was removed when a footway was created under the tower in 1762. The existing south wall of the church therefore provides a fixed point. On the plan of 1633 there is a black shape edged in red dots against the south wall of St Magnus (Fig. 8), and its width corresponds reasonably well to that recorded for PE1 – about 21½ feet compared with 22 feet 5 inches. The distance on the 1633 plan between the southern edge of PE1 and the southern end of the principal east part corresponds to that for which leases were granted in 1683 (341 feet 1 inch). Each lease in 1683 was for a pier and a gullet, and the distance between PE1 and the southern edge of the first pier corresponds to that for which Thomas Kentish obtained leases in 1683 (44 feet).[37]

PE1's dimensions are recorded as follows:

1633: on the plan, width about 21½ feet, depth about 23½–24 feet.

1644: width 22 feet 5 inches, depth 32 feet, including 11 feet 3 inches over the cloister of St Magnus.

1667: width 23 feet 9 inches 'from the corner of the church wall to the corner of the peeres of the narrow gullie conveying the water to for [sic] the waterhouse'; before the fire, it jutted over the cloister 11 feet 3 inches.

1668: as in 1644.

1725: as in 1644, but the 32-feet depth including 11 feet 3 inches over the cloister was at first-floor level; the depth of the ground-floor shop was 20 feet 9 inches, behind which was a little room belonging to St Magnus parish.[38]

So different storeys were of different sizes, and the 32-feet depth did not apply to the ground floor. The shape shown on the 1633 plan could be that of a cellar.

PE1 can be traced back to the survey of 1358, when it was the 34th and 35th houses on the principal east part. These were combined in 1409, and the combined house was rebuilt in about 1572.[39] In the reign of Elizabeth, not later than 1583, the City acquired from St Magnus parish the right to extend two bridge houses over the cloister of St Magnus (Fig. 121), in return for a quit rent of 18s.[40] The tenants named in 1583 indicate that these were PE1 and PE2. PE1 was burnt in 1633 but patched

Fig. 121 Detail from Wyngaerde's view of *c*. 1544, showing St Magnus and its cloister.

up afterwards. The Privy Council ordered its demolition in 1635, describing it as

> standinge betweene the wharfe called freshe wharfe and the church ruinous and ready to fall were it not under-propped and shoared up with tymber and beinge soe situate as that it impeaches and dammes up some of the manie lights and windowes of the said churche.[41]

The pre-fire lessee spent £20 on repairs and rent never stopped being paid for it.[42] By 1644 it may have fallen down, as there was said to have been a house there until four years before. It was then agreed that William Viner, citizen and goldsmith (probably the same person as William Vyner, haberdasher, who had occupied it in 1633) should build a house of 3½ storeys there.[43] In 1645 the tenant leased from St Magnus parish a little room at shop-floor level and described as over the cloister, and this was apparently not the renewal of an earlier lease.[44] The house was burnt again in 1666 and was rebuilt in brick afterwards.[45] It is shown next to St Magnus's church on Ogilby and Morgan's map of 1676 and Morgan's panorama of 1682 (Figs 63, 122).

PE2 shared a party wall with PE1,[46] and was the other house which extended over the cloister, as shown on plans of 1683 (Figs 123, 124). The cloister was at the house's cellar level, and it was the ground-floor shop which extended over the cloister. The ground fell steeply here, as indicated by the stairs shown on the 1633 plan and by a later painting (Fig. 125), and that is presumably why the space over the cloister obtained

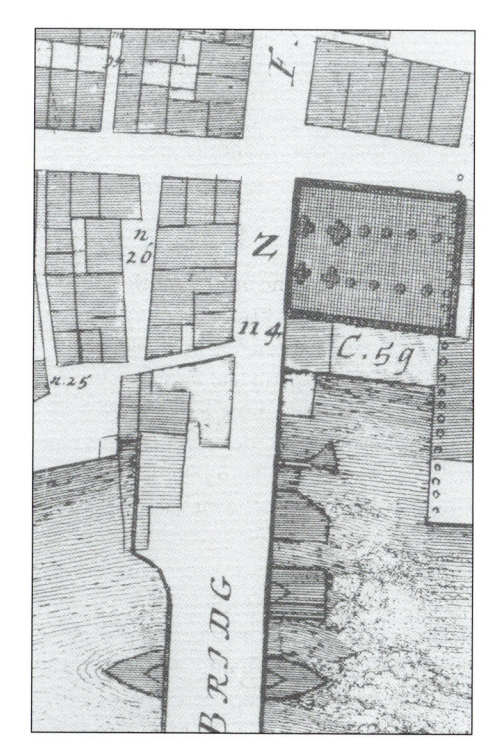

Fig. 122 Detail from Ogilby and Morgan's plan of the city in 1676, showing the north end of the bridge.

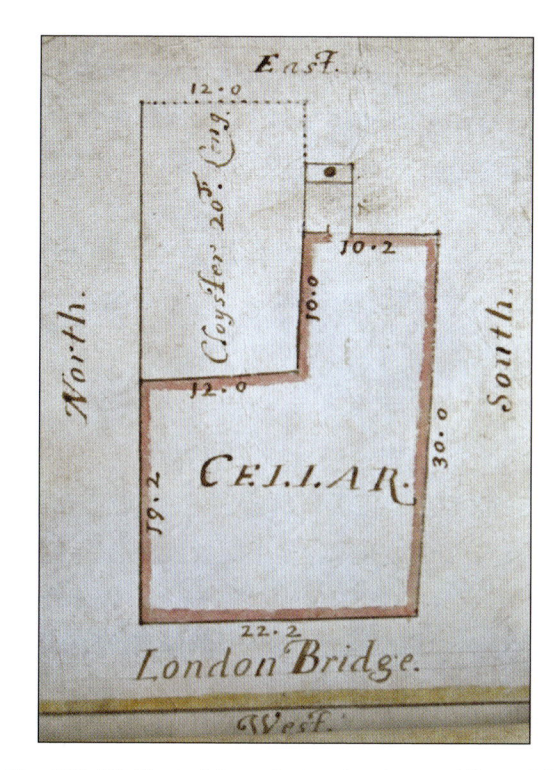

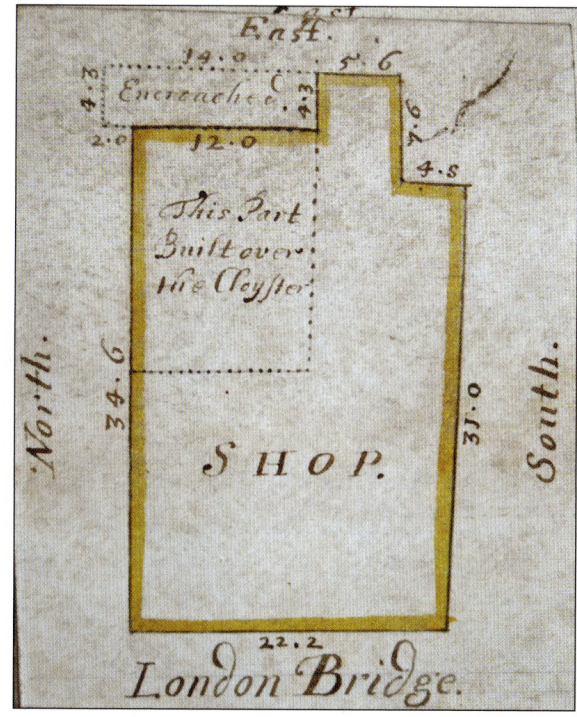

Figs 123–24 Plans of the cellar level and ground floor of PE2, drawn by William Leybourn in 1683 for Thomas Kentish's lease.

182 LONDON BRIDGE AND ITS HOUSES, c. 1209–1761

Fig. 125 Painting by William Marlow of Fresh Wharf, the north end of the bridge and St Magnus in about 1763, showing the different levels.

The west side

On the west side there are no fixed points like the south wall of St Magnus's church, and extra property was acquired and then partly lost in the seventeenth century. Using the 1633 plan as the basis (Fig. 8), we will start with the rebuilding of 1683 and work backwards in time. The leases of 1683 for the principal west part covered 341 feet 1 inch on the east side (excluding PE1) and 337 feet 6 inches on the west side (including the main grant to Thomas Collett but not some additional land referred to later).[50] As the southern limit was presumably the same on both sides, the northern limit must have been 4 feet 6 inches further south on the west side than on the east – that is, about 4 feet 6 inches further south than the southern boundary of PE1 and about 1 foot 6 inches north of the dotted red line on the south side of the grey L-shaped plot west of the bridge on the 1633 plan. This is confirmed by the plan on Collett's lease (Fig. 126).[51]

To the north of this, land had been lost after the Great Fire. The most northerly of the new houses of 1645–49 on the west side was let to Richard Shelbury, citizen and scrivener, in 1649 and sub-let to John Johnson, merchant taylor, from 1657.[52] It was burnt in the Great Fire. By 1668 part of the site had been staked out for public use, and only 6½ feet was said to be left.[53] The public area was evidently the passage linking the bridge approach to the new 40-foot wharf by the Thames. The passage is shown on Ogilby and Morgan's map opposite PE1, running not quite at right angles to Bridge Street (Fig. 122), and is named on Rocque's map as Red Cross Alley. It had taken most of the southern part of Shelbury's house, leaving a plot to the north which was 4 feet 4 inches wide at the front, 6 feet 8 inches wide at the back (perhaps the

that it 'will much preserve the arch there', whereas not rebuilding would be 'prejudicall to the arch'.[49] This has implications for any archaeological work in the area.

in Elizabethan times was added to the first floor at PE1 but the ground or shop floor at PE2. 'Encroached' on Figure 124 refers to the fact that St Magnus parish had built its minister's house over part of the cloister granted to the City.[47]

The reason PE1 belonged to the Bridge House was probably that it stood over the bridge's northern abutment and the first arch. In 1534 a breast of stonework was newly made under it.[48] When the case for rebuilding it was considered in 1667, one argument in favour was

APPENDIX 6: THE NORTHERN END OF THE BRIDGE

Fig. 126 Plan of the north-west part of the bridge, drawn by William Leybourn in 1683 for Thomas Collett's building lease. North is at the top.

6½ feet of 1668), and 24 feet from front to back.[54] The plot continued to be let out by the Bridge House (it was Collett's additional land mentioned above), but was combined by the lessee with land owned by others to the north and west. It included vaults under Red Cross Alley and rooms over it, which were 9 feet 2 inches wide at the east end and 8 feet 2 inches wide at the west end.[55] The trajectory of Red Cross Alley matched the northern boundary of the main site granted to Collett in 1683 (Figs 122, 126). On the 1633 plan, the street frontage from the northern edge of the first pier to the northern edge of the structure coloured grey measured about 25 feet, which can be accounted for in 1683 as follows: from south to north, about 10 feet for Collett's new houses (Fig. 126), 9 feet 2 inches for Red Cross Alley and 4 feet 4 inches for the left-over part of the plot formerly held by Shelbury, totalling 23 feet 6 inches, which, while not an exact match, is close enough for this purpose. The northern edge of the structure coloured grey on the 1633 plan was therefore the northern edge of the new houses of 1645–49.

That northernmost part of the west side was a relatively recent purchase by the Bridge House, made in three stages. First, a cellar appears in the rental in 1598, let to Nicholas Skinner and described as a little cellar. From 1616 to 1625 the rent was paid by Alexander Baker, for a cellar demised to Nicholas Skinner.[56] Secondly, in 1618 the bridge wardens were ordered to purchase from Alexander Baker a tenement near the staples, on the grounds that there was a cellar belonging to the City under it and there was no access to the cellar except through the tenement. The purchase was made in 1620. Nicholas Skinner had leased the tenement from Baker in 1615, and appears in the Bridge House rental in 1621 for a tenement lately purchased. He was succeeded by John Brooke in both the tenement and the little cellar in 1626.[57] Thirdly, in 1628 the bridgemasters were authorised to purchase from William Thomas the 'parcell of ground or cellar roome' under Brooke's house and to rebuild the whole property, which they did, the rebuilding being in progress in 1630. The dimensions of the cellar were 24 feet 4 inches from east to west, 11 feet at the east end and 15½ feet at the west end ('from a stone wall there'), which matches closely the structure coloured grey on the 1633 plan.[58]

Now we must place these three acquisitions on the map. We already have the northern limit, which must therefore be the northern edge of the tenement. Given its dimensions, the cellar purchased in or about 1628, situated underneath that tenement, can only be the grey shape on the 1633 plan. The strong likelihood is that the outline of the tenement itself is marked by the red dots on the plan, indicating that the tenement extended slightly beyond the cellar and was partly over the gullet between the abutment and the first pier. In fact the red dots almost certainly mark one of the two houses which the Privy Council wanted removed in 1635 – 'the one at the west end beinge partely burned downe'.[59] (Probably it was removed, as no rent was paid for it to the Bridge House after 1633.) The remaining problem is the little cellar of 1598, but, as it could be accessed only from the tenement, it was almost certainly the remaining area within the red dots not included in the cellar of c. 1628, measuring about 11 feet by 6 feet. The fact that it was first recorded in 1598 is a clue. Once the channel approaching the first arch had been leased for a waterwheel in 1581, there was no need to keep it clear for navigation, and therefore the space over the channel could be used for cellars, just as PE2 later had a cellar which would have obstructed any navigation through the same arch (Figs 123, 127).

Until 1620, therefore, the northern limit of the bridge houses on the west side was the line of red dots on the 1633 plan south of the structure coloured grey. The northernmost house prior to 1620 can be traced back to the 32nd house on the principal west part in

1358. There is no obvious reason why the Bridge House held less on the west side than the east, and why on that side the bridge houses did not even quite reach the abutment.

The roadway

In 1633 the roadway of the principal part of the bridge was said to have been 15 feet wide before the fire of that year. After the fire it was widened to 18 feet, and the Privy Council wanted it widened further to 20 feet, as shown on the plan of 1633. The plan suggests, however, that PE1 was set back slightly, in line with the west wall of St Magnus's church, and that at that point the roadway was more than 20 feet wide.[60]

A fixed point is provided by the second arch of the bridge, excavated in 1921.[61]

The reconstruction plan (Fig. 127)

Parts of the sites of PE1 and 2 are within the present churchyard of St Magnus, while PW1 and 2 are within the curtilage of Adelaide House. The churchyard also includes part of the first gullet. St Magnus parish was granted part of the roadway of the widened bridge in 1832 to use as a churchyard as compensation for a detached churchyard taken for the approach to the new London Bridge (Fig. 104).[62] The back wall of the ground belonging to St Magnus parish south of the church is the back wall of the cloister, which had at least two walks, each 11 to 12 feet wide. The present waterfront runs through the site of the bridge's fourth pier.

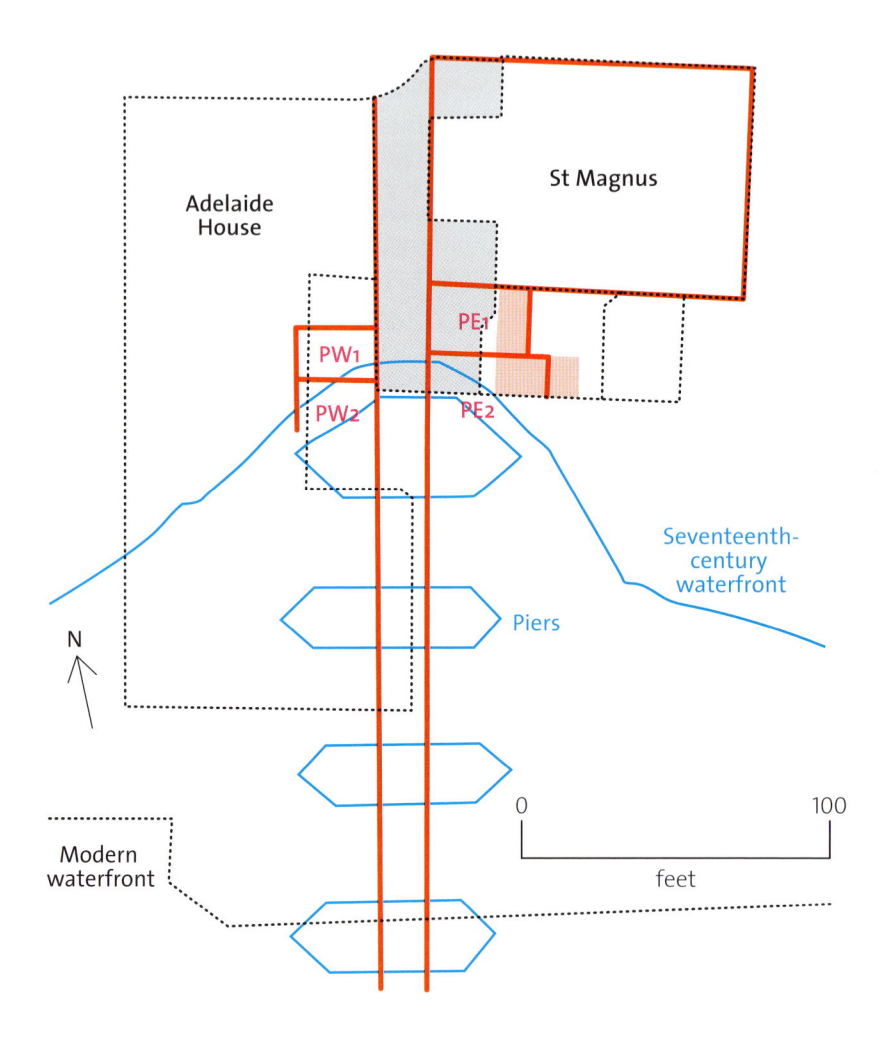

Fig. 127 Reconstruction plan of the north end of the bridge. Modern features are marked by black dotted lines, and the present churchyard of St Magnus is shaded grey. The seventeenth-century waterfront and the bridge piers are marked in blue. St Magnus as it was in the seventeenth century, the bridge roadway as widened in the 1680s and the northernmost bridge houses are marked in red, and the part of St Magnus's cloister for which there is good evidence is shaded pink. The placing of past features is approximate.

Notes

Chapter 1 – Introduction

1. See Peter Murray and Mary Anne Stevens (eds), *Living bridges: the inhabited bridge, past, present and future* (1996).
2. BHR; LMA, CLA/007/EM/04/003/A.
3. BHR. There are also weekly accounts for certain periods (LMA, CLA/007/FN/03/001 onwards), which have been used sparingly in this study.
4. CCLD, 02479 (see Survey, MW7–8, 1613) was summarised by Welch without dimensions or reference, and that summary has hitherto been the basis for reconstructions of the bridge houses (Charles Welch, *History of the Tower Bridge* (1894), p. 83; Home, p. 87; Peter Jackson, *London Bridge* (1971), p. 21). The leases are held by the Comptroller and City Solicitor, and can be consulted at LMA by arrangement.
5. See below, pp. 12–13.
6. Alan Cooper, *Bridges, law and power in medieval England, 700–1400* (2006), pp. 111–13; David Harrison, *The bridges of medieval England: transport and society 400–1800* (2004), p. 112.
7. Watson, p. 91; *British Journal*, 25 July 1730. The datestone was found 'next door to the Golden Still on London Bridge over the water-works'.
8. Labelye's measurement of length, from Wiltshire and Swindon History Centre, 2057-F6-12 a. There was apparently an additional pier and arch at the north end on part of the riverbed later reclaimed; see Appendix 6.
9. Cooper, *Bridges*, pp. 112, 117–19. For earlier French experience building houses on bridges, see Marjorie Nice Boyer, *Medieval French bridges: a history* (1976), pp. 74–76.
10. Wiltshire and Swindon History Centre, 2057-F6-12 a.
11. Home, pp. 36, 251.
12. Nicholas Hawksmoor, *A short historical account of London-Bridge* (1736), pp. 8–9.
13. Harrison, *Bridges*, pp. 114–17.
14. Hawksmoor, *Short historical account*, pp. 12–13.
15. Watson, pp. 84, 123; Tony Sharp, 'History of London Bridge: the origins of the Bridge House Yard and Bridge House estates; a review of their early history as civic and religious institutions' (2010), on the academia.edu website [accessed on 20 March 2021].
16. For the relationship with the City, see Caroline M. Barron, 'The government of London and its relations with the Crown 1400–1450' (PhD thesis, University of London, 1970), pp. 184–92; Harding, pp. ix–x; Mark Latham, 'The London Bridge Improvement Act of 1756: a study of early modern urban finance and administration' (DPhil thesis, University of Leicester, 2009), ch. 2.
17. Cooper, *Bridges*, pp. 109–10; Harrison, *Bridges*, pp. 204–06.
18. Harding, p. xvii; BHR.
19. Below, pp. 18, 143–66.
20. e.g. BHR, 004, ff. 247a, 260b; BHR, 007, f. 153a.
21. BHJ, 006, p. 5; James Peller Malcolm, *Anecdotes of the manners and customs of London during the eighteenth century* (1808), pp. 232–33.
22. Derek Keene, 'London Bridge and the identity of the medieval city', *Transactions of the London & Middlesex Archaeological Society*, vol. 51 (2000), pp. 148–54; Watson, pp. 114–15.
23. L. Grenade, *The singularities of London, 1578*, London Topographical Society No. 175 (2014), pp. 89–90.
24. Quoted in Keene, 'London Bridge', p. 148; quoted in Patricia Pierce, *Old London Bridge* (2001), p. 161.
25. BHR, 010, f. 73a.
26. LMA, COL/CC/LB1/02/001, 21 June, 19 July 1757; LMA, COL/CC/LBI/04/001, pp. 52–53, 98, 102.
27. LMA, London Picture Archive 21502.
28. BHP, 007, 1731, plan.
29. Wiltshire and Swindon History Centre, 2057-F6-12. That item includes another plan showing the piers improved by being encased in 3 or 4 feet of Portland stone and one showing every other pier and starling removed. The plan reproduced in Home, opposite p. 84, is a copy of the one showing the piers improved.
30. Among other things he adds three extra arches between the stone gate and the Southwark bank.

Chapter 2 – Reconstructing the bridge and its houses

1. See Dorian Gerhold, *London plotted: plans of London buildings c.1450–1720*, London Topographical Society No. 178 (2016), pp. 11–12.
2. BHP, 003, 1684, account of the lessees' names etc. Leybourn recorded making such a set of measurements, which were then checked by John Oliver and workmen

on the bridge itself (TNA, C 24/1144, No. 60). It had a different title from the paper that survives, but it seems unlikely that the measuring would have been repeated.
3 John Strype, *A survey of the cities of London and Westminster* (1720), vol. 1, book 1, p. 57; Home, pp. 214, 244.
4 Watson, p. 85.
5 For example, one of the cellars at the southern end received light from the roadway in 1725 (BHP, 006, 1723 [*sic*], petition of Philip Oddy and Joseph Bennett; BHP, 006, 1726, reply to petition).
6 BHP, 003, 1684, measurements made at the south end.
7 LMA, COL/CC/BHC/05/001, p. 113.
8 BHJ, 003, p. 186.
9 Below, pp. 36–37; LMA, COL/CCS/PL/01/203/35; BHP, 007, 1727–28, design for plaque, and plan of stone gate.
10 David Harrison, *The bridges of medieval England: transport and society 400–1800* (2004), p. 145.
11 Below, p. 115.
12 Michael J. Chandler, 'London Bridge before the Great Fire', *Guildhall Miscellany*, 1 (1952), p. 21. William Knight's 20 feet was the width at a single place, supported by a reference to Stow, whose 20 feet was actually the distance of the arches from each other (*Archaeologia*, 23 (1831), p. 118; Stow, vol. 1, p. 26). Stow said the breadth of the arches was 30 feet, but this was clearly wrong, and perhaps was measured at the Square, which was wider than the rest of the bridge (about 33 feet); see Fig. 8. Thomson's 20 feet was based on measurements made in 1725, possibly at the south end following the fire of that year (Richard Thomson, *Chronicles of London Bridge* (1827), p. 486).
13 BHP, 003, 1684, measurements made at the south end (dated 12 January 1685 but relating to the houses before rebuilding).
14 Below, pp. 26–27.
15 See the Survey.
16 Below, p. 30.
17 Home, pp. 86–87; Peter Jackson, *London Bridge* (1971), pp. 20–21.
18 Watson, p. 101.
19 Below, pp. 118, 122.
20 BHP, 003, 1684, measurements made at the south end.
21 Text on Fig. 1.
22 L. Grenade, *The singularities of London, 1578*, London Topographical Society No. 175 (2014), p. 90.
23 Repertories, vol. 51, f. 332b. In 1647 the Bridge House was providing 'great lanterns' and candles for them on the bridge (LMA, CLA/007/FN/03/017, 19 January 1646/47, 30 October 1647).
24 Thomas Pennant, *Some account of London* (1790), p. 320.
25 BHJ, 003, p. 107.
26 CCLD, 02670. There is a plan showing hammer beams parallel to the roadway (BHP, 007, 1731); and much other comment indicates that neighbouring houses might share a hammer beam (e.g. BHP, 008, 1745, decision of 19 July 1745).
27 See Home, opposite p. 84, for a plan; Jackson, *London Bridge*, pp. 14, 21, 28 for reconstructions making the piers too short.
28 Peter Murray and Mary Anne Stevens (eds), *Living bridges: the inhabited bridge, past, present and future* (1996), pp. 18, 53, 55, 57, 59, 71, 73.
29 Research on Bristol Bridge published by Nick Howes on Twitter and Facebook; Murray, *Living bridges*, pp. 28, 37, 38.
30 Stewart Brown, *The medieval Exe Bridge, St Edmund's Church, and excavation of waterfront houses, Exeter* (2018), p. 61. I am grateful to Stewart Brown for allowing me to see the text of this before publication.
31 CCLD, 02566, 02572, 02535, 02484 and 02566; TNA, C 106/85, articles of agreement 1684.
32 CCLD, 02706. 16 inches by 14 inches had earlier been intended (BHP, 010, 1746, particulars for builders of new houses – probably of 1745 or earlier).
33 Watson, p. 124.
34 BHJ, A, f. 78a.
35 L.F. Salzman, *Building in England down to 1540* (1979 edn), pp. 217–19.
36 TNA, C 106/85, box 1, articles of agreement; CCLD, 02566.
37 See also BHP, 005, 1724, petition of W. Hasleham, which requests two upright beams to support the hammer beams.
38 CLA/007/FN/07/001, 4 March 1618/19; BHJ, 006, p. 192.
39 e.g. LMA, CLA/007/FN/07/001, March 1624/25; BHJ, 009, p. 15; BHP, 008, 1744, view of 31 October 1745, James Brooke.
40 e.g. £9.13s.10d. in 1745 (BHP, 008, 1745, view of 31 October 1745, James Brooke); about £20 for seven houses in 1750 (BHJ, 010, p. 185).
41 BHP, 003, 1688, petition of Andrew Dandy.
42 It is not clear that the ribs contributed any extra strength to the piers, and they potentially created an unbalanced load on the most westerly of the piers concerned.
43 BHP, 002, 1682; BHR, 028, 1682–83, expenses by order of court.
44 BHJ, 003, pp. 219, 235.

Chapter 3 – The houses from c. 1209 to 1358

1 Marjorie Nice Boyer, *Medieval French bridges: a history* (1976), pp. 74–76.
2 BHJ, 009, p. 154. The piers in the drawbridge area are the most likely to have been enlarged, as they apparently did not bear houses at first, and perhaps Dance was referring to these.
3 BHR, 060, pp. 492, 704, 746. The piers enlarged in the latter two years were the fifth and sixth piers from the north.
4 Quoted in LMA, CLA/007/EM/04/011, p. 17, and described as Maitland's translation.
5 Stow, vol. 1, p. 24; Watson, p. 97.
6 Charles Welch, *History of the Tower Bridge* (1894), p. 78; LMA, CLA/007/EM/04/008 (especially A50, B87 and C7) and LMA online catalogue for CLA/007/EM/02; LMA, CLA/007/EM/04/001, f. 233.
7 Richard Thomson, *Chronicles of London Bridge* (1827), p. 127.
8 BHJ, 002, p. 23. See also LMA, COL/CC/BHC/05/001, pp. 209–10.
9 LMA, COL/CC/BHC/05/001, pp. 209–10; BHP, 002, 1682, petition of William Gray.
10 Gustav Milne and others, *Timber building techniques in London c. 900–1400*, London & Middlesex Archaeological Society Special Paper 15 (1992), pp. 99, 135–36.

11 Derek Keene, 'Shops and shopping in medieval London', in Lindy Grant (ed.), *Medieval art, architecture and archaeology in London*, BAA Conference Transactions 10 (1990), p. 36.
12 LMA, CLA/007/EM/04/008, Nos A12, A24, A50, B6, B40, C7; LMA, CLA/007/EM/03/157; Reginald R. Sharpe (ed.), *Calendar of wills proved and enrolled in the Court of Husting, London, A.D. 1258–A.D. 1688*, part 1 (1889), p. 86; CLA/007/EM/04/001, f. 233, No. 244. See also CLA/023/DW/01/61, No. 101, for 1338.
13 Below, p. 54.
14 Below, pp. 56–57.
15 Survey. The reason for dating MW10 to before 1460 is that no date of building is recorded; see p. 45 below. The Pepys view shows a larger building at MW10, unless the hall was more than a storey high (Fig. 112).
16 LMA, CLA/007/EM/04/003/A, ff. 64–67.
17 Any mergers by the time the drawbridge houses were built would have reduced the figure below 138.
18 Apart from some short-lived houses north of the stone gate; see below, p. 42.
19 See Maurice Beresford, *New towns of the Middle Ages* (1988 edn), ch. 5.
20 Keene, 'Shops and shopping', p. 34.
21 Derek Keene, 'The property market in English towns, A.D. 1100–1600', in *D'une ville á l'autre: structures matérielles et organisation de l'espace dans les villes Européennes (XIIIe–XVIe siècle)*, Collection de l'École Française de Rome, 122 (1989), p. 216; Derek Keene, 'Landlords, the property market and urban development in medieval England', in Finn-Einar Eliassen and Geir Atle Ersland (eds), *Power, profit and urban land* (1996), p. 102.
22 Below, pp. 82–83.
23 Peter Jackson, *London Bridge* (1971), pp. 20–21; Watson, p. 101.
24 i.e. explicit references in leases for PW6A and PW9; dimensions in leases indicating cross buildings for PW4, PW5A/PE5A, PW14/PE12B, PW16A, PW18/PE16; visual evidence for PW21B/PE19. The drawbridge houses and their hautpas are not compared here because there was no continuity in the houses on that part of the bridge.
25 Survey, PE9 and 12, PW4, 14 and 16, ME7 and 9.

Chapter 4 – The major buildings

1 Watson, p. 110.
2 Harding, p. 107; Journals, vol. 13, f. 274a; BHR, 006, ff. 75a, 117a, 136b.
3 Above, p. 5.
4 Christopher Wilson, 'L'architecte bienfaiteur de la ville, Henry Yevele et la chapelle du London Bridge', *Revue de l'Art*, 166 (2009), pp. 46–48.
5 Survey, ME2; LMA, COL/CCS/PL/01/208/054.
6 Richard Thomson, *Chronicles of London Bridge* (1827), p. 83.
7 British Library, Add. MS 71008, ff. 64b–65a.
8 Wilson, 'L'architecte', p. 47.
9 Watson, pp. 112, 114.
10 BHR, 007, ff. 126b, 135a, 147a, 401b.
11 BHR, 008, f. 19b.
12 Survey, ME2.
13 Fig. 27; BHR, A, f. 144a; CCLD, 02768.
14 CCLD, 02768; LMA, CLA/007/FN/03/017, 29 January 1647/48, 13 January 1648/49.
15 CCLD, 02600.
16 BHV 2, p. 121.
17 BHP, 003, 1685, petition of Nicholas Smith.
18 CCLD, 02801; British Library, Add. MS 71008, f. 65a.
19 LMA, CLA/007/EM/04/008, No. A24; Watson, pp. 105–06, 108–09. See also Henry Thomas Riley (trans.), *Chronicles of the mayors and sheriffs of London* (1863), p. 42, for 1258.
20 John Rees, *The Leveller revolution* (2016), p. 194; LMA, CLA/007/FN/03/017, 7 August 1647.
21 LMA, CLA/007/FN/01/019, pp. 137, 144.
22 Harding, p. xxi.
23 BHR, 060, pp. 260, 276, 318, 413, 459.
24 http://www.british-history.ac.uk/survey-london/bk9/pp69-84 [accessed on 2 July 2018].
25 BHR, 060, pp. 589, 631, 722, 732.
26 BHR, 005, ff. 228b, 242b, 269b, 282b; BHR, 006, f. 33b.
27 Home, p. 232; E. S. de Beer (ed.), *The diary of John Evelyn* (1955), vol. 4, p. 382, vol. 5, p. 235.
28 What was done in 1634, at a cost of £220, was general repairs rather than further widening (compare James Robertson, 'Persuading the citizens? Charles I and London Bridge', *Historical Research*, 79 (2006), p. 531, and Repertories, vol. 48, f. 424a).
29 Fig. 34; BHP, 007, 1727–28, design for plaque; BHJ, 006, p. 205. For the first postern being on the west side, see also BHJ, 006, pp. 173, 225; BHP, 006, 1725, report on enlarging the gate. Only BHP, 007, 1727–28, report on work on the gate, refers to a new postern on the west side.
30 BHP, 007, 1727–28, passim.
31 Sharpe LB, *Letter-Book H* (1907), p. 447; Sharpe LB, *Letter-Book I* (1909), p. 259. Either the whole gate or part of it was granted to John Dustone, Mayor's Serjeant, in 1382–83 (Sharpe LB, *Letter-Book H*, p. 212).
32 BHJ, 001, pp. 162a, 167a; BHP, 004, 1695–1700, view of bridge gate; BHJ, 004, pp. 60, 61, 71.
33 BHJ, 007, p. 9.
34 BHR; LMA, COL/CC/BHC/05/001, pp. 75–76.
35 BHR; LMA, COL/CC/BHC/05/001, pp. 75–76; below, pp. 93–95.
36 Survey, SE8.
37 BHR, 040, rental 1731; BHJ, 007, pp. 120–21; BHJ, 008, p. 40.
38 *Holinshed's chronicles of England, Scotland and Ireland*, vol. 4 (1808), p. 18.
39 Below, p. 54.
40 Riley, *Chronicles*, p. 42; Watson, p. 107; Stow, vol. 1, p. 25.
41 Home, pp. 77–79.
42 BHR, 008, f. 67a.
43 BHR, 004; Alfred B. Beavan, *The aldermen of the City of London* (1908), vol. 2, p. 21.
44 Repertories, vol. 5, f. 201.
45 Harding, p. xxii.
46 Journals, vol. 8, f. 248; BHR, 004, f. 12a; Home, p. 190.
47 BHR, 004, ff. 74b, 148b, 188a; Watson, p. 107.
48 Watson, pp. 108–09.
49 Below, pp. 50–53.
50 Dorian Gerhold, *London plotted: plans of London buildings c.1450–1720*, London Topographical Society No. 178 (2016), pp. 211–12.
51 A. H. Thomas (ed.), *Calendar of early Mayor's Court rolls … 1298–1307* (1924), p. 247.

52 LMA, CLA/007/FN/01/018, p. 68; BHR, 060, p. 184. The 1383 reconstruction followed an order by the Common Council that the bridge wardens keep the latrine on the bridge in repair (Sharpe LB, *Letter-Book H*, p. 212).
53 LMA, CLA/007/EM/04/003/A, f. 72a.
54 British Library, Harley MS 6016, p. 159. The latter is an undated survey of Bridge House lands (not including the houses on the bridge) copied in 1654. In the 1460s the Bridge House was receiving quit rent from three shops with solars at the staples on the east side between land late of Roger Clovile to the north and the public latrine to the south (BHR, 060, p. 112). The exact location of these shops and why only quit rent was paid for them is unclear.
55 Journals, vol. 8, f. 237b.
56 Stow, vol. 1, p. 25; BHR, 060, p. 990.
57 LMA, COL/CC/CLC/07/003, p. 14.
58 BHR, 004, ff. 255a, 258a.
59 Martha Carlin, *Medieval Southwark* (1996), pp. 236–37.
60 BHR, 010, f. 105b and rental 1591/92. In 1659 SE14 did not have a cellar at all, perhaps indicating that the cellar was not under Muschampe's house or that it was subsequently let separately to someone else (Survey).
61 Lena Cowen Orlin, *Locating privacy in Tudor London* (2007), pp. 161–62.
62 Repertories, vol. 22, f. 320.
63 BHV 2, p. 118.
64 BHJ, 006, p. 205.
65 LMA, CLA/007/FN/03/017, 1 September 1649.
66 BHR, 004, ff. 92a, 104a; BHJ, 006, p. 292.
67 Peter Jackson, *London Bridge* (1971), p. 31; Stow, vol. 1, p. 188; BHJ, 005, pp. 88–93; BHJ, 007, p. 170.
68 Journals, vol. 22, f. 446; British Library, Lansdowne MS 18, No. 61. These were evidently the mills of which a model was made, with a box for it (BHR, 010, ff. 95b, 105a). Old and new mills at the bridge are mentioned in 1527–28, but what form they took is unknown (BHR, 006, f. 46b); see also Repertories, vol. 5, f. 19.
69 Watson, p. 116.

Chapter 5 – The houses from 1358 to 1633

1 LMA, CLA/007/FN/01/018, p. 108. In two cases a tenant of 1404 in this area paid an entry fine before that date (Richard Chaumberleyn in 1388 and Richard Lambard in 1395) but in both these cases the property was described as 'below the stone gate'.
2 It is an addition to the 1358 rental at the south end of the principal west part, which was then regarded as extending from the chapel northwards. ME1 may have been extended northwards, as it was double the usual width, but if this happened it could have been before 1358 rather than afterwards.
3 BHR, 060, pp. 489–90.
4 Ibid. Stow gives the number as thirteen plus the gate (Stow, vol. 1, pp. 42, 60).
5 BHR, 060, pp. 489–90.
6 Derek Keene, *Cheapside before the Great Fire* (1985), pp. 13, 19.
7 Repertories, vol. 5, f. 201.
8 CCLD, 02672.
9 These figures include mergers among the drawbridge houses, later destroyed.
10 Survey; BHP, 003, 1684, abstract of all the leases.
11 One new house is listed in the 1404–21 rental (PW3B), and one is mentioned in 1420 (PW2 or 3A) (BHR, 058, f. 172). Large increases in rents may have reflected rebuilding: increases exceeded 80% in 1421–60 for PE3A, PE11, PW4A and B, MW2 and MW4, as well as the two houses in the drawbridge tower. The reconstruction of the southern abutment, apparently some time between 1445 and 1460 (Watson, p. 132), presumably led to the rebuilding of the houses there.
12 *Holinshed's chronicles of England, Scotland and Ireland*, vol. 3 (1808), pp. 531–32.
13 BHJ, A; Repertories, vol. 9, f. 49b; Repertories, vol. 10, f. 86a.
14 BHR, 004, f. 244a–b.
15 BHJ, A, ff. 35b, 44a–b.
16 BHR, 060, pp. 704, 740, 742–43, 746, 784; BHR, 004, ff. 2nd 75b, 87a, 94b, 99b; BHR, 006, f. 116a. For another example of a pier rebuilt without the house on it being rebuilt, see LMA, CLA/007/FN/03/006, f. 36b.
17 BHJ, A, ff. 43b–44b. See also BHP, 005, 1713, report on Mr Amy's hammer beam; BHP, 009, 1745.
18 LMA, COL/CC/BHC/05/001, p. 111.
19 BHR, 007, f. 124b.
20 The figures exclude houses in the stone gate and PW1 (not yet acquired).
21 Below, p. 54.
22 In 1464 three adjoining houses, ME7 to ME9, had been vacated, together with MW7, but the accounts give no indication that they were being rebuilt.
23 Harding, p. xiii.
24 BHR, 004, f. 296a.
25 Harding, p. xiii.
26 BHR, 004, f. 234b; BHR, 005, f. 48b; H.M. Colvin, *The history of the King's Works*, vol. 3, *1485-1660*, part 1 (1975), p. 408.
27 Survey, PW21; BHR, 005, ff. 58a, 72b.
28 Above, p. 32.
29 BHR, 007, f. 12a–b.
30 BHV 2, p. 120.
31 Simon Thurley, *The royal palaces of Tudor England* (1993), p. 43; Nicholas Cooper, *Houses of the gentry 1480–1680* (1999), pp. 93–94; John Schofield, *Medieval London houses* (1994), p. 104; Simon Thurley, *Hampton Court* (2003), pp. 57, 59 (illustrations).
32 Colvin, *King's works*, vol. 3, *1485-1660*, part 1, p. 409; Bower Marsh (ed.), *Records of the Worshipful Company of Carpenters*, vol. 3 (1915), p. 211. Ambrose died in 1557 (BHR, 008, f. 38a).
33 Doreen Leach, *Carpenters in medieval London c.1240–c.1540*, (PhD thesis, University of London, 2017), pp. 191, 235; BHR, 004, f. 225b.
34 BHR, 007, ff. 107b, 113b, 114b, 115a, 118a–119a, 125b, 133a, 135b, 137a, 147b.
35 Survey, SE7 and SW6.
36 LMA, CLA/007/FN/03/017, 29 May, 26 June 1647.
37 LMA, Remembrancia, vol. 1, No. 65; Stow, vol. 1, p. 60; BHR, 009, f. 246b; BHJ, A, f. 18a–b.
38 Stow, vol. 1, p. 60.
39 I am indebted to Stephen Conlin for pointing out that

much of what appears to be the original fenestration of Nonsuch House is visible in the later views.
40 Mark Girouard, *Elizabethan architecture: its rise and fall, 1540-1640* (2009), pp. 147, 196–99.
41 BHR, 008, f. 138b; BHR, 009, f. 248a; Colvin, *King's works*, vol. 3, *1485–1660*, part 1, p. 406; Simon Thurley, *Somerset House: the palace of England's queens 1551–1692*, London Topographical Society No. 168 (2009), p. 19. Stockett was preceded in 1560–63 as chief carpenter to the Bridge House by John Revell, also Surveyor of the Queen's Works. The builder of Nonsuch House was Thomas Strutt (mis-named as 'Stynte' in the accounts for 1579), who had worked for the Bridge House since about 1560 and was paid 3s. per week in addition to his usual 6s. per week for thirty-six weeks in 1577–78 and forty weeks in 1578–79.
42 Richard Thomson, *Chronicles of London Bridge* (1827), pp. 347–48.
43 Apparently initiated in [Edward Hatton], *A new view of London* (1708), vol. 2, p. 790.
44 BHJ, A, f. 18a–b; LMA, Remembrancia, vol. 1, Nos 64, 65.
45 LMA, CLA/007/FN/09/001, pp. 10, 21.
46 Survey, ME12 and MW13.
47 BHV 2, p. 12.
48 LMA, CLA/002/02/01/1230.
49 Derek Keene, 'Shops and shopping in medieval London', in Lindy Grant (ed.), *Medieval art, architecture and archaeology in London*, BAA Conference Transactions 10 (1990), p. 36.
50 Sarah Pearson, 'Rural and urban houses 1100–1500: "urban adaptation" reconsidered', in Kate Giles and Christopher Dyer (eds), *Town and country in the Middle Ages* (2007), p. 50; John Schofield, *Medieval London houses* (1994), pp. 66, 71; Roger H. Leech, *The town house in medieval and early modern Bristol* (2014), pp. 26–28.
51 Harding, p. 42.
52 BHR, 004, f. 215a; CCLD, 02583.
53 BHJ, A, f. 61a; Survey.
54 For this paragraph, see the Survey. See also Survey, SE3, SW5.
55 Derek Keene, 'The property market in English towns, A.D. 1100–1600', in *D'une ville á l'autre: structures matérielles et organisation de l'espace dans les villes Européennes (XIIIe–XVIe siècle)*, Collection de l'École Française de Rome, 122 (1989), pp. 211, 213.
56 In 1404–12 they averaged 89% of annual rents (BHR, 001).
57 Sharpe, *Letter-Book K*, pp. 268–69.
58 BHR, 004, f. 211b.
59 BHR, 005, ff. 157b, 217b; BHR, 006, ff. 86a, 169b; Keene, 'Property market', p. 211.
60 BHR, 060, p. 300; BHR, 004, ff. 50b, 105a.
61 e.g. Sharpe LB, *Letter-Book F*, pp. 244–45; Sharpe LB, *Letter-Book G*, p. 37. See also next paragraph.
62 BHJ, A.
63 BHR, 008, f. 44b; BHJ, A; Keene, 'Property market', pp. 216-17.
64 BHR, 008, f. 67a; BHJ, 001, f. 94b. A lease granted in 1592 to William Jackson and his wife was for twenty-one years if they lived so long (BHJ, A, f. 46a).
65 BHJ, A, ff. 82b, 84a.
66 BHJ, A, f. 39.
67 LMA, Remembrancia, vol. 1, No. 247; BHJ, 001, f. 24a.
68 Harding, p. 39; BHR, 058, f. 125.
69 See BHJ, A. For fines or confiscation for unlicensed subletting, see Harding, p. 42; BHR, 058, f. 61.
70 e.g. BHR, 005, f. 178b; BHR, 007, f. 109a.
71 CCLD, 02498.
72 BHR, rentals, with Figs 66, 71; CCLD, 02498.
73 LMA, CLA/007/FN/010/008; LMA, CLA/007/EM/05/02/009. Upon rebuilding, existing leases were usually extended to sixty-one years.
74 BHR, 060, pp. 118, 256, 295, 345.
75 BHR, 004, f. 223a.
76 e.g. BHJ, A, f. 43b.
77 Keene, 'Property market', pp. 216–18; BHJ, A.
78 BHJ, A, ff. 42a–b, 78a; CCLD, 02681 and 02773.
79 Repertories, vol. 44, f. 57a. For hanging cellars, see CCLD, 02573; BHJ, 001, f. 77a.
80 BHP, 001, 1636–49, order about repairs.

Chapter 6 – Inside the houses in the seventeenth century

1 The inventories of pre-1680s houses are TNA, PROB 4/1104, 2773, 4790, 8224, 11506, 20950 and 25942; TNA, PROB 5/1984; LMA, CLA/002/02/01/1230, 1678, 1934, 1990 and 2275.
2 e.g. Survey, ME3.
3 CCLD, 02655; BHV 2, p. 87; LMA, CLA/007/EM/05/02/009. p. 269.
4 C.C. Knowles and P.H. Pitt, *The history of building regulation in London 1189–1972* (1972), p. 22.
5 BHR, 004, expenses.
6 TNA, C 24/1144, No. 60, pp. 1–2.
7 e.g. BHV 2, p. 85.
8 BHV 1, 1650, 1655.
9 John Schofield, *Medieval London houses* (1994), p. 106; Harding, p. 38.
10 Below, p. 66. See also above, pp. 29–30.
11 Survey, PE18, PW8, PW17.
12 BHP, 003, 1684, measurements made at the south end.
13 Dorian Gerhold, *London plotted: plans of London buildings c.1450-1720*, London Topographical Society No. 178 (2016), pp. 20, 22.
14 BHV 2, p. 83.
15 e.g. CCLD, 02566.
16 Below, p. 67.
17 e.g. BHR, 009, f. 282a; BHP, 006, 1723, petition of Philip Oddy and Joseph Bennett.
18 Richard Thomson, *Chronicles of London Bridge* (1827), p. 511. This seems not to account for the full height of the piers.
19 BHJ, A, f. 142a. There was a similar problem in 1684 (Repertories, vol. 89, f. 130b). The lessee of ME11 in 1623 was forbidden to dig into or deface the stonework, and this was not a standard provision (CCLD, 02664).
20 BHR, 005, f. 2a; BHR, 006, f. 58b.
21 There is one example of a cellar described as being on the same floor as the shop (Survey, ME1), which was probably an error.
22 LMA, CLA/007/EM/05/02/009, p. 231. See also BHP, 006, 1726, proposals for Mr Davis's house.

23 George Dance referred in 1756 to 'the vacuities of the several arches, where the hanging-cellars are now fixed', which he proposed to fill in in order to extend the arches to the new width of the bridge (LMA, COL/CC/LBI/03/001, report of July 1756).
24 Survey, MW7, ME7 and MW12. See also Survey, PE17, ME3, ME4 and SE13.
25 Survey, ME4, ME9, SE2, SE10 and SE13.
26 TNA, C 24/1144, No. 60, p. 5.
27 See Derek Keene, 'Shops and shopping in medieval London', in Lindy Grant (ed.), *Medieval art, architecture and archaeology in London*, BAA Conference Transactions 10 (1990), p. 43; Gerhold, *London plotted*, pp. 72–76.
28 BHR, 005, f. 242a; BHR, 006, f. 147a; BHV 1, August 1652, October 1660.
29 LMA, City Letter-Books, vol. Z, f. 119b. See Keene, 'Shops and shopping', pp. 35–6.
30 Below, pp. 86–87. See Nancy Cox, *The complete tradesman: a study of retailing, 1550–1820* (2000), pp. 81–87.
31 e.g. Harding, p. 38; BHR, 004, ff. 105a, 205a; LMA, CLA/007/FN/03/006, ff. 5a, 7a, 8b, 16b. See Cox, *Complete tradesman*, pp. 80–81.
32 Kathryn A. Morrison, *English shops and shopping: an architectural history* (2003), p. 34; Harding, p. 38; BHR, 060, p. 745.
33 LMA, CLA/002/02/01/1934; TNA, PROB 4/20950. See also BHV 1, 1659, Rucke; CCLD, 02617, schedule; LMA, CLA/002/02/01/1990.
34 LMA, CLA/007/FN/01/018, p. 113; BHR, 060, p. 164; BHR, 008, f. 165b; LMA, CLA/007/FN/07/001; BHJ, 001, f. 2b. See also LMA, CLA/007/FN/07/001, 27 February 1620/21; BHR, 028, 1683/84, casual receipts, 10 and 17 December 1683; BHP, 004, 1709, report of 11 November 1709 on Mr Amy's cellar; BHJ, 011, p. 15.
35 Same position on more than one floor, PW17, ME3; different positions on different floors, MW1, MW2, MW6, SE13, SW6; at corner, MW5, MW12; dimensions given, PE7, PE12, PW12 or 13, SE5–6 (1649); rebuilt, 1650 (SE5–6).
36 Respectively: PW3, SE1, SW1 and SW6; ME3 and ME12; and MW12, SE12 and SW2.

37 TNA, PROB 4/11506. See also TNA, PROB 4/1104.
38 Roger H. Leech, *The town house in medieval and early modern Bristol* (2014), pp. 109–12, 122.
39 MW10 in 1640 and probably SW7.
40 In Ralph Treswell's surveys of 1607–12, there were only a few houses of one-room plan with a shop on the ground floor, and in all but three of these cases there was no kitchen at all. Of those three, in one the kitchen was on the third floor, above a hall on the first floor and a chamber on the second; in one it was on the second floor, above two chambers on the first floor; and in one it was in the cellar; in other words there was no consistent response (John Schofield (ed.), *The London surveys of Ralph Treswell*, London Topographical Society No. 135 (1987), pp. 70–71, 115, 132–33).
41 The exceptions were PW12, PW16 and PW21. For the latter, see Fig. 54.
42 BHJ, 010, p. 65.
43 At PW3 (CCLD, 02693).
44 Schofield, *Medieval London houses*, p. 149.
45 Survey, ME9, ME10, MW9 and SE3.
46 TNA, PROB 4/8224.
47 LMA, CLA/002/02/01/1934.
48 LMA, CLA/002/02/01/1990; above, p. 53.
49 BHV 1, 1649 Lardyn, 1650 Phillipps, 1656 Finch, 1666 Allen (for ME8, SW8, MW12, SE10 respectively).
50 TNA, PROB 4/11506.
51 BHR, 060, pp. 34, 80, 126, 175, 178, 360. Both pulleys and 'shevers' are mentioned, but they were perhaps the same thing.
52 e.g. BHR, 005, ff. 7a, 8b.
53 e.g. BHR, 060, pp. 698, 740.
54 Quoted in Patricia Pierce, *Old London Bridge* (2001), p. 172; I have changed 'eating house' to 'kitchen', and omitted the rest of the sentence, where he indicates that fish were caught using lines.
55 Gerhold, *London plotted*, p. 26.
56 See also Survey, ME7 to 9, MW3, MW5, MW6, SW8, SW11, and the discussion in Schofield, *London surveys*, p. 17. In several cases discrepancies seem to indicate that only part of a divided house is recorded (ME2, ME3, SE14, SW12).

57 Schofield, *Medieval London houses*, p. 115. Chimneys were being built at bridge houses in the 1460s, but whether they were being added to houses which previously lacked them is unknown (BHR, 060, pp. 132, 275).
58 Survey, PW19, ME3B, SE1, SE4, SW1. Several houses (SW5, SW6) had a mix of chimneys in side walls and north–south walls, which could indicate corner chimney stacks, which are more clearly indicated in the hall of SW3.
59 Both Norden's view from the west and the Pepys view show a chimney on the west side of SW6, and the lease description of 1634 confirms that placing; Norden shows one on the east side of SE7. Another possible chimney on the outer edge of a house is at ME9 in Norden's view.
60 BHP, 001, 1630–35, Privy Council order of 21 January 1634/35.
61 BHV 1; LMA, COL/CC/BHC/05/001, p. 209.

Chapter 7 – Fires and rebuildings 1633–82

1 British Library, Sloane MS 1457, pp. 91–94; order of paragraphs altered, and capitalisation modernised here.
2 LMA, COL/CC/BHC/05/001, p. 113; Fig. 56.
3 LMA, CLA/007/FN/07/002, oak timber 14 March 1634 (see note under oak timber 1632–33 indicating that the sums should have been charged in 1633).
4 See James Robertson, 'Persuading the citizens? Charles I and London Bridge', *Historical Research*, 79 (2006), pp. 512–33.
5 LMA, COL/CC/BHC/05/001, pp. 115, 131–32; BHP, 001, 1630–35, Privy Council communication and estimate of costs; Dorian Gerhold, *London plotted: plans of London buildings c.1450–1720*, London Topographical Society No. 178 (2016), pp. 135–37.
6 BHJ, 001, ff. 64b–65b; BHR, 017, rentals; Appendix 6.
7 LMA, CLC/W/GE/001/MS03461/001, 1634; CCLD, 02696; BHJ, 001, f. 110b. See also John Greene in CCLD, 02613.
8 Repertories, vol. 57/2, f. 63.
9 He was described as Anthony Jerman the younger, but it was certainly Edward Jerman who was appointed, as

he was described as master carpenter to the City (an office Edward shared with his father, Anthony), and it was Edward who was later paid for the plan; there was no Anthony Jerman the younger in the family at that date (Repertories, vol. 57/2, ff. 67, 135b; Helen Collins, *Edward Jerman 1605–1668: the metamorphosis of a master-craftsman* (2004), pp. 26–28, 48–51; LMA, CLA/007/FN/03/017, 12 January 1649/50).

10 Collins, *Edward Jerman*, passim.
11 Repertories, vol. 57/2, ff. 113, 135b; BHR (for Darvoll); LMA, CLA/007/FN/03/017, 12 January 1649/50, 12 October 1650. £2.10s.0d. was paid to William Field for assistance with Darvoll's plot (ibid., 27 April 1650).
12 Unless otherwise indicated, the rest of this section is based largely on the weekly accounts (LMA, CLA/007/FN/03/017, 1645–49), the record of leases granted (BHJ, 001, ff.105–13) and the leases calendared at Survey, pp. 165–66.
13 Repertories, vol. 59, f. 58b.
14 Not the second pier as shown in the reconstruction in Home, opposite p. 352.
15 Peter Jackson, *London Bridge* (1971), p. 40.
16 PW6 had been 32 feet from east to west, of which about 29½ feet remained after the widening of the roadway, whereas the new house there was only 24 feet deep.
17 LMA, CLA/007/FN/03/017, 1 December 1646.
18 CCLD, 02649.
19 Below, pp. 125–26.
20 For the yard at PW2, see BHV 1, 1655, 1656, 1659, 1661.
21 LMA, CLA/007/FN/03/017, 28 March, 13 June, 5 September 1646, 29 January 1647/48, 9 December 1648; CCLD, 02727.
22 John Strype, *A survey of the cities of London and Westminster* (1720), vol. 1, book 1, p. 57. See also James Howell, *Londinopolis* (1657), p. 22.
23 Matthew Davies *et al.* (eds), *London and Middlesex 1666 hearth tax*, British Record Society hearth tax series 9.2 (2014), p. 702. From 1655 to 1661 the Bridge House was worried about Richard Westbrooke at PE3 keeping salt in the shop, which it said was rotting the foundations (BHV 1).
24 BHJ, 001, ff. 113a, 134a.
25 BHJ, 001, ff. 163b, 167b. The journal for 1658–63 is missing.
26 LMA, CLA/007/FN/03/017, 6 January 1648/49; Robert Latham and William Matthews (eds), *The diary of Samuel Pepys*, vol. 7 (1972), p. 22; Strype, *Survey*, vol. 1, book 1, p. 56.
27 Latham and Matthews, *Diary*, vol. 7, p. 268.
28 BHJ, 002, pp. 67–71, 84.
29 Nicholas Smith and Joshua Lasher to PW3 and PW5 respectively.
30 BHJ, 002, p. 15; BHP, 002, 1682.
31 BHP, 002, 1666, decision; BHP, 002, 1667 and 1671–72, decisions on leases; BHP, 002, 1682, lists of sheds.
32 LMA, COL/CHD/LA/03/025/009/015.
33 BHP, 002, 1682, petition of Locke and lists of sheds; LMA, COL/CHD/LA/03/067/003; BHV 2, p. 88.
34 See Appendix 6.
35 LMA, P69/MAG/B/001/MS02791/001, p. 21; J.R. Woodhead, *The rulers of London 1660–1689* (1965), p. 79.
36 BHP, 002, 1683, judgment.
37 British Library, Sloane MS 1457, p. 92; BHJ, 001, f. 109a; BHV 1, 1658; https://www.british-history.ac.uk/no-series/cromwell-army-officers/surnames-f [accessed on 8 April 2019]; LMA, P69/MAG/B/018/MS01179/001, p. 929. Finch was a clothworker by company (p. 165 below).
38 BHV 2; CCLD, 02727; LMA, COL/CHD/LA/03/067/003; CCLD, 02591; TNA, PROB 11/381/175. William Finch held several houses in Croydon.

Chapter 8 – Trading on the bridge

1 The two possible exceptions are Alderman Hayes in the larger part of the chapel house in about 1670 (LMA, COL/CHD/LA/03/025/009/015) and Peter Daniel at SE5–6 around 1678 (below, p. 105).
2 TNA, C 7/442/24; TNA, C 6/111/125. John Weld, citizen and fishmonger, was a silkman (CCLD, 02553; Appendix 6), as was Jeremy Tawke, citizen and clothworker (CCLD, 02587; LMA, CLA/002/02/01/1934).
3 Ian Archer, *The history of the Haberdashers' Company* (1991), pp. 2, 26. The Bridge House accounts record haberdashers supplying lead, iron and tiles.
4 Archer, *History of the Haberdashers' Company*, pp. 2–3; Eilert Ekwall, *Two early London subsidy rolls* (1951), p. 141.
5 Archer, *History of the Haberdashers' Company*, pp. 8, 11, 19, 30.
6 Ekwall, *Two early London subsidy rolls*, pp. 141, 146, 213, 216; Reginald R. Sharpe (ed.), *Calendar of wills proved and enrolled in the Court of Husting, London, A.D. 1258–A.D. 1688*, part 1 (1889), p. 86; Ralph W. Waggett, *A history of the Worshipful Company of Glovers of London* (2000), p. 98; Sharpe LB, *Letter-Book F*, pp. 244–45; LMA, CLA/007/FN/01/019, p. 196.
7 Ekwall, *Two early London subsidy rolls*, pp. 213–14; Sharpe LB, *Letter-Book G*, pp. 81, 293; LMA, CLA/007/FN/01/018, p. 218. See also Sharpe LB, *Letter-Book G*, p. 37, for William Hunte in 1355.
8 Waggett, *History ... Glovers*, pp. 8–9, 15.
9 Sharpe LB, *Letter-Book C*, p. 76; Charles Welch, *History of the Cutlers' Company of London*, vol. 1 (1916), pp. 1, 19, 36, 41, 64, 195, 202, 207, 244–45; BHR.
10 It is too early to have been a result of the decline of the Weald's iron industry.
11 Barbara E. Megson, 'The bowyers of London 1300–1500', *London Journal*, 18 (1993), pp. 1–3, 5.
12 Justin Colson, 'Commerce, clusters, and community: a re-evaluation of the occupational geography of London, c.1400–c.1550', *Economic History Review*, 2nd ser., 69 (2016), p. 119. The evidence from London Bridge suggests that the concentration there was not, as suggested by Colson (pp. 119–20), a new feature of the late fifteenth century.
13 Megson, 'Bowyers', p. 7; James E. Oxley, *The fletchers and longbowstringmakers of London* (1968), pp. 13–14; CLA/007/FN/01/019, p. 51. John Verne, also a fletcher, was living at ME6A by 1404.
14 Oxley, *Fletchers*, p. 103; BHR.
15 Oxley, *Fletchers*, p. 148; BHR.
16 Barbara Megson, *Such goodly company: a glimpse of the life of the bowyers of London 1300–1600* (1993), pp. 74, 79,

80, 84; BHR. They may have included John Derneford, the first known Warden (ibid., p. 27), as a John Derneford was a lessee on the bridge in 1404 (at MW8).

17 Megson, 'Bowyers', p. 10; Oxley, *Fletchers*, pp. 35, 104; BHR; BHJ, A, ff. 24a, 33b; TNA, PROB 11/90/288.
18 Ekwall, *Two early London subsidy rolls*, p. 141; Sharpe, *Calendar of wills*, part 1, p. 519.
19 BHR; Marian K. Dale, 'The London silkwomen of the fifteenth century', *Economic History Review*, 1st ser., 4 (1933), pp. 324, 331–33; Kay Lacey, 'The production of "narrow ware" by silkwomen in fourteenth and fifteenth century England', *Textile History*, 18 (1987), p. 187.
20 BHR, 058, p. 140.
21 Caroline M. Barron, 'The "golden age" of women in medieval London', *Reading Medieval Studies*, vol. 15 (1989), pp. 47–49.
22 Clé Lesger, 'Patterns of retail location and urban form in Amsterdam in the mid-eighteenth century', *Urban History*, 38 (2011), pp. 26, 31.
23 Sharpe LB, *Letter Book E*, p. 131.
24 Peter Murray and Mary Anne Stevens (eds), *Living bridges: the inhabited bridge, past, present and future* (1996), pp. 24–25; Marjorie Nice Boyer, *Medieval French bridges: a history* (1976), p. 76.
25 BHR, 004, f. 134b; Survey, p. 150.
26 BHP, 002, 1667 and 1671–72.
27 Claire Walsh, 'Shop design and the display of goods in eighteenth-century London', *Journal of Design History*, 8 (1995), p. 175.
28 Daniel Defoe, *The complete English tradesman* (Alan Sutton 1987 edn), p. 7.
29 Megson, *Such goodly company*, p. 45.
30 Below, p. 135.
31 Derek Keene, 'London Bridge and the identity of the medieval city', *Transactions of the London & Middlesex Archaeological Society*, 51 (2000), p. 153.
32 Stow, vol. 1, pp. 81, 211; Archer, *History of the Haberdashers' Company*, pp. 18–19.
33 See Archer, *History of the Haberdashers' Company*, pp. 238–42.
34 Anne F. Sutton, *The mercery of London: trade, goods and people, 1130–1578* (2005), p. 450.
35 Lacey, 'Production of "narrow ware"', p. 187.
36 https://en.wikipedia.org/wiki/Simon_Lowe_alias_Fyfield [accessed on 18 January 2019].
37 LMA, CLA/007/FN/01/019, p.121.
38 S. Thrupp, 'The grocers of London, a study of distributive trade', in Eileen Power and M.M. Postan (eds), *Studies in English trade in the fifteenth* century (1933), pp. 248–50, 263–65, 269–70, 283; Pamela Nightingale, *A medieval mercantile community: the Grocers' Company & the politics & trade of London 1000–1485* (1995), pp. 1, 227.
39 J. Aubrey Rees, *The Worshipful Company of Grocers* (1923), p. 146. Henry Coke, a lessee on the bridge, was described as 'grocer otherwyse barber surgeon' in 1550 (BHR, 007, f. 147b).
40 Drew Mompesson, lessee of the chapel house and a mercer trading in silk, had himself transferred from the Mercers to the Grocers in the 1560s (Sutton, *Mercery of London*, p. 451), but he seems to have inherited a grocery business and the chapel house from William Bridger (TNA, C 3/106/95).
41 Thrupp, 'Grocers', pp. 274–76.
42 L. Grenade, *The singularities of London, 1578*, London Topographical Society No. 175 (2014), pp. 109–12, 169.
43 Repertories, vol. 3, f. 66b; Repertories, vol. 98, f. 213a.
44 BHV 2, p. 118; BHR, 060, p. 25; BHR, 006, f. 241b.
45 e.g. TNA, C 8/8/92.
46 Quoted in Margaret Spufford, *Small books and pleasant histories* (1981), p. 111.
47 LMA, CLA/002/02/01/1678.
48 BHV 2; Richard Thomson, *Chronicles of London Bridge* (1827), p. 374. There was a pitching block for porters near the north end of the bridge in 1753 (BHJ, 010, p. 324).
49 Spufford, *Small books*, pp. 116–17; Margaret Spufford, *The great reclothing of rural England* (1984), p. 16.
50 TNA, C 8/33/148, C 8/46/65, C 6/111/125, C 6/117/166, C 7/47/113, C 11/1794/20, C 11/1320/56, C 11/1290/15, C 11/1683/17.
51 TNA, PROB 4/11506.
52 TNA, C 104/263, bundle 18.
53 TNA, PROB 4/2773.
54 R.B. McKerrow (ed.), *A dictionary of printers and booksellers in England, Scotland and Ireland, and of foreign printers of English books 1557–1640* (1910), pp. 114–15; BHR, 007 to 019, rentals; CCLD, 02618; BHR, 015, f. 95a; BHJ, 001, ff. 43b, 45a; Henry R. Plomer, *A dictionary of the booksellers and printers who were at work in England, Scotland and Ireland from 1641 to 1667* (1907), p. 79; Survey, SE8. Thomas Gosson was admitted to the Stationers' Company by Thomas Purfoote in 1577 (McKerrow, *Dictionary*, p. 115), and Purfoote was the lessee of SW7 from 1597 to 1612. In 1630, Henry Gosson was citizen and grocer in the committee journal (BHJ, 001, f. 32b) but citizen and stationer in the lease. The occupant of the former Three Bibles in 1654, John Meadowes, was a tallow chandler (CCLD, 02632; TNA, PROB 11/316/145). Other early booksellers seem not have been on the bridge itself, i.e. William Pickering, Hugh Astley and John Tapp, 'under St Magnus's church' or at St Magnus Corner 1556–1631 (Home, p. 223; McKerrow, *Dictionary*, p. 263).
55 McKerrow, *Dictionary*, pp. 213, 252–53.
56 Plomer, *Dictionary ... 1641 to 1667*, pp. 145, 185; *Notes and Queries*, 6th ser., vol. 5, p. 222, vol. 6, p. 446; BHV 1, 1660; TNA, PROB 4/8224; Spufford, *Small books*, pp. 92–98. In 1663 Tyus had some sort of business arrangement with F. Coles (*Notes and Queries*, 6th ser., vol. 5, p. 222).
57 Plomer, *Dictionary ... 1641 to 1667*, pp. 145, 185; BHV 2, p. 120; LMA, COL/CHD/LA/03/014/017; Spufford, *Small books*, pp. 83, 111; TNA, PROB 11/391/380; Henry R. Plomer, *A dictionary of the printers and booksellers who were at work in England, Scotland and Ireland from 1668 to 1725* (1922), pp. 232–33.
58 Plomer, *Dictionary ... 1668 to 1725*, p. 294; Home, pp. 226–27; *British Apollo*, 9-11 March 1709; *Notes and* Queries, 6th ser., vol. 5, p. 223; LLT 1715–27.
59 Plomer, *Dictionary ... 1668 to 1725*, pp. 77–78, 230–31; LMA, COL/CHD/LA/03/067/003; LMA, COL/CHD/LA/03/014/017; LLT 1705; LMA, CLA/007/FN/09/001, p. 6. The Angel was the sign used jointly by Collier and Stephen Foster in 1679, but, as it was described as a little below the gate, it may have been elsewhere (*Notes and Queries*, 6th ser., vol. 5, p. 223).

60 Plomer, *Dictionary ... 1668 to 1725*, p. 285. Mrs Taylor is recorded as the bookseller there in 1678. Home, p. 224, refers to Taylor succeeding Parkhurst at the Bible in 1680, but it is not clear on what authority.
61 Below, p. 112; Home, p. 224; British Library catalogue (for Vousden); LMA, COL/CHD/LA/04/01/048.
62 Plomer, *Dictionary ... 1668 to 1725*, pp. 120, 127, 317; British Library catalogue for John Gilbertson and Henry Green; LMA, COL/CHD/LA/03/014/017. No reference to Green has been found in the land taxes.
63 Plomer, *Dictionary ... 1668 to 1725*, p. 34; LLT 1705; *Notes and Queries*, 6th ser., vol. 5, p. 223, vol. 7, pp. 104, 462; British Library, catalogue entry for *A proper memorial for the 29th of May ...* (1715).
64 On the east side seven from the south end.
65 Home, p. 224; BHP, 002, 1682, lists of sheds; LMA, COL/CHD/LA/03/067/003; Plomer, *Dictionary ... 1668 to 1725*, p. 38; LMA, COL/CHD/LA/03/014/017; Spufford, *Small books*, pp. 88–89, 99; LMA, CLA/002/02/01/2747.
66 Plomer, *Dictionary ... 1668 to 1725*, pp. 38, 220–21; LLT 1705–48; Home, p. 224; Henry R. Plomer and others, *A dictionary of the printers and booksellers who were at work in England, Scotland and Ireland from 1726 to 1775* (1922), pp. 67–68, 116, 127–28; British Library catalogue, entries for Looking Glass; *Notes and Queries*, 6th ser., vol. 7, pp. 104, 462; *General Advertiser*, 10 October 1746, 12 May 1747; *Public Advertiser*, 17 December 1759. Midwinter married Norris's daughter.
67 Plomer, *Dictionary ... 1668 to 1725*, pp. 12–13, 162; *Notes and Queries*, 6th ser., vol. 5, p. 223, vol. 6, p. 532, vol. 7, p. 103; LMA, COL/CHD/LA/03/014/017; LLT 1705–22. John Bush was also recorded as a bookseller at the Black Boy in 1692–96.
68 Spufford, *Small books*, p. 111.
69 Ibid., p. 101.
70 LMA, CLA/007/FN/09/001; LLT 1705–22.
71 LMA, CLA/007/FN/09/001; LMA, COL/CHD/LA/03/014/017; Charles Humphries and William C. Smith, *Music publishing in the British Isles* (1970), pp. 234, 326; TNA, PROB 11/696/336 (Elizabeth Miller); TNA, PROB 31/268, No. 85.
72 Home, pp. 315–16; TNA, PROB 11/776/234 (Joseph Collier).
73 TNA, C 104/62; TNA, C 11/1231/46; TNA, PROB 11/750/225 (Gerrard Pitham).
74 LMA, CLA/007/FN/09/001, pp. 1, 5; TNA, PROB 11/610/462 (Richard Durnford); R. Campbell, *The London tradesman* (1747), p. 256; TNA, PROB 11/698/352 (Richard Durnford); BHR; LMA, COL/CCS/CO/06/004, list of lessees' and occupiers' names.
75 *Weekly Journal or British Gazetteer*, 28 February 1730; TNA, catalogue entry for ADM 106/863/177 and 178.
76 Home, pp. 323–24.
77 Home, pp. 310–11, 317, 318, 322.
78 TNA, PROB 31/8, No. 698.
79 Home, p. 321.
80 TNA, PROB 11/784/231; LLT 1705.
81 TNA, PROB 11/307/411 (Simon Leeson); BHV 2, p. 121; LMA, COL/CCS/CO/06/004, list of houses; LLT 1744.
82 Below, pp. 121–22.
83 Bryant Lillywhite, *London coffee houses* (1963), p. 792; LMA, COL/CHD/LA/03/014/017; LMA, COL/CHD/LA/04/01/048 and 108; LLT 1705–11; LMA, CLA/007/FN/09/001, pp. 28, 81. For Hamet's in 1705, see BHJ, 004, p. 139. Needham's was run by widow Green by 1724 (CCLD, 02670).
84 LMA, CLA/002/02/01/1230, 1934, 1990 and 2275; TNA, PROB 4/2773, 11506, 20950, 25942; above, pp. 95, 98, 99.
85 BHV 1, 1659; BHV 2, p. 116; TNA, PROB 4/4790; LMA, CLA/002/02/01/2275; TNA, PROB 4/20950; BHP, 010, 1748, petition of Anne Putham.
86 Home, pp. 310, 312–15, 317, 318, 321. Vincent was at SW13B from about 1752 to 1756. Stedman was at SE5 from about 1751 to 1753.
87 Thomas Pennant, *Some account of London* (1790), p. 320; Mark Latham, 'The death of London's "living bridge": financial crisis, property crash and the modernization of London Bridge in the mid-eighteenth century', *London Journal*, 35 (2010), p. 170.
88 Kathryn A. Morrison, *English shops and shopping: an architectural history* (2003), pp. 33, 36, 43. The increase in the size of London shops seems to have occurred only after the bridge houses were removed.

Chapter 9 – Families and community

1 The main source for this section is BHR, rentals and entry fines.
2 BHR, 058, ff. 95, 131; BHR, 005, f. 217b.
3 LMA, CLA/007/FN/01/019, pp. 160, 192; BHR, 001; LMA, MS 9171/3, f. 32a, will of William Moger.
4 Barbara Megson, *Such goodly company: a glimpse of the life of the bowyers of London 1300–1600* (1993), p. 80.
5 Harding, p. 174.
6 BHR, 008, f. 120a; http://socrates.berkeley.edu/~ahnelson/SUBSIDY/252k.html [accessed on 8 April 2019]; LMA, MS 9052/4, No. 68, Mary Langham; British Library, Sloane MS 1457, p. 93.
7 TNA, PROB 11/136/34 (William Richbell); BHJ, 001, ff. 43b, 45a; TNA, C 2/ChasI/S43/26; TNA, C 8/39/20.
8 Harding, pp. xx–xxi.
9 TNA, catalogue entry for SP 46/17, f. 25; Ian Archer, *The history of the Haberdashers' Company* (1991), pp. 55, 259; LMA, catalogue entry for HO1/ST/A/102/001.
10 LMA, COL/CC/BHC/05/01, pp. 12, 33; LMA, P69/MAG/B/018/MS01179/001, p. 5; CCLD, 02770; TNA, C 8/195/86; J.R. Woodhead, *The rulers of London 1660–1689* (1965), p. 123.
11 Archer, *History of the Haberdashers' Company*, pp. 240–41; TNA, C 8/195/86; TNA, C 8/39/20; Woodhead, *Rulers*, p. 123; LMA, COL/CHD/LA/03/067/003; BHP, 002, 1677, petition of William Osbalston; TNA, C 5/438/69; TNA, PROB 11/359/156 (William Osbolston).
12 TNA, C 2/JasI/R12/36; CCLD, 02479 and 02567; TNA, PROB 4/11506; LMA, CLC/W/GE/001/03461/001, 1634; BHV 1, 1660; LMA, P69/MAG/B/018/MS01179/001, p. 929; TNA, PROB 11/338/308. He may have been the 'Thomas Ruske' who was Master of the Girdlers' Company in 1661 (T.C. Barker, *The Girdlers' Company: a second history* (1957), p. 167).
13 LMA, COL/CHD/LA/03/067/003; CCLD, 02566;

14 BHP, 003, 1684, account of fines; LMA, COL/CHD/LA/03/044/009; LMA, CLA/007/FN/09/001, p. 9; LLT 1711, 1715.
14 British Library, Sloane MS 1457, p. 93; Archer, *History of the Haberdashers' Company*, p. 241; Woodhead, *Rulers*, p. 56; Timothy Walker, *The first Clapham saints* (2016), pp. 100–01, 121, 124, 223–24; TNA, PROB 11/357/188 (Peter Daniel); BHJ, 001, ff. 117a, 119b–20a; LMA, COL/CHD/LA/03/067/003; CCLD, 02566; LMA, COL/CC/BHC/05/001, p. 241; BHJ, 003, pp. 33, 35.
15 Matthew Davies *et al.* (eds), *London and Middlesex 1666 hearth tax*, British Record Society hearth tax series 9.2 (2014), p. 702; TNA, E 179/258/4; M.J. Power, 'The social topography of Restoration London', in A.L. Beier and Roger Finlay (eds), *London 1500–1700: the making of the metropolis* (1986), p. 214.
16 BHV 2; LMA, COL/CHD/LA/03/067/003; BHP, 002, 1682, petition of Cornelius Herbert; TNA, PROB 11/513/345; BHP, 008, 1735, arrears; BHJ, 010, pp. 138, 142–3, 221; TNA, PROB 11/790/49; CLA/007/FN/09/001, p. 4; below, p. 115; LLT 1705–44; Brian Loomes, *Clockmakers of Britain, 1286–1700* (2014), p. 241; Home, p. 315; LMA, P69/MAG/C/001/MS02785/046 to 059. Cornelius junior was described as a goldsmith in 1725, possibly in error (BHJ, 006, p. 170). A third Cornelius Harbert was apprenticed to his father in 1727 (Loomes, p. 241), but this seems too late for him to have been the Cornelius whose daughter-in-law succeeded him in 1751.
17 John Strype, *A survey of the cities of London and Westminster* (1720), vol. 2, book 5, pp. 133–34.
18 BHR, 008, f. 86a.
19 The numbers listed on the middle part of the bridge were 140 in 1678, 98 in 1689, 99 in 1690, about 134 in 1692/93 and 174 in 1695. It is unlikely that there were many (if any) people exempt; see Tom Arkell, 'An examination of the poll taxes of the later seventeenth century, the Marriage Duty Act and Gregory King', in Kevin Schurer and Tom Arkell (eds), *Surveying the people* (1992), pp. 142–80.
20 LMA, COL/CHD/LA/03/067/003.
21 Craig Spence, *London in the 1690s: a social atlas* (2000), p. 90.
22 LMA, COL/CHD/LA/04/01/048 and 108.
23 Reported in Patricia Pierce, *Old London Bridge* (2001), p. 202.
24 LMA, P69/MAG/A/001/MS11361; LMA, X015/005.
25 Above, pp. 17, 57; below, p. 117.
26 H.F. Westlake, *The parish gilds of mediaeval England* (1919), p. 186; Reginald R. Sharpe (ed.), *Calendar of wills proved and enrolled in the Court of Husting, London, A.D. 1258–A.D. 1688*, part 2.II (1890), p. 550.
27 TNA, PROB 11/179/337.
28 TNA, PROB 11/326/174.
29 TNA, PROB 11/171/58 (Samuel Armitage); TNA, PROB 11/82/374 (William Chambers); TNA, C 2/Eliz/W10/54; LMA, P69/MAG/A/001/MS11361, 1597 marriages; TNA, C 3/447/128.
30 TNA, C 2/JasI/C25/1; TNA, C 8/5/59. See also TNA, PROB 11/123/542 (Avery Dransfield).
31 Charles Welch, *History of the Cutlers' Company of London*, vol. 1 (1916), p. 195; Walker, *First Clapham saints*, pp. 98, 100–01, 224; TNA, PROB 11/326/174; TNA, PROB 4/25942; TNA, PROB 4/25558; LMA, CLA/002/02/01/2275; TNA, C 11/1231/46; above, p. 95.
32 https://www.bellhouse.co.uk/wright-family [accessed on 19 March 2021].

Chapter 10 – The great rebuilding of 1683–96

1 BHJ, 002, p. 155.
2 BHP, 002, 1682, report to committee of 5 May 1682.
3 BHP, 002, 1682, reasons for letting.
4 BHP, 002, 1682, report to committee of 5 May 1682.
5 BHP, 002, 1682; BHP, 003, 1684, abstract of all the leases.
6 BHJ, 003, pp. 33–36; BHP, 002, 1682, petition of William Gray; CCLD, 02519, 02535, 02572, 02596 and 02655; BHP, 003, 1684, receipt by Sheldon to Norman; BHP, 009, 1742, view of tenements leased to Hatchett; BHP, 002, 1682, list of sheds; TNA, C 6/522/126; TNA, C 6/389/70. For Foltrop, see Dorian Gerhold, *London plotted: plans of London buildings c.1450–1720*, London Topographical Society No. 178 (2016), p. 243.
7 BHP, 002, 1682, report to committee of 5 May 1682; Gerhold, *London Plotted*, pp. 268, 270, 273.
8 BHP, 002, 1683; CCLD, 02572; Harrison, quoted in Richard Thomson, *Chronicles of London Bridge* (1827), pp. 472–73; Thomas Pennant, *Some account of London* (1790), p. 320.
9 LMA, COL/CCS/PL/01/128/A to N; LMA, COL/CCS/PL/01/203/58/B; LMA, COL/CCS/PL/01/203/29/C. Caseby said his houses on the west side were 30 feet deep, while his builder said the eastern ones were shallower (TNA, C 6/522/126; TNA, C 6/389/70).
10 BHP, 003, 1684, petitions of Thomas Gray and John Foltrop; TNA, C 6/389/70. The work done is described in BHR, 028, 1681–82 to 1683–84, expenses by order of court.
11 Repertories, vol. 89, ff. 67a–68b.
12 TNA, C 6/522/126; TNA, C 6/389/70.
13 TNA, C 6/522/126; BHP, 006, 1724, letter of W. Hasleham; BHJ, 006, pp. 159–60; LMA, COL/CC/LBI/03/001, valuation.
14 BHP, 003, 1684, abstract of all the leases.
15 Roger Finlay and Beatrice Shearer, 'Population growth and suburban expansion', in A.L. Beier and Roger Finlay (eds), *London 1500–1700: the making of the metropolis* (1986), p. 49. All London population figures are subject to a large margin of error.
16 Above, p. 71: LMA, COL/CC/BHC/05/01, pp. 113–14.
17 Journals, vol. 41, f. 193b.
18 Repertories, vol. 80, f. 254b.
19 Peter Kincaird, *The rule of the road: an international guide to history and practice* (1986), pp. 2–8; M.G. Lay, *Ways of the world: a history of the world's roads and of the vehicles that used them* (1992), pp. 197–99.
20 Repertories, vol. 127, p. 216; statutes, 1756 cap XL, s. 17, 1835 cap L, s. 78; BHJ, 006, p. 16; BHJ, 010, p. 293.
21 BHJ, 003, pp. 178–83; BHP, 003, 1684, committee reports of 5 and 21 February 1683/84. There is no evidence of any widening of the bridge superstructure in the seventeenth

century, suggested as 'probable' by Bruce Watson (Watson, p. 158), and such an expensive and disruptive undertaking would have left plentiful traces in the records.
22 BHP, 003, 1684, petition of John Greene, and notes of 6 March 1683/84; BHR, 028 and 030, rentals.
23 TNA, C 106/85, articles of agreement 1684 (for ME8); CCLD, 02566 (for ME5); LMA, CLA/007/EM/03/222 (for ME10–11). For sizes of hammer beams, see p. 19 above.
24 CCLD, 02566, 02588, 02590, 02591, 02592, 02658 and 02671; TNA, C 24/1144, part 2, No. 60, p. 8; TNA, C 106/85, agreement of 1684. These cover ME4 to 8 and MW9 to 12. The exceptions were 30 feet at ME3 and 28 feet 6 inches and 30 feet 6 inches at the two houses which replaced ME1 (CCLD, 02568 and 02600).
25 BHP, 003, 1684, petition of Antrim and Styleman.
26 Repertories, vol. 89, f. 48b; BHP, 003, 1684, committee business 19 November 1684; BHR, 028, 1685/86, expenses by order of court, March and November 1685.
27 Above, p. 34; BHP, 003, 1684, committee business 19 November 1684; *London Gazette*, 17 August 1685.
28 BHP, 003, 1687, petition of Richard Norman.
29 BHP, 003, 1684, petition of Andrew Dandy; BHP, 003, 1686, petition of Dandy, Norman and Jones; BHP, 003, 1687, petition of Richard Norman; BHP, 003, 1688, petition of Andrew Dandy; BHJ, 003, pp. 84–85. See also BHP, 003, 1685, petition of Andrew Dandy.
30 Survey; CCLD, 02566 and 02658. 6 inches was transferred from MW1 to MW2 (BHJ, 003, p. 54).
31 i.e. ME10–11, MW2–4, MW9–12, but in the latter case, apart from MW12 being replaced by two houses, all the new buildings conformed to the earlier boundaries (CCLD, 02588 and 02590 to 02592).
32 BHP, 003, 1684, committee of 28 July 1684; BHJ, 003, p. 107; BHP, 003, 1688, petition of Andrew Dandy; BHR, 030, 1686/87, expenses by order of court.
33 BHP, 004, 1693, order of 14 September 1693 and committee report of 10 October 1693; BHJ, 003, pp. 184, 187, 190, 191; CCLD, 02568.
34 BHP, 003, 1685, report of Robert Geffery; CCLD, 02600; BHP, 003, 1684, petition of Henry Foot Hamett.
35 CCLD, 02595, 02600 and 02755. Foltrop's shops had been combined into a single shop by 1743 (BHP, 009, 1743, committee report on east side of middle part).
36 BHP, 008, 1744, petition of St Magnus inhabitants.
37 BHV 2, pp. 88, 120; BHP, 003, 1684, petition of Henry Thurston; BHP, 003, 1685, petition of Henry Thurston; TNA, C 6/262/54; LMA, COL/CHD/LA/03/044/009.
38 BHP, 003, 1684, committee business 19 November 1684; BHJ, 003, pp. 66, 68; below, p. 162.
39 BHJ, 003, pp. 61, 62, 68, 81; LMA, CLA/007/FN/010/008; BHP, 003, 1687, petition of Christopher Flower.
40 BHP, 003, 1686, petition of Nathaniel Blagrave.
41 BHP, 003, 1687, petition of Lucy Phillips.
42 BHV 2, 1682; LMA, COL/CHD/LA/03/044/009.
43 Repertories, vol. 90, f. 114a; BHP, 003, 1687, names of tenants at the south end 5 April 1687; BHP, 003, 1688, committee of 26 March 1688.
44 Repertories, vol. 93, f. 79b; BHJ, 003, p. 105; BHJ, 006, p. 173; BHP, 006, 1726, petition of Francis Wilkinson. Wilkinson's lease of 1690 (CCLD, 02796) indicates only that the house had already been rebuilt.
45 BHJ, 004, pp. 8, 21, 25–27, 338; TNA, C 6/414/26; statutes, 8 & 9 William III c. 37, section VII. For the site, see Fig. 114. The City later had to compensate St Bartholomew by the Exchange parish, Evans's landlord, for the ground taken into the roadway (BHJ, 008, pp. 3–4, 72, 85, 96).
46 BHP, 004, 1693, report of 6 October 1693; BHJ, 003, pp. 219, 227; LMA, CLA/007/EM/05/02/009, pp. 312–13; CCLD, 02598.
47 John Strype, *A survey of the cities of London and Westminster* (1720), vol. 1, book 1, p. 57.
48 BHP, 003, 1684, abstract of all the leases; BHP, 008, 1739, schedule of movables.
49 TNA, PROB 4/8532 and 25558; TNA, PROB 31/8, No. 698; LMA, CLA/002/02/01/2747; TNA, C 104/263, bundle 18; TNA, C 11/1231/46. Of the two closets, one was 'on the stairs' and one on the second floor.
50 TNA, PROB 4/25558. Locke's house is identified as PE2 in CCLD, 02655 and LMA, CLC/W/GE/001/03461/002.
51 Above, pp. 73–74; BHJ, 003, p. 20; BHP, 003, 1684, committee business 19 November 1684.
52 CCLD, 02645 and 02693.
53 Philip R. Björling, *Pumps: their history and construction* (1888), pp. 6, 14.
54 TNA, PROB 4/25942. Part of the inventory including the name is missing, but the unknown person was in partnership with John Sheldon at the White Lion; William and John Sheldon were lessees of ME6 from 1667 and ME6 was the White Lion in 1660 and 1675–82 (BHV 1; BHV2).
55 TNA, PROB 31/8, No. 698. Walkden's house is identified from the placing of his widow in the land tax assessment of 1722 (LLT 1722).
56 TNA, PROB 3/56/28. Mitchell's house is identified from LMA, P69/MAG/C/001/MS02785/050 to 054.

Chapter 11 – From the fire of 1725 to the removal of the houses

1 BHP, 006, 1725, report on the fire. The house formerly of Evan Evans was destroyed too, but that was held by the Bridge House only on lease.
2 BHP, 006, 1725, reference of the petition, report on the fire, and case of Gerrard Pitham; BHJ, 006, pp. 192, 196; LMA, CLA/007/EM/05/02/009, p. 269; BHP, 005, 1723 [sic], petition of Philip Oddy and Joseph Bennett
3 BHJ, 006, pp. 190–91, 252–3, 255, 274, 278, 292.
4 BHJ, 006, pp. 335, 349–50; BHJ, 007, p. 254; BHP, 008, 1741, petition of William Kinleside.
5 BHJ, 006, pp. 173, 175, 188, 206; above, p. 37.
6 For the last years of the houses, see Mark Latham, 'The death of London's "living bridge": financial crisis, property crash and the modernization of London Bridge in the mid-eighteenth century', *London Journal*, 35 (2010), pp. 164–84, though some of his conclusions are disagreed with here.
7 Peter Murray and Mary Anne Stevens (eds), *Living bridges: the inhabited bridge, past, present and future* (1996), pp. 29–30, 54–56, 59; above, p. 70; Ralph and Hawksmoor, quoted in Latham, 'Death', p. 167.
8 George and Michael Dewe, *Fulham Bridge 1729–1886*

(1986), p. 24; R.J.B. Walker, *Old Westminster Bridge* (1979), pp. 60, 205–06, 283.
9. BHP, 006, 1722, petition.
10. BHJ, 008 and 009, *passim*; BHP, 009, 1742 to 1744.
11. LMA, CLA/007/EM/05/02/009, pp. 231–35, 271–91.
12. BHJ, 008, pp. 161–62; Howard Colvin, *A biographical dictionary of British architects 1600–1840* (1995), p. 1150.
13. BHJ, 008, p. 175; BHJ, 009, pp. 3, 31, 33, 36, 39–40.
14. BHJ, 009, pp. 7, 16.
15. J. Parry Lewis, *Building cycles and Britain's growth* (1965), pp. 14, 17; Latham, 'Death', p. 175.
16. BHJ, 009, p. 15. The fourteen houses had been thirteen before MW12 was divided into two in the 1680s rebuilding.
17. BHP, 009, 1743, reference of Gerrard Pitham's petition; BHJ, 009, pp. 39–40.
18. BHJ, 009, pp. 40, 45, 47, 49–51; LMA, COL/CC/LBI/03/001, Dance's estimate.
19. CCLD, 02706. An undated list of proposed scantlings for new houses on the bridge has hammer beams 16 by 14 inches, and differs in several respects from what was agreed in the contract (BHP, 010, 1746). Dance received £222.10s.0d. for his surveying and drawing plans of the new houses (BHR, 043, f. 30b).
20. BHP, 009, 1745, report of 19 July 1745.
21. Ibid.; BHJ, 009, pp. 152, 209.
22. Home, p. 266.
23. Latham, 'Death', pp. 172–75, 178–79.
24. BHJ, 009, pp. 210–11, 217–19; Home, p. 311; BHP, 010, 1748, petition of Anne Putham; BHJ, 010, pp. 66–67, 179, 324. The bridge estates committee indicated in April 1747 that it was willing to take responsibility for maintaining the piers and hammer beams, though the Hurds' lease made them wholly responsible for repairs (BHJ, 009, p. 211; CCLD, 06251).
25. BHJ, 010, passim. For Ellgott and Deakin, ibid., pp. 65, 80, 121.
26. Above, p. 130; BHR, 010, p. 28 (for Reynolds' additional £200); LMA, CLA/007/EM/05/02/009, pp. 236–44.
27. BHJ, 009, pp. 128–29; BHR, 043, tenants at will 1754.
28. cf. Latham, 'Death', pp. 176–77.
29. LMA, COL/CCS/CO/06/004, rents 1743–53; BHJ, 009, pp. 128–29; BHJ, 010, p. 19. The committee did not in December 1750 reverse its earlier decision about abating rents, other than in a few cases in return for the tenant undertaking repairs (BHJ, 010, p. 197; cf. Latham, 'Death', p. 177).
30. BHJ, 010, pp. 84, 148, 185, 197; BHJ, 009, p. 149. See also BHP, 010, 1749, report of June 1749; BHP, 010, 1750; BHJ, 010, pp. 100, 142–3. Latham is wrong to say that the tenants were unwilling or unable to repair. The report of 1750 about defective houses referred to by Latham related only to repairs to seven houses (Latham, 'Death', p. 177; BHJ, 010, p. 185).
31. LMA, CLA/007/EM/05/02/009, p. 247; Lewis, *Building cycles*, p. 14.
32. LMA, COL/CCS/CO/06/003, Dance's estimate for repairs 1754; BHJ, 010, pp. 168, 176, 282.
33. Journals, vol. 60, ff. 179a, 189a, 263a; Journals, vol. 61, ff. 31a, 67a.
34. *Journals of the House of Commons*, 1754–57, pp. 349, 520–21, 618; Journals, vol. 61, ff. 58b–59a, 67a–69a, 70b, 72a; BHP, 011, petitions of Henry Barber and William Urlwyn.
35. LMA, COL/CC/LBI/03/001, estimate of 8 April 1758.
36. LMA, COL/CC/LBI/02/001, 2 and 22 June, 29 March 1757.
37. The phasing is based mainly on the dates when the materials of the houses were advertised for sale, in LMA, COL/CC/LBI/04/001. See also BHR, 044, rentals; LMA, P69/MAG/C/001/MS02785/054 to 059; LMA, CLC/W/GE/001/03461/004.
38. Home, pp. 310, 314, 315, 317, 320–22, 324; *London Gazette*, 19 August 1981, p. 10729.
39. Latham, 'Death', p. 181.
40. Watson, pp. 164–66.

Survey of the houses on London Bridge, 1604–83

1. CCLD. Surviving leases were identified from a list made in 1787 (CLA/007/EM/04/015); only a few of those listed then are now missing, and none of those requested which were not on this list were found.
2. A few names of individuals recorded elsewhere have been standardised.
3. TNA, E 179/188/504.
4. BHP, 003, 1684, account of the lesseess' names etc.
5. BHP, 006, 1723, petition of Philip Oddy and Joseph Bennett.
6. LMA, CLA/007/EM/04/003/A, f. 66.
7. e.g. ME4, ME10, MW4, SE3.
8. CCLD, 02655.
9. BHP, 006, 1725, report of 3 September 1725.
10. BHJ, 001, f. 93b. The same dimensions were stated in a lease of 1668 (CCLD, 02781).
11. CCLD, 02672.
12. CCLD, 02809.
13. BHR, 006, f. 249a.
14. CCLD, 02692.
15. CCLD, 02573.
16. LMA, CLA/007/FN/07/001.
17. CCLD, 02528.
18. CCLD, 02549.
19. CCLD, 02677.
20. CCLD, 02636.
21. LMA, CLA/007/EM/03/186.
22. CCLD, 02550.
23. CCLD, 02773.
24. CCLD, 02579.
25. CCLD, 02624.
26. CCLD, 02612.
27. LMA, COL/CC/BHC/05/01, p. 66.
28. CCLD, 02564.
29. CCLD, 02804.
30. CCLD, 02485.
31. CCLD, 02765.
32. CCLD, 02699.
33. BHR, 005, f. 263b.
34. CCLD, 02623.
35. CCLD, 02498.
36. CCLD, 02575. Calverley does not appear in the rentals, because his lease was not due to begin until 1636, but he was the occupant of this house in 1633. His widow's

executor was Thomas Freebody, clearly from the family which leased the house before Calverley (LMA, COL/CC/BHC/05/001, p. 157).
37 LMA, CLA/007/FN/07/002, sales of new lead 6 October 1632.
38 BHR, 004, f. 215a.
39 CCLD, 02583.
40 CCLD, 02816.
41 CCLD, 02626.
42 CCLD, 02576.
43 CCLD, 02779.
44 CCLD, 02676.
45 CCLD, 02563.
46 BHR, 009, ff. 278a, 282a, and rentals; TNA, C 6/262/54.
47 CCLD, 02617.
48 CCLD, 02812.
49 British Library, Add. MS 71008, f. 65a.
50 LMA, COL/CHD/LA/03/025/009/006 and 015.
51 CCLD, 02768. The kitchen, buttery and coal-house are assigned to the first floor here on the basis that otherwise there are too few square feet on the first floor and too many on the second floor.
52 CCLD, 02767.
53 CCLD, 02801.
54 BHJ, A, f. 61a.
55 CCLD, 02568.
56 CCLD, 02503.
57 BHJ, A, f. 48a.
58 CCLD, 02517.
59 CCLD, 02673.
60 CCLD, 02567.
61 CCLD, 02620.
62 CCLD, 02611.
63 CCLD, 02792.
64 TNA, C 24/1144, part 2, No. 60.
65 A storey could be described as the third either counting the ground floor (e.g. MW9) or not counting it (e.g. PW9).
66 CCLD, 03076. The rooms and dimensions were identical in the 1654 lease, except that the chamber on the third floor was described (clearly in error) as 19′ × 19′ (TNA, C 106/86).
67 CCLD, 02521.
68 CCLD, 02538.
69 CCLD, 02496. The description in the 1639 lease is a cut-down version of that of 1616, except for the dimensions of the cellar (18′ × 8′) and the second-floor chamber towards the street (19½′ × 11½′) (CCLD, 02696).
70 LMA, CLC/522/MS23766 (lease of 1684 reciting earlier details).
71 CCLD, 02664.
72 LMA, CLC/522/MS23766 (lease of 1666 reciting earlier details); 1639 information from CCLD, 02663, giving identical measurements except the length of the shop (27½′) and the omission of dimensions for one of the little rooms over the street; it does not mention a hanging cellar.
73 BHV 1, 1647.
74 CCLD, 02810.
75 BHV 1.
76 BHP, 003, 1684, petition of John Greene.
77 CCLD, 02613.
78 CCLD, 02617. See also CCLD, 02608, covering both MW1 and MW2 in 1617.
79 CCLD, 02577.
80 CCLD, 02580.
81 BHV 1, 1667.
82 CCLD, 02690.
83 CCLD, 02622.
84 CCLD, 02695.
85 CCLD, 02791.
86 CCLD, 02611.
87 CCLD, 02790.
88 CCLD, 02784.
89 BHV 1, 1659.
90 CCLD, 02819.
91 BHR; BHJ, A, ff. 123–4.
92 CCLD, 02479.
93 CCLD, 02629.
94 CCLD, 02674.
95 CCLD, 02501.
96 CCLD, 02481.
97 BHV 1, 1667.
98 CCLD, 02614.
99 CCLD, 02588 (lease of 1685 reciting earlier details).
100 BHV 1, 1656.
101 CCLD, 02581.
102 TNA, E 179/252/23, m. 14.
103 CCLD, 02591 (lease of 1685 reciting earlier details).
104 CCLD, 02795.
105 CCLD, 02777.
106 BHP, 003, 1687, petition of Lucy Phillips.
107 CCLD, 02788.
108 CCLD, 02811. BHP, 003, 1687, petition of Lucy Phillips, recites a lease of 1653 to Henry Phillips which is to similar effect, except that 20′ is the north–south dimension of the hanging cellar, and the shop is east–west 25′ besides the counting house and breadth 12′4″.
109 BHJ, 001, f. 44b.
110 BHP, 003, 1684, measurements at south end of bridge.
111 CCLD, 02667.
112 CCLD, 02797.
113 BHJ, 001, ff. 38b, 43b, 45a, 59b–60a.
114 CCLD, 02518.
115 CCLD, 02807. The lease of 1653 is to similar effect, except that the hall and chamber are together 33′ east–west and 19½′ in breadth, and the kitchen and chamber above are said to be of the same length and breadth (CCLD, 02799).
116 BHJ, 001, ff. 117a, 119b–120a.
117 CCLD, 02507.
118 CCLD, 02515.
119 BHV 2.
120 CCLD, 02553.
121 BHJ, 001, ff. 45a, 118b.
122 CCLD, 02618.
123 CCLD, 02632.
124 BHV 1, 1667.
125 CCLD, 02662.
126 LMA, CLA/007/EM/05/01/001, f. 132b; BHJ, 001, f. 30a.
127 CCLD, 02551.
128 CCLD, 02548.
129 LMA, CLA/007/EM/05/02/009, p. 231.
130 BHP, 005, 1712, reports on tenements on south-east end.

131 Ibid.
132 CCLD, 02494.
133 LMA, CLA/007/EM/05/02/009, p. 231.
134 BHP, 005, 1712, reports on tenements on south-east end; BHP, 006, 1726, petition of Gerrard Pitham.
135 CCLD, 02666.
136 CCLD, 02537.
137 CCLD, 02625.
138 BHV 2, p. 83.
139 CCLD, 02800.
140 CCLD, 02539.
141 CCLD, 02771.
142 CCLD, 02686.
143 CCLD, 02808.
144 CCLD, 02482.
145 CCLD, 02483.
146 CCLD, 02681.
147 CCLD, 02582.
148 CCLD, 02534.
149 CCLD, 02557.
150 CCLD, 02813.
151 TNA, C 2/JasI/I&J8/66.
152 CCLD, 02621.
153 CCLD, 02492.
154 LMA, CLA/007/EM/05/01/001, f. 140b; CCLD, 02610.
155 CCLD, 02584.
156 CCLD, 02511.
157 LMA, CLA/007/EM/05/02/009, p. 312.
158 BHJ, 001, f. 93a.
159 CCLD, 02497.
160 LMA, CLA/007/EM/05/02/009, p. 312.
161 CCLD, 02803. Identified as SW11 rather than SW12 (also held by Ward) because the existing lease had nine years to run, and was therefore the lease granted in 1633 (see BHJ, 001, f. 60b).
162 CCLD, 02490.
163 BHJ, 001, ff. 98a, 115b.
164 CCLD, 02787.
165 BHJ, 001, f. 23a.
166 CCLD, 02514. The lease of 1670 gives the same dimensions (CCLD, 02502).
167 CCLD, 02645.
168 CCLD, 02727.
169 Two extant leases relate to this house (CCLD, 02561 and 02571), but neither lists rooms or provides dimensions.
170 CCLD, 02649.
171 CCLD, 02687.
172 CCLD, 02565.
173 BHV 1, 1656, 1659 and 1661.
174 CCLD, 02693.
175 CCLD, 02635.
176 BHV 1, 1656.
177 CCLD, 02680.
178 CCLD, 02656.
179 CCLD, 02587.

Appendices

1 Home, illustration opposite p. 305.
2 Fig. 8; above, p. 34.
3 BHP, 007, 1731, plan.
4 Watson, pp. 136–37.
5 BHP, 006, 1723, petition of Philip Oddy and Joseph Bennett.
6 East side: 341 feet 1 inch (length leased in 1683) plus 22 feet 5 inches (width of PE1). West side: 337 feet 6 inches (length leased in 1683, including about 1½ feet formerly part of PW1) plus 14 feet (remaining part of PW1). See Appendix 6.
7 See Survey, PE9 and 12 and PW4, 14 and 16 (widths from 10 to 11½ feet).
8 Below, pp. 173–75.
9 BHR, 060, pp. 544, 552, 742, 743.
10 Above, p. 63.
11 LMA, CLA/007/FN/07/002, new lead sold 1632/33.
12 In BHR, 001, printed in Harding, pp. 38–43, but with the following errors: p. 39, last entry (Hallary/Sampton), rent is 26s.8d., not 16s.8d.; p. 41, last entry (Burton/Miles), rent is 20s.; p. 42, five entries from end (Bray), rent is 21s.8d., not 32s., and should be followed by additional entry, '(Margia Lyne) <Robert Bray> Alice Bray 32s.' The 1404 rental itself seems to omit one house, in Harding, p. 39, No. 131, between 11th entry (Hert/Spene), numbered 6 Mid E in the accounts, and 12th entry (Verne/Dyngewyk or Tyngewyk), numbered 8 Mid E.
13 BHR, 002.
14 For Cheapside, see Derek Keene, *Cheapside before the Great Fire* (1985), p. 20. I am grateful to Derek Keene for additional information on Cheapside rents.
15 See CLA/007/EM/04/012. Two houses in Old Change were sold in 1512 and two in Paternoster Row were acquired in 1513.
16 E.H. Phelps Brown and Sheila V. Hopkins, 'Seven centuries of building wages', *Economica*, n.s., 22 (1955), p. 205.
17 Gregory Clark, 'Farm wages, population, and economic growth, England 1209–1869', *Economic History Review*, 2nd ser., 60 (2007), pp. 97–135.
18 Above, p. 88.
19 Done using the statutory rate of interest and current length of leases (1570s, 10%, 22 years; 1653, 6%, 61 years; 1744–45, 5%, 21 years) and the tables in Isaac Steell, *Tables for computing the whole value of leases, and fines to be paid* (1770).
20 LMA, COL/CC/LBI/03/001, valuation of houses.
21 In 1654, the entry fine for the eastern part of Nonsuch House agreed the previous year was reduced from £170 to £130 because the transfer of responsibility for repairs meant the fine paid was more than the house was worth (BHJ, 001, f. 149b).
22 BHP, 008, 1742, view of Mr Gray's houses.
23 CCLD, BHR, 001.
24 LMA, CLA/022/01/01/003, houses charged to the land tax.
25 The two parts of Nonsuch House have been excluded because they would dominate the results and were exceptional.
26 BHJ, A.
27 BHP, 008, 1742 to 1744.
28 LMA, CLA/007/EM/05/02/009, pp. 271–91.
29 LMA, COL/CC/LBI/03/001, valuation of houses.
30 BHP, 006, 1726, list.
31 T.C. Dale, *The inhabitants of London in 1638* (1931), pp. 94–95. A quarter of the rent was said to have been abated, and so is adjusted upward by a third here.

32 BHP, 003, 1684, list.
33 See note 14 above.
34 http://estate.rbt.org.uk/estate/London/rent%20tables.asp [accessed on 17 Aug 2018].
35 BHR, 006, f. 177a; BHP, 003, 1688, arbitration between St Magnus parish and John Vyner.
36 Paul Jeffery, *The City churches of Sir Christopher Wren* (1996), p. 257.
37 BHP, 003, 1684, abstract of all the leases. Norden's view shows that the southern limit of the houses on the principal part was between the southern edge of the seventh pier and the southern edge of its starling, and this seems to have been unchanged in the 1680s.
38 BHJ, 001, f. 93b; BHJ, 002, p. 23; CCLD, 02781; BHP, 006, 1725, report of 3 September 1725.
39 BHR, 009, f. 158a.
40 BHP, 003, 1688, arbitration between St Magnus parish and John Vyner; BHR, 010, f. 291a.
41 LMA, COL/CC/BHC/05/001, p. 132.
42 BHJ, 001, f. 67a; BHR, rentals. The continuing payment of rent for PE1 has misled some writers into stating that one house on the bridge was rebuilt in 1639 (e.g. Home, p. 215).
43 BHJ, 001, f. 93b.
44 BHP, 003, 1688, arbitration between St Magnus parish and John Vyner; LMA, P69/MAG/B/018/MS01179/001, pp. 75, 83, leases at end and accounts for 1644–48.
45 CCLD, 02781 and 02655; BHV 2, p. 87.
46 BHP, 002, 1683, report by Mr Oliver.
47 BHJ, 003, p. 15.
48 BHR, 006, f. 177a.
49 BHJ, 002, p. 23. See also LMA, COL/CC/BHC/05/01, pp. 209–10.
50 BHP, 003, 1684, abstract of all the leases.
51 CCLD, 02572.
52 BHJ, 001, f. 113a; Philip E. Jones, *The Fire Court*, vol. 2 (1970), pp. 287–88. Johnson's is identified as the northernmost of Shelbury's two houses in Matthew Davies *et al.* (eds), *London and Middlesex 1666 hearth tax*, British Record Society hearth tax series 9.2 (2014), p. 702.
53 Jones, *Fire Court*, vol. 2, pp. 287–88.
54 BHP, 007, 1732, plan; CCLD, 02487.
55 CCLD, 02487.
56 BHR, 012 to 014, rentals; BHJ, A, f. 67a.
57 BHJ, A, f. 135a; LMA, COL/CC/BHC/05/001, p. 8; LMA, CLA/023/DW/01/295, No. 28; BHR, 014, f. 53b and rentals.
58 LMA, COL/CC/BHC/05/001, p. 66; BHR, 015, rental for 1629–30. It seems to have been part of a larger cellar, divided into two or possibly three parts in 1628, which had belonged to a house called the Key (LMA, CLA/023/DW/01/304 (formerly 305), Nos 14 and 15).
59 LMA, COL/CC/BHC/05/01, p. 132.
60 St Magnus lost some land at its west end to the roadway in 1667, described as being 15 feet from north to south (LMA, P69/MAG/B/018/MS01179/001, leases at end, 1667 and 1669), which suggests that only a projecting area, such as part of the site of the tower, had been taken.
61 *Transactions of the London & Middlesex Archaeological Society*, 2nd ser., 4 (1922), plan opposite p. 395.
62 LMA, COL/CC/LBC/04/02/014, No. 3093.

IMAGE CREDITS

Illustrations not listed below have been provided by the author

Frontispiece (and details, 23, 31, 38, 44, 121) © Ashmolean Museum, University of Oxford

1 (and details, 26, 32, 107, 109, 113) Used by permission of the Folger Shakespeare Library (STC 18643 Copy 1)

2 (and details, 108, 111) By permission of the Pepys Library, Magdalene College Cambridge

3 MOLA (Museum of London Archaeology)

4, 6 Look and Learn/Peter Jackson Collection

8 (and details, 59, 85) London Metropolitan Archives, City of London (London Picture Archive 21502)

9 Reproduced by permission of the 18th Earl of Pembroke and Montgomery and the Trustees of the Wilton House Trust, Wilton House (Wiltshire and Swindon History Centre, 2057-F6-12)

10 (and details, 46, 56, 117) © Trustees of the British Museum (1864,0611.437)

11 London Metropolitan Archives, City of London (COL/CC/BHC/03/003, 1684)

15 (and details, 49, 53) Illustration by Stephen Conlin based on research by Dorian Gerhold; artwork commissioned by *Country Life* magazine)

16 By permission of the Comptroller and City Solicitor, City of London (CCLD, 02535)

18 London Metropolitan Archives, City of London (CLA/007/EM/04/003/A)

21 Illustration by Stephen Conlin based on research by Dorian Gerhold; artwork commissioned by *Country Life* magazine)

22 (see also 43) © The British Library Board (Royal MS 16 F II, f. 73)

24, 25, 27 © Trustees of the British Museum (G,10.44, 1880,1113.1534 and 1880,1113.1548)

28 (see 84)

29 Courtesy of The Lewis Walpole Library, Yale University

30 London Metropolitan Archives, City of London (COL/CCS/PL/01/203/54)

33 (see 84)

34, 35 London Metropolitan Archives, City of London (COL/CCS/PL/01/128Q and COL/CCS/PL/01/203/35)

36, 40 © Trustees of the British Museum (Heal, Topography.42 and Heal,Topography. 107)

41, 42 © The British Library Board (Yates Thompson 47, ff. 94v, 97)

43 (see also 22) © The British Library Board (Royal MS 16 F II, f. 73)

45 (and detail, 109) © Trustees of the British Museum (1880,1113.1120)

47 (and 63 and 118) Reproduced with the permission of the Society of Antiquaries of London

48 London Metropolitan Archives, City of London (COL/CCS/PL/01/202/23)

57 (and 61) © Trustees of the British Museum (Q,6.58)

58 London Metropolitan Archives, City of London (London Picture Archive 4235)

60, 62 © Museum of London (57.54 and 35.190)

65 Efforts to trace the copyright holder for this image have been unsuccessful

67 Mark Smith collection of seventeenth-century London tokens

70, 72–75 © Trustees of the British Museum (Heal,17.152, 1935,0522.7.137, Banks, 97.13.+, Heal,52.54 and Heal,24.7)

76 © The Stationers' Company

77, 78 Efforts to trace the copyright holder for these images have been unsuccessful

79–81 Sotheby's

82 © Trustees of the British Museum (1862, 1011.598)

84 (and details, 28, 33, 86, 87, 92, 115) © Trustees of the British Museum (1880, 1113.1531)

88 (see 98)

89 Look and Learn/Peter Jackson Collection

91, 93, 94 © Trustees of the British Museum (G,10.34, 1880,1113.1197 and Heal,Topography.91)

96, 97 London Metropolitan Archives, City of London (COL/CCS/PL/01/128E and COL/SVD/PL/03/0002)

98 (and detail, 88) © DAE Picture Library/Age Fotostock

99, 100 © Trustees of the British Museum (1909,0406.4 and 1880,1113.3872)

101 © Trustees of the British Museum (1866,0407.270)

102, 103 © Trustees of the British Museum (G.13,13 and 1880,1113.1575)

104 London Metropolitan Archives, City of London (COL/CC/LBC/04/02/002, No. 307)

105 © Trustees of the British Museum (1880, 1113.3858)

106, 114 London Metropolitan Archives, City of London (London Picture Archive 28779 and COL/CC/BHC/03/007, 1731)

116 © Trustees of the British Museum (1882,0211.603)

123, 124 By permission of the Comptroller and City Solicitor, City of London (CCLD, 02655)

125 © Museum of London (50.31)

126 By permission of the Comptroller and City Solicitor, City of London (CCLD, 02572)

INDEX

All references are to pages; numbers in *italics* refer to illustrations and their captions.
Under 'Occupations', references are sometimes to company affiliation rather than necessarily to the trade practised.

Abchurch Lane *100*, 142
Abyndon, John *84*
Adams, John *97*
Adelaide House 184, *184*
Agas map *39*
Akers, William 136
Aldermanbury 85
Aldermen, Court of 40, 44, 71, 90, 118
alehouses, *see* London Bridge shops
Allen, Henry 54, 159–60, Nathaniel 160
Ambrose (Ameros), Richard 49
Amell, John 85, 111
Amey (Amie), Henry 164, 177
Amy, John 21
Angell, William 164
Anselm the furbisher 86
Apjohn, William 104
Appleby, William 91
apprentices 107, *108*, 109
archery 85–86
Armitage, Joan 110, Samuel *90*, 110, 145
Army, clothing contractor 123
Arnold, Francis 149, Richard *84*, Thomas 158
Arundell, John *108*
Asgill, Henry *114*, 115
Ashford, Kent 92
Assheby, Alice 86
Astley, Hugh 192
Austin, Edward 176, Jane 109, widow *97*

Ayers, Elizabeth *108*
Ayloffe, Joseph 125

Babyngton, Agnes 86
Back, John 91, 95–96, *108*
Baker, Alexander 183, John *97*
Ballad Partners 94
Balsam of Chili 94
Barber, Henry 139
Barnaby, Isabella *84*, 86
Barnard, Dr E. 109
Barnes, Jane *108*
Barton, Richard *108*, Robert 176, William *84*
Basinghall Street 130
Basse, Agnes *84*
Basset, Henry *84*
Bateman, John 160, 177
Bath, Pulteney Bridge 19
Bayley, John *108*
Beale, Stephen *90*, Valentine *90*, 145
Bear Tavern, Southwark 123, *159*, *162*
Becket, Thomas 31, 32
Bedford, Earl of 70
Bedwood, Joanna *108*
Bekyngham, Robert 56
Bettesworth, Arthur 95
Bigg, Thomas 115, 116
Billingsgate 40
Bishop, James 92

Black Death 28–29, 43, 88, 109
Blackfriars Bridge 136–37
Blackwell, Timothy 65, *97*, 101, 159
Blagrave, Nathaniel 122
Blancher, John 163
Blare, Elizabeth 95, Joseph/Josiah 95, 96, 101
Blower, John *108*
Blundell, Ann *108*
Boarne, Elizabeth *108*, Robert *108*
Bodman, Ralph 91, *97*, *108*, 109
bogemen 45
Bohemia, Queen of 55
bookshops, *see* Occupations, booksellers
Boorne, William 149
Borham, de, Robert 85
Borough, Southwark *39*, 126, 142, 167
Bouth, Andrew 90
Bowles, John, prints by *123*, *135*, 171
Bowyers' Company 86, 103
Boxley, Kent 100
Bradway, Mary *108*
Branches, Robert 39
brass wire 96, 98
Brathwaite, John 73
Bray, Alice 86, Anthony 53, Richard 86
Brett, Thomas 165
bridge estates committee 43, 55, 57, 75, 104, 116, 129–30, 158

Bridge House 5
  accounts 1, 44
  chief/master carpenters, *see* carpenters
  estate 5
  finances 5, 45, 56, 74, 88, 129, 130, 142
  ownership of the bridge houses 55
  records 1–2
  rent gatherer 104
  repairs and rebuilding by 34, 44, 54, 57
Bridge Street 31, 95, 182
Bridge Ward 8
  beadle 37–38, 41, 163
  meetings 110
bridge wardens 5, 31, 38, 74, 103
Bridger, William 33, 192
bridges, medieval
  chapels on 31
  inhabited 1, 3–4, 19, 23
  piers 19
  widths 13–14
Briggs (Brigges), John 69, *90*
Bright, John 45, Thomas *84*
Bristol 65, 85
  Bristol Bridge 19
Britt, Sarah 176
Broad Street 27
Bromley, Kent 104
Brooke, James 100, John 146, 177, 183
Brookes, Mrs *90*

Broome, John *90*, Mrs John *90*
Brown, John *84*
Browne, Robert 104–05, *114*, 115, 120, Samuel 153, Thomas *97*, *108*, 109
Buck, Nathaniel and Samuel, panorama by *122*, 171
Buckham, Thomas 176
Buckingham, Duke of 49
Buckingham, Francis *108*
Buckstead, William 86
Bull, Cornelius 67, *97*, 101
Burleigh, Lord 53, 55
Burr, Olyffe 107
Burrow, Robert 166
Burvylde, Thomas 107
Burwash, Sussex 92
Bury, Henry 151
Busbridge, John *64*, 110, 150
Bush, John 193
Butlar, Sir William 36
Butler, Elizabeth 146
Butlin, Edward 101
Byfleet, Surrey 98

Cade's rebellion 36, 42
Cadman, Michael 91
Caernarvon, Wales 92
Calcott, Edward jun. 75
Calverley (Coverley), John *65*, *90*, 149
Camberback, Joshua *108*
Camberwell 111, 125
Campbell, Robert 98
Canaletto *134*, 171
Canterbury 92
  Cathedral Priory 29
Capper, John *97*
Carlile, Henry *84*
carpenters, Bridge House's chief/master carpenter of the land works
  Ambrose (Ameros), Richard 49, 50
  Coke, Humphrey 45–49
  Darvoll, Joseph 71, 73, 74

Gray, William *114*, 115, 118
  Maunsey, Thomas 49
  Revell, John 189
  Stockett, Lewis 52
Carpenters' Company 49
Caseby, Humphrey *21*, 75, *114*, 115, 116, 129
Cater, John *108*
Catherine Wheel Alley 93
Chamber of London, rent gatherer 104
Chamberlin, Henry 146
Chambers, Abraham *90*, Elizabeth 110, John 110, Mrs sen. *90*, Susanna 110, William 110
Chamley, Jeremiah *90*
Champney, Jeremy/Jeremiah 63, *90*, 145, Thomas 149
Change Alley, Cornhill 142
chapel, *see* London Bridge, chapel
Chapelier, le, William 81
Chapman, John sen. and jun. 103, Samuel 103
Charles I 70, 71, 117, 128
Charles II 105
Charlton, Martha *15*, 156, William 146
Cheapside 24, 27, 43, 54, 63, 85, 88–90, 95, 178–79, *178–79*
Cheshire, John 176
Chester 85, 153
Child, Coles 98, 142, John 165
Christie, Mr 101, 136
Church Yard Alley *140*
Churcher and Christie 101
Clapham 105, 111
Clarke, Edmund 121, 154, John 162, Robert 54, *97*, 101, 111, 160, *160*, 177
Clayton, Margaret 110, William 53, 110
Clearke, Mr 176
Clegate, Richard 176
Cliffe, Philadelphia *108*
Clockmakers' Company 106
Clovile, Roger 40
clustering of trades 87, 101

coaches 117, 118, 128
coal 62, 66, 147
Cocker, John 128
Codde, John 63, *84*
coffee houses 83, 100, 101, 128
Coke, Henry 192, Humphrey 45–49
Coleburne, Richard *97*
Coles, F. 192
Collett, Thomas *114*, 115, 182–83, *183*
Collier, Joseph 94, *97*
Common Council of City of London 136–39
Coney, John 166
Conlin, Stephen, drawings by *20*, *29*, *52*, *62*
Conney, Daniel 75, *90*
Cooke, E.W., drawings by *139*, *141*
Cooper, Dennison and Walkden 142
Cornhill 27, 142
Cornwall 89
Cotiler, le, Simon 85
Cotton, Lawrence 40
Covent Garden 70, 73
Coventry 52–53
Coverley, *see* Calverley
Cowper, John *84*
Cranbrook, Kent 92, 104
Crane, John *84*
Crosby, Sir John 36
Crowder, Stanley 95
Croydon 92
Crull (Crulle), Alice 103, John 103, Master 103, Richard 103, Robert 86, 103, Thomas 84, 103
Curette, John *84*
Curle, Samuel *108*
Cutlers' Company 85

Danbrooke, Christopher 160
Dance, George sen. 23, 61, 129–31, 135, 136, jun. 14
Dandy, Andrew 120, 121
Daniel (Daniell), Elizabeth 103, Lionel *90*, 105, Mary *105*, Peter *97*, 105, 109, 110, 177, Roger 152, William 105, *105*, 110, 111, 158, 177
Daniell, William, print by *138*
Dannold, Samuel 162
Darvoll, Joseph 71, 73–74
Davis, Mary *108*
Davison, Charles *108*
Dawling, Charles 109, Elizabeth 109, John 136
Deakin, William 135
Defoe, Daniel 87
Denn, Basil jun. 101
Derneford, John 192
Dickins, Mr 100
Dixson, Thomas 177
Dobson, Thomas 109, 176
Dorking 91
Downes, Robert *108*
Drake, Timothy *90*
Dranfield, Avery 110
Dransfield, John *90*
Ducey, John 160
Dudson, Nicholas *97*
Dunkin (Dunkyn), James *90*, 91, 156
Dunton, John 95
Durnford, John 98, Richard sen. and jun. 98, Thomas 92, 98
Dustone, John 187
Dye, Anne 34

Earle, John 149
Ebmede, Thomas *84*
Edmeade, John 45
Edmund, Saint *43*
Edward the Confessor 35
Edward IV 35
Edward VI 32
Elleston, Joseph *97*
Ellgott, William 135
Ellis, Randall 165
Elsey, Jane *108*

Elwood, Thomas 164
Elyott, Henry 162
English, Richard 156
Erfurt, Germany, Krämerbrücke 19
Est, William 37
Estgarston, John *84*
Eton, John *84*
Eunuch, Bridget *108*
Evans, Evan 123, *159*
Exeter, Exe Bridge 19

Fairfax, Sir Thomas 35
Faryngton, Thomas *84*
Fauconberg, Thomas, rebellion by 35, 36, 42
Felde, Henry *84*
Ferun, le, Andrew 23, Eufemia 23
Fillett, Peter 52
Finch, Francis 77–79, *90*, 156, 165, 176, Joyce 79, William 79, *97*, *108*
firearms 65, 86
fires, see London Bridge, fires on
Fish Street Hill 69, 118, *135*, 142
fishing 98
Fitzherbert, William 165
Fitzhugh (Fitzhughs), William *97*, 165, 177
Fleet, River or Ditch 85, 136
Fletchers' Company 85–86
Flitcroft, Henry 139
Foltrop, John 79, *114*, 115, 119, 121, 122, 124, 125
Forman, Gilbert *84*
Foster, Stephen 95
Fourbour, le, Reginald 86
Fowler, Richard 98
Foxe's *Book of Martys* 41
Foxhall, Thomas 110
fraternities 31, 110
Frecok, Isabella *84*, Richard 46
Freebody, Thomas 197
Fresh Wharf 181, *182*
frost fair *78*
Fuse, Mary *108*

Gamage, Nicholas 93
Gandre, Ralph 85, Thomas 85
Gardiner, Abraham 152, 154, 155
Gardner, Sarah 156
Gardyner, Richard 46
Garitte, John *84*
Garnell, Richard 42
Gatcliffe, Russell 96
Genvey, Felix *84*
George, Edward 118
Gibson, Richard *84*
Gilbertson, John 95
Giles (Gyles), William 92, *92*, *97*, 101
Gill, William 100, *100*; see also Wright and Gill
Gille, William *84*
Girdlers' Company 194
Gloucestre, de, Thomas 81
Glovers' Company 85
Goldesburgh, de, John 81, Robert 81
Goldham, James *91*, 177; see also Houldinge
Goodenough, Edmond 161
Goodere, John *97*
Goodhew, John *108*
Gosson, Alice 93, Henry 93, *159*, Joseph 93, Thomas 93, 192
Goudhurst, Kent 92
Gould, widow *97*
Gouldham (Golding), Henry *97*, 177, 181
Gover, John *90*, 110, 146
Grant, John 98, *99*, 101, 130
Gravel Lane 111
Gravesend 91
Gray, Henry 163, Rice 146, 164, Thomas *114*, 115, 121, 124, William *114*, 115, 118
Great Fire of London 75, *76*, *77*, 181, 182
Great Queen Street 73
Green (Greene, Grene) *97*, 176, Cicely *108*, Edward *90*, 176, Henry 95, John 75, *90*, 118, 148, 150, 153, 176, Thomas 54, 151, widow 193, William *84*

Gregory, Arthur 8
Grenade, L. 8, 17, 90
Grocers' Company 36, 89
Grover, Samuel 98, *99*, 101
Gryffen, Edwin 145
Gyles, see Giles

Haberdashers' Company 88, 104, 105
Hall, Thomas 153
Halle, John 86
Hamett, Henry Foot 100, Susanne 100
Hamond, John *84*
Hampton Court 21, 49
Harbert (Herbert), Cornelius sen. *97*, 106, *106*, 115, Cornelius jun. 106, Elizabeth 106, Margaret 106, William 96, 106, *107*, *137*, 142
Harding, Matthew 90
Hardy, Robert *84*
Harrington, Mary *108*
Harris, Thomas 95
Harrison (Harreson), Nicholas 177, Ralph/Raphe 110, 156, Robert 176
Harwill, Daniel *108*
Hastyng, John 37
Hatchett, Thomas *114*, 115, 116
Hawksmoor, Nicholas 5, 128
Hayborne, John 86
Hayes, Alderman 191
Hayward, Mrs *108*
Head, William *97*
heads of traitors 35, 36–37, 39, *39*, 48
hearth tax 67–68, 75, 105, 150–66, 176–77
Heath, Thomas 159
Hellingly, Sussex 92
Henry VII 39
Henry VIII 32, 50
Herbert, see Harbert
Hertwell, William *84*, 85
Hewett, Anne 106–07, William 106–07
Hickman, Thomas 145
Higgins, Mary *108*

Highways Act 1835 118
Hill, Edward *108*, Elizabeth *108*, John 176
Hilliard, Richard 176
Hinxhill, Kent 95
Hobart, William *97*
Hobbs, Thomas 165
Hodges, F. 95, James 95, 137–38
Holden, James 177
Hollar, Wenceslaus, prints by *10*, 11, 49–51, *50*, 60, *70*, 71–72, *72*, *77*, *163*, 170–71
Hollier, Thomas 166
Holloway 95, 111
Holte, William *84*
Hondius, Abraham *78*
Hooke, William 65, 145
Horne, Mary *108*
Horsbeke, Robert *84*
Horton, Mary *108*
Hotham, Matthew 96
Houldinge (Goldham?), James 177
Howard, James 101, John 142, William 176
Humfrey, John *84*
Hunte, George 155
Hurd, Christopher 130, Francis 130
Hutchenson, William 149
Hytherpool 42

Ince, Robert *108*
ink powder 100
inventories, probate 53–54, 62–67, 93, 100–01, 124, 126
Isembert of Saintes 3–4, 18, 23

Jackson, Peter, drawings by *4*, *6*, *117*
James I 70
James, John 96, Richard *84*, Thomas 53
Jenkins, Grace *108*
Jerman, Edward 71, 191
John (King) 3, 23
Johnson, Helena *108*, Isebrande 48, John *114*, 115, 176, 182
Jones, Inigo 70, 71

Jongh, Claude de 11
Jonson, Benjamin 93
Juse, Mrs *97*

Kellow, William *84*
Kentish Men, Society of 96
Kentish, Thomas *114*, 115, 118, 180, *181*
Kenton, William 166
Kidder, Thomas 156
King (Kinge, Kynge), John *84*, Ralph 177, Richard *97*
Kinleside, William 128
Kirby Hall, Northants. 49
Kirby, Francis 74, 165
Kirke, Robert *108*
Knight, Thomas 177, William *5*

La Rochelle 4
Labelye, Charles *9*, 10–11, 167, 171
Lancaster, John *97*, *108*
Langham, Benjamin 104, Jane *90*, 104, 150, John 103, 104, Mary 104, 150
Langstone, Thomas 86
Lardine, John 152
Lasher (Lusher), James 55, 152, Joshua *97*, *108*, 166, 176, Nathaniel 109, 176
Latham, William 156
lattices 63
Lawrence, James *108*
Lawrymore, John *90*
Leadenhall Street *99*, 102, 142, 179, *179*
Leather, Mary 162
Leathersellers' Company 85
Leaver, Edmond 145
Lee, Arthur *90*, 110, 143
Leeson, Simon 119, 152
left-hand driving 117–18
Legge, George 177
Lever, Mrs 21
Lewis, Alice 45, Thomas 45
Leybourn, William 12
 plans by *21*, *181*, *183*

lighthouses 104
Ligoe, George *108*
Little Eastcheap 69
Little Moreton Hall, Cheshire 50
Living, Edward *108*
Locke, Gervase 75, 111, 115, 125
Lombard Street 90
London
 changing character of City 111, 126
 identity, contribution of bridge to 8
 population of 117
 property market in 129, 130, 136
 shopping in 88, 90, 101–02
London Bridge
 arches 5, 22
 cage 41, *41*
 chapel 5, 7, 23, 25–26, 31–34, *32–34*, 49, 110; *see also* London Bridge houses, chapel house
 closures at night 8
 collapses of 5, 21, 35–36, 42
 construction of 3–4, *4*
 corbels 21, 119
 datestones 3, 46
 demolition of *141*, 142
 drawbridge 5, 7, 8, *28*, 38–39, 119
 drawbridge tower 7, 35, 38–40, *39*, 46, 50, 175
 excavation of arch 167, 184
 fires on
  1212/13, 23, 31
  1504, 44–45
  1633, *9*, 69–71, *90*
  1666, 75, *76*, *77*, 181, 182
  1725, 37, 127–28
 fishpond at chapel 34
 foreign visitors, observations on the bridge 8
 gate keepers 37, 38, 85, 86
 hammer beams 19–20, *20*, 57, 61–62, 73, 112, 116, 119, 127, 129, 130, 136

heads of traitors *35*, 36–37, 39, *39*, 48
keep-left and keep-right rules 117–18, *117*
length of 3
lighting 17, 186
maintenance of 5
mills on 188
northern end of 180–84
piazza *34*, 129, *131*
piers 4–5, *5*, 14, 18, *18*, 19, 22–24, 45, 61, *139*, 142, 167
plans of 8, *9*, 10–11, *18*, *21*, *27*, 70, *140*, *159*
privies, public 40
reconstruction of plan 10–11, 17–18, *18*, 27, *27*, 30, 167–69
Rennie's bridge 142
road chain 41
roadway 12–14, *16*, 70
 gutter 68
 height 15, 37, 117
 not straight 8, 10, 18, 167
 steepness reduced 128
 width 12–14, 37, 115, 117, 167, 184
 widening of 34, 36–37, 70–71, 73, 105, 115, 117–19, 123–24, 139, 142, 167, 184
royal arms 37, *37*
Square, the 7, 14, 25–26, 121, 150
staples 36, 41
starlings 4–5, *5*, 142
stocks 41, *41*, 91
stone gate 7, 13, 23, 35–38, *35–37*, 93, 127, 128, 138, 159, 163, 168
stone ribs 21–22, *21*
street keepers 117, *117*, 118, 128
temporary bridge *137*, 139
tolls 5, 39, 104, 161
traffic growth 117, 128
traffic management 117–18
views of the bridge 11
 reliability of 143, 170–71

waterworks and water wheels *9*, 41, *70*, 125, *134*
widening of bridge 137–39
winds, impact on bridge 17, 75
See also bridge estates committee; Bridge House; bridge wardens; London Bridge houses; London Bridge shops
London Bridge Act 1756, 137–39
London Bridge Coffee House 100
London Bridge houses
 balconies 74, 116, 143
 boundaries between houses, longevity of 14, 120
 brick, use of 58, 127, 130, 143, 181
 building agreements and leases 21, 56, 112, 115, 119, 121, 122, 130
 building materials 58, 60
 cellars 9, 12, 17, 32–34, 61–62, 168
 chapel house *9*, 32–34, *33–34*, 55, 60, 61, 64–66, 100, *100*, 104, 119, 136, 139, 150–51, 167, 168; *see also* London Bridge, chapel
 chimneys 58, 67–68, 74, 120
 coal holes 66
 collective action by occupants 109–10
 cost of building 73, 74, 116, 120, 122, 130, 135
 counting houses 62, 64
 cross buildings 15–16, *15*, *18*, *20*, 29–30, 45, 49, 60, 66, 74, 115, 117, 121, 122, 130, 143, *149*, 168
 damage by boats 63
 dates of building 46
 depths of 14, 18, 48, *114*, 115–16, 119, *119*, 121, 122, 130, 168
 dining rooms 53, 64, 67, 74, 124, *124*
 drawbridge houses 14, 25, *26*, 27, 29, 42–43, *122*, *162–64*
 enlargement of 14, 54, 157, 162
 entry fines 33, 53, 55, 129, 135, 136, 172, 178
 fire insurance 127, 129

INDEX

fire risk 115, 121, 127–28; *see also* London Bridge, fires on
forges and furnaces 88, 101
galleries 33, 66, 150
gardens 74, 121
garrets 24, 65–66
grouping of 7, *7*, 25
halls 64–66, 126
hautpas, *see* cross buildings
heating 67–68
house with many windows 39, *48*, 49–50, *50*, 63, 122, 158, 163, *163*, *164*, 170
households and household size 107, *108*, 109
intermixed tenancies 60
jettying 60, 123–24, 143, 157
kitchens 54, 58, *63*, 65, 74, 125
leads 66, 74, 119, 130
leases 1–2, 17, 23, 55–57, 58, 143
mergers of 18, 26, 43–44, 173–75
Nonsuch House, *see* Nonsuch House
number of 25, 27, 43, 45
numbering systems 172
origins of 23–24
ovens 65, 88, 135, 149
parlours 64
party walls 58, 143, 168
plans of *51*, *125*, *131*, *181*
plot size, variation in 60
population of 107, 109
privies 68, 74, 124, 130
rebuilding of houses 44–54, 57, 152, 155, 158, 183
  houses of 1645–49, 71–75, *72*, *73*, 165–66
  houses of 1683–96, 19, 44, 112–24, *113–14*, *119*, *121–25*
  houses of 1740s, 19, 130, *131*, *133*, 135
  building by contractors 72–73, 130
  building by tenants 46, 57
reconstructed cross sections of *15*, *24*, *53*, *61*, *64*, *65*, *124*, *149*

removal of 139
rentals of 1, 172, 178–79
  rental of 1358, 24–30, *26*, 172
rents 6–7, 25, 27, 29, 88, 90, 102, 127, 172, 178–79, *178*, *179*
repair of 24, 30, 56–57, 112, 136
scaffolding 45, 56–57
sagging of 81, 116, 117, 130
sheds built after Great Fire 24, 75, 77, *78*, *79*, 87, 95, 107, 112, 115
shops, *see* London Bridge, shops
solars 24
stairs 63, 74, 116
storey heights 115, 119, 130
storeys 24, 54, 60, 73, 170
sub-letting 56
tapestries in 53, 67
tenants at will 55, 135
waterhouses and water supplies 65, 67, 73–74, 125–26, 143
weaponry displayed 64–65
weatherboarding 46, 58, 60
wheelage house 41, 104, 122, 161
widths of 14, 26–27, 43–44, 73, 173–75
windows 49, 60, 63, 74, 126, 150, 154
yards 74
London Bridge shops 24, 62–63, 80–102
  alehouses 87, *99*, 100, 122, 136, *148*, 150
  Bridge House policy on trades 87, 88, 135
  clustering of trades 87, 101
  customers of 91–93, *92*
  furnishings 63, 126
  glass windows 63
  lattices 63
  occupations conducted in 29, 74, 82–83
  single-storey shops of 1680s, *78*, *119*, 121–22, 130
  See also signs of London Bridge shops
Longbowstringmakers' Company 86
Love, Richard 67, 176
Lowe, Simon/Symonde 46, 63, 89

Lower Thames Street 142
Ludgate 85
Lusher, *see* Lasher
Lutman (Luttman), Thomas *97*, *108*
Lydgate, Jon *43*

Maidstone 92, 100
Major, *see* Moger
Man, Thomas 176
Manfeld, Germanus *84*
Margate 92
Marlow, William, painting by *182*
marriage tax 107, 109
Marshall, Arthur *97*
Marten, Abraham *90*
Mary I 35
Maunsey, Thomas *49*
Maye, Susan 153
Maynard, John *49*
Meadowes, John 159, 192
Mells, Somerset *92*
Mercers' Company 89, 104
Merchant Taylors' Company 88
Merci, Luigi 96
Middleton, Thomas 93
Midmore, Ellis *90*, 145, Joyce 155
Midwinter, Edward 95
Miles, John *84*
Milk Street 89
Miller, Elizabeth 96, John 96
Milton, John sen. 56, 148, jun. 56
Mitchell, Daniel 126, Edmond *108*, John *108*
Mitton, Edward *97*, *108*
Moger (Major), John 103, Juliana 103, Katherine 103, Thomas *84*, 101, William sen. and jun. 103
Moldeson, Thomas *84*
Mompesson, Drew 192
Moreton Corbet, Shropshire 52
Morgan, William, panorama by *51*, *78*, *164*, 171

Morris, Peter 41
Morteyn, Thomas *84*
Motham, William 109
Mott, Roger *97*
Mountjoy, Edmond 164
Munns (Muns, Munnes), Edward *91*, 111, 164–65
Murchard, Henry 110
Muschampe, Edward 40
music shops 83, 96

Nash, George 159
Navy, supplies to 98
Needham, Thomas *97*, Mr 100
Negoose, Joseph 157
Nethersoll, Alice 153, William 153, family 104
New England 92
New Model Army 35
Newcastle Bridge 129
Newcomen Street, Southwark 37, *37*
Newenton (Newyngton), Simon *84*, 85
Newland, Peter *97*
Newnham (Newman), William *90*, 148
Newport, Essex 149
Newport Pagnell, Bucks. *92*
Newton, William *84*
Nicholas, Giles *84*
Nicholls, John *97*
Nicholls, Sutton, print by 11, *33*, *35*, 54, *113*, *114*, 121, *160*, 171
Nicholson, Edmund 110, Margaret 110
Nonsuch House 7, 12–14, 17, *20*, 40, *48*, 50–54, *51–53*, 55, 57, 60, 62, 63, 67, 100–01, 110, 119, *120*, 129, 153, 156, *164*, 171
Nonsuch Palace 50
Norden, John 17
  view of London 11, *48*, 148, 154
  view of London Bridge *1*, 11, *33*, 34, *35*, 63, 93, *144*, 150, *151*, 157, 168, 170–71

Norman, Richard *114*, 115, 120
Norris, Thomas 95, 111
North Foreland, Kent 104
Norton, Francis 160

occupations 29, 74, 82–83
    alesellers 87, 100, 122; *see also* publicans; victuallers
    apothecaries 63, 82, 89, 90, *97*, 101, 111, 128, 160, 177
    apple sellers 41, 90–91
    armourers 82–83, *84*, 86
    barbers, barber chirurgeons and barber surgeons 82, 152, 166, 192
    beavermakers 105
    Blackwell Hall factors 87
    blue shops, owners of 83, 100
    bodice sellers 83, 96, *97*
    booksellers 66, 82–83, 87, 90, 91, 93–96, *94*, *97*, 98, 99, 101, *108*, 111, 176, 177, 192–93
    bottlemakers 83
    bowyers 29, 42, 81–83, *84*, 85, 86, 103
    boxmakers 83, 98, 176
    brasiers 83
    breeches maker 101, 142
    bricklayer 73, 115
    broochmakers 83, *84*
    brushmakers 83, 98, *99*, 101, 129–30
    cappers 83
    carpenters 46, 52, 72, 79, 87, 115, 118, 130
    carvers 72
    chaplains 83
    chapmakers 83
    chapmen 89, 91, 93–96
    clockmakers and watchmakers 83, *97*, 98, 106, 115
    clothworkers 45, 74, 83, 88, 89, 106, 145, 149, 154, 156, 157, 159, 165, 166
    cobblers 83, *84*; *see also* cordwainers; shoemakers
    coffeemen 83, 100, 101, 128, 130
    combmakers 83, 176
    cooks 83, 87, 100; *see also* pastry cooks
    coppersmiths 83, 107
    cordwainers 83, 156; *see also* cobblers; shoemakers
    cork-cutters 83
    costermongers 117
    cutlers 29, 80–83, *84*, 85, 87, 90, 91, 96, *97*, 111, 139, 145, 151, 153, 158, 162
    distillers 83, *90*, 130
    drapers 53, 74, 82–83, 86–88, 90, *90*, 91, *91*, *97*, 104, 105, *108*, 111, 123, 156, 157, 160, 163–65, 176
    drysalters 53, 83, *97*
    fellmongers 83
    fishmongers 83, 109, 152, 154, 155, 160, 163, 165
    flaxmen 83
    fletchers 29, 46, 81, 82, *84*, 85–87
    footmen 83
    founders 83
    furbers 83, 86
    girdlers 74, 80–82, *84*, 86, *90*, 91, 104, 110, 115, 143, 145, 146, 152, 155, 166
    glassmen 83, 176
    glaziers 72, 73
    glovers 29, 74, 81–85, *84*, 87, 88, *90*, *97*, *108*, 111, 176
    goldsmiths 71, 82–83, *84*, 86, 88, 90, 92, 96, *97*, 101, 143, 181
    grocers 33, 34, 39, 53, 56, 74, 81–83, *84*, 86–91, *90*, 96, 104, *108*, 110, 148, 155, 158, 176, 192
    haberdashers 81–83, *84*, 88, 89, *90*, 96, *97*, *98* and *passim*
    hair merchants 83
    hatters 83, 92; *see also* haberdashers; milliners
    hempshops, owners of 83
    hop merchants 83
    horners 83
    hosiers 74, 77, 79, 87, 89–91, *90*, *97*, *108*, 176, 177
    instrument makers 83; *see also* mathematical instrument makers; surgical instrument makers
    ironmongers 74, 83, *84*, 90, *97*, *108*, 176
    jewellers 82–83, 86, 88, 101
    joiners 48, 49
    leathersellers 53, 82–83, 85, *97*, 100–01, 145, 152
    looking glass makers 83, *97*, 98
    marblers 83
    masons 35, 74, 83
    mathematical instrument makers 83, 98, 99, 101, 142
    mercers 53, 74, 75, 81, 83, 87, 88, 90, *90*, 91, *97*, 104, 111, 115, 144, 150, 153, 163, 176, 177
    merchants 83, 104, 105, 115
    merchant taylors 83, 88, 89, 103, 115, 145, 146, 149, 156, 159, 161, 177, 182
    metalworkers 82–83, 96; *see also* individual trades
    milliners 74, 83, 87, *90*, 176; *see also* haberdashers; hatters
    music shops, owners of 83, 96
    necklace makers 83, 96, 101, 142
    needlemakers 69, 83, *90*, 96, *97*, 98, 101, 142
    painters 36, 49, 72, 83
    painter stainers 83, 115
    paper hangings makers 101
    pastry cooks 65, 83, 100, 135; *see also* cooks
    pepperers 83, 89
    perfumers 83, 100
    periwig makers 83, 96
    pewterers 83, *84*, 96, *97*, 101, 128, 159, 160, 177
    pinmakers/pinners 82, *84*, 92, 96, 97, *99*, 101, 111
    plasterers 73
    pointmakers 83
    pouchmakers 85
    printmakers and print sellers 96, 106, *107*, 142
    publicans 130, 135; *see also* alesellers; victuallers
    pursers 81, 83, 85
    salesmen 83, *97*, 123
    salters 74, 83, *90*, 100, 151, 163, 176
    sawyers 72
    scale makers 83, 98, 101, 142
    scriveners 56, 71, 74, 83, *90*, 103, 104, 148, 155, 177, 182
    sempsters 83, 176
    sergeants 83, *84*
    sheathers 83, 85
    shoemakers 87, *90*, 176; *see also* cobblers; cordwainers
    shopkeepers, country 91–92, 100
    silkmen and women 63, 67, 74, 82, *84*, 86, 89, 90, *90*, 92, *97*, 100, 101, *108*, 111, 176
    silversmiths 83
    skinners *63*, 74, 83, 150, 165
    slopshops, owners of 53, 83, 96
    snuffmakers 83, 100
    spectacle makers 83, 98
    spurriers 82, *84*, 86
    stationers 53, 74, 82–83, 87, 94, *97*, 99–101, 109, 111, 126, 142, 159, 166, 177
    stringers 81, 83, 85, 86
    strong water shops, owners of 83
    surgeons 82
    surgical instrument makers 98, *99*, 101
    tailors *84*, 101, 130
    tallow chandlers 83, *84*, 192
    textile dealers 88–89, 96; *see also* individual trades
    tinmen 83, 95, 96, 177
    tobacconists 87

trunkmakers 83, 91, *97*, 98, *108*, 109
turners 52, 69, 72, 75, 83
victuallers 82–83, 87, *97*, 100, 101, *108*, 176; see also alesellers; publicans
vintners 15, 53, 74, 82–83, 115, 149, 152, 155, 162, 166
watchmakers, see clockmakers and watchmakers
water bailiffs 83
waxchandlers 83
weavers 92
whalebone sellers 83, 96, *97*
worsted shops, owners of 83
yarnmen 83, 176
Odye, Richard 86
Ogilby and Morgan's map *181*
Old Change 178, *178*
Old London coffee house 100
Oliver, John 120, 186, William 91
Osbolston (Osburton), Lambert 104, Robert 34, 104, 110, 150, 151, 157, William 104, 177
Osborne, Edward 107
Otehill, Richard 86

Pall Mall 126
Palmer, Agnes 55
Panne, Ralph *90*
Paris, bridges of 19
Parkhurst (Purchas), Thomas 94–95, 177
Parton, Ann *108*
Partriche, William *84*
Partridge, Gabriel 80, 151, 166, 176
Parys, widow *84*
Passinger, Charles 95, John 94, Sarah 94, Thomas sen. 49, 94, 96, *97*, *108*, 153, 176, Thomas jun. 94
Paternoster Row 93, 95, 178, *178*
Peere, John 38
Pemble, John *97*, *108*
Pengfeild, Thomas 163
Penhertgart (Penhertgard), Henry *84*, 85

Pennant, Thomas 101
Pepys Library view of London Bridge *2–3*, 11, 14, 38, 41, 47, 49, 58, 62, *64*, 66, 67, 146, *147*, 148–50, 153, *154*, 157, 161, *162*, 168, 170–71
Pepys, Samuel 75
Pernell, Margery 160, Stephen 93
Peter of Colechurch 3, 31
Peter, Matthew 36
Peters, James 177
Pettit, Thomas 177
Petty, Samuel *90*
Phillips, Henry 157, Lucy 122, Stephen 163
Phippes, Edmund 148
Phipps, Robert 110
Pickering, William 192
pickpockets 91
Pierse, Edward 165, Mary 165
Pikeman, Henry 86, John 86, William 86
pilgrims 31
Pilling, William 73
Pitham, Gerrard *99*, 127, 129–30
Pitt, Edward 53–54, 67, 100–01, 176
plague 109; see also Black Death
Plessington, Humphrey 55
poll tax 107, *108*, 109
Pope, Daniel 126
Porteridge (Portresse), John *97*, *108*
Poultry 27
Powell, Alice *61*, 152, Hugh *90*, 110, 146, Thomas *97*, *108*, 111, 176
Price, James sen. 96, 98, 101, 111, jun. 98
privies, public 40
Privy Council 8, *9*, 181, 183
Pullen, Thomas 40
pumps 125–26
Purchas, see Parkhurst
Purfoote, Thomas 192
Pursers' Company 85
Putham, Anne 130–31, Isaac 101, 130
Putney Bridge 128

Pye Corner *84*, 94
Pye, William *84*
Pyke, Edmond 165

Quant, John *84*
Queenhithe 7, 38
quit rents 5

Ralph, James 128
Randolph, Henry 177
Raves, John *84*
Ray, Sarah *108*
Raymant, St Cleere 176
Read, John *97*
rebellions 25, 35, 36, 38–40, 42
reconstructed cross sections of London Bridge houses 15, *24*, *53*, *61*, *64*, *65*, *124*, *149*
reconstruction drawings of London Bridge *4*, *6*, *16*, *20*, *28*, *29*, *52*, *59*, *62*, *117*
reconstruction plan of London Bridge 10–11, 17–18, *18*, 27, *27*, 30, 167–69
Red Cross Alley 75, 182–83
Reede, Richard *84*
Rennie, John 142
Revell, John 189
Reynolds, James 92, *92*, Thomas 130, William 86, *97*
Richard II 35
Richardson, Hannah *108*, Richard 136
Richbell, Timothy 104, 158, William 104
Richers, Robert *84*
Robegent, John *84*
Rocque, John, map by 167, 182
Roe, James 177
Rogers, Walter 71
Roofe, Jane *108*
Roundtree, Robert 176
Rownang, Richard 47
royal arms 37, *37*
Royal Exchange 71
Ruck (Rucke), Hanna *108*, Thomas (1st, 2nd and 3rd), 64, 67, 68, 92, *97*, 101, 104–05, *108*, *114*, 115, 152, 155, 176
Rudd, William 152
Rudgwick, Sussex 92
Rusk, Francis 98
Russell, Thomas *84*
Rust, Daniel *108*
Rye, Sussex 91

St Dionis Backchurch parish, London 178, *178*
St Ives, Cambs. 31
St Magnus the Martyr, London
    church 75, *77*, *135*, *140*, 142, 180, *182*, 184
    churchyard *140*, 184, *184*
    cloister 143, 180–82, *180*, *181*, 184
    fraternity 110
    parish 8, 121–22
St Mary Colechurch, London 3
St Mary Overy, Southwark *78*
St Olave, Southwark, church *78*, parish 8, 23
St Paul's Cathedral 70, *72*
St Thomas Becket 5, 31, 32
St Thomas the Martyr, fraternity of 110
St Thomas's Hospital 104
Safford, Joseph *108*
Salesbury, Stephen *84*
Salisbury 91
Saltonstall, Sir Richard *1*
Salve Regina, fraternity of 110
Sampson, John *84*
Sancroft, Elizabeth *108*
Sandwich, Kent 92
Santon, Stephen 86
Sauston, Alice *84*
Savage, John 34, *97*, *108*
Scalticke (Scaltike), Anne 154–55, Anthony 110, 154
Scott, Joseph *108*
Scott, Samuel, painting by *116*, *120*, *132–33*, 171
Scotte, Richard *84*

INDEX

Searel, Humfrey 90
Sedere (Sethere), Stephen 85
Selde, Robert *84*
Sertayn, William 86
servants 104, 105, 107, *108*, 109
Shakemaple, John 91, 101
Shanke, Matthew *97*, 101
Sheerness, Kent 92
Shelbury, Richard 71, *90*, 182
Sheldon, John 100, 111, William *97*, *108*, 176
Shepard, John *108*
Shepherd, George, drawing by *140*
Sheppard, Matthew 161, William *97*
Sherley, John 71, *90*, Mary 146
Sheter, Thomas *84*
Shoreditch 92
signs on London Bridge houses
    Anchor 91, *97*, 109
    Angel 95, 192
    Beehive 95
    Bell 53, *97*
    Bible 95, *97*
    Black Boy 91, 96
    Blue Boar *90*
    Bunch of Grapes 122
    Castle *97*
    Clock *97*, 106
    Cross Keys 34, *97*, 100, 136
    Crown and Bell *97*
    Dial 106
    Dog 109
    Dog's Head and Porridge Pot 78
    Dog's Head in the Pot 78, *97*
    Frying Pan *97*
    Frying Pan and Saw *97*
    Gate *97*
    Globe 99
    Golden Anchor *97*
    Golden Bell 104
    Golden Bible 95
    Golden Globe 106, *106*
    Golden Salmon and Spectacles 98
    Golden Still 185
    Golden Violin 96
    Green Dragon *97*
    Hand and Beads 101
    Hand and Bible 95
    Hand and Scales 98
    Hat and Feather 92, *97*
    Horseshoe *97*
    King's Arms 93, *97*
    Looking Glass 95, *97*
    Maidenhead *97*
    Old Three Bibles 94
    Panier 44
    Pedlar and Pack 91, *97*
    Pigeon and Parrot *97*, 109
    Plough and Harrow *97*
    Red Lion 95, *97*
    Salmon and Spectacles 98
    Sceptre and Hart 98
    Seven Stars 95
    Ship *97*
    Ship and Anchor *97*
    Ship and Pinnace *97*
    Star *97*, 104
    Sugar Loaf *91*, *97*
    Sun 96
    Sun and Bible 95
    Sun Tavern 87
    Sussex House 122
    Swan 34, *97*
    Talbot *97*
    Three Bibles *15*, 93–94, *94*, *97*, 192
    Three Bibles and Ink Bottles 94
    Three Cranes *97*
    Three Cups *97*
    Three Needles and Coronets *97*
    Three Pigeons *97*
    Trunk *97*
    Two Cocks *97*
    Violin and Hautboy 96
    White Hart *97*
    White Horse *97*
    White Lion *97*
    White Swan *97*
    Whitstone and Dripping Pan *97*
Sion College 93
Skailes, Edward 177
Skinner, Nicholas 183
Smith (Smyth), Edward 155, 176, Elizabeth 95, Jeremy 155, Nathaniel 177, Nicholas 34, *97*, *108*, 165, 166, 176, Samuel *108*
Smither, Thomas *97*, *108*
Smithers, John 99
Smithfield Market 96
Snayleham, John *84*
Somer, Henry *84*
Somerset House, London 52
Somerset, Duke of 52
Soper (Soap), Thomas 63, *97*, 101, 110, 177
Souch, John 98
South Foreland, Kent 104
Southwark
    customers of bridge shops 91
    fair 91
    fires 23, 127
    growth of 142, 179
    privy, public 40
    warehouse in 96
    water supply 125
    water wheels 41
    See also Bear Tavern, Borough, Newcomen Street, St Mary Overy, St Olave, Tooley Street
Spencer, John 93
Stanyon, Abraham 73
Stapleton, Anthony 144
Stationers' Company 95, 192
Staveley, Babington *114*, 115
Stede, William 39, *84*
Stedman, Christopher 99, 101, 142
Stephens, Elizabeth 109
Stevyns, John *84*
Stileman, Francis 75
Stockett, Lewis 52
Stocks Market 5
Stockwell, Daniel *15*, 152
Stockwood, Daniel 176
Stony Stratford, Bucks. 92
Stortford, de, Margery 81, Ralph 81, William sen. and jun. 81
Stow, John 38, 40, 50, 88, 186
Strand, the 52
Stratton, Susanna *108*
Streatham 111
street trading 90–91
Streete, Robert 91
Strutt, Thomas 52, 189
Strype, John 12, 74, 107, 124
Stuart, John 94
Styvar, John 40
suburban retreats 111
Sudbury, Suffolk 92
Sun Fire Office 129
Surveyor of Queen's Works 52, 189
Sutton, Baptist 73
Sweeting (Sweting), George *97*, *108*

Takeneswell, Walter 86
Taillour, John *84*, Thomas *84*
Tallman, James 98
Tange, William *84*
Tapp, John 192
Tawke, Jeremy/Jeremiah 63, 67, *97*, 101, 166
Taylor (Tayler), Edward 110, Jane *108*, Mary *108*, Thomas 95, William 73, 74
Temple Bar 37
Tenterden, Kent 92
Terrill, John *90*
Terry, William *84*
Thackerye, William 94
Thames Street, Upper and Lower 70, 142
Thomas, William 183
Thomson, Henry *84*
Thornbury Castle, Glos. 49
Thornton, John *84*, William *84*

Thorpe (Thorp), Mr 136, Thomas *84*, *108*
Thurston, Henry 122
Tiby, John *84*
Tilles, Philip 157
Timewell, Mrs 129
Tipperary 104
Tixall Gatehouse, Staffs. 51
Toker, John 63, *84*
tolls 5, 39, 104, 161
Tooley Street, Southwark 12, *39*, 93, 123, 127, 128, 167
Tower of London, Master Carpenter at 49
Tracy, Ebenezer 94, Henry 94, John 94, *94*, widow 94
trade cards 98–99, *99*, 101, *107*
Treswell, Ralph 190
Troughton, Miles 152
Turner (Tournor), John 86, Mrs 21, Thomas 145
Turpin, William 155
Tutty, John 122
Tyus (Tias), Charles 66–67, 93–94, 96, Sarah 94

Ulfe, Alice *84*
Upper Thames Street 142
Urlwyn, William 139
Urmston, Pete, drawings by *16*, *28*, *59*

Vane, Anne 127
Verne, Robert 85
Vertue, George, engravings by *32*
Vincent, Robert 98, 101, 142
Vousden, John 95
Vyner (Viner), Anne 177, James 176, William *90*, 143, 181

Wakefield, Yorks. 31
Walcott, Edmond 110, 111, 157, William 157
Walkden, Charles 99, 101, 126, 142, Richard 99–101, *100*, 142
Walker, George 177
Wall, Richard *108*, widow 143
Wallace, Sir William 39
Walle, Isabella *84*
Waller, John 92
Wallington, Nehemiah 69
Walsingham, Sir Francis 8
Walton, John *84*
Walworth 111
Wandsworth 92
Warbleton, Sussex 91
Ward, Mary 161, Ned 4–5, Thomas 165
Wareham, Thomas 46
Waren, John *84*
Warkeman, Robert 176
Warkman, Joan 110, Lawrence *15*, 110, 152, 155
Warnett, Edmund 80, 91, 158, Edward *90*
Watkins, Walter 139, 142
Weatherfield, Essex 164
Weatherhead, William *97*

Weaver, John 53, Samuel 96, Thomas 176
Webb, Michael 150, 176
Weedon, Jane 156
Weld, John *97*, 177, Josias 92
Welding, *see* Wilding
West End, shopping in 101–02
West, William 53
Westbrooke, Richard 191
Westminster Bridge 128, 136
Westminster Hall 21, 35
wheelage, *see* tolls
Whetstone, Richard 55
Whittington, Richard 56
Wilding (Welding, Wildeinge), John 68, *90*, 100, *108*, 109, 152, 176, Richard 110, 155, Zabulon 165
Wilkins, Walter 101
Wilkinson, Francis 123
Willcoxe, Richard 146
Williamot, Edward 110, 144, Samuel 153, Susan 153
Williamson, John 95
Willin, Mary *108*
Wimborne, Mr *108*
windows, cant and compass 49, 150, 154
Witherall, Rowland 156
Wollat, Ann *108*
Woller, John 21, Mr 63
Wolsey, Cardinal 49
women
  apprentices 109
  households headed by 86, 107, 109
  inhabitants on the bridge 107, 109
  lessees 86
  servants 107, *108*, 109
  silkwomen *84*, 86, 89
Wood Street 89
Wood, Joan 161, Samuel *90*, Thomas *108*, 177, Zelderhaes 153
Woodfall, Anne 157, Henry 157
Worger, John 110
Worley (Wyrley), Thomas *97*, *108*
Worth, John *84*
Wrenke, Thomas 35
Wright and Gill 142
Wright, Andrew 36, Robert 145, Thomas *97*, 100, *100*, 109, 111, 177
Wyatt, Sir Thomas, rebellion by 35, 38–40
Wyngaerde, Anthonis van den, drawing by ii, 11, 30, *32*, *35*, 36, *39*, 45, 47, *47*, 49, 63, *180*
Wyrley, *see* Worley

Yardley, Thomas 177
Yate, John *108*, Samuel 163
Yates, William *97*, *108*
Yeoman of the Channel 38
Yeoman, William *84*
Yeomans, Richard *97*
Yevele, Henry 31
Young (Younge, Yonge), Edward 143, Henry 86, William 158